Canadian Guide to Uniform Legal Citation

5ᵗʰ edition

Manuel canadien de la référence juridique

5ᵉ édition

McGill Law Journal
Revue de droit de McGill

CARSWELL

A THOMSON COMPANY

National Library of Canada Cataloguing in Publication

Canadian guide to uniform legal citation-Manuel canadien de la référence juridique.—5th ed.-5e éd.

"McGill law journal-Revue de droit de McGill".
Text in English and French.
Includes bibliographical références and index.
ISBN 0-459-24068-4 (bound).—ISBN 0-459-24042-0 (pbk.)

1. Citation of legal authorities—Canada. I. Title: Manuel canadien de la référence juridique.

KE259.C35 2002   808'.06634   C2002-903667-4E

Catalogage avant publication de la Bibliothèque nationale du Canada

Canadian guide to uniform legal citation-Manuel canadien de la référence juridique.—5th ed.-5e éd.

"McGill law journal-Revue do droit de McGill".
Texte en anglais et en français.
Comprend des références bibliographiques et un index.
ISBN 0-459-24068-4 (rel.).—ISBN 0-459-24042-0 (br.)

1. Recueils juridiques faisant autorité—Citation—Canada. I. Titre: Manuel canadien de la référence juridique.

KE259.C35 2002   808'.06634   C2002-903667-4F

CARSWELL
A THOMSON COMPANY

One Corporate Plaza	**Customer service/Service à la clientele:**
2075 Kennedy Road	Toronto 1-416-609-8000
Toronto, Ontario	Elsewhere in Canada/U.S.—Ailleurs au Canada/É.-U. 1-800-387-5164
M1T 3V4	Fax/Télécopieur 1-416-298-5094

Summary Table of Contents

McGill Law Journal
Revue de droit de McGill

Preface

This bilingual *Guide* has been compiled by *McGill Law Journal* editors and associate editors, all of whom are students at the Faculty of Law, McGill University. Since its first edition in 1986, the *Guide* has become an essential reference tool for judges, lawyers, professors, and law students across Canada. It is used in legal methodology programs across the country, and has been officially adopted by almost thirty law journals in Canada and Singapore. Subsequent editions in 1987, 1992, and 1998 have ensured that the *Guide* has kept pace with changes in citation format and have allowed editors to add citation rules for jurisdictions and materials.

This edition of the *Guide* was revised over the course of one academic year, in addition to the four regular issues of the *Journal*. During the summer of 2001, members of volume 47 conducted preliminary research on several chapters and edited our electronic copy of the *Guide* to ensure that its content accurately reflected the printed version of the fourth edition. Editing for the fifth edition began in the fall, with members of volume 47 updating most of the examples of the *Guide* and researching the proper citation format for jurisdictions and materials not included in the fourth edition. These changes were carefully reviewed throughout the winter term. As a result, further research was conducted, and changes to many sections were made. Meanwhile, work commenced on the appendix, introduction, Singapore sections, the neutral citation, and the electronic sections. A final draft was ready by the end of March, and further proofreading and corrections were complete a little more than a week before our final exams!

We found it especially challenging this year to weave the rules on new jurisdictions and material into the pre-existing web of compromises made in previous editions to suit the different standards and practices of two languages and several legal cultures and traditions. It has also proven to be very difficult to achieve the right balance between ensuring the stability of our present citation system and meeting the need to update material and make legal citation more efficient, pragmatic, and uniform. In general, where a rule served a clear purpose, was widely accepted, or where changes to it might cause too much confusion, we felt it was not our mandate to change it in order to increase efficiency and consistency, but instead tried to explain it more clearly. We did feel justified in making changes to a rule if it had become outdated as a result of new developments in citation practices. Where no one single rule was being followed, we chose the rule that was most efficient and consistent with the rest of the *Guide*.

Special thanks must be extended to Professors Gary F. Bell, Michael Hor, and Victor V. Ramraj of the Faculty of Law, National University of Singapore, for so generously conducting all the research on Singapore sections in this edition. It was no easy feat to integrate previous Singapore citation practices with the system presented in this *Guide*, and we are extremely grateful to them for their thoughtful analysis of these difficulties and their many helpful suggestions. The *Guide* has benefited enormously from their contribution.

Me Daniel Boyer (Wainright Librarian, Nahum Gelber Law Library, McGill University) and Professor René Provost (McGill Faculty of Law) very kindly agreed to review portions of the *Guide*, and we are also grateful for the many thoughtful suggestions from Professor John Swan (McGill Faculty of Law) and Janet Moss (Administrative Librarian, Gerard V. La Forest Law Library, University of New Brunswick). The chapter on Government Documents would not have been possible without the unfailing help of librarians at the Government Documents Section of the McLennan Library at McGill University, especially Phyllis Rudin. Our production assistant, Nicole Leger, spent countless hours entering in editors' corrections to the fourth edition, and we are extremely grateful for her patience and dedication. We also gratefully acknowledge the Nahum Gelber Law Library at McGill, the York University Law Library, and the Great Library of the Law Society of Upper Canada, where most of the research was conducted. The dedicated staff of the McGill Law Information Management Centre provided much-needed technical assistance.

We appreciate the insightful suggestions of members of previous *Journal* boards, whose efforts laid the groundwork for this edition, and we want to emphasize how grateful we are to all who contributed to the first, second, third, and fourth editions of the *Guide*. The fifth edition is very much the product of years of co-operative effort of *Journal* members and countless others—judges, legislative counsel, research directors, professors, librarians, editors, lawyers, and students—who so generously took time to respond to our questions and submitted extensive comments upon the various drafts of all five editions. Also, we were thrilled to see the number of academic publications that have officially adopted this *Guide* more than double since the last edition, and we would like to thank all of these journals and judicial institutions for agreeing to be associated with this project.

Finally, I would like to thank all of my fellow members of the *Journal*, because this project could never have been accomplished had it not been for their enthusiasm, team spirit, attention to detail, and unwavering commitment.

Timothy Reibetanz
Citation Guide Editor
McGill Law Journal, vol. 47

COMMENTS:

If you have comments and suggestions on how we can improve this *Guide*, we would appreciate hearing from you. Please write, fax, or e-mail us:

> McGill Law Journal
> 3644 Peel Street
> Montreal QC H3A 1W9 Canada
> Tel: (514) 398-7397
> Fax: (514) 398-7360
> E-mail: journal.law@mcgill.ca
> http://www.journal.law.mcgill.ca

NEW TO THE FIFTH EDITION

IMPORTANT CHANGES

Neutral citation. A recent innovation in citation of case law, the neutral citation, has been included. Unlike traditional citations, neutral citations are issued directly by courts. They are independent of the electronic databases or printed reporters that publish case law. The integration of neutral citation with traditional citation is explained in chapter 3. See the new roadmap at 3.1 to assist users in determining which source of jurisprudence to cite.

Authors' Name. Authors' given names are now to be included in citations as they appear in the publication being cited. The former practice of reducing authors' names to initials did not allow for gender identification of authors nor did it reflect the plurality of cultural practices governing names. For examples, see especially chapter 6.

Style of Cause. The "v." in the style of cause should be italicized. This change reflects modern citation practice. See section 3.2.2.

The Hereinafter Rule. Short forms in footnotes should now be included in brackets, without the word "hereinafter". See section 1.4.1.

Electronic Media. The chapter on electronic media has been simplified and integrated into the other chapters.

NEW ADDITIONS

New Sections. The Introduction chapter now describes bibliographies in more detail, as well as in-text citations. Sections have been added on citation of materials from Canada's newest territory, Nunavut. A section has been added on citation of U.S. government documents. Recent changes in the distribution of legislative power in the U.K. are reflected in sections on citation of legislation from Northern Ireland and Scotland. There are new sections on citing legal materials from Australia, New Zealand, Singapore, and South Africa. Lastly, more materials are now covered by chapter 6 (Secondary Sources and Other Materials), notably historical legal materials and archival materials.

Appendices. The appendices have been greatly enlarged. They now include more periodicals, yearbooks, jurisdictions, and courts. The list of case law reporters has been expanded to include the jurisdiction and dates of the cases within each reporter.

Table of Contents

1

INTRODUCTION

The rules in this *Guide* apply to footnotes, in-text citation, and bibliographies. Use the rules from the English section when writing in English, even if the source being referred to is written in another language. Use the French rules only when writing in French. When the example requires a comma, use a comma; if the rule says that parentheses "( )" must be used, brackets "[   ]" are not an acceptable substitute. There is one exception: in accordance with well-established convention, underlining may always be used in lieu of italics. While it is always preferable to provide parallel citations to a case, parallel citations have been omitted from most examples in this *Guide* to simplify presentation. Finally, though bold-faced font has been used to make some examples in this *Guide* explicit, it should not be reproduced.

1.1 BIBLIOGRAPHIES

Examples
LEGISLATION *Anti-terrorism Act*, S.C. 2001, c. 41. *Aggregate Resources Act*, R.S.O. 1990, c. A-8. *National Arts Council Act* (Cap. 193A, 1992 Rev. Ed. Sing.). *Tobacco Product Control Act*, R.S.C. 1985 (4th Supp.), c. 14.

JURISPRUDENCE

Delgamuukw v. British Columbia, [1997] 3 S.C.R. 1010, 153 D.L.R. (4th) 193.
Kendle v. Melsom, 1998 HCA 13.
Létourneau c. Laflèche Auto Ltée, [1986] R.J.Q. 1956 (Sup. Ct.).
R. v. Marshall (No. 2), [1999] 3 S.C.R. 533, 179 D.L.R. (4th) 193.

SECONDARY MATERIAL: MONOGRAPHS

Macklem, Patrick. *Indigenous Difference and the Constitution of Canada* (Toronto:
    University of Toronto Press, 2001).
Nadeau, Alain-Robert. *Vie privée et droits fondamentaux* (Cowansville, Qc.: Yvon Blais,
    2000).
Smith, Graham J.H. *Internet Law and Regulation*, 3d ed. (London: Sweet & Maxwell,
    2002).
Tan, Cheng Han. *Matrimonial Law in Singapore and Malaysia* (Singapore: Butterworths
    Asia, 1994).

SECONDARY MATERIAL: ARTICLES

Borrows, John. "With or Without You: First Nations Law (in Canada)" (1996) 41
    McGill L.J. 629.
————. "Wampum at Niagara: The Royal Proclamation, Canadian Legal History, and
    Self-Government" in Michael Asch, ed. *Aboriginal and Treaty Rights in Canada:
    Essays on Law, Equity, and Respect for Difference* (Vancouver: UBC Press, 1997)
    155.
Deleury, E. "Naissance et mort de la personne ou les confrontations de la médecine et du
    droit" (1976) 17 C. de D. 265.
Wang Sheng Chang. "Combination of Arbitration with Conciliation and Remittance of
    Awards – with Special Reference to the Asia-Oceana Region" (2002) 19 J. Int. Arb. 51.

Bibliographies and tables of authorities of legal texts should be divided into sections (*e.g.* legislation, jurisprudence, and secondary materials). Within each section, the entries should be in alphabetical order. If some material does not fit into a defined section, a residual section entitled "other material" may be used. It may be useful to divide the "secondary material" section into sub-sections (*e.g.* articles and books). It may also be useful to divide material between domestic sources and foreign sources.

While bibliographical citation of legislation and jurisprudence should follow the rules indicated in this *Guide*, references to secondary materials are made differently in the context of a bibliography or list of authorities than in the context of footnotes.

For secondary material included in a bibliography, the author's family name appears first. Note that a family name may appear before, after, or in between given names, depending on cultural conventions. In order to determine which name to place first in a bibliography, consult the cataloguing data on the back of the first page of a monograph or consult other references to the author (for example, in an introduction to a book, in library catalogues, or in other scholarship referring to the author). If the family name does not normally appear first in the author's name, place a comma after it followed by given names and/or any initials included in her or his name, as they appear in the publication.

Except for the name of the author or editor, all other information provided in the bibliographical citation of secondary material should be organized according to rules established in this *Guide*. If a citation directly follows a citation to another work by the same author, replace the author's names with a 3-em dash. Cite a work by a single author before citing a work by that author and others. Each citation should have a hanging indent of ¼ inch or .63 cm (all lines except the first line should be indented).

1.2   IN-TEXT REFERENCES

In some forms of writing, *e.g.* facta and memos, it is permissible to leave citations directly in the text rather than to use footnotes. Sources may be cited in parentheses in the text or, alternatively, all of the sources referred to in one paragraph may be cited immediately following the paragraph. In the latter case, indent both the left and right margins for the references, and use a smaller font size. It is not necessary to establish a short form for cases if they are not referred to in any subsequent paragraph (see the *Robitaille* example, below). If *supra* is used in subsequent citations, it refers to the page on which the reference was made (*e.g.* "*Nixon, supra* page 4").

Examples
In addition to the requirement of an "actionable wrong" independent of the breach sued upon, punitive damages will only be awarded "where the defendant's misconduct is so malicious, oppressive and high-handed that it offends the court's sense of decency" (*Hill v. Church of Scientology of Toronto*, [1995] 2 S.C.R. 1130 at para. 196, 186 N.R. 1, Cory J. [*Hill*]). Such behaviour has included defamation (*Hill*), failure to provide medical care (*Robitaille v. Vancouver Hockey Club* (1981), 124 D.L.R. (3d) 228 (B.C.C.A.)), and an insurer's reprehensible conduct in contesting a claim (*Whiten v. Pilot Insurance*, 2002 SCC 18 [*Whiten*]).

In addition to the requirement of an "actionable wrong" independent of the breach sued upon, punitive damages will only be awarded "where the defendant's misconduct is so malicious, oppressive and high-handed that it offends the court's sense of decency" (*Hill*). Such behaviour has included defamation, failing to provide medical care, and an insurer's reprehensible conduct in contesting a claim.
 	
        Hill v. Church of Scientology of Toronto, [1995] 2 S.C.R. 1130 at para. 196, 184 N.R. 1, Cory J. [*Hill*].
        Robitaille v. Vancouver Hockey Club (1981), 124 D.L.R. (3d) 228 (B.C.C.A.).
Whiten v. Pilot Insurance, 2002 SCC 18 [*Whiten*].

1.3   GENERAL RULES FOR FOOTNOTING

In legal writing, the two most common forms of footnotes are *textual footnotes* and *citation footnotes*. *Textual footnotes* contain matter of related interest to the subject, but that is sufficiently peripheral that its presence in the body of the paper would detract from the thrust of the argument. *Citation footnotes* are used to indicate sources from which the argument or quotation has been drawn. Citation and textual footnotes can be mixed, and both can occur within the same footnote.

1.3.1   When to footnote

When writing a legal research paper, create footnotes only under the following circumstances: (1) at the first reference to the source; (2) at every subsequent quotation from the source; (3) at every subsequent reference or allusion to a particular passage in the source. The full citation should be provided in the first footnote referring to a source.

1.3.2   How to indicate a footnote in the text

In legal writing, footnotes are indicated by superscripted numbers, starting at 1 and increasing in sequential order by positive whole integers. Special characters such as *, †, and ‡ are not used. Generally, place the footnote number at the end of the sentence after the punctuation.[1] When referring to one word, place the footnote number[2] directly after the word. When quoting from a source, place the footnote number after "the quotation marks"[3] and/or "the punctuation".[4] Note that this is contrary to the rule applicable in French, where the footnote number always precedes the punctuation.

1.3.3   Where footnotes appear

Footnotes appear on the same page (if possible) below the text to which they refer. They should be differentiated from the body of the text in some way, *e.g.* set in a smaller font with a horizontal line separating them from the body of the text.

1.3.4   When to combine footnotes

Never place more than one footnote number at any given point in the text. Instead, combine the references into one footnote. Citations to two or more sources in a footnote are separated by a semi-colon and the entire footnote must end with a period. If the result is not confusing, citations to a few materials may generally be combined into one footnote with the footnote number placed at the end of the paragraph. Avoid combining footnotes that refer to several quotations from different sources.

1.3.5 How to cite non-English sources

Examples
[27]Jean-Louis Baudouin & Pierre-Gabriel Jobin, *Les obligations*, 5th ed. (Cowansville, Qc.: Yvon Blais, 1998) at 240.
[60]*Loi n° 94-653 du 29 juillet 1994*, J.O., 30 July 1994, 11056, Gaz. Pal. 1994. 2e sem. Lég.576.

If writing in English, use the English citation rules regardless of the language of the source. Though the title of the source should remain in the original language and follow that language's rules on capitalization, all other items in the citation should follow the English rules, particularly English rules on use of punctuation.

1.3.6 Introductory signals

Examples
See *Egan v. Canada*, [1995] 2 S.C.R. 513. **See generally** *McKinney v. University of Guelph*, [1990] 3 S.C.R. 229. **But see** *Miron v. Trudel*, [1995] 2 S.C.R. 418.

An introductory signal is sometimes appropriate to explain the logical relationship between the source cited and the proposition stated in the text. Only e.g. and contra should be italicized (because they are the only non-English words in the list); all other signals should be in Roman font. While not exhaustive, the following list presents some introductory signals:

Examples	
Egan	There is no introductory signal when the authority cited is being quoted or directly referred to in the text.
See *Egan*	The authority cited directly supports the proposition given in the text.
See especially *Egan*	The authority cited is the strongest of several that support the proposition in the text. Use this when listing only the best of many possible sources.
See e.g. *Egan*	The authority cited is one of several that support the proposition given in the text, but the other supporting authorities are not cited.

See generally *Egan*	The authority cited supports and provides background information to the proposition in the text.
See also *Egan*	The authority cited provides added support for the proposition in the text, but is not the most authoritative or is not directly on point.
Accord *Egan*	As with "See also", the authority cited provides added support for the proposition in the text. However, in this instance, the authority directly supports the proposition in the text and is as authoritative as the authority first cited. "Accord" is also used to indicate that the law of one jurisdiction accords with the law of another.
Compare *Egan*	The authority cited provides a useful contrast to illustrate the proposition being discussed in the text. Do not confuse this with "cf."
But see *Egan*	The authority cited is in partial disagreement with the proposition in the text, but does not directly contradict it.
Contra Egan	The authority cited directly contradicts the proposition given in the text.

1.3.7 Parenthetical information

Examples
Roncarelli v. Duplessis, [1959] S.C.R. 121, 16 D.L.R. (2d) 689, Rand J. (a discretionary decision must "be based upon a weighing of considerations pertinent to the object of the administration" at 140); *Oakwood Development Ltd. v. St. François Xavier (Municipality)*, [1985] 2 S.C.R. 164, 20 D.L.R. (4th) 641, Wilson J. ("the failure of an administrative decision-maker to take into account a highly relevant consideration is just as erroneous as the improper importation of an extraneous consideration" at 174).
See *Lawson v. Wellesley Hospital* (1975), 9 O.R. (2d) 677, 61 D.L.R. (3d) 445, aff'd [1978] 1 S.C.R. 893, 76 D.L.R. (3d) 688 (duty of hospital to protect patient); *Stewart v. Extendicare*, [1986] 4 W.W.R. 559, 38 C.C.L.T. 67 (Sask. Q.B.) [*Stewart*] (duty of nursing home to protect resident).

- In addition to introductory signals, it may be helpful to provide a brief description or quotation in parentheses following the citation, especially if the proposition affirmed or denied is unclear.
- Parenthetical information refers to the citation immediately preceding it. Therefore, in the *Lawson* example, the parenthetical information would be placed immediately before "aff'd" if it were meant to refer only to the appeal decision.

- Parenthetical information follows any reference to online services.

1.4 PRIOR AND SUBSEQUENT REFERENCES TO A CITATION

A single source is often repeatedly referred to. The full citation should be indicated in the footnote accompanying the first reference to the source. Subsequent references refer back to this initial citation.

1.4.1 Establishing a Short Form

1.4.1.1 *General Form*

Examples
[4] *Kadlak v. Nunavut (Minister of Sustainable Development)*, [2001] Nu. J. No. 1 (Nu. Ct. J.) (QL) *[Kadlak]*.
[21] *Kadlak, supra* note 4 ¶ 15.

- If the title of a source is short, the full title may be used in all subsequent references. If the title of a source is long, a short title should be created for subsequent references.
- Place the short title in brackets directly after the citation but before the final punctuation. Be careful not to italicize the brackets.
- The short title should follow electronic references (*e.g.* (QL)) but should precede parenthetical information (as in the case of *Stewart* in section 1.3.7, above).
- In subsequent footnotes, use the appropriate cross-referencing symbols (*e.g. supra, ibid.*) and the short title to direct the reader back to the footnote containing the full citation.

1.4.1.2 *Legislation*

Examples
[3] *Museums Act*, S.C. 1990, c. 3.
[8] *Nordion and Theratronics Divestiture Authorization Act*, S.C. 1990, c. 4 *[Nordion Act]*.
[10] *Canadian Charter of Rights and Freedoms*, Part I of the *Constitution Act, 1982*, being Schedule B to the *Canada Act 1982* (U.K.), 1982, c. 11 *[Charter]*.
[12] *Charter of the French language*, R.S.Q. c. C-11 *[Bill 101]*.

- If a statute has an official short title, it should always be used in the initial citation. If the short title is brief, it may also be used in subsequent references (*e.g.* the *Museums Act* example).
- If a statute has no official short title, or if the official short title is too long for subsequent references, a distinctive short title should be created and indicated in brackets at the end of the citation.

1.4.1.3 Cases

Examples

---

[3] *R. v. Van der Peet*, [1996] 2 S.C.R. 507, 137 D.L.R. (4th) 289 [***Van der Peet* cited to S.C.R.**].

[7] *Van der Peet, supra* note 4 at 510.

- Create a short form by choosing one of the parties' names or a distinctive part of the style of cause.
- If the initial citation includes parallel references, indicate the reporter to which subsequent pinpoint references will be made by including "cited to" followed by the abbreviation of the reporter.

1.4.1.4 Secondary materials

Examples

---

[3] G. Blaine Baker, "The Reconstitution of Upper Canadian Legal Thought in the Late-Victorian Empire" (1985) 3 Law & History Rev. 219 [**Baker, "Reconstitution"**].

[6] John Humphrey, *No Distant Millennium: The International Law of Human Rights* (Paris: UNESCO, 1989).

[9] G. Blaine Baker, "The Province of Post-Confederation Rights" (1995) 45 U.T.L.J. 77 [**Baker, "Post-Confederation Rights"**].

[12] **Humphrey**, *supra* note 6 at 25.

[26] Rebecca Veinott, "Child Custody and Divorce: A Nova Scotia Study, 1866-1910" in Philip Girard & Jim Phillips, eds., *Essays in the History of Canadian Law,* vol. 3 (Toronto: University of Toronto Press, 1990) 273.

[43] **"Baker, "Post-Confederation Rights"**, *supra* note 9 at 86.

[86] Kimberley Smith Maynard, "Divorce in Nova Scotia, 1750-1890" in **Girard & Phillips**, *supra* note 26, 232 at 239.

- Use the author's name to make subsequent references to the source (*e.g.* notes 6 and 12).

- If more than one work by a particular author is cited, the short form should consist of the author's name and a shortened form of the title of the work (preferably only one or two words) separated by a comma. In the short form of the title, maintain the same formatting as the full title—italics for books and quotation marks for articles (*e.g.* note 43).
- If two essays from the same book are cited, cite the second essay by referring to the original citation of the collection of essays using the name of the editor(s) (*e.g.* note 86).

1.4.2 *Ibid.*

Examples
[12] See *Canada (Labour Relations Board) v. Local 1764 of the International Longshoremen's Association, Steamship Checkers, Cargo Repairmen, Weighers and Samplers*, [1983] 1 S.C.R. 245 [*I.L.A.*].
[13] ***Ibid.*** at 260. See also *Fraser v. Canada (Public Service Staff Relations Board)*, [1985] 2 S.C.R. 455 at 463 [*Fraser*].
[14] *Fraser*, ***ibid.*** at 460.
[15] ***Ibid.***
[16] ***Ibid.*** at 464-65.
[98] But see *Union des employés de service, Local 298 v. Bibeault*, [1988] 2 S.C.R. 1048, where the Court cited a "patently unreasonable" standard of review (***ibid.*** at 1084-85).
[138] See *Business Corporations Act*, R.S.S. 1978, c. B-10, s. 18; Paul Martel with Luc Martel, *Les conventions entre actionnaires*, 7th ed. (Montreal: Wilson & Lafleur and Martel, 1999).
[139] See *Business Corporations Act, ibid.*, s. 22.

- *Ibid.* is an abbreviation of the Latin word *ibidem*, meaning "in the same place".
- Use *ibid.* to direct the reader to the immediately preceding reference. Do not provide the number of the footnote being referred to.
- *Ibid.* may be used after a full citation (*e.g.* note 13) or even after another use of *ibid.* (*e.g.* note 16). Use a short form to identify the source only if there is more than one source mentioned in the previous footnote (*e.g.* note 14).
- If using *ibid.* without providing a pinpoint reference, the *ibid.* is assumed to refer to the same pinpoint as in the previous footnote (*e.g.* note 15).
- When the same source is referred to twice in one note, place the *ibid.* reference in parentheses (*e.g.* note 98).

1.4.3 *Supra*

Examples

[17] *McMillan Bloedel Ltd. v. British Columbia (A.G.)* (1996), 22 B.C.L.R. (3d) 137 (C.A.) [*McMillan*]; *Towne Cinema Theatres Ltd. v. R.*, [1985] 1 S.C.R. 494, 18 D.L.R. (4th) 1 [*Towne Cinema*].

[72] *McMillan*, ***supra*** note 17 at 147.

[73] *Ibid.* at 150. See also *Towne Cinema*, ***supra*** note 17.

[77] ***Supra*** note 43 at 120.

[94] See also ***supra* note 24 and accompanying text**.

- *Supra* is a Latin word meaning "above".
- Use *supra* and the short form to refer a reader to a previous footnote containing the original full citation. *Supra* must always refer the reader to the original citation, not to another *supra* or *ibid.*
- If the source being referred to is clearly identified in the text, it is unnecessary to identify it in the footnote (*e.g.* note 77).
- To refer to a previous footnote and the accompanying text, use "*supra* note 24 and accompanying text".
- To refer only to the text and not to the footnote, use "above" not *supra*. See section 1.4.5.

1.4.4 *Infra*

Examples

[16] For another example of restrictions on leasing, see ***infra*** note 76.

[76] The *Civil Code of Québec* sets out a specific regime for residential leases at arts. 1892ff. This regime is much more protective of a tenant than the regular system of Quebec lease law, and is administered by a special bureaucracy.

- *Infra* is a Latin word meaning "below".
- Use *infra* to refer a reader to a subsequent footnote.
- *Infra* should be generally avoided by providing the full citation at the first reference.
- To refer only to the text and not to the footnote, use "below" not *infra*. See section 1.4.5.

1.4.5 Above and below

Examples
[21] See Part III.A, **above,** for more on this topic.
[52] Further discussion of this case will be found at 164-70, **below**.
[70] For further analysis of the holding in *Oakes*, **see text accompanying note 41**.

- Use the words "above" and "below" to direct the reader to a portion of the text and not to the footnotes.
- If there are no easily identifiable section or paragraph markers, or if the final pagination of the text is unclear at the time of writing, use the formulation "see text accompanying note".

1.5 CITING SOURCES THAT QUOTE OR REPRINT THE ORIGINAL SOURCE

Examples	
Cited in	*Papers Relating to the Commission appointed to enquire into the state and condition of the Indians of the North-West Coast of British Columbia*, British Columbia Sessional Papers, 1888 at 432-33, **cited in** Hamar Foster, "Honouring the Queen's Flag: A Legal and Historical Perspective on the Nisga'a Treaty" (1998) 120 B.C. Studies 11 at 13.
Reprinted in	George R. to Governor Arthur Phillip, Royal Instruction, 25 April 1787 (27 Geo. III), **reprinted in** *Historical Documents of New South Wales*, vol. 1, part 2 (Sydney: Government Printer, 1892-1901) 67.
	International Covenant on Civil and Political Rights, (19 December 1966), 999 U.N.T.S. 171, 1976 Can. T.S. No. 47.
	NOT *International Covenant on Civil and Political Rights*, (19 December 1966), 999 U.N.T.S. 171, 1976 Can. T.S. No. 47, reprinted in Hugh M. Kindred *et al.*, eds., *International Law Chiefly as Interpreted and Applied in Canada: Documentary Supplement* (N.p.: Emond Montgomery, 2000) 87.

It is always preferable to cite directly to an original source. If an original source is quoted in part in a secondary work, every effort must be made to consult the original work in order to verify the context and accuracy of the reference. The original source, however, may sometimes be difficult to find or may have been destroyed. Therefore, in such exceptional circumstances, it may be necessary to cite to the original source as cited in a secondary work. Provide as much of a complete citation to the original work as is possible, followed by "cited in" and the citation of the secondary work.

In certain cases, reference may be made to a document fully reprinted in a collection. Such is the case for collections reprinting debates, letters, or manuscripts that would usually otherwise be available only in archives. Provide as much of a complete citation to the original work as is possible, followed by "reprinted in" and the citation of the secondary material. Do not cite to books reprinting excerpts from original sources that are readily available, *e.g.* textbooks.

1.6   GENERAL RULES FOR QUOTATIONS

Examples

It was clear from this moment that "[t]he center ..of American jurisprudence had changed."[32]

"[A] mixed question of fact and law" must be appealable.[42]

[53]*Norris, supra* note 21 **[emphasis added]**.

- These rules apply to both text and footnotes.
- Short quotes of four lines or less should be placed in quotation marks and directly incorporated into the text. Quotes of more than four lines should be indented from both margins and single-spaced. Quotation marks should not be used. Legislative provisions may be indented even if they are less than four lines long.
- Spelling, capitalization, and internal punctuation in a quote must be exactly the same as in the original source; any additions must be clearly indicated in brackets. If material that starts with a lower case letter is used to start a sentence, change it to upper case and enclose the changed letter in brackets. Use an ellipsis ("..") to indicate the omission of any part of a quoted passage. Note that this rule differs from the rule applicable in French.
- Where the original source contains an error, enclose the correction in square brackets. Do not use "[*sic*]", which should only be used to draw attention to the original error.
- Text may be emphasized by using italics and placing "[emphasis added]" at the end of the citation. If the text was emphasized in the original copy, place "[emphasis in original]" at the end of the citation. If the footnotes of the original text are omitted, place "[footnotes omitted]" at the end of the citation. (Note that the placement of such expressions after the citation in the footnote is contrary to the rule applicable in French, where such expressions are placed after the quote and not in the footnote.) Such expressions should follow the establishment of a short form (*e.g. Kadlak v.*

Nunavut (Minister of Sustainable Development), [2001] Nu. J. No. 1 ¶ 9 (QL) [*Kadlak*] [emphasis added]).

1.6.1 Quoting a Source in Another Language

Example
[96] Jacques Ghestin & Gilles Goubeaux, *Traité de droit civil: Introduction générale*, 4th ed. (Paris: Librairie générale de droit et de jurisprudence, 1994) at para. 669 **[translated by author]**.

- If at all possible, use an English version of a source when writing in English and a French version when writing in French. Remember that every Canadian jurisdiction passes statutes in English.
- If quoting in another language, a translation may be provided. Translating sources from other languages is not required. Any translation should be clearly indicated in the footnote, and the translator identified. If the work is translated by a professional, then the translator's name should be indicated (see section 6.2.2.5.1). If the work is translated by the author of the essay, include the phrase "translated by author" in brackets.

2

LEGISLATION

2.1 CANADA

2.1.1 Statutes

2.1.1.1 General Form

Examples						
Title,	Statute volume	jurisdiction	year	(session or supplement),	chapter,	pinpoint.
Criminal Code,	R.S.	C.	1985,		c. C-46,	s. 745.
Income Tax Act,	R.S.	C.	1985	(5th Supp.),	c. 1,	s. 18(1)(m)(iv)(c).
Charter of human rights and freedoms,	R.S.	Q.			c. C-12,	s. 10.

- There is no space between the statute volume and the jurisdiction.
- At the time of printing, federal and provincial governments still regard electronic copies of statutes and regulations as unofficial and as being intended for research

purposes only. To indicate that an unofficial electronic copy was used, follow the rules set out at section 2.9.

2.1.1.2 Title

Examples
Manitoba Claim Settlements Implementation Act, S.C. 2000, c. 33. *Reciprocal Enforcement of Maintenance Orders Act*, S.Y. 1980, c. 25, s. 5(2).

- Italicize the title of the statute and place a non-italicized comma after the title.
- Provide the official short title of the statute. If no official short title is provided, use the title found at the head of the statute. Include "The" only if it forms part of the title.
- If the title of the statute is provided in the text, do not repeat it in the citation.
- Follow the capitalization of words in the title as set out in the statute. Note that many English titles of Quebec statutes follow French capitalization rules. Do not capitalize letters in these titles so that they conform with English language capitalization rules.
- A year that is part of the title of the statute should be included in italics within the title.

N.B. Change *"Ordinance"* to *"Act"* in the title when citing the Northwest Territories or Yukon Territory legislation originally enacted as an ordinance.

N.B. The statutes of the following jurisdictions are adopted in both English and French: Canada, Manitoba, New Brunswick, Ontario, Quebec, Nunavut, the Northwest Territories, and the Yukon Territory. However, statutes adopted prior to a certain date may exist only in English.

2.1.1.3 Statute Volume

- Canadian statutes appear in bound volumes of revised or sessional statutes. The looseleaf volumes contain the statutes in their most revised form, up to the date indicated at the bottom of the looseleaf (*i.e.* the revised statutes, including all amendments subsequent to the revision). See section 2.1.1.3.1.
- For common law jurisdictions, cite to the Revised Statutes (in Manitoba, the Re-enacted Statutes) whenever possible. Cite to the sessional or annual volumes only when citing a section that has been added or amended since the revision date, or if citing a statute that was enacted since the last revision was published.
- For Quebec statutes, cite to the looseleaf whenever possible. See section 2.1.1.3.2.

2.1.1.3.1   Revised Statutes and Sessional Volumes

Examples	
Revised statutes	*Children's Law Reform Act*, **R.S.**O. 1990, c. C-12.
	Bees Act, **R.S.Q.** c. A-1, s. 17.
Sessional volumes	*Access to Education Act*, **S.**B.C. 2001, c. 1.

- Both "Revised Statutes" and "Re-enacted Statutes" are abbreviated to "R.S." For citations to sessional volumes, simply abbreviate "Statutes" to "S."
- Use "S." for "Statutes" (not "O." for "Ordinances") when referring to any volume, past or present, of Northwest Territories or Yukon Territory legislation.

N.B. If a statute cannot be found in the current Revised Statutes, do not assume that it does not exist or that it is no longer relevant. For example, the *Canada Corporations Act* has been replaced by the *Canada Business Corporations Act* for profit-making corporations, but is still in force for non-profit corporations. The *Canada Corporations Act* was not brought forward into the 1985 revision of the *Revised Statutes of Canada*, but is found in the 1970 revision. The 1970 version as amended is still valid law.

2.1.1.3.2   Looseleafs

- Only cite the looseleaf version of the jurisdictions indicated in the table below.
- When citing the looseleaf editions of the statutes of Manitoba (C.C.S.M.) or Quebec (R.S.Q.), do not place a comma between the name of the volume and the chapter number.
- Do not cite the looseleaf of the Statutes of Canada, Alberta, British Columbia, Prince Edward Island or Saskatchewan. These publications are not official.
- No looseleaf edition presently exists for the statutes of Newfoundland and Labrador, the Northwest Territories, Nunavut, Ontario, and the Yukon Territory.
- See generally Mary Jane T. Sinclair, *Updating Statutes and Regulations for all Canadian Jurisdictions* (Toronto: Carswell, 1995) and consult the *Interpretation Acts* of the various jurisdictions.

2—Legislation

Examples	
Manitoba	*Retirement Plan Beneficiaries Act*, S.M. 1992, c. 31, **C.C.S.M. c. R138**, s. 14. Referring to the looseleaf is optional. If used, it must be preceded by the reference to the bound issue of sessional volumes. The pinpoint is placed at the end of the citation. Acts included in the *Continuing Consolidation of the Statutes of Manitoba* are cited "C.C.S.M." followed immediately by the chapter number, with no indication of the year. Statutes included in the Re-enacted Statutes are designated by the same chapter number in the C.C.S.M.
New Brunswick	The looseleaf consolidation is official; however, when citing a statute enacted since the last bound version of the *Revised Statutes of New Brunswick* (presently 1973), cite to the annual volume, *e.g. Hospital Act*, S.N.B. 1992, H-6.1 (in most cases, the annual volume need not be consulted, however, because the looseleaf consolidation is official). When referring generally to a statute included in the bound version of the *Revised Statutes*, but that has since been amended, refer only to "R.S.N.B. 1973", which is deemed to be the amended version of the *Act*. However, if the amendment is relevant to the point being discussed in the text, cite the original statute in the *Revised Statutes* first, followed by "as am. by" and the citation for the amending statute in the annual volumes.
Nova Scotia	The looseleaf consolidation is official; however, when citing a statute enacted since the last bound version of the *Revised Statutes of Nova Scotia* (presently 1989), cite to the annual volume, *e.g. Fisheries and Coastal Resources Act,* S.N.S. 1996, c. 25, s. 11 (in most cases, the annual volume need not be consulted, however, because the looseleaf consolidation is official). When referring generally to a statute included in the bound version of the *Revised Statutes*, but that has since been amended, refer only to "R.S.N.S. 1989", which is deemed to be the amended version of the *Act*. However, if the amendment is relevant to the point being discussed in the text, cite the original statute in the *Revised Statutes* first, followed by "as am. by" and the citation for the amending statute in the annual volumes.
Quebec	*Securities Act*, **R.S.Q. c. V-1.1**, s. 15. Statutes in their current form should always be cited to the looseleaf. "R.S.Q." followed immediately by the chapter number, with no reference to the year, refers to the looseleaf. The citation "R.S.Q. 1977" followed by the chapter number refers to the unamended form of the *Revised Statutes* as found in the bound volumes.

2.1.1.4 *Jurisdiction*

Examples
Proceeds of Crime (Money Laundering) Act, S.**C.** 2000, c. 17.
Workers Compensation Act, S.**P.E.I.** 1994, c. 67.

- Place the jurisdiction immediately after the statute volume.
- When citing legislation, certain jurisdictions are abbreviated differently than in other contexts (*e.g.* "N." for "Newfoundland", rather than "Nfld.").

Abbreviate the jurisdictions as follows:

Alberta	A.
British Columbia	B.C.
Canada	C.
Lower Canada	L.C.
Manitoba	M.
New Brunswick	N.B.
Newfoundland (Statutes – before 6 December 2001 / Regulations – before 13 December 2001 / Gazette – before 21 December 2001)	N.
Newfoundland and Labrador (Statutes – 6 December 2001 and after / Regulations – 13 December 2001 and after / Gazette – 21 December 2001 and after)	N.L.
Northwest Territories	N.W.T.
Nova Scotia	N.S.
Nunavut (1 April 1999 and after)	Nu.
Ontario	O.
Prince Edward Island	P.E.I.
Province of Canada	Prov. C.
Quebec	Q.
Saskatchewan	S.
Upper Canada	U.C.
Yukon Territory	Y.

2—Legislation

2.1.1.5 Year, Session, and Supplement

Examples	
Year	*Animal Protection Act*, R.S.A. **1988**, c. A-42.1.
Session spanning more than one year	*Government Organization Act, 1983*, S.C. **1980-81-82-83**, c. 167.
More than one session in a year	*An Act to amend the Business Licence Act*, S.N.W.T. **1985 (3d Sess.)**, c. 1.
Supplement	*Customs Act*, R.S.C. **1985 (2d Supp.)**, c. 1.
Regnal Year	*An Act respecting the Civilization and Enfranchisement of certain Indians*, S.Prov. C. 1859 **(22 Vict.)**, c. 9.

- Place the year after the jurisdiction. Place a comma after the year, unless a session or supplement follows the year, in which case the comma is placed after the session or supplement.
- For federal statutes enacted before 1867, and for provincial statutes enacted before the province entered Confederation, give the regnal year in parentheses following the calendar year. Otherwise give the calendar year and not the regnal year.
- Omit the year when citing the looseleaf editions of the statutes of Manitoba (C.C.S.M.) or Quebec (R.S.Q.), and do not place a comma between the name of the volume and the chapter number. See section 2.1.1.3.2.
- When a session spans more than one year, cite the full date span of the volume.
- If a statute volume is divided into several sessions with independent chapter numbering, place the number of the session (*e.g.* "1st", "2d", "3d", "4th") and the abbreviation "Sess." in parentheses following the year.
- Cite to the supplement for acts and amendments that were passed during the year in which the Revised Statutes were issued but were not included in the revision. Place the supplement number and the abbreviation "Supp." in parentheses after the date.

2.1.1.6 Chapter

Examples
Holocaust Memorial Pay Act, S.B.C. 2000, **c. 3**.
Law Reform Act, S.N.B. 1993, **c. L-1.2**.
Child Welfare Act, 1972, S.N. 1972, **No. 37**.

- Include the numeric or alphanumeric chapter designation exactly as shown in the statute volume.
- Abbreviate "chapter" to "c."

N.B. Between 1934 and 1975-76 statutes in Newfoundland sessional volumes are designated by number. Abbreviate "Number" to "No."

2.1.1.7 Pinpoint

Examples
Environmental Protection and Enhancement Act, S.A. 1992, c. E-13.3, **ss. 2, 38-42, 84**.
Legal Profession Act, 1990, S.S. 1990, c. L-10.1, **ss. 4(1), 6(2)(b)(i)-(ii), 9**.
Peddlers Act, R.S.Q. c. C-30, **s. 8, para. 3**.
Charter of the French language, R.S.Q. c. C-11, **Preamble**.
Access to Information Act, R.S.C. 1985, c. A-1, **Sch. II**.

- To refer to a specific section of a statute, place the pinpoint reference after the chapter indication but preceded by a comma.
- Do not insert "at".
- Abbreviate "section" to "s." and "sections" to "ss." in the footnotes but not in the text. Further subdivisions of sections (*e.g.* subsections, paragraphs, subparagraphs) are also abbreviated to "s." or "ss."
- Place numbered or lettered subsections in parentheses immediately after the section number.
- Refer to an unnumbered or unlettered subdivision as a "paragraph", abbreviated as the symbol ¶ or "para." in the singular and "paras." in the plural.
- Never abbreviate the word "Preamble".
- Abbreviate "Schedule" to "Sch."
- Separate consecutive sections by a hyphen; if the sections are non-consecutive, separate them with commas (*e.g.* the *Succession Law Reform Act* example).
- The provisions of Quebec codes are "articles" not "sections". Abbreviate "article" and "articles" to "art." and "arts." respectively. See section 2.1.3.

2.1.1.8 Amendments, Repeals, and Re-enactments

Examples	
Assumed to be amended	*Crown Liability Act*, R.S.C. 1985, c. C-38.
Indicating amended status	*Emergency Measures Act*, S.M. 1987, c. 11, **as am. by S.M. 1997, c. 28**. *Municipal Taxation Act*, R.S.A. 1980, c. M-31, s. 24(1)(b), **as am. by** *School Act***, S.A. 1988, c. S-3.1, s. 249(a)**.
Indicating repealed status	*Family Benefits Act*, R.S.O. 1990, c. F-2, **as rep. by** *Social Assistance Reform Act, 1997***, S.O. 1997, c. 25, s. 4(1)**.
Act amending an earlier act	*An Act to Amend the Labour Standards Act*, S.N.W.T. 1999, c. 18, **amending R.S.N.W.T. 1988, c. L-1**.
Act repealing an earlier act	*An Act respecting the James Bay Native Development Corporation*, R.S.Q. 2000, c. S-9.1, **repealing** *An Act to incorporate the James Bay Native Development Corporation***, S.Q. 1978, c. 96**.

- Citations are presumed to be to the statute as amended.
- Indicate that the statute has been amended only if it is relevant to the point being discussed in the text. When indicating an amendment, cite the original statute first, followed by "as am. by" and the citation for the amending statute.
- When an act has been repealed, always indicate the repeal in the citation. Abbreviate "as repealed by" to "as rep. by".
- Use "amending" when referring specifically to a statute that amends an earlier statute, and use "repealing" when citing a statute that repeals an earlier one.
- In all cases, the title of the second statute is indicated only if it is different from the title of the first statute, or if it is not included in the title of the first statute cited.
- If a statute or part of a statute was repealed and another substituted, cite the original statute first, followed by "as re-en. by" and the citation for the new replacement section. Use this term only if the repeal and substitute provision are found in the same section.

2.1.1.9 Appendices

Example
Canadian Bill of Rights, S.C. 1960, c. 44, **reprinted in R.S.C. 1985, App. III**.

- For statutes that appear in an appendix, always provide the official citation rather than citing the appendix alone.

- Introduce the appendix reference with the phrase "reprinted in".
- Indicate the statute revision or volume to which the appendix is attached, followed by a comma and the appendix number.
- Abbreviate "Appendix" to "App."

2.1.1.10 Statutes Within Statutes

Example
Enterprise Cape Breton Corporation Act, s. 25, **being Part II of the *Government Organization Act, Atlantic Canada, 1987*, S.C. 1988, c. 50**.

- Refer first to the title of the statute within the statute. Indicate the relevant part of the containing act and its full citation, introduced by a comma and "being".
- Pinpoint references to section numbers are placed before the citation to the containing act.

2.1.2 Constitutional Statutes

Examples	
Constitution Act, 1867	*Constitution Act, 1867* (U.K.), 30 & 31 Vict., c. 3, reprinted in R.S.C. 1985, App. II, No. 5.
Canada Act 1982	*Canada Act 1982* (U.K.), 1982, c. 11.
Constitution Act, 1982	*Constitution Act, 1982*, being Schedule B to the *Canada Act 1982* (U.K.), 1982, c. 11.
Charter	*Canadian Charter of Rights and Freedoms*, Part I of the *Constitution Act, 1982*, being Schedule B to the *Canada Act 1982* (U.K.), 1982, c. 11.
Other constitutional statutes	*Saskatchewan Act*, S.C. 1905, c. 42.

Many constitutional statutes were enacted under different names than those used today. Consult the Schedule to the *Constitution Act, 1982* to determine the new title for the statute, and use the new title. If it is necessary for the argument, provide the old title in parentheses at the end of the citation.

- As the *Canada Act 1982* is a British statute, it is cited according to the rules for the United Kingdom, at section 2.2.1.

2—Legislation

- Since the *Charter* is not an independent enactment, it is cited as Part I of the *Constitution Act, 1982*.
- A reference to Appendix II of R.S.C. 1985 may be included after the official citation. (Most Canadian constitutional statutes are reprinted in Appendix II.)

2.1.2.1 Pinpoint

Examples	
Constitution Act, 1867	*Constitution Act, 1867* (U.K.), 30 & 31 Vict., c. 3, **s. 91**, reprinted in R.S.C. 1985, App. II, No. 5.
Canada Act 1982	*Canada Act 1982* (U.K.), 1982, c. 11, **s. 1**.
Constitution Act, 1982	*Constitution Act, 1982*, **s. 35**, being Schedule B to the *Canada Act 1982* (U.K.), 1982, c. 11.
Charter	*Canadian Charter of Rights and Freedoms*, **s. 7**, Part I of the *Constitution Act, 1982*, being Schedule B to the *Canada Act 1982* (U.K.), 1982, c. 11.
Other constitutional statutes	*Saskatchewan Act*, S.C. 1905, c. 42, **s. 2**.

- Place pinpoint references to the *Charter* and the *Constitution Act, 1982* directly after the title.
- Place pinpoint references to the *Canada Act 1982* and other constitutional statutes after the chapter number.

2.1.3 Codes of Quebec

Examples	
Civil Code of Québec	Art. 1260 **C.C.Q.**
Civil Code of Québec (1980)	Art. 435 **C.C.Q. (1980)**.
Civil Code of Lower Canada	Art. 1131 **C.C.L.C.**
Code of Civil Procedure	Art. 477 **C.C.P.**
Code of Penal Procedure	Art. 104 **C.P.P.**

- Full citations are never used when referring to codes; simply cite them as illustrated here.

N.B. To cite the Minister's Comments see section 4.1.2.2.1.

N.B. The "C.C.Q. (1980)" refers to a series of family law enactments implemented in 1980: *An Act to establish a new Civil Code and to reform family law*, S.Q. 1980, c. 39. Do not confuse this with the *Civil Code of Quebec*, S.Q. 1991, c. 64 (C.C.Q.), which came into force on 1 January 1994, replacing the *Civil Code of Lower Canada* of 1866 (C.C.L.C.).

2.1.4 Nunavut

At the time of printing, a territorial Queen's Printer for Nunavut does not yet exist. Thus there is no "official" print publication for Nunavut statutes. Those seeking "official" copies of Nunavut statutes may contact the Nunavut Legislative Assembly by telephone, toll-free, at (877) 334-7266. "Unofficial" Nunavut statutes may be found online from the Nunavut Court of Justice Web site <http://www.nunavutcourtofjustice.ca/library/legislation.htm>, on Quicklaw, on Legis at <http://www.legis.ca>, and at <http://www.lex-nu.ca>.

2.1.4.1 Statutes Enacted by Nunavut

Example
Flag of Nunavut Act, S.Nu. 1999, c. 1.

- For statutes enacted by Nunavut after 1 April 1999, provide the standard citation following the general form as described in section 2.1.1.

2.1.4.2 Statutes Enacted by the Northwest Territories for Nunavut

Example
Nunavut Judicial System Implementation Act, S.N.W.T. 1998, c. 34, as enacted for Nunavut, pursuant to the *Nunavut Act*, S.C. 1993, c. 28.

- For statutes enacted specifically for Nunavut by the Northwest Territories prior to 1 April 1999 and that were only to apply to Nunavut, provide the standard citation followed by "as enacted for Nunavut, pursuant to the *Nunavut Act*, S.C. 1993, c. 28."

2—Legislation

2.1.4.3 *Statutes Duplicated by Canada for Nunavut*

Example
Official Languages Act, R.S.N.W.T. 1998, c. O-1, as duplicated for Nunavut by s. 29 of the *Nunavut Act*, S.C. 1993, c. 28.

- Under section 29 of the *Nunavut Act*, S.C. 1993, c. 28, laws from the Northwest Territories were duplicated for Nunavut to take effect on 1 April 1999 to the extent they would apply in relation to Nunavut.
- Provide the standard citation followed by "as duplicated for Nunavut by s. 29 of the *Nunavut Act*, S.C. 1993, c. 28."

2.1.5 Bills

Examples								
	Number,	*title,*	session,	legislature,	Jurisdiction,	year,	pinpoint	(additional information) (optional).
Canada	Bill C-7,	*An Act in respect of criminal justice for young persons and to amend and repeal other Acts,*	1st Sess.,	37th Parl.,		2001,	cl. 2	(as passed by the House of Commons 29 May 2001).
	Bill S-33,	*An Act to amend the Carriage by Air Act,*	1st Sess.,	37th Parl.,		2001,	cl. 42(1)(h)	(as passed by the Senate 6 November 2001).
Provinces and territories	Bill 161,	*An Act to establish a legal framework for information technology,*	2d Sess.,	36th Leg.,	Quebec,	2001		(assented to 21 June 2001), S.Q. 2001, c. 32.

- Bills originating in the House of Commons are preceded by "C-" and bills originating in the Senate are preceded by "S-".
- Always use the long title of the bill. Italicize the title and follow the bill's capitalization.
- When referring to a provincial bill, include the jurisdiction.
- Do not provide the regnal year.
- The subdivisions of a bill are "clauses", abbreviated to "cls." and "cl." in the singular.
- Additional information may be included (*e.g.* the date of first reading or the state which the bill has reached at the time of writing); place it in parentheses at the end of the citation.
- If the chapter number of the bill is known, the future statute citation may be included after the date of assent.

2.1.6   Regulations

Jurisdiction	Unrevised	Revised or Reenacted
Canada	S.O.R./2000-111, s. 4.	C.R.C., c. 1035, s. 4.
Alberta	Alta. Reg. 184/2001, s. 2.	
British Columbia	B.C. Reg. 362/2000, s. 4.	
Manitoba	Man. Reg. 155/2001, s. 3.	Man. Reg. 368/97R, s. 2.
New Brunswick	N.B. Reg. 2000-8, s. 11.	
Newfoundland	Nfld. Reg. 78/99, s. 4.	
Newfoundland and Labrador	N.L.R. 08/02, s. 2.	
Northwest Territories	N.W.T. Reg. 253-77, s. 3.	R.R.N.W.T. 1990, c. E-27, s. 16.
Nova Scotia	N.S. Reg. 24/2000, s. 8.	
Nunavut	Nu. Reg. 045-99, s. 2.	
Ontario	O. Reg. 426/00, s. 2.	R.R.O. 1990, Reg. 1015, s. 3.
Prince Edward Island	P.E.I. Reg. EC1999-598, s. 3.	
Quebec	O.C. 868-97, 2 July 1997, G.O.Q. 1997.II.3692, s. 2.	R.R.Q. 1981, c. E-12, r. 1, s. 4.

2—Legislation

Saskatchewan	S. Reg. 67/2001, s. 3.	R.R.S. 2000, c. C-50-2, Reg. 21, O.C. 359/2000, s. 6.
Yukon	Y.O.I.C. 2000/130, s. 9.	

2.1.6.1   Federal Regulations

2.1.6.1.1   Revised Regulations

Example				
Title,	C.R.C.,	chapter,	pinpoint	(year) (optional).
Migratory Birds Regulations,	C.R.C.,	c. 1035,	s. 4	(1978).

- When citing revised regulations, abbreviate Consolidated Regulations of Canada to "C.R.C."
- Indication of the year of revision of the revised regulations is optional; unless a year is specified, references are assumed to be to the latest revision.

2.1.6.1.2   Unrevised Regulations

Example			
Title,	S.O.R./	year-regulation number,	pinpoint.
Canadian Aviation Security Regulations,	S.O.R./	2000-111,	s. 4.

- Federal regulations promulgated after the Consolidation are in Part II of the *Canada Gazette*. It is not necessary to include a direct reference to the Gazette in the citation.
- "Statutory Orders and Regulations" is abbreviated to "S.O.R."
- Indication of the title is optional.

2.1.6.2   Provincial and Territorial Regulations

- The title of the regulations may be included in italics at the beginning of the citation, followed by a comma.

N.B. Alberta, British Columbia, New Brunswick, Newfoundland and Labrador, Nova Scotia, Nunavut, Prince Edward Island, and the Yukon Territory do not publish revised versions of their regulations.

2.1.6.2.1   Alberta

Example			
Jurisdiction	Reg.	number/year,	pinpoint.
Alta.	Reg.	184/2001,	s. 2.

2.1.6.2.2   British Columbia

Example			
Jurisdiction	Reg.	number/year,	pinpoint.
B.C.	Reg.	362/2000,	s. 6.

- The British Columbia looseleaf consolidation is cited in the same manner as unrevised regulations.

2.1.6.2.3   Manitoba

Examples	Jurisdiction	Reg.	number/year,	pinpoint.
Not re-enacted	Man.	Reg.	155/2001,	s. 3.
Re-enacted	Man.	Reg.	468/88R,	s. 2.

- Most of Manitoba's regulations were re-enacted in English and in French in 1987 and 1988. There has been no revision since.
- To indicate a re-enacted regulation, insert "R" immediately following the last two digits of the year.

2.1.6.2.4   New Brunswick

Example			
Jurisdiction	Reg.	year-number,	pinpoint.
N.B.	Reg.	2000-8,	s. 11.

- The New Brunswick regulations were last revised in 1963.
- The looseleaf of the New Brunswick regulations is not an official revision.

2—Legislation

2.1.6.2.5   Newfoundland and Labrador

Examples				
	Jurisdiction	Reg. or R.	number/year,	pinpoint.
Before 13 December 2001	Nfld.	Reg.	78/99,	s. 4.
13 December 2001 and after	N.L.	R.	8/02,	s. 2.

2.1.6.2.6   Northwest Territories

2.1.6.2.6.1   Unrevised

Example			
Jurisdiction	Reg.	number-year,	pinpoint.
N.W.T.	Reg.	253-77,	s. 3.

2.1.6.2.6.2   Revised

Example			
R.R.N.W.T.	year of revision,	chapter,	pinpoint.
R.R.N.W.T.	1990,	c. E-27,	s. 16.

2.1.6.2.7   Nova Scotia

Example			
Jurisdiction	Reg.	number/year,	pinpoint.
N.S.	Reg.	24/2000,	s. 8.

2.1.6.2.8   Nunavut

Example			
Jurisdiction	Reg.	number-year,	pinpoint.
Nu.	Reg.	045-99,	s. 2.

- The *Nunavut Gazette* should be consulted for all regulations made on or after 1 April 1999.
- The *Revised Regulations of the Northwest Territories* (1990) and *The Northwest Territories Gazette*, Part II, should be consulted for all regulations made prior to 1 April 1999.
- No revised version of the Nunavut Regulations has been issued.

2.1.6.2.9   Ontario

2.1.6.2.9.1   Unrevised

Example			
Jurisdiction	Reg.	number/year,	pinpoint.
O.	Reg.	426/00,	s. 2.

2.1.6.2.9.2   Revised

Example				
R.R.O.	year of revision,	Reg.	number,	pinpoint.
R.R.O.	1990,	Reg.	1015,	s. 3.

2.1.6.2.10 Prince Edward Island

Example			
Jurisdiction	Reg.	ECyear-number	pinpoint.
P.E.I.	Reg.	EC1999-598,	s. 3.

- "EC" is the abbreviation for "Executive Council".

2—Legislation

2.1.6.2.11 Quebec

2.1.6.2.11.1 Unrevised

Example				
O.C.	Number-year,	date,	gazette citation,	pinpoint.
O.C.	1240-2000,	25 October 2000,	G.O.Q. 2000.II.6817,	s. 2.

- To cite the *Gazette officielle du Québec*, see section 2.1.7.1.

2.1.6.2.11.2 Revised

Example			
R.R.Q. 1981,	number,	rule number,	pinpoint.
R.R.Q. 1981,	c. C-11,	r. 9,	s. 10.

2.1.6.2.12 Saskatchewan

2.1.6.2.12.1 Unrevised

Example			
Jurisdiction	Reg.	number/year,	pinpoint.
S.	Reg.	67/2001,	s. 3.

2.1.6.2.12.2 Revised

Example					
R.R.S.	year of revision,	chapter,	number,	O.C. number/year (if available),	pinpoint.
R.R.S.	2000,	c. C-50.2,	Reg. 21,	O.C. 359/2000,	s. 6.

2.1.6.2.13 Yukon

Example			
Jurisdiction	O.I.C.	year/number,	pinpoint.
Y.	O.I.C.	2000/130,	s. 9.

- Abbreviate "Order in Council" to "O.I.C."

2.1.7   Other Information Published in Gazettes

2.1.7.1   General Form

Examples					
Title (additional information),	gazette abbreviation	year.	part of gazette.	page	(additional information) (optional).
Ministerial Order 36/91,	A. Gaz.	1991.	I.	1609.	
Notice (Town of Wallaceburg),	C. Gaz.	1995.	I.	4400.	
O.C. 309/2001,	A. Gaz.	2001.	I.	1752	(*Provincial Parks Act*).

- *N.B.* There is a space between the gazette abbreviation and the year (*e.g.* "C. Gaz. 1995"). However, there is no space between the year and the part of the gazette; nor is there a space between the part of the gazette and the page number (*e.g.* "1995.I.4400").
- Indicate the title of the item if appropriate. If the item is numbered in some way, include the number with the title, as it appears in the gazette. The number may include the year or the last two digits of the year. Include the statutory instrument number ("S.I.") if there is one. The name of the person or body concerned by a notice may be included in parentheses after the title.
- Indicate the part of the gazette following the year. If the gazette is not published in parts, cite the page number directly after the period that follows the year (*e.g.* "1991.74").
- Additional information may be included if helpful. For example, give the name of the statute under which an order in council is made (see *The Provincial Parks Act* example above).

Abbreviate the gazettes as follows:

The Alberta Gazette	A. Gaz.
The British Columbia Gazette	B.C. Gaz.
Canada Gazette	C. Gaz.
Gazette officielle du Québec	G.O.Q.
The Manitoba Gazette	M. Gaz.
New Brunswick: *The Royal Gazette*	N.B. Gaz.
Northwest Territories Gazette	N.W.T. Gaz.
The Newfoundland Gazette (before 21 December 2001)	N. Gaz.
The Newfoundland and Labrador Gazette (21 December 2001 and after)	N.L. Gaz.
Nova Scotia: *Royal Gazette*	N.S. Gaz.
Nunavut Gazette	Nu. Gaz.
The Ontario Gazette	O. Gaz.
Prince Edward Island: *Royal Gazette*	P.E.I. Gaz.
The Saskatchewan Gazette	S. Gaz.
The Yukon Gazette	Y. Gaz.

2.1.7.2 Orders in Council

2.1.7.2.1 Federal

Examples			
Title (if available),	P.C. year-number or S.I./year-number,	gazette citation	(additional information) (optional).
	P.C. 1997-627,	C. Gaz. 1997.II.1381.	
Withdrawal from Disposal Order (North Slave Region N.W.T.),	S.I./97-42,	C. Gaz. 1997.II.1338.	

- Include the title in italics, if there is one.
- Abbreviate "Privy Council" to "P.C."
- Include the statutory instrument ("S.I.") number, if there is one.
- Additional information such as the title of the act under which the order in council is made may be provided in parenthesis.

2.1.7.2.2   Provincial and Territorial

Examples			
Title (if available),	Order in Council number,	gazette citation	(additional information) (optional).
Town of Paradise Order,	O.C. 99-529,	N. Gaz. 1999.II.451	(*Municipalities Act*).
	O.I.C. 1989/19,	Y. Gaz. 1989.II.57.	
Regulation respecting the lifting of the suspension and the application of section 41.1 of the Act respecting labour standards for certain employees,	O.I.C. 570-93,	G.O.Q. 1993.II.2607	(*Act respecting labour standards for certain employees*).

- Include the title of the instrument, if applicable.
- Cite the abbreviation for "Order in Council" as it appears in the relevant gazette.
- Cite the number as it appears in the gazette; this may include the year or the last two digits of the year.
- Additional information, such as the title of the act under which the order in council is made, may be provided.

2—Legislation

2.1.7.3 *Proclamations and Royal Instructions*

Examples				
Citation of law that entered into force or issuer of proclamation or instruction,	type of document,	date,	S.I. year-number,	gazette or other citation.
Canadian Space Agency Act, S.C. 1990, c.13,		Proclaimed in force 14 December 1990,	S.I./91-5,	C. Gaz. 1991.I.74.
	Proclamation,	1 April 1991,		S. Gaz. 1991.I.1174.
George R.,	Proclamation,	7 October 1763 (3 Geo. III),		reprinted in R.S.C. 1985, App. II, No. 1.
George R. to Governor Arthur Phillip,	Royal Instruction,	25 April 1787 (27 Geo. III),		reprinted in *Historical Documents of New South Wales*, vol. 1, part 2 (Sydney: Government Printer, 1892-1901) 67.

- When citing proclamations, the words "Proclamation" or "Royal Instruction" may be used as titles if it is appropriate in the context.
- Include the date, followed by the gazette or other citation.
- For federal proclamations dating from 1972 or after, include the statutory instrument ("S.I.") number.

2.1.8 Municipal By-laws

	Municipality,	By-law	number,	*title*	(date),	pinpoint.
Examples						
Unrevised	City of Whitehorse,	By-law	No. 97-42,	*Zoning By-law*	(11 May 1998),	s. 1.
Revised	City of Montreal,	Revised By-law	C. S-0.1.1,	*By-law Concerning Collection Services,*		s. 5.

- Include the by-law number. Provide the full title if no short title is provided.

2.1.9 Rules of Court

Jurisdiction,	*title,*	pinpoint.
Examples		
	Federal Court Immigration Rules,	r. 18.
Manitoba,	*Court of Queen's Bench Rules,*	r. 275.2.

- Include the jurisdiction unless it is part of the title of the rules.
- It is not necessary to indicate "Canada" for the rules of the Supreme Court of Canada or the Federal Court.
- Abbreviate "rule" to "r."
- To cite to the Quebec *Code of Civil Procedure* or *Code of Penal Procedure*, see section 2.1.3.

2.2 UNITED KINGDOM

With the exception of the differences noted below, cite United Kingdom legislation in the same manner as Canadian legislation.

2—Legislation

2.2.1 Statutes

Examples	
Before 1963	*Statute of Westminster, 1931* (U.K.), 22 & 23 Geo. V., c. 4, s. 2.
1 January 1963 and after	*Terrorism Act 2000* (U.K.), 2000, c. 11, s. 129.

- Include "(U.K.)" after the title of the statute to indicate its origin.
- **Before 1963:** When the title includes a year, place a comma before the year. Cite the regnal year in Arabic numerals. The number following the abbreviation for the monarch should be in Roman numerals (*e.g.* "Geo. V").
- **1 January 1963 and after:** When the title includes a year, do not place a comma before the year. Indicate the calendar year after "(U.K.)", preceded by a comma.

2.2.1.1 Northern Ireland

2.2.1.1.1 Legislation Passed by the United Kingdom

Examples	
Before 1963	*Public Health (Ireland) Act, 1878* (U.K.), 41 & 42 Vict., c. 52.
1 January 1963 and after	*Northern Ireland Act 1998* (U.K.), 1998, c. 47, s. 5.

- Cite legislation applying to Northern Ireland passed by the United Kingdom in the same manner as United Kingdom legislation.

2.2.1.1.2 Legislation Passed by Northern Ireland

Examples	
1921-1972	*Criminal Law Amendment (Northern Ireland) Act*, R.S.N.I. 1923, c. 8.
	National Insurance Act, N.I. Pub. Gen. Acts 1946, c. 23, s. 7.
1999-present	*Family Law Act (Northern Ireland) 2001*, (N.I.), 2001, c. 12.

- Abbreviate "Northern Ireland Public General Acts" to "N.I. Pub. Gen. Acts".
- Abbreviate "Statutes Revised, Northern Ireland" to "R.S.N.I."

- The United Kingdom passed legislation for Northern Ireland from 1972-1999. On 19 November 1998, the Northern Irish Assembly was created and empowered to pass legislation as of 2 December 1999. For legislation passed by the Assembly after 1999, include "(N.I.)" after the title of the statute to indicate its origin. Otherwise cite in the same manner as United Kingdom legislation. Note that after 2 December 1999, the United Kingdom can still pass legislation affecting Northern Ireland.

2.2.1.2 Scotland

Examples	
Before 1998	*Contract (Scotland) Act 1997* (U.K.), 1997, c. 34.
	Scotland Act 1998 (U.K.), 1998, c. 46, s. 4.
1998-present	*Standards in Scotland's Schools etc. Act*, A.S.P. 2000, c. 6, s. 2.

- Before 1998, cite in the same manner as United Kingdom legislation.
- Note that Acts passed by the United Kingdom still apply to Scotland if the legislation pertains to a reserved or non-devolved matter.
- From 19 November 1998, abbreviate "Acts of Scottish Parliament" to "A.S.P."

2.2.1.3 Wales

Example
Government of Wales Act 1998 (U.K.), 1998, c. 38, s. 3.

- The United Kingdom passes legislation pertaining to Wales. Cite this legislation in the same manner as United Kingdom legislation.

2—Legislation

2.2.2 Bills

2.2.2.1 United Kingdom

Examples					
Bill no.,	*title,*	session,	year,	pinpoint	(additional information) (optional).
Bill 49,	*Anti-terrorism, Crime and Security,*	2001-2002 Sess.,	2001		(1st reading 19 November 2001).
Bill 40,	*British Overseas Territories Bill [HL],*	2001-2002 Sess.,	2001,	s. 2.	

- Bills that originate in the House of Lords have "[HL]" in the title.

2.2.2.2 Northern Ireland

Example					
Number,	*title,*	session,	year,	pinpoint	(additional information) (optional).
NIA Bill 15/00,	*A bill to amend the Game Preservation (Northern Ireland) Act 1928,*	2001-2002 Sess.,	2001,	s. 2	(Committee Stage 29 October 2001).

2.2.2.3 Scotland

Example					
Number,	*title,*	session,	year,	pinpoint	(additional information) (optional).
SP Bill 36,	*Freedom of Information (Scotland) Bill,*	Sess. 1,	2001,	s. 16.	

2.2.3 Regulations

2.2.3.1 United Kingdom

Examples			
	Title (optional),	S.R. & O. or S.I.	year/number.
Before 1948	*Public Health (Prevention of Tuberculosis) Regulations 1925,*	S.R. & O.	1927/757.
1948 and after	*The Community Legal Service (Costs) Regulations 2000,*	S.I.	2000/441.

- Including the title of the regulation is optional.
- Before 1948: Abbreviate "Statutory Rules & Orders" to "S.R. & O."   After 1948: Abbreviate "Statutory Instruments" to "S.I."

2.2.3.2 Northern Ireland

Examples			
Title (optional),	S.R. & O. or S.I.	year/number	(N.I. number).
The Proceeds of Crime (Northern Ireland) Order 1996,	S.I.	1996/1299	(N.I. 9).
Tax Credits (Miscellaneous Amendments No. 8) (Northern Ireland) Regulations,	S.I.	2001/3086.	
Cheese Regulations (N.I.) 1970,	S.R. & O.	1970/14.	
Dangerous Substances in Harbour Areas Regulations (Northern Ireland) 1991,	S.R.	1991/509.	

- Including the title of the regulation is optional.
- If the regulation or order is passed by the U.K., it is contained in the *Statutory Instruments*.
- Some regulations passed by the Northern Irish Assembly are also included in the *Statutory Instruments*. These regulations include "(N.I.)" and a number at the end of the title of the regulation.
- If the regulation is passed by the Northern Irish Assembly it is called a "Statutory Rule", which is abbreviated "S.R."

2—Legislation

- Northern Ireland regulations are also included in *Statutory Regulations and Orders* (abbreviated "S.R. & O.") beginning in 1922.
- If there is a Northern Ireland Order number, include it after the year/number to indicate that the order was passed by the Northern Ireland Assembly.

2.2.3.3 Scotland

- Cite Scottish regulations in the same manner as United Kingdom regulations.

2.2.3.3.1   Regulations Passed by the United Kingdom

Example		
Title (optional),	S.R. & O. or S.I.	year/number.
Employment Tribunals (Constitution and Rules of Procedure) (Scotland),	S.I.	2001/1170.

2.2.3.3.2   Regulations Passed by the Scottish Parliament

Example		
Title (optional),	Scot. S.I.	year/number.
National Health Service (General Ophthalmic Services) (Scotland) Amendment Regulations,	Scot. S.I.	2001/62.

- Abbreviate "Scottish Statutory Instruments" to "Scot. S.I."

2.2.3.4 Wales

Example			
Title (optional),	S.R. & O. or S.I.	year/number	(W. number).
Children's Homes Amendment (Wales) Regulations 2001,	S.I.	2001/140	(W. 6).

- After the year/number, include the Welsh regulation number to indicate that the regulation was passed by the National Assembly for Wales.

2.3   UNITED STATES

2.3.1 Federal and State Constitutions

Examples
U.S. Const. art. III, § 2, cl. 3.   U.S. Const. amend. XIV, § 1.   N.M. Const. art. IV, § 7.

- Abbreviate "article" to "art.", "section" to "§.", and "sections" to "§§."
- A paragraph within a section is labeled a "clause", and abbreviated to "cl." or "cls." in the plural.
- Abbreviate "amendment" to "amend."
- Abbreviate "preamble" to "pmbl."
- Indicate article and amendment numbers in capital Roman numerals. Indicate section and clause numbers in Arabic numerals.

See Appendix B for a list of state abbreviations.

2.3.2 Statutes

In descending order of preference, cite statutes to:

1. An official code.
2. An unofficial code.
3. An official reporter of session laws.
4. An unofficial reporter of session laws.
5. A looseleaf service.

2.3.2.1 Codes

A code in the United States is a consolidation and codification by subject matter of the general and permanent laws of the United States. To determine whether a state code is official or unofficial consult *The Bluebook: A Uniform System of Citation*, 17th ed. (Cambridge, Mass.: Harvard Law Review Association, 2000).

An official code is a code of the laws of the United States organized under 50 subject titles, prepared under the supervision of an appropriate government authority (*e.g.* federal Department of Justice). The official federal code is the *United States Code* ("U.S.C.").

An unofficial code is a code of the laws of the United States prepared by private publishers. Unofficial federal codes include the *United States Code Service* ("U.S.C.S.") and the *United States Code Annotated* ("U.S.C.A.").

2—Legislation

Examples								
	Title (exception-ally),	division of code (if applicable)	Abbreviat-ed code name	title number (if applicable)	section	(publisher	supplement (if applicable)	year).
Official codes	*Americans with Disabilities Act,*	42	U.S.C.		§ 12101			(1990).
			Minn. Stat.		§ 169.947			(1990).
			I.R.C.		§ 61			(1994).
Non-official codes		8	U.S.C.A.		§ 1182	(West		1997).
			Pa. Stat. Ann.	tit. 63	§ 425.3	(West	Supp.	1986).
			Wis. Stat. Ann.		§ 939.645	(West	Supp.	1992).

- Once a statute has been codified, its original title is not usually cited. Include the title only for a special reason (*e.g.* because it is commonly known by that name). Italicize the title.
- If the code is divided into separate numbered titles, chapters, or volumes, the number of that division must be included. When citing the federal code, indicate the division before the code abbreviation. When citing state codes, consult *The Bluebook: A Uniform System of Citation*, 17th ed. (Cambridge, Mass.: Harvard Law Review Association, 2000).
- Do not italicize the abbreviated name of the code. Citations to the Internal Revenue Code can replace "26 U.S.C." with "I.R.C."
- When citing to an unofficial code, include the name of the publisher before the year, or before "Supp." where applicable.
- When citing a supplement found in a pocket insert, place "Supp." before the year indicated on the title page of the supplement.
- Include the year of publication of the code in parentheses at the end of the citation. When citing a bound volume, provide the year that appears on the spine of the volume. When citing a supplement, provide the year that appears on the title page of the supplement.

2.3.2.2 Session laws

Session laws are the statutes passed by a session of Congress, bound and indexed chronologically. Session laws track the historical development of a law.

Examples								
Title (or date of enactment),	public law number or chapter number,	section (optional),	session laws reporter	first page of act	pinpoint to reporter	(year) (if not in title)	(codification information) (optional).
The Indian Child Welfare Act of 1978,	Pub. L. No. 95-608,		92 Stat.	3069			(codified as amended at 25 U.S.C. § 1901-1963 (1988)).
Antiterrorism and Effective Death Penalty Act of 1996,	Pub. L. No. 104-132,	§ 327,	110 Stat.	1214	at 1257	(1997).	
Act of 25 April 1978,	c. 515	§ 3,	1978 Ala. Acts	569	at 570.		

- Provide the name of the statute in italics. If it has no name, identify it by the date of its enactment (*e.g.* "Act of 25 April 1978"). If no date of enactment is available, identify it by the date on which the act came into effect (*e.g.* "Act effective [date]").
- Provide the public law number, introduced by the abbreviation "Pub. L. No.", or the chapter number of the statute. The number before the hyphen is the session. The number following the hyphen is the identifier.
- To refer to a particular section, indicate the section number directly after the public law number or the chapter number. If referring to a particular section, also include a pinpoint to the reporter.
- For federal statutes, the official reporter is the *Statutes at Large*, abbreviated to "Stat." The abbreviation of the reporter is preceded by the volume number, followed by the first page of the act. *N.B.* To determine whether a reporter of state session laws is official or unofficial consult *The Bluebook: A Uniform System of Citation*, 17th ed. (Cambridge, Mass.: Harvard Law Review Association, 2000).
- Indicate a pinpoint following the citation to the first page of the act. If including a pinpoint to the reporter, also include a pinpoint to the particular section after the public law number or the chapter number.
- Indicate the year the statute was enacted in parentheses at the end of the citation, unless the year is part of the name of the statute. The year in the title might not coincide with the year in which the statute was published, in which case you must provide both. See *Antiterrorism and Effective Death Penalty Act of 1996* example above.
- Codification information for the law should be provided if it is available. Often a single statute is divided and codified under many subject headings of the code. If so,

2—Legislation

indicate this with parenthetical information at the end of the citation "(codified as amended in scattered sections of 26 U.S.C.)".

2.3.2.3 Unofficial Reporters of Session Laws

Example						
Title,	public law number,	[volume]	U.S.C.C.A.N.	pinpoint,	session law citation.
Veteran's Benefits Improvements Act of 1996,	Pub. L. No. 104-275,	[1996]	U.S.C.C.A.N.	3762,	110 Stat. 3322.

- The most important unofficial reporter of session laws is the *United States Code Congressional and Administrative News* abbreviated to "U.S.C.C.A.N."
- When citing to the U.S.C.C.A.N., indicate the volume and page number of *Statutes at Large* ("Stat.") in which the law will subsequently appear.

2.3.3 Uniform Codes, Uniform Acts, and Restatements

Uniform Codes and Uniform Acts are proposed legislation, published by the National Conference of Commissioners of Uniform State Laws, to be adopted in all state legislatures, districts, and protectorates. Restatements are reports of the state of American common law on a given topic and interpretation of statutes, published by the American Law Institute.

Examples		
Title	section	(year of adoption).
U.C.C.	§ 2-012	(1995).
Uniform Partnership Act	§ 23	(1969).
Restatements of Security	§ 51	(1941).
Restatement (Second) of the Law of Property	§ 15	(1977).

- Italicize the title, unless it is a code.
- Do not place a comma after the title of a code or a restatement.
- When more than one restatement has been produced, indicate the number in parentheses.

- At the end of the citation, in parentheses, indicate the year of adoption, promulgation, or latest amendment, which often appears on the title page.

2.3.4 Bills and Resolutions

2.3.4.1 Federal Bills

Examples								
U.S.,	Bill	house	number,	*title,*	Congress number,	year,	pinpoint	(status, if enacted).
U.S.,	Bill	H.R.	6,	*Higher Education Amendments of 1998,*	105th Cong.,	1997		(enacted).
U.S.,	Bill	S.	7,	*Educational Excellence for All Learners Act of 2001,*	107th Cong.,	2001,	s. 103.	

- Abbreviate House of Representatives as "H.R." and Senate as "S."

2.3.4.2 Federal Resolutions

Examples						
U.S.,	type of resolution	number,	*title,*	Congress number,	year	(status, if enacted).
U.S.,	H.R. Con. Res.	6,	*Expressing the Sense of the Congress Regarding the Need to Pass Legislation to Increase Penalties on Perpetrators of Hate Crimes,*	107th Cong.,	2001.	
U.S.,	H.R. Res.	31,	*Designating Minority Membership on Certain Standing Committees of the House,*	104th Cong.,	1995	(enacted).

2—Legislation

Abbreviate the type of resolution as follows :

House Concurrent Resolutions	H.R. Con. Res.
House Resolutions	H.R. Res.
House Joint Resolutions	H.R.J. Res.
Senate Concurrent Resolutions	S. Con. Res.
Senate Resolutions	S. Res.
Senate Joint Resolutions	S.J. Res.

2.3.4.3 State Bills and Resolutions

Examples									
U.S.,	type of bill or resolution	number,	*title,*	year or legisla-ture number,	number or designation of legislative session,	state,	year,	pinpoint	(status, if enacted).
U.S.,	A.B.	31,	*An Act to Add Section 51885 to the Education Code, Relating to Educational Technology,*	1997-98,	Reg. Sess.,	Cal.,	1996,	s. 1.	
U.S.,	S.R.	10,	*Calling for the Establishment of a Delaware State Police Community Relations Task Force,*	141st Gen. Assem.,	Reg. Sess.,	Del.,	2001		(enacted).

- In addition to Regular Sessions, state legislatures may hold First, Second and Third Extraordinary Sessions. Abbreviate these as "1st Extra Sess.", "2d Extra. Sess.", and "3d Extra. Sess.", respectively. Special Sessions may be abbreviated "Spec. Sess."
- Abbreviate the state according to the list in Appendix B.

2.3.5 Rules and Regulations

2.3.5.1 The Code of Federal Regulations

The *Code of Federal Regulations* is the codification of the regulations of the United States, organized under the same 50 subject titles as the United States Code.

Examples				
Title (exceptionally),	volume	C.F.R.	section	(year).
EPA Effluent Limitations Guidelines,	40	C.F.R.	§ 405.53	(1980).
	47	C.F.R.	§ 73.609	(1994).

- Indicate the title of the rule or regulation when it is commonly known under such a name.
- When possible, cite federal rules and regulations to the *Code of Federal Regulations* ("C.F.R.").

N.B. For a list of official state administrative compilations, consult *The Bluebook: A Uniform System of Citation,* 17th ed. (Cambridge, Mass.: Harvard Law Review Association, 2000).

2.3.5.2 Administrative Registers

Administrative registers report, among other things, administrative regulations enacted by government authorities.

Example						
Title (if applicable)	volume	Fed. Reg.	page	(year)	(codification information	pinpoint for codification information).
	44	Fed. Reg.	124,37221	(1979)	(to be codified at 29 C.F.R.	§ 552).

- When rules and regulations have not been codified, cite them to an administrative register.
- For federal rules and regulations, refer to the *Federal Register* ("Fed. Reg.").
- Include the number of the volume, the abbreviation of the register, the page number, and the year.
- When possible, at the end of the citation indicate where the rule or regulation will appear in the official compilation.

N.B. To identify state administrative registers, and for more information on citing American legislation, consult *The Bluebook: A Uniform System of Citation,* 17th ed. (Cambridge, Mass: Harvard Law Review Association, 2000).

2.4   FRANCE

2.4.1   Statutes and Other Legislative Instruments

Examples					
Title,	J.O.,	publication date	(N.C.) (if applicable),	page	parallel citation.
Loi n° 99-493 du 15 juin 1999,	J.O.,	16 June 1999,		8759,	D. 1999.Lég.3.7.
Ordonnance n° 2001-766 du 29 août 2001,	J.O.,	31 August 2001,		13946,	D. 2001.Lég.2564.
Décret du 5 décembre 1978 portant classement d'un site pittoresque,	J.O.,	6 December 1978	(N.C.),	9250.	

- Cite the title of the statute in French, but provide all information pertaining to the date of the actual enactment in English. If the legislation has a number, then its descriptive title is optional. If the legislation does not have a number, include its descriptive title in full.
- Always cite first to the *Journal officiel de la République française*, abbreviated to "J.O.", followed by the publication date and the page number. For J.O. supplements, place "(N.C.)" for *numéro complémentaire* after the publication date. For a list of earlier versions of the *Journal officiel*, consult section 4.4.2.
- When possible, provide a parallel citation to a French reporter, according to the rules at section 3.5.4.

2.4.2 Codes

Code civil des Français (1804-1807)	Art. 85 **C.c.F.**
Code Napoléon (1807-1814)	Art. 85 **C.N.**
Code civil (1815-)	Art. 1536 **C. civ.**
Code pénal	Art. 30 **C. pén.**
Nouveau Code de procédure civile	Art. 1439 **N.C. proc. civ.**
Code de propriété intellectuelle	Art. 123(8) **C.P.I.**
Code de procédure pénale	Art. 144(2) **C. proc. pén.**

- Full citations are never used when referring to codes; simply cite them as illustrated here. Note that the abbreviations are in the original language.

2.5   AUSTRALIA

2.5.1 Statutes

Examples		
Title	(jurisdiction),	pinpoint.
Corporations Act 2001	(Cth.).	
Electricity Reform Act 2000	(N.T.).	
Marine Pollution Act 1987	(N.S.W.),	s. 53(1)(d).

- Acts should be referred to by their official short title in italics. Include the year of the act as part of the title.
- The abbreviation for the jurisdictional statutory compilation should be placed immediately after the title.

Australian jurisdictions should be abbreviated as follows:

Commonwealth	Cth.
Australian Capital Territory	A.C.T.
New South Wales	N.S.W.
Northern Territory	N.T.
Queensland	Qld.
South Australia	S.A.
Tasmania	Tas.
Victoria	Vic.
Western Australia	W.A.

Legislation is found in the following statutory compilations:

Acts of Parliament of the Commonwealth of Australia
Laws of the Australian Capital Territory, Acts
Statutes of New South Wales
Northern Territory of Australia Laws
Laws of the Northern Territory of Australia
Queensland Acts
Queensland Statutes
South Australia Statutes
Tasmanian Statutes
Acts of the Victorian Parliament
Victorian Statutes
Statutes of Western Australia

2.5.2 Delegated Legislation (Regulations)

Examples		
Title	Regulatory compilations / session laws,	pinpoint.
Admiralty Rules 1998	(Cth.),	r. 5(b).
Income Tax Regulations (Amendment) 1996	(Cth.).	
Supreme Court Rules (Amendment) 1996	(A.C.T.),	r. 2.

• Regulations and Rules generally follow the same style as statutes.

Regulations are found in the following compilations:

Commonwealth Statutory Rules
Laws of the Australian Capital Territory, Subordinate Legislation
New South Wales Rules, Regulations, and By-Laws
Queensland Subordinate Legislation
Tasmanian Statutory Rules
Victorian Statutory Rules, Regulations, and By-Laws
Western Australia Subsidiary Legislation

2.6   NEW ZEALAND

With the exception of the differences noted below, cite New Zealand legislation in the same manner as Canadian legislation.

2.6.1 Statutes

Examples				
Title	(N.Z.),	year/number,	RS	first page.
Abolition of the Death Penalty Act 1989	(N.Z.),	1989/119,	41 RS	1.
Kiwifruit Industry Restructuring Act 1999	(N.Z.),	1999/95.		

2—Legislation

- Include "(N.Z.)" after the title of the statute to indicate its origin.
- Provide volume number followed by "RS" (for Reprint Series).

2.6.2 Delegated Legislation (Regulations)

Examples					
Title	(N.Z.),	year number or Gazette year,	Gazette page	RS	page.
Kiwifruit Export Regulations 1999	(N.Z.),	1999/310.			
Ticketing of Meat Notice 1979	(N.Z.),	Gazette 1979,	2030.		
High Court Amendment Rules (No 2) 1987	(N.Z.),	1987/169,		40 RS	904.

- Include "(N.Z.)" after the title of the statute to indicate its origin.
- Provide volume number followed by "RS" (for Reprint Series).

2.7   SINGAPORE

2.7.1 Constitutional Documents

Constitution of the Republic of Singapore (1999 Rev. Ed.), art. 12(1).
Independence of Singapore Agreement 1965 (1985 Rev. Ed.).
Republic of Singapore Independence Act (1985 Rev. Ed.), No. 7 of 1965, art. 2.

- Cite the constitutional amendments in the same form as ordinary legislation.
- Revised Edition is abbreviated to "Rev. Ed."

2.7.2 Legislation

Examples	
Statutes from the Revised Edition	Penal Code (Cap. 224, 1985 Rev. Ed. Sing.), s. 34.
Statutes not yet assigned a Revised **Edition** chapter number	United Nations Act 2001 (No. 44 of 2001, Sing.), s. 2.

- Revised Edition of the Statutes of the Republic of Singapore is abbreviated to "Rev. Ed. Sing."

- "Cap." refers to Chapter.
- For recent acts that have not yet been assigned a chapter number in a revised edition, use the act number as in the example above. The act number is not to be confused with the "Acts Supplement" number, which is a number given to each supplement of the Government Gazette publishing recent enactments.
- For legislation prior to 15 August 1945, the following abbreviations should be inserted after the title of the statute:
  - for legislation during the Straits Settlements period (1 April 1867 to 15 February 1942) use (S.S.)
  - for legislation by the Japanese Military Administration during the occupation of Singapore (15 February 1942 to 15 August 1945) use (J.M.A.)
- For legislation after 15 August 1945, use (Sing.) to refer to legislation passed during the following periods:
  - British Military Administration
  - Colony of Singapore
  - State of Singapore, both before and during federation with Malaysia
  - Republic of Singapore

2.7.3 Amendments and Repeals

Example
Penal Code (Cap. 224, 1985 Rev. Ed. Sing.), s. 73, as am. by *Penal Code (Amendment) Act*, No. 18 of 1998, s. 2.

- For further details, see section (Canadian amendments and repeals) 2.1.1.8.

2.7.4 English Statutes Applicable in Singapore

Example
Misrepresentation Act (Cap. 390, 1994 Rev. Ed. Sing.), s. 2.

- English statutes now applicable in Singapore under the *Application of English Law Act* (Cap. 7A, 1994 Rev. Ed. Sing.), may be cited to their Singapore revised edition in the same manner as Singapore statutes.

2—Legislation

2.7.5 Subsidiary Legislation (Regulations)

Examples After 1965		
Title	(Rev. Ed. or S. number),	regulation number
Housing and Development Conveyancing Fees Rules	(1999 Rev. Ed. Sing.),	r. 2
United Nations (Anti-Terrorism Measures) Regulations 2001	(S. 561/2001 Sing.),	r. 3

- The revised editions of subsidiary legislation are not numbered.
- Revised Edition is abbreviated to "Rev. Ed."

2.8   SOUTH AFRICA

2.8.1 Statutes

Examples			
Title,	Number	of year,	pinpoint.
Constitution of the Republic of South Africa 1996,	No. 108	of 1996.	
National Environmental Management Act, 1998,	No. 107	of 1998,	s. 3.

2.8.2 Bills

Number,	title,	session,	parliament,	year,	pinpoint.
B50-2000,	*Conventional Arms Control Bill,*	2d sess.,	2d Parl.,	2001.	
B03-2001,	*Unemployment Insurance Bill,*	2d sess.,	2d Parl.,	2001,	s. 2.

- Cite South African bills in the same manner as Canadian bills.
- Additional information may be added in parentheses at the end of the citation.

2.9   LEGISLATION FROM ELECTRONIC SERVICES

Note that most jurisdictions consider electronic reprints of legislation as unofficial copies for research purposes only. The authoritative text of legislation and regulations is contained in the official printed copies.

2.9.1   Electronic Services

Examples	
Full citation of legislation	(Electronic service and database (optional)).
Crown Liability Act, R.S.C. 1985, c. C-38	(QL, R.S.C.).
Americans with Disabilities Act, 42 U.S.C. § 12101 (1990)	(Lexis).
United Nations Act 2001 (No. 44 of 2001, Sing.), s. 2	(Lawnet).

- Provide the full citation, followed by the electronic service in parentheses.
- If the document cannot be readily found on the service without knowing the database within the electronic service, indicate the database in which the document can be found (*e.g.* "(QL, R.S.C.)").
- This form of citation should be used only for electronic services that require a subscription, or for Internet sites that are similarly organized with comprehensive indexes, search tools, professional editors, and recognizable abbreviations. Citation to government Internet sites should include the full Internet address (see section 2.9.2).
- Include a paragraph number as a pinpoint reference, if available. If the page numbering of a printed source is reproduced in the electronic source, reference may be made to those page numbers. Do not pinpoint to the electronic service's screen number or page number, as these are specific to the service used and can vary in different formats (*e.g.* text, html).
- If possible, do not cite to an electronic service to which the majority of readers will not have access. For example, do not cite to Azimut when writing for an audience outside of Quebec.

2—Legislation

The following is a list of abbreviations of acceptable electronic services:

Australian Legal Information Institute	AustLII
Azimut (produced by SOQUIJ)	Azimut
British and Irish Legal Information Institute	BILII
Butterworths Services	Butterworths
Canadian Legal Information Institute	CanLII
*e*Carswell	eC
Lawnet	Lawnet
Legifrance	Legifrance
LexisNexis	Lexis
LexUM	LexUM
Quicklaw	QL
Westlaw	WL

2.9.2 Internet Sites

Example			
Full citation,	online:	name of Web site	<URL>.
An Act respecting the protection of personal information in the private sector, R.S.Q. c. P-39.1, s. 11,	online:	Publications du Québec	<http://www.publicationsduquebec. gouv.qc.ca>.

- Provide the full traditional citation, followed a comma, "online:", the name of the Web page, and the URL.
- Cite the full Web address of the document you are citing unless the address is specific to one Web session. In this instance, cite the home page of the Web site.
- Internet sources differ in their reliability. Judgment must be exercised when citing to these sources.

- Many online articles expire after a short period of time. Cite to online sources only if the source provides an archive of material for a reasonable period of time, preferably several years.
- Include a paragraph number as a pinpoint reference, if available. If the page numbering of a printed source is reproduced in the electronic source, reference may be made to those page numbers.

2—Legislation

3

JURISPRUDENCE

This chapter refers to the neutral citation on several occasions. Neutral citation permits permanent identification of a case independent of the electronic database or printed reporter in which it is published. For further information on neutral citation and citation to electronic sources, see sections 3.10 and 3.11.

3.1 WHICH SOURCE TO CITE FROM

Examples	
Neutral citation available, not yet published in any printed reporter: cite to neutral citation only (do not cite to an electronic service).	*Whiten v. Pilot Insurance*, 2002 SCC 18.
Neutral citation available, published in printed reporter(s): cite to printed reporter(s), include neutral citation as final parallel citation.	*R. v. Latimer*, [2001] 1 S.C.R. 3, 193 D.L.R. (4th) 577, 2001 SCC 1 [*Latimer* cited to S.C.R.].
No neutral citation available, published in both official and other reporter: cite to official reporter, preferably including the other reporter as a parallel citation.	*Baker v. Canada (Minister of Citizenship and Immigration)*, [1999] 2 S.C.R. 817, 174 D.L.R. (4th) 193, L'Heureux-Dubé J. [*Baker* cited to S.C.R.].

No neutral citation available, not published in official reporter: cite to semi-official (preferred) or unofficial reporter, preferably including a parallel citation where available.	*Wigle v. Allstate Insurance Co. of Canada* (1984), 49 O.R. (2d) 101 (H.C.).
No neutral citation available, published in printed reporter accessed through electronic service or Internet: if quoted or pinpointed, identify electronic service or URL after traditional citation.	*Lachine General Hospital v. Québec (A.G)*, [1996] R.J.Q. 2804, 142 D.L.R. (4th) 659 at 665, Robert J., (QL) [*Lachine* cited to D.L.R.].
No neutral citation available, not published in printed reporter, accessed through electronic service: cite to number assigned by electronic service.	*R. v. Leimanis*, [1992] B.C.J. No. 2280 (Prov. Ct.) (QL).
No neutral citation available, unreported decision, not accessed through electronic service: follow rules for unreported decisions.	*Commission des droits de la personne du Québec c. Brasserie O'Keefe* (13 September 1990), Montreal 500-05-005826-873 (Qc. Sup. Ct.).

3.2   CANADA—CITATION TO PRINTED REPORTERS

3.2.1 General Form

Examples							
Style of cause	(year of decision),	[year of reporter]	volume	reporter	(series) (if any)	page	(jurisdiction and/or court) (if required).
R. v. Latimer,		[2001]	1	S.C.R.		3.	
R. v. Macki	(2001),		199	D.L.R.	(4th)	178	(B.C.S.C.).
Griffiths v. Zambosco	(2001),		54	O.R.	(3d)	397	(C.A.).

Example				
First citation	pinpoint,	parallel citation,	judge (optional)	(establishment of a short form).
R. v. Sharpe, [2001] 1 S.C.R. 45	at 97,	194 D.L.R. (4th) 1, 2001 SCC 2,	McLachlin C.J.C.	[*Sharpe* cited to S.C.R.].

3.2.2 Style of Cause

- If the style of cause is written in the text, do not repeat it in the footnote.
- Italicize both the names of the parties and the "v." or "c." that separates the names of the parties.
- In order to accord with the rules governing the neutral citation standard, the use of the "v." and "c." in the style of cause may now indicate the language of the decision being cited. If the decision of the tribunal is in English, use "v." If the decision of the tribunal is in French, use "c." If the decision is bilingual, use "v." if you are writing in English, use "c." if you are writing in French, and use either if you are writing in another language.

Examples		
	If you are writing in English	If you are writing in French
Decision written in English	*Pacific Developments Ltd. v. Calgary (City of)*	*Pacific Developments Ltd. v. Calgary (Ville de)*
Decision written in French	*Traverse Trois-Pistoles Escoumins Ltée c. Quebec (Commission des Transports)*	*Traverse Trois-Pistoles Escoumins Ltée c. Québec (Commission des Transports)*
Bilingual decision	*Committee for the Equal Treatment of Asbestos Minority Shareholders v. Ontario (Securities Commission)*	*Comité pour le traitement égal des actionnaires minoritaires de la Société Asbestos Ltée c. Ontario (Commission des valeurs mobilières)*

- Capitalize the first letter of a party name and the first letter of all words, other than prepositions, conjunctions, and words in procedural phrases.
- Translate descriptions such as "city" but do not translate words forming part of the name of a party, such as "University", and do not translate abbreviations such as "Ltd." or "LLP".

- Omit "The", "Le", "La", "L'", or "Les" as the first word of any party name, whether part of a company name or not. However, include any of these words if they are part of the name of an object proceeded against *in rem* (*e.g.* aircraft or ships, such as *The Mihalis Angelos*).

3.2.2.1 Names of Parties

Examples	
	Toneguzzo-Norvell v. Savein *Best v. Best*
NOT	*Jessica Teresa Toneguzzo-Norvell v. Nelson Savein* *Theodore Clifford Best v. Marlene Shirley Best*

- Use only last names; omit first names or first initials.
- Where more than one person is on either side of the action, use only the first person's name.
- Omit expressions such as "*et al.*" that indicate multiple parties.

3.2.2.2 Person Represented by Guardian or Tutor

Examples
*Williams (**Guardian ad litem of**) v. Canadian National Railway*
*Dobson (**Litigation guardian of**) v. Dobson*

3.2.2.3 Names of Companies and Partnerships

Examples	
	*Sloan v. **Union Oil Co. of Canada Ltd.***
	*Metson v. **R.W. de Wolfe Ltd.***
	*Prowse Chowne **LLP** v. Northey*
	*National Party of Canada v. Canadian Broadcasting **Corp.***
NOT	*Sloan v. Union Oil* *Metson v. de Wolfe*
BUT	*Wickberg v. **Shatsky & Shatsky***

- Always include "Ltd.", "ltée", "Limited", "s.r.l.", or "LLP". Do not translate these identifying words or abbreviations.
- If it is clear from the name that a party is a company, do not include "Inc." or "Co." However, if it is not clear from the name that the party is a company, or if these identifying words or abbreviations do not come at the end of the name of the company (*e.g.* "Union Oil Co. of Canada"), include the appropriate identifying words. These words are also included if they form an integral part of the name of the company. In such cases, "Corporation" is abbreviated "Corp."
- Include given names and initials that form part of a company or firm name. Also include the names of all partners in a partnership.
- When a company has a bilingual name, use the name of the company in the language of the decision you are citing. If the decision is bilingual, use the name of the company in the language in which you are writing. If you are writing in a language other than English or French, use either language version of the name of the company.

3.2.2.4 *Countries, Federal Units, Provinces, and Municipalities*

Examples	
Country	*United States v. Burns*
NOT	*The United States of America v. Burns*
Province, State	*Mercier v. Alberta (A.G.)*
Municipality	*Bay Colony Ltd. v. Wasaga Beach (Town of)*
	Toronto (City of) v. Toronto (Metropolitan)
	Toronto Dominion Bank v. Alfred (Township of)

- Use the common name of a country, not its formal name or abbreviation.
- Omit "Province of", "State of", "People of", or any other similar identifiers.
- Include identifiers such as "City of", "County of", "District of", or "Township of" in parentheses.

3.2.2.5 *Wills and Estates*

Examples	
Name of Estate	*Kipling v. Kohinsky Estate*
Name of Estate if no plaintiff or defendant is included	*Re Eurig Estate*

- Do not use the names of executors.

3.2.2.6 Bankruptcies and Receiverships

Examples
Chablis Textiles (***Trustee of***) *v. London Life Insurance*
Confederation Trust Co. (***Liquidator of***) *v. Donovan*

- Use the name of the bankrupt or company in receivership followed by "Trustee of", "Receiver of", or "Liquidator of" in parentheses.

3.2.2.7 Statute Titles

Examples	
If the jurisdiction is obvious from the name of the statute	*Re Canadian Labour Code*
If the jurisdiction cannot be discerned from the name of the statute	*Reference Re Fisheries Act (Canada)*

3.2.2.8 The Crown—Criminal Cases

Example
R. *v. Blondin*

- Use "R." to refer to the Crown in criminal cases, and to replace expressions such as "The Queen", "Regina", "The Crown", "The Queen in Right of" or other such terms.

3.2.2.9 The Crown—Civil Cases

Examples	
A.G.	*Schreiber v. Canada* (***A.G.***)
M.N.R.	*Buckman v.* ***M.N.R.***
Other Government Bodies	*Susan Shoe Industries Ltd. v. Ontario* (***Employment Standards Officer***)
Do not repeat the name of the jurisdiction	*Laurentian Bank of Canada v. Canada* (***Human Rights Commission***) ***NOT:*** *Laurentian Bank of Canada v. Canada* (***Canadian Human Rights Commission***)

Do not include the name of an individual representing a government body	Canada **(Combines Investigation Acts, Director of Investigation and Research)** v. Southam **NOT:** Lawson A.W. Hunter (Director of Investigation and Research of the Combines Investigation Branch) v. Southam

- In civil cases, use the name of the jurisdiction to signify the Crown in right of Canada or a province.
- Abbreviate the Minister of National Revenue to "M.N.R", the Deputy Minister of National Revenue to "Deputy M.N.R.", and "Attorney-General" to "A.G."
- Use the name of the jurisdiction followed by the name of the government body (such as an agency, commission, or department) in parentheses.
- When citing a federal or provincial administrative tribunal, refer to the rule in Appendix F.

3.2.2.10 Crown Corporations

Example
Westaim Corp. v. **Royal Canadian Mint**

- Do not include the name of the jurisdiction before the name of the Crown corporation.

3.2.2.11 Municipal Boards and Bodies

Example
Johnson v. Sarnia (City of) **Commissioners of Police**

3.2.2.12 School Boards

Example	
	Prince Albert **Rural School Division No. 56** v. Teachers of Saskatchewan
NOT	Board of Education of Prince Albert Rural School Division No. 56 v. Teachers of Saskatchewan

- Omit such terms as "Board of Education", "Board of Trustees", or "Governors of"; include only the name of the institution.

3—Jurisprudence

3.2.2.13 Unions

Example	
	Canadian Autoworkers' Union, Local 576 *v. Bradco Construction*
NOT	*C.A.U., Local 576 v. Bradco Construction*

- Do not abbreviate union names, as such abbreviations vary widely.

3.2.2.14 Social Welfare Agencies

Examples
*Doe v. **Metropolitan Toronto Child and Family Services***
*E.P. v. **Winnipeg (Director of Child and Family Services)***

- Include the name of the community where the aid agency is based unless it forms part of the name of the agency, *e.g.*: *Doe v. Metropolitan Toronto Child and Family Services*.

3.2.2.15 Parties' Names That Are Undisclosed

Examples
Droit de la famille—1544
M. v. H.

- If the names of the parties are not disclosed in the case, use initials where available, or the title and numerical description provided by the reporter.

3.2.2.16 The Case Is Known Under Two Names—The Sub nom. *Rule*

Example
Reference Re Resolution to Amend the Constitution, [1981] 1 S.C.R. 753, **(*sub nom.* Reference Re Amendment of the Constitution of Canada (Nos. 1, 2 and 3))** 125 D.L.R. (3d) 1.

- Start the cite using the party names as provided in the first-cited reporter.
- If a parallel citation refers to the parties by different names, enclose this style of cause in parentheses introduced by the phrase "*sub nom.*" Place the parentheses immediately before the citation for the reporter using those names.

- *Sub nom.* is the abbreviated version of *sub nomine*, which is Latin for "under the name of".

3.2.2.17 One Party Is Acting for Someone Else—The Ex rel. Rule

Example
Ryel v. Quebec (A.G.) **ex rel. Société immobilière du Québec**

- Where a third party enters the suit to act on behalf of one of the parties, note this by using the phrase *ex rel.*
- *Ex rel.* is the abbreviated version of *ex relatione*, which is Latin for "upon relation or information".

3.2.2.18 Procedural Phrases and Constitutional References

Examples	
Constitutional	**Reference Re** Firearms Act
Other	**Re** Gray **Ex parte** James: Re Condon

- Use "*Reference Re*" for constitutional cases only; in all other cases, use "*Re*" alone.
- Shorten "*In re*", "In the matter of", and "Dans l'affaire de" to "*Re*".
- Write "*Ex parte*" in full. The expression *ex parte* in the style of cause indicates that the named party is the one that has brought the action.

3.2.3 Year

Parentheses are used to indicate the year of the decision. Brackets are used to indicate the year of the reporter.

3.2.3.1 Year of decision

General rule:	Provide the year of decision in parentheses	R. v. Borden (**1993**), 24 C.R. (4th) 184 (N.S.C.A.).
Year of reporter and year of decision different:	Provide both years	Joyal v. Hôpital du Christ-Roi (**1996**), [1997] R.J.Q. 38 (C.A.).
Year of reporter and year of decision are the same:	Do not provide the year of decision	Raymond v. Adrema Ltd., [**1962**] O.R. 677 (H.C.J.). NOT Raymond v. Adrema Ltd. (1962), [**1962**] O.R. 677 (H.C.J.).

- Provide the year of the decision in parentheses after the style of cause and followed by a comma.
- If the year of the decision is the same as the year of the reporter, do not provide the year of the decision.

3.2.3.2 Year of reporter

Reporter organized by year, one volume published per year	Raymond v. Adrema Ltd., [**1962**] O.R. 677 (H.C.J.).
Reporter organized by year, several volumes published per year	Reference re Secession of Quebec, [**1998**] 2 S.C.R. 217.
Reporter published in volumes numbered in series: no year of reporter can be given	R. v. Borden (1993), 24 C.R. (4th) 184 (N.S.C.A.).

- Reporters are published either in volumes numbered in series (*e.g.* D.L.R., C.C.C.) or in volumes organized by year of publication (*e.g.* S.C.R., R.J.Q.).
- If the reporter volumes are numbered in series, no year is needed to identify the reporter volume.
- If the reporter volumes are numbered by year of publication, then the year is needed to identify the reporter volume. Enclose the year in brackets.
- Some reporters currently organized by year of publication (*e.g.* S.C.R.) publish several volumes per year. Thus, indicate the year in brackets followed by the volume number.
- Some reporters have changed their mode of organization. The *Supreme Court Reports* are organized by numbered volume from 1877-1923 (*e.g.* 27 S.C.R.), by yearly volume from 1923-1974 (*e.g.* [1950] S.C.R.), and by year with several volumes per year since 1975 (*e.g.* [1982] 2 S.C.R.). Similarly, the Ontario Reports are organized by

year prior to 1974 (*e.g.* [1973] O.R.), and by numbered series since 1974 (*e.g.* 20 O.R.).

3.2.4 Reporter

Example
Blakley v. Horsman (2001), 206 **Sask. R.** 132 (Q.B.).

- Abbreviate the name of the reporter according to the list in Appendix G.

3.2.4.1 Official Reporters
- Official reporters are those published by the Queen's Printer.
- Where a judgment has been reported in an official reporter, the citation must be to that reporter.
- Whenever there is a discrepancy between two versions of the same case, the version in the official case reporter takes precedence.

The following is a list of the official reporters:

Canada Supreme Court Reports (1970-present) *Canada Law Reports: Supreme Court of Canada* (1923-1969) *Canada Supreme Court Reports* (1876-1922)	S.C.R.
Canada Federal Court Reports (1971-present)	F.C.
Exchequer Court of Canada Reports (1923-1970) *Exchequer Court of Canada Reports* (1875-1922)	Ex. C.R.

3.2.4.2 Semi-Official Reporters
- Cite to a semi-official reporter when a judgment has not been reported in an official reporter.
- Semi-official reporters are published under the auspices of a provincial or territorial bar association.

The following is a list of the semi-official reporters published in 2002:

Alberta	*Alberta Reports* (1976-present) *N.B.*: *Alberta Law Reports* (3d) ("Alta. L.R. (3d)") is unofficial.	A.R.
British Columbia	No semi-official reporter was published in 2002.	
Manitoba	No semi-official reporter was published in 2002.	
New Brunswick	*New Brunswick Reports* (2d) (1969-present)	N.B.R. (2d)
Newfoundland and Labrador & Prince Edward Island	*Newfoundland & Prince Edward Island Reports* (1971-present)	Nfld. & P.E.I.R.
Nova Scotia	*Nova Scotia Reports* (2d) (1969-present)	N.S.R. (2d)
Nunavut	No semi-official reporter was published in 2002.	
Ontario	*Ontario Reports* (3d) (1991-present)	O.R. (3d)
Quebec	*Recueils de jurisprudence du Québec* (1986-present)	R.J.Q.
Saskatchewan	No semi-official reporter was published in 2002.	
Northwest Territories	No semi-official reporter was published in 2002.	N.W.T.R.
Yukon	No semi-official reporter was published in 2002.	

For a complete listing of all semi-official reporters, including those published prior to 2002, see Appendix G.

3.2.4.3 *Unofficial Reporters*

*   Where a judgment is not reported in either an official or semi-official reporter, cite to an unofficial reporter.
*   Whenever possible, the following guidelines should be followed:

- General reporters (*e.g. Western Weekly Reports*) are preferred to specific reporters (*e.g. Canadian Criminal Cases*).
- Reporters covering a large geographic area (*e.g. Dominion Law Reports*) are preferred to reporters covering a smaller geographic area (*e.g. Saskatchewan Reports*).
- Reporters that are most readily available are preferred (*e.g. Dominion Law Reports*).

See Appendix G for a list of unofficial reporters.

3.2.5 Series

Examples	
Series number	*Bohun v. Similco Mines Ltd.* (1995), 6 B.C.L.R. **(3d)** 22 (C.A.).
New series	*Citizen's Mining Council of Newfoundland and Labrador Inc. v. Canada (Minister of the Environment)* (1999), 29 C.E.L.R. **(N.S.)** 117 (F.C.T.D.).

- If the reporter has been published in more than one series, indicate the series in parentheses, between the reporter abbreviation and the first page of the judgment.
- Do not put the series number in superscript.
- Abbreviate "New Series" or *"Nouvelle série"* to "N.S."

3.2.6 First Page

Example
Reference re Secession of Quebec, [1998] 2 S.C.R. **217**.

- Indicate the number of the first page of the decision.

3.2.7 Pinpoint

Examples
R. v. Proulx, [2000] 1 S.C.R. 61, 2000 SCC 5 **at para. 27.**
Bousquet v. Barmish Inc. (1991), 37 C.P.R. (3d) 516 **at 527** (F.C.T.D.).
Rebus v. McLellan (1992), [1993] N.W.T.R. 186 **at 189ff** (S.C.).
Vriend v. Alberta (A.G.), [1998] 1 S.C.R. 493 **at 532-34**, 156 D.L.R. (4th) 385.
Quebec (P.G.) c. Germain, [1995] R.J.Q. 2313 **at 2320, 2322** (C.A.).

- Place the pinpoint reference after the first page of the reporter.
- Paragraph pinpoints are preferred to page pinpoints. Begin a page or paragraph pinpoint with "at" unless using ¶. Do not place a comma before "at". Refer to paragraphs by using "para.", "paras.", or ¶. Do not use "p." to indicate the page number.
- Always pinpoint to the first reporter cited.
- To indicate a general area rather than a specific set of pages or paragraphs, place "ff" immediately after the number, which is the abbreviation of "and following". It is preferable, however, to cite a specific set of pages or paragraphs.
- Separate consecutive page or paragraph numbers by a hyphen, retaining at least the two last digits at all times (*e.g.* "32-35", not "32-5").
- Non-sequential page numbers are separated by a comma (*e.g.* 160, 172).

3.2.8 Parallel Citations

Examples
R. v. Sharpe, [2001] 1 S.C.R. 45 at para. 24, **2001 SCC 2** [*Sharpe*].
R. v. Bain, [1992] 1 S.C.R. 91 at 93, **87 D.L.R. (4th) 449** [*Bain* **cited to S.C.R.**].
Vanderburgh v. ScotiaMcLeod Inc. (1992), 4 Alta. L.R. (3d) 138, **[1992] 6 W.W.R. 673** (Q.B.).

- Include at least one parallel citation whenever possible.
- Separate parallel citations with commas.
- Indicate the reporter to which subsequent references will be directed (*e.g.* [*Bain* cited to S.C.R.]), preferably to the first and most official reporter.
- If referring to paragraph numbers, it is not necessary to indicate the reporter to which subsequent references are directed. It is never necessary to indicate that all further references are directed to the neutral citation.
- Include the volume year of the reporter used for the parallel citation even when it repeats the year of the decision. See the *Vanderburgh* example.
- Do not provide pinpoint references for each of the parallel citations.

3.2.9 Jurisdiction and Court

Examples
Taylor v. Law Society of Prince Edward Island (1992), 97 D.L.R. (4th) 427 **(P.E.I.S.C. (A.D.))**.
Ballard v. Ballard (2001), 201 Nfld. & P.E.I.R. 352 **(Nfld. S.C. (T.D.))**.
O'Brien v. Centre de location Simplex ltée (1993), 132 N.B.R. (2d) 179 **(C.A.)**.
Boisjoli c. Goebel, [1982] **C.S.** 1 **(Qc.)**.
Dobson (Litigation Guardian of) v. Dobson, [1999] 2 **S.C.R.** 753.

- Indicate the jurisdiction and court in parentheses after the first page or pinpoint reference. Additionally, references to the jurisdiction and court should follow all parallel citations unless the parallel citation is a neutral citation.
- If the jurisdiction is evident from the name of any reporter, reference is made only to the level of court. If both the jurisdiction and the level of court are evident from the title of the reporter, reference does not need to be made to either.
- The jurisdiction and level of court are always obvious from a neutral citation. If a neutral citation stands alone or if it is included as a parallel citation, never include another abbreviation for the jurisdiction and level of court.
- When the court is bilingual, use English abbreviations. If the court only renders judgments in French, use the French abbreviations.
- There should be no space between any abbreviations of courts consisting solely of upper case letters. Leave a space when an abbreviation consisting of upper case letters is placed next to an abbreviation consisting of both upper case and lower case letters (*e.g.* B.C.C.A., Ont. Div. Ct., N.S. Co. Ct., Alta. Q.B.).

Refer to the abbreviations found in the Appendices.

3.2.10 Judge

Example
R. v. Sharpe, [2001] 1 S.C.R. 45 at 61, 2001 SCC 2, **McLachlin C.J.C.**
Gosselin c. Québec (P.G.), [1999] R.J.Q. 1033 (C.A.), **Robert J., dissenting**.

- If relevant, a reference to the name of the judge may be included.
- Do not insert a comma between the name of the judge and the office.

3—Jurisprudence

Abbreviate offices as follows:

C.J.C.	Chief Justice of Canada
C.J.A.	Chief Justice of Appeal
C.J.	Chief Justice, Chief Judge
J.A.	Justice of Appeal, Judge of Appeals Court
JJ.A.	Justices of Appeal, Judges of Appeals Court
J.	Justice, Judge
JJ.	Justices, Judges
L.J.	Lord Justice
L.JJ.	Lord Justices
Mag.	Magistrate

3.2.11 History of Case

3.2.11.1 Prior History

Examples	
Affirmed	*Law v. Canada (Minister of Employment and Immigration)*, [1999] 1 S.C.R. 497, **aff'g (1996), 135 D.L.R. (4th) 293 (F.C.A.).**
Reversed	*Wilson & Lafleur ltée c. Société québécoise d'information juridique*, [2000] R.J.Q. 1086 (C.A.), **rev'g [1998] R.J.Q. 2489 (Sup. Ct.).**

- Cite the prior history of the case if it is relevant to the argument.
- Place the prior history of the case as the last element of the citation.
- Separate different decisions with a comma.
- Abbreviate "affirming" to "aff'g". Abbreviate "reversing" to "rev'g".
- Both "aff'g" and "rev'g" refer to the first citation.
- If the decision is affirming or reversing the prior decision on grounds other than those being discussed, use "aff'g on other grounds" or "rev'g on other grounds".
- Parallel citations to the prior history may be included.

3.2.11.2 Subsequent History

Examples	
Affirmed	*Granovsky v. Canada (Minister of Employment and Immigration)*, [1998] 3 F.C. 175 (C.A.), **aff'd [2000] 1 S.C.R. 703, 2000 SCC 28**.
Reversed	*Ontario English Catholic Teachers' Association v. Ontario (A.G.)* (1998), 162 D.L.R. (4th) 257 (Ont. Gen. Div.), **rev'd (1999), 172 D.L.R. (4th) 193 (Ont. C.A.)**, rev'd **[2001] 1 S.C.R. 470, 2001 SCC 15**.

- Cite the subsequent history of the case if it was subsequently appealed to other courts.
- Place the subsequent history of the case as the last element of the citation.
- Separate different decisions with a comma.
- Abbreviate "affirmed" to "aff'd" and "reversed" to "rev'd".
- If the decision was affirmed or reversed on grounds other than those being discussed, use "aff'd on other grounds" or "rev'd on other grounds".
- Parallel citation to subsequent history may be included.
- Both "aff'd" and "rev'd" refer back to the first citation. In the *Ontario English Catholic Teachers' Association* example, the use of "rev'd" before the Supreme Court decision indicates that the Supreme Court decided that the judgment of the Ontario Court's General Division should have been reversed; it did not reverse the decision of the Ontario Court of Appeal.

3.2.11.3 Prior and Subsequent History

Examples	
Affirmed	*Ardoch Algonquin First Nation v. Ontario* (1997), 148 D.L.R. (4th) 126 (Ont. C.A.), **rev'g [1997] 1 C.N.L.R. 66 (Ont. Gen. Div.), aff'd [2000] 1 S.C.R. 950, 2000 SCC 37**.
Reversed	*Canada v. Canderel Ltd.*, [1995] 2 F.C. 232 (C.A.), **rev'g [1994] 1 C.T.C. 2336 (T.C.C.), rev'd [1998] 1 S.C.R. 147**.

- Apply the rules for prior and subsequent history listed above.
- All affirming and reversing decisions refer back to the first citation. In the *Canderel Ltd.* example, the Federal Court of Appeal reversed the decision of the Tax Court of Canada, but was itself reversed by the Supreme Court of Canada (*i.e.* the Supreme Court of Canada upheld the tax court's decision).
- Place prior history before subsequent history.

3.2.11.4 Leave to Appeal

Examples				
	Citation of the decision for which leave to appeal is requested,	court		citation of the decision as to the appeal.
Requested	*White Resource Management Ltd. v. Durish* (1992), 131 A.R. 273 (C.A.),	leave to appeal to S.C.C. requested.		
Granted	*Westec Aerospace v. Raytheon Aircraft* (1999), 173 D.L.R. (4th) 498 (B.C.C.A.),	leave to appeal to S.C.C. granted,		[2000] 1 S.C.R. xxii.
Refused	*Sinclair v. Law Society of Manitoba* (1997), 124 Man. R. (2d) 145 (C.A.),	leave to appeal to S.C.C. refused,		[1998] 3 S.C.R. vii.
As of Right	*Whiten v. Pilot Insurance* (1996), 132 D.L.R. (4th) 568. (Ont. Gen. Div.),	appeal as of right to the C.A.		

- Include the citation of the decision for which leave to appeal is requested.
- Indicate the court to which appeal is requested. If available, indicate whether leave was granted or refused and include the citation for that decision.

3.2.12 Unreported Judgments

3.2.12.1 Common Law

Example				
Style of cause	(date),	judicial district	docket number	(jurisdiction and court).
R. v. Crète	(18 April 1991),	Ottawa	97/03674	(Ont. Prov. Ct.).

- For cases from common law provinces, indicate the style of cause, the full date of the decision in parentheses followed by a comma, the judicial district, and the docket number. Place the jurisdiction and court in parentheses at the end of the citation.

3.2.12.2 Quebec

Example					
Style of cause	(date),	judicial district	docket number,	J.E. number (if available)	(jurisdiction and court).
Lalancette c. Gagnon	(18 April 1995),	Montreal	500-02-019902-944,	J.E. 95-1255	(C.Q.).

- For Quebec cases, indicate the style of cause, the full date of the decision in parentheses followed by a comma, the judicial district, and the docket number. Place the jurisdiction and court in parentheses at the end of the citation. If available, include the *Jurisprudence Express* number preceded by a comma after the docket number.

3.2.13 Administrative Bodies and Tribunals

3.2.13.1 Decisions in Printed Reporters

Examples	
Adversarial	*Clarke Institute of Psychiatry v. O.N.A. (Aduseri Grievance)* (2001), 95 L.A.C. (4th) 154 (OLRB).
Non-adversarial	*Re Writers' Union of Canada Certification Application (Certification)* (1998), 84 C.P.R. (3d) 329 (Canadian Artists and Professional Relations Tribunal).

- Indicate the style of cause and whether it is adversarial or non-adversarial, as shown by the particular reporter cited. Where there is no style of cause, use the decision number instead.
- Include the abbreviation of the body or tribunal in parentheses at the end of the citation if it is not evident from the title of the cited reporter (if an abbreviation cannot be found, use the full name). Use the abbreviation as it is provided by the administrative body. These acronyms usually do not contain periods. Note that most acronyms consist of single letters for each important word in the name. Provinces and territories are usually abbreviated to the shortest provincial abbreviations (*e.g.* Ontario Securities Commission: OSC; Newfoundland and Labrador Human Rights Commission: NLHRC). However, note that abbreviations of a printed reporter (*e.g.* O.S.C. Bull.) may be different from the abbreviation of the agency (*e.g.* OSC).
- Include one or more parallel citations if available.

3.2.13.2 Online Decisions

Examples
Extending the availability of alternative formats to consumers who are blind (8 March 2002), Telecom Decision CRTC 2002-13, online: CRTC <http://www.crtc.gc.ca/archive/ENG/Decisions/2002/dt2002-13.htm>.
Canada (Commissioner of Competition) v. Superior Propane (4 April 2002), 2000 Comp. Trib. 16, online: Comp. Trib. <http://www.ct-tc.gc.ca/english/cases/propane/0238a.pdf>.
Re: 2950995 Canada Inc. (9 May 2000), OSC Decision, online: OSC <http://www.osc.gov.on.ca/en/Enforcement/Decisions/decisions_list.html#2001decisions>.
Re: Foresight Capital Corporation (22 August 2001), 2001 BCSECCOM 848, online: BCSC <http://www.bcsc.bc.ca/Enforcement/default.asp>.
Re: Bourse de Montréal (30 November 2001), CVMQ Decision 2001-C-0553, *Bulletin hebdomadaire* 33 : 12 (29 March 2002), online: <http://www.cvmq.com/en/decision/membre.asp>.

- Enclose the date of the decision in parentheses after the style of cause. Place a comma after the date.
- Include the decision number and indicate the abbreviation used by the administrative body or tribunal. These acronyms usually do not contain periods. Note that most acronyms consist of single letters for each important word in the name. Provinces and territories are usually abbreviated to the shortest provincial abbreviations (*e.g.* Ontario Securities Commission: OSC; Newfoundland and Labrador Human Rights Commission: NLHRC).

3.2.14 Citation of Arguments and Documents at a Hearing

Examples	
Factum	*Reference re Secession of Quebec*, [1998] 2 S.C.R. 217 **(Factum of the Appellant at para. 16)**.
Oral pleading	*Vriend v. Alberta*, [1998] 1 S.C.R. 493 **(Oral argument, appellant)**.
Settlement Agreement	*Mulroney v. Canada (A.G.)* **[Settlement Agreement]**, [1997] Q.J. No. 45 (Qc. Sup. Ct.) (QL).
Evidence	*R. v. Swain*, [1991] 1 S.C.R 933 **(Evidence, Dr. Fleming's recommendation that the appellant be released in the community)**.

- When referring to a factum, provide the full citation of the case, then indicate the party and the page number or paragraph number in parentheses. Use the full names of the parties. A short form can always be established following the first reference to the document (*e.g.* Factum of the Appellant at para. 16 [FOA].).
- When referring to an oral argument, provide the full citation of the case, then place "Oral argument" and the party in parentheses.
- When referring to a public settlement agreement, provide the style of cause, followed by "Settlement Agreement" in brackets before the other elements of the citation. If the agreement was announced through a news release, see section 6.14.
- When referring to evidence, provide the full citation of the case, followed by "Evidence" in parentheses and a brief statement identifying the item.
- When referring to a trial transcript, use the rules for citing unreported judgments from section 3.2.12.

3.3 UNITED KINGDOM—CITATION TO PRINTED REPORTERS

3.3.1 General Form

Examples						
Style of cause	(year of decision),	[year of reporter]	vol.	reporter	page	court.
R. v. Woollin	(1998),	[1999]		A.C.	82	(H.L.).
Burgess v. Home Office	(2000),	[2001]	1	W.L.R.	93	(C.A.).

- Cite United Kingdom cases using the same format as Canadian cases.
- If the year of the decision and the year of the reporter are the same, do not provide the year of the decision.
- Cite the *Law Reports* in preference to the *Weekly Law Reports* ("W.L.R.") or the *All England Law Reports* ("All E.R.").
- Cite a general before a specialized reporter.
- Include parallel citations, if available.

See Appendix G for a list of United Kingdom reporters and their abbreviations. See Appendix F for a list of courts and their abbreviations.

3—Jurisprudence

3.3.2 Reporter

3.3.2.1 Law Reports

* *Law Reports* are divided into series. Do not refer to the *Law Reports*, but rather to the series.
* There is no separate reporter for the Court of Appeal; therefore, include "C.A.", the abbreviation of "Court of Appeal", at the end of each reference to a case heard in that court.

Abbreviate the series for the *Law Reports* as follows:

Appeal Cases (House of Lords and Judicial Committee of the Privy Council)	A.C.
Chancery (Chancery Division and appeals therefrom in the Court of Appeal)	Ch.
Queen's (King's) Bench (Queen's (King's) Bench Division and appeals therefrom in the Court of Appeal)	Q.B. (K.B.)
Probate (1891-1971) (Family Division, Probate, Divorce, and Admiralty Division, appeals therefrom, and Ecclesiastical Courts)	P.
Family (1972 to present)	Fam.
Industrial Courts Reports (1972-1974) and *Industrial Cases Reports* (1975 to present)	I.C.R.
Law Reports Restrictive Practices (1957-1972) (National Industrial Relations Court and Restrictive Practices Court, appeals therefrom, and decisions of the High Court relevant to industrial relations)	L.R. R.P.

3.3.2.2 Form for a Case from 1875-1890

Example
Akerblom v. Price, Potter, Walker & Co. (1881), 7 **Q.B.D.** 129 (C.A.) [*Akerblom*].

* Include "D." for "Division" after the reporter to distinguish the 1875-1890 series of reporters from the later series with the same name.

3.3.2.3 Form for a Case from 1865-1875

Example
Rylands v. Fletcher (1868), **L.R.** 3 H.L. 330.

- Include "L.R." for "Law Reports" before the volume number to distinguish the 1865-1875 series of reporters from the later series with the same name.

3.3.2.4 Form for a Case from 1537-1865

Example
Lord Byron v. Johnston (1816), 2 Mer. 28, 35 E.R. 851 (Ch.).

- Cite to the nominate reporter whenever possible and always provide a parallel citation to *English Reports* ("E.R.") where available.
- The *English Reports* and *All England Reports Reprints* are reprints.

3.3.2.5 Yearbooks

Example							
Style of cause	(year),	yearbook	term	regnal year	monarch,	plea number,	folio number.
Waldon v. Marshall	(1370),	Y.B.	Mich.	43	Edw. III,	pl. 38,	fol. 33.

- Abbreviate "Michaelmas" to "Mich.", "Hilary" to "Hil.", "Easter" to "Pach.", and "Trinity" to "Trin."
- Indicate the regnal year in Arabic numerals.
- Refer to the monarch using Roman numerals.
- Abbreviate "plea" to "pl."
- Abbreviate "folio" to "fol."

3.3.2.6 Reprints

Example		
Yearbook citation	reprinted in	citation
Beauver v. Abbot of St. Albans (1312), Y.B. Mich. 6 Edw. II,	reprinted in	(1921) 38 Selden Soc. 32.

- When citing to a reprint, provide as much information about the original yearbook entry as possible. Cite to the location where the reprint is found.

3.3.3 Scotland, Ireland to 1924, and Northern Ireland

Examples	
Scotland	*M'Courtney v. HM Advocate*, [1977] J.C. 68 (H.C.J. **Scot.**).
Ireland	*Johnson v. Egan*, [1894] 2 **I.R.** 480 (Q.B.D.).
Northern Ireland	*R. v. Crooks*, [1999] **N.I.** 226 (C.A.).

- Where the jurisdiction is not obvious from the title of the reporter, abbreviate "Scotland" to "Scot.", "Ireland" to "Ir.", and "Northern Ireland" to "N.I." and enclose the abbreviation in parentheses at the end of the citation.
- As each volume is divided according to the court reported and each section is paginated separately, include the name of the court.
- See Appendix F for relevant court abbreviations and Appendix G for relevant reporter abbreviations.

3.3.4 Judge

Lord Justice	L.J.
Lord Justices	L.JJ.
Master of the Rolls	M.R.
Lord Chancellor	L.C.
Vice Chancellor	V.C.
Baron	B.
Chief Baron	C.B.

N.B. For more information on citing jurisprudence from the United Kingdom, consult Donald Raistrick, *Index to Legal Citations and Abbreviations*, 2d ed. (London: Bowker-Saur, 1993).

3.4   UNITED STATES—CITATION TO PRINTED REPORTERS

3.4.1   General Form

Examples								
Style of cause,	vol.	reporter	series	page	pinpoint	(jurisdiction and/or court	year of decision)	(other information) (if applicable).
Texas Beef Group v. Winfrey,	11	F.Supp.	2d	858		(N.D. Tex.	1998).	
Dell Computer Corp.,	121	F.T.C.		616	at 619		(1996).	
Distribution Center of Columbus,	83	Lab. Arb. Rep. (BNA)		163			(1984)	(Seidman, Arb.).

- Administrative adjudications and arbitrations are cited in the same manner as other cases.
- For arbitrations, place the name of the arbitrator followed by a comma and "Arb." in parentheses at the end of the citation.

3.4.2   Style of Cause

Examples	
	California v. United States *Larez v. Los Angeles (City of)*
NOT	*State of California v. United States of America* *Larez v. L.A.*

- Indicate the style of cause according to the rules for Canadian decisions.
- Where one of the parties is a state or country, use the common name, not the full formal name or abbreviation.
- If the case involves a city whose name could be mistaken for a state, enclose the relevant identifying information in parentheses: "New York (City of)" or "Washington (D.C.)".

3.4.3 Reporter and Series

Examples
Lotus Development v. Borland International, 140 **F.3d** 70 (1st Cir. 1998) [*Lotus*]. *Scott v. Sanford*, 60 **U.S.** (19 How.) 393 (1857).

- After the style of cause, provide the volume number, the reporter abbreviation, the series number, and the first page of the case. There is no space between the reporter abbreviation and the series number.
- *U.S. Reports* prior to 1875 are also numbered consecutively for each editor. Place this number and the editor's name in parentheses after "U.S."

With the exceptions of Cranch and Black, the editor's name is abbreviated as follows:

Wallace	Wall.
Black	Black
Howard	How.
Peters	Pet.
Wheaton	Wheat.
Cranch	Cranch
Dallas	Dal.

The principal reporters are abbreviated as follows:

Atlantic Reporter	A.
California Reporter	Cal.
Federal Reporter	F.
Federal Supplement	F.Supp.
Lawyers' Edition	L. Ed. 2d
New York Supplement	N.Y.S.
North Eastern Reporter	N.E.
North Western Reporter	N.W.

Pacific Reporter	P.
South Eastern Reporter	S.E.
South Western Reporter	S.W.
Southern Reporter	So.
Supreme Court Reporter	S. Ct.
United States Reports	U.S.
United States Law Week	U.S.L.W.

- For the United States Supreme Court, cite reporters in the following order of preference: U.S., S. Ct., L. Ed. 2d., U.S.L.W.
- For federal courts, cite to F. or F.Supp.
- For state courts, cite to a regional reporter in preference to a state reporter.

See Appendix G for a list of common reporters and their abbreviations.

3.4.4 Pinpoint

Examples
United States v. McVeigh, 153 F.3d 1166 **at 1170** (10th Cir. 1998).
McVeigh, *supra* note 1 **at 1173**.

- Place "at" before a pinpoint reference.

3.4.5 Court

3.4.5.1 *Federal Courts*

Examples	
United States Supreme Court	*Bush v. Gore*, 531 U.S. 98 (2000). *Boy Scouts of America v. Dale*, 68 U.S.L.W. 4625 (**U.S.** 28 June, 2000).
Courts of Appeal	*United States v. Kaczynski*, 154 F.3d 930 (**9th Cir.** 1998).
District Courts	*A&M Records v. Napster*, 114 F. Supp. 2d 896 (**N.D. Cal.** 2000).

3—Jurisprudence

- The United States Supreme Court does not require an abbreviation unless citing to the *United States Law Week* ("U.S.L.W."). When citing to the "U.S.L.W.", put "U.S." and the date in parentheses at the end of the citation.
- For Courts of Appeal refer to the numbered circuit.
- Abbreviate the District of Columbia Circuit Court to "D.C. Cir." and the Federal Circuit Court to "Fed. Cir."
- For district courts provide the abbreviated name of the district.

3.4.5.2 State Courts

Examples
Peevyhouse v. Garland Coal & Mining, 382 P.2d 109 (**Okla. Sup. Ct.** 1963).
Truman v. Thomas, 165 **Cal.** Rptr. 308 (**Sup. Ct.** 1980).
Hinterlong v. Baldwin, 308 **Ill. App.** 3d 441 (1999).

- Provide the court and the jurisdiction in parentheses, using the abbreviations from Appendices B and F.
- Omit the jurisdiction if it is obvious from the name of the reporter.
- Omit the court if it is the highest court in its jurisdiction.

3.4.6 Year of decision

- Place the year of decision in parentheses at the end of the citation even if there are parallel citations.

N.B. For more information on citing jurisprudence from the United States, consult *The Bluebook: A Uniform System of Citation*, 17th ed. (Cambridge, Mass.: Harvard Law Review Association, 2000).

3.5 FRANCE—CITATION TO PRINTED REPORTERS

3.5.1 General Form

Examples									
	Court (if applic-able)	city (if applic-able),	date,	*style of cause* (if applic-able),	reporter	year of publication.	section. (if applic-able)	page and/or decision number	(annota-tion)(if applic-able).
Cour de Cassation	Cass. civ. 2ᵉ,		14 June 2001,		D.	2001.	Jur.	3075	(Annot. Didier Cholet).
Court of Appeal		Paris,	12 January 2000,		J.C.P.	2000.	II.	10433	(Annot. Philippe Pierre).
Court of First Instance	Trib. gr. inst.	Mans,	7 September 1999,		J.C.P.	2000.	II.	10258	(Annot. Colette Saujot).

N.B. There is no space between the year of publication, the section, and the page (*e.g.* "2000.II.10258").

3.5.2 Court

3.5.2.1 *Courts of First Instance*

Examples									
Court	city,	date,	*style of cause* (if applic-able),	reporter	year of publication.	session (if applic-able).	section (if applic-able).	page	(anno-tation) (if applic-able).
Trib. admin.	Nantes,	27 November 1981,	*Mme Robin*,	Rec.	1981.			544.	
Trib. gr. inst.	Paris,	10 September 1998,		Gaz. Pal.	1999.	1ᵉ sem.	Jur.	37.	

- Indicate the city where the court sits.
- When referring to the *Gazette du Palais* (Gaz. Pal.), the spaces between the reporter, session, section, and page should be indicated as follows: "Gaz. Pal. 1983. 2ᵉ sem. Jur.623".

3—Jurisprudence

Abbreviate the names of the courts as follows:

Tribunal administratif	Trib. admin.
Tribunal civil or *Tribunal de première instance* (Civil court of original general jurisdiction, prior to 1958)	Trib. civ.
Tribunal commercial	Trib. com.
Tribunal correctionnel	Trib. corr.
Tribunal de grande instance (Civil court of original general jurisdiction, after 1958)	Trib. gr. inst.
Tribunal d'instance (Small claims court, after 1958)	Trib. inst.

For a complete list of court abbreviations, see Appendix F.

3.5.2.2 Court of Appeal

Example							
City,	date,	reporter	year of publication.	session. (if applicable)	section	page	(annotation).
Orléans,	23 October 1997,	Gaz. Pal.	1999.	1er sem.	Jur.	217	(Annot. Benoît de Roquefeuil).

- Omit the name of the court.
- Indicate only the city in which the court sits.

3.5.2.3 Cour de cassation

Example						
Chamber,	date,	reporter	year of publication.	section.	page,	decision number (if applicable).
Cass. Civ. 1re,	30 March 1999,	Bull. civ.	1999.	I.	77,	No. 118.

Abbreviate the chambers as follows:

Chambre civile, depending on whether the decision is from the first, second, or third chamber (after 1952)	Cass. civ. 1re, Cass. civ. 2e, Cass. civ. 3^{e}
Chambre commerciale	Cass. com.
Chambre sociale	Cass. soc.
Chambre criminelle	Cass. crim.
Chambre des requêtes	Cass. req.
Chambres réunies (before 1967)	Cass. Ch. réun.
Assemblée plénière (after 1967)	Cass. Ass. plén.
Chambre mixte	Cass. mixte

3.5.2.4 Conseil d'État

Example					
Court,	date,	*style of cause,*	reporter	year of publication.	page.
Cons. d'État,	27 January 1984,	*Ordre des avocats de la Polynésie française,*	Rec.	1984.	20.

- Abbreviate *Conseil d'État* to "Cons. d'État".

3.5.2.5 Conseil constitutionnel

Example						
Court,	date,	*style of cause,*	reporter	year of publication.	page,	decision number.
Cons. constitutionnel,	25 June 1986,	*Privatisations,*	Rec.	1986.	61,	86-207 DC.

- Abbreviate *Conseil constitutionnel* to "Cons. constitutionnel".
- Indicate the decision number at the end of the citation.

3—Jurisprudence

3.5.3 Style of Cause

Example
Cass. civ. 1re, 5 February 1968, *Ligny-Luxembourg*, Gaz. Pal. 1968. 1re sem. Jur.264.

- Omit the style of cause when citing a French case except in the following circumstances:
    - when citing a decision from an administrative tribunal or the Conseil d'État;
    - when citing an unpublished decision or one that is summarized in the "Sommaire" section of a reporter;
    - to avoid confusion (*e.g.* where two decisions were rendered on the same day by the same court);
    - when the case is better known by the names of the parties than by the usual information.
- When the style of cause is included, italicize it and place it after the date, set off by commas.

3.5.4 Reporter

Examples						
Court	date,	reporter	year of publication of reporter.	session number (if applicable).	section.	page and/or decision number.
Cass. Civ. 3^{e},	23 June 1999,	J.C.P.	2000.		II.	10333.
Cass. soc.,	3 February 1998,	Gaz. Pal.	1998.	1re sem.	Jur.	176.

- There is a space between the reporter and the year (*e.g.* Gaz. Pal. 1990). However, there is no space between the year and the section; nor is there a space between the section and the page number (*e.g.* 1993.II.22063).

Some common French reporters:

Actualité juridique de droit administratif	A.J.D.A.
Bulletin de la Cour de cassation, section civile	Bull. civ.
Gazette du Palais	Gaz. Pal.
Recueil Dalloz and *Recueil Dalloz et Sirey* (1945-present)	D.
Recueil des décisions du Conseil d'État or *Recueil Lebon*	R.C.E. or Rec.
Semaine Juridique (1937-present)	J.C.P.

See Appendix G for more French reporter abbreviations.

3.5.5 Year

Example
Paris, 5 February 1999, Gaz. Pal. **1999**. 2ᵉ sem. Jur.452.

- Include the year of publication of the reporter after the abbreviated title of the reporter.

3.5.6 Session

- Indicate the session number after the year of publication when citing the *Gazette du Palais* (Gaz. Pal.).

3.5.7 Section

- When the sections in the volume are numbered, indicate the section number in Roman numerals after the year of publication.
- When the sections are not numbered, provide the abbreviation of the section title.
- Exception: Do not include the section when citing the *Recueil Lebon* (Rec.) or the *Actualité juridique de droit administrif* (A.J.D.A.).

Abbreviation of section titles:

Assemblée plénière	Ass. plén.
Chambre mixte	Ch. mixte
Chambres des requêtes	Req.

Chambres réunies	Ch. réun.
Chroniques	Chron.
Doctrine	Doctr.
Informations rapides	Inf.
Jurisprudence	Jur.
Législation, Lois et décrets, Textes de lois, etc.	Lég.
Panorama de jurisprudence	Pan.
Sommaire	Somm.

3.5.8 Page and Decision Number

Examples	
Semaine Juridique	Ass. plén., 6 November 1998, J.C.P., 1999.II.**10000 bis**.
Bulletin de la Cour de cassation	Cass. civ. 2e, 7 June 2001, Bull. civ. 2001, II.**75, No. 110**.

- Indicate the page number after the section reference or the year of publication.
- For the *Semaine Juridique* provide the decision number (*e.g.* 10000 bis).
- For the *Bulletin de la Cour de cassation* cite both the page and decision number separated by a comma.

3.5.9 Pinpoint

Example
Trib. gr. inst. Narbonne, 12 March 1999, Gaz. Pal. 1999. 1er sem. Jur.405 **at 406**.

- Pinpoint citations are rarely used given the brevity of most decisions. If required, it is always placed after the page number and introduced by "at".

3.5.10 Parallel Citation

Example	
First citation,	parallel citation.
Cass. civ. 1re, 26 May 1999, Bull. civ. 1999.I.115, No. 175,	J.C.P. 1999.II.10112.

- Parallel citations may be included.

3.5.11 Annotations, Reports, and Conclusions

Example
Cass. civ. 1re, 6 juillet 1999, J.C.P. 1999.II.10217 **(Annot. Thierry Garé)**.

- Any annotation or other writing appended to or included with a case must be indicated at the end of the citation, in parentheses.
- Refer to "Annot.", Rep.", or "Concl." followed by the author's name.

3.6   AUSTRALIA—CITATION TO PRINTED REPORTERS

3.6.1   General Form

Examples						
Style of cause	(year of decision),	[year of reporter]	volume	reporter	page	(jurisdiction and/or court) (if required).
C.D.J. v. V.A.J.	(1998),		197	C.L.R.	172	(H.C.A.).
Standard Portland Cement Company Pty. Ltd. v. Good	(1983),		57	A.L.J.R.	151	(P.C.).
Thwaites v. Ryan	(1983),	[1984]		V.R.	65	(S.C.).
Bentley v. Furlan,		[1999]	3	V.R.	63	(S.C.).

- Cite Australian cases using the same format as Canadian cases.
- If the year of the decision and the year of the reporter are the same, do not provide the year of the decision.
- Cite to a general before a specialized reporter.

3.6.2 Reporter

3.6.2.1 Law Reports

Abbreviate the series for the *Law Reports* as follows:

Commonwealth Law Reports (1903-present)—Official	C.L.R.
Australian Law Reports (1973-present)	A.L.R.
Federal Court Reports (1984-present)—Official	F.C.R.
Federal Law Reports (1956-present)	F.L.R.
Australian Law Journal Reports (1958-present)	A.L.J.R.
New South Wales Law Reports (1971-present)—Official	N.S.W.L.R.
Queensland State Reports (1902-1957)—Official	Qd. S.R.
Queensland Reports (1958-present)—Official	Qd. R.
South Australia State Reports (1922-present)—Official	S.A.S.R.
Tasmanian Law Reports (1896-1940)—Official	Tas. L.R.
Tasmanian State Reports (1941-1978)	Tas. R.
Tasmanian Reports (1979-present)—Official	Tas. R.
Victorian Law Reports (1886-1956)	V.L.R.
Victorian Reports (1957-present)—Official	V.R.
Western Australia Law Reports (1899-1959)	W.A.L.R.
Western Australia Law Reports (1960-present)—Official	W.A.R.
Australian Capital Territory Reports (1973-present)	A.C.T.R.
Northern Territory Reports (1978-present)	N.T.R.
Northern Territory Law Reports (1992-present)	N.T.L.R.

- For Privy Council (P.C.) and High Court of Australia (H.C.A.) decisions, cite to (in order of preference): C.L.R., A.L.R., A.A.L.R.
- For other federal court decisions, cite to the official F.C.R. before F.L.R.
- For Australian States and Territories, cite to the official state or territorial court reporter when possible, otherwise cite to an unofficial reporter.

3.6.3 Court

Include the name of the federal, state, or territorial court in parentheses at the end of the citation, as follows:

Privy Council (Australia)	P.C.
High Court of Australia	H.C.A.
Federal Court of Australia	F.C.A.
Supreme Court of Queensland—Court of Appeal	Qld. C.A.
Supreme Court of Queensland	Qld. S.C.
Supreme Court of the Australian Capital Territory	A.C.T.S.C.
Supreme Court of New South Wales	N.S.W.S.C.
Supreme Court of New South Wales—Court of Appeal	N.S.W.C.A.
Supreme Court of Tasmania	Tas. S.C.
Supreme Court of Victoria—Court of Appeal	Vic. S.C.A.
Supreme Court of Victoria	Vic. S.C.
Supreme Court of Southern Australia	S.A.S.C.
District Court of Southern Australia	S.A.D.C.
Supreme Court of Western Australia	W.A.S.C.
Supreme Court of Western Australia—Court of Appeal	W.A.S.C.A.
Supreme Court of the Northern Territory	N.T.S.C.

- For state and territorial courts, if the jurisdiction is evident from the reporter cited, only indicate the level of court.

3—Jurisprudence

3.7   NEW ZEALAND—CITATION TO PRINTED REPORTERS

3.7.1   General Form

Examples						
Style of cause	(year of decision),	[year of reporter]	volume	reporter	page	(jurisdiction and/or court) (if applicable).
Erbium Ltd. v. Gregory,		[1998]		D.C.R.	1119.	
Ryde Holdings Ltd. v. Sorenson,		[1988]	2	N.Z.L.R.	157	(H.C.).

- Cite New Zealand cases using the same format as Canadian cases.
- If the year of the decision and the year of the reporter are the same, do not provide the year of the decision.
- Cite a general before a specific reporter.

3.7.2   Reporter

3.7.2.1   *Law Reports*

- *Law Reports* are divided into series. Reference is not made to the *Law Reports* but rather to the series.
- There is no separate reporter for the Judicial Committee of the Privy Council (post-1932), the Court of Appeal, or the High Court; therefore, include abbreviations "P.C.", "C.A.", or "H.C." at the end of each reference to a case heard in that court.

Abbreviate the series for the *Law Reports* as follows:

New Zealand Law Reports (1883-present) (Privy Council, Court of Appeal, High Court)	N.Z.L.R.
New Zealand Privy Council Cases (1840-1932)	N.Z.P.C.C.
Gazette Law Reports (1898-1953) (Court of Appeal, Supreme Court (High Court), Court of Arbitration)	G.L.R.
District Court Reports (1980-present)	N.Z.D.C.R.
Magistrates' Court Decisions (1939-1979)	M.C.D.
Magistrates' Court Reports (1906-1953)	M.C.R.
Book of Awards (1894-1991) (Arbitration Court, Court of Appeal)	B.A.
Employment Reports of New Zealand (1991-present) (Court of Appeal, Labour Court, Aircrew Industrial Tribunal)	E.R.N.Z.
New Zealand Industrial Law Reports (1987-1990) (Labour Court, Court of Appeal, Aircrew Industrial Tribunal)	N.Z.I.L.R.
Judgments of the Arbitration Court of New Zealand (1979-1986) (Arbitration Court, Court of Appeal)	N.Z.A.C.
New Zealand Family Law Reports (1981-present) (Privy Council, Court of Appeal, High Court, Family Court, Youth Court, District Court)	N.Z.F.L.R.
Criminal Reports of New Zealand (1993-present) (Court of Appeal, High Court)	C.R.N.Z.

3—Jurisprudence

3.7.3 Court

Privy Council (New Zealand)	P.C.
New Zealand Court of Appeal	N.Z.C.A.
New Zealand High Court	N.Z.H.C.
District Court of New Zealand	D.C.N.Z.
Magistrates' Court of New Zealand	Mag. Ct. N.Z.
Coroners Court	Cor. Ct.
New Zealand Employment Court	N.Z. Empl. Ct.
Environment Court	Env. Ct.
Family Court of New Zealand	Fam. Ct. N.Z.
Maori Land Court / *Te Kooti Whenua Maori*	Maori Land Ct.
Maori Appellate Court	Maori A.C.
New Zealand Youth Court	N.Z.Y.C.
Waitangi Tribunal / *Te Rōpū Whakamana i te Tiriti o Waitangi*	Waitangi Trib.

3.8   SINGAPORE—CITATION TO PRINTED REPORTERS

3.8.1 General Form

Examples						
Style of cause	(year of decision),	[year of reporter]	volume	reporter	page	(jurisdiction and/or court) (if applicable).
Er Joo Nguang v. Public Prosecutor,		[2000]	2	Sing. L.R.	645	(H.C.).
Jeyaretnam Joshua Benjamin v. Lee Kuan Yew,		[1991]	2	M.L.J.	135	(Sing. C.A.).
Re Ong Yew Teck	(1960),		26	M.L.J.	67	(Sing. H.C.).

- In Singapore, because of the plurality of cultural practices governing names, always provide the full name of individuals.
- Include the abbreviation "Sing." unless the citation is from the *Singapore Law Reports*.
- If the year of the decision and the year of the reporter are the same, do not provide the year of the decision.

3.8.2 Unreported Decisions

Example			
Style of cause	(date),	case no.	(jurisdiction and/or court) (if applicable).
Public Prosecutor v. Loh Chai Huat	(31 May 2001),	D.A.C. No. 36923 of 2000	(Sing. Dist. Ct.).

3.8.3 Reporters

The principal reporters are abbreviated as follows:

Singapore Law Reports	Sing. L.R.
Malayan Law Journal	M.L.J.
Criminal Law Aid Scheme News	C.L.A.S.N.
Straits Settlements Law Reports	S.S.L.R.

3.8.4 Court

Abbreviate the name of the court as follows:

Court of Appeal	C.A.
High Court	H.C.
District Court	Dist. Ct.
Magistrates' Court	Mag. Ct.

- District Courts in Singapore have no subdivisions.

3—Jurisprudence

3.9   SOUTH AFRICA—CITATION TO PRINTED REPORTERS

3.9.1   General Form

Examples						
Style of cause	(year of decision),	[year of reporter]	volume	reporter	page	(jurisdiction and/or court) (if applicable).
Oosthuizen v. Stanley,		[1938]		A.D.	322	(S. Afr. S.C.).
Messina Associated Carriers v. Kleinhaus,		[2001]	3	S. Afr. L.R.	868	(S.C.A.).

- Cite South African cases in the same manner as Canadian cases.
- Cite to the *South African Law Reports* or *Butterworths Constitutional Law Reports*, if possible.
- If the year of the decision and the year of the reporter are the same, do not provide the year of the decision.

3.9.2   Reporters

The principal reporters are abbreviated as follows:

Butterworths Constitutional Law Reports	B. Const. L.R.
South African Law Reports, Appellate Division (1910-1946)	A.D.
South African Law Reports (1947-present)	S. Afr. L.R.

For a complete listing of all reporters, see Appendix G.

3.9.3 Court

Abbreviate the name of the court as follows:

Bophuthatswana High Court	Boph. H.C.
Cape Provincial Division	Cape Prov. Div.
Ciskei High Court	Ciskei H.C.
Constitutional Court of South Africa	S. Afr. Const. Ct.
Durban and Coast Local Division	D&C Local Div.
Eastern Cape Division	E. Cape Div.
Labour Court of South Africa	S. Afr. Labour Ct.
Labour Court of Appeal of South Africa	S. Afr. Labour C.A.
Land Claims Court of South Africa	S. Afr. Land Claims Ct.
Natal Provincial Division	Natal Prov. Div.
Northern Cape Division	N. Cape Div.
Orange Free State Provincial Division	O.F.S. Prov. Div.
South-Eastern Cape Division	S.E. Cape Div.
Supreme Court of Appeal of South Africa	S. Afr. S.C.
Transkei High Court	Transkei H.C.
Transvaal Provincial Division	Transv. Prov. Div.
Witwatersrand Local Division	Wit. Local Div.
Venda High Court	Venda H.C.

3.10 NEUTRAL CITATION

3.10.1 Relationship with Traditional Citation

A neutral citation permits permanent identification of a case independent of the electronic database or printed reporter in which it is published. Courts assign the neutral citation when they render decisions. Because neutral citations emanate directly from the court, a case cannot be cited by neutral citation if no neutral citation is presented in the decision.

The Canadian Citation Committee, which created the neutral citation system for Canada, suggested that it would be convenient for users to include the neutral citation as a parallel citation following a traditional citation to a printed reporter once the decision is published in a printed reporter. The Committee suggested that the neutral citation only appear on its own when the decision to which it refers has yet to be published in a printed reporter.

There are two primary disadvantages to the Committee's suggestion. First, once a decision is published, authors will have to add a parallel neutral citation after traditional citations to the case in a printed reporter. This additional step was not necessary before the introduction of the neutral citation. Second, another purpose of the neutral citation is to provide a permanent and universal identification for a case. Requiring that the neutral citation be used as a parallel citation once the decision is published in a printed reporter suggests that the more permanent method of identification is the traditional citation to the printed reporter, and implies that the neutral citation is primarily a replacement for citation to electronic sources.

However, the clear advantage of using the neutral citation as a parallel citation, rather than using it as the only citation, is that it is easier for readers to find cases in printed reporters when they have a direct citation to the specific volume and page of the printed reporter. In contrast, a reader who only has a neutral citation will have to search in the indexes of printed reporters in order to find the case. These indexes do not, as of yet, list cases by neutral citation.

We therefore feel it is most efficient to follow the committee's suggestion until such time as printed reporters make it easier to search for a case using a neutral citation.

N.B. When a neutral citation is available for a case, it must appear as a parallel reference when the decision to which it refers is published in a printed reporter (either official, semi-official, or unofficial). A neutral citation may only be included on its own if, at the time of writing, the decision to which it refers has not been published in a printed reporter.

3.10.2 General Form

Examples						
Style of cause,	traditional citation (if published),	core of neutral citation			optional elements.	
		year	tribunal identifier	ordinal number of decision	paragraph number	notes.
R. v. Law,		2002	SCC	10	¶ 22.	
R. v. Sangha	(2001), 288 A.R. 170,	2001	ABQB	373	para. 8.	
R. v. Rezvi,		2002	UKHL	3.		
Ordre des arpenteurs- géomètres du Québec c. Tremblay		2001	QCTP	24		note 14.
Preston v. Chow,		2002	MBCA	34	¶ 29-30, 33.	

- The core of the citation is assigned by the court and cannot be changed.
- There are no periods in the tribunal identifier.
- The jurisdiction and level of court are always obvious from a neutral citation. Whether a neutral citation stands alone or is included as a parallel citation, never include other abbreviations of jurisdictions and courts.
- When the neutral citation is included as a parallel reference, it should follow any other parallel references to printed reporters.
- Cite neutral citations from all countries in the same manner.
- When a neutral citation is available, never include an electronic service identifier (*e.g.* QL).

3.10.2.1 Style of Cause

The style of cause is the same as that which is used in citing to printed reporters (see section 3.2.2).

3.10.2.2 Core of the Citation—Year

The year is the year in which the decision was rendered by the court. If the date of the decision is fixed later, the year may be the year the case is entered into the court register.

3.10.2.3 Core of the Citation—Tribunal Identifier

The tribunal identifier is assigned by the court, and can be up to eight characters in length. The identifier begins with a prefix of two characters that, with the exception of the Northwest Territories, correspond to the standard two-letter jurisdiction code:

Alberta	AB
British Columbia	BC
Manitoba	MB
New Brunswick	NB
Newfoundland and Labrador	NF (NL?)
Northwest Territories	NWT or NT
Nova Scotia	NS
Nunavut	NU
Ontario	ON
Prince Edward Island	PE
Quebec	QC
Saskatchewan	SK
Yukon	YK

- The natural acronym of the tribunal or court follows this prefix, but should omit the reintroduction of any letters representing the jurisdiction. For example, Le Tribunal des professions du Québec is "QCTP" and not "QCTPQ."
- At the time of printing, the two-letter prefix for Newfoundland and Labrador is "NF". As the province's name changed in 2001, this prefix may change to "NL".

One Tribunal Identifier:

One identifier will be used when:

- a tribunal usually renders decisions in only one official language,

- a tribunal is not bilingual, or
- if a tribunal is bilingual, it uses the same acronym for decisions in English and French. In this case, the tribunal may add a suffix code to the tribunal identifier indicating the language of the decision. For example, a CRTC decision in English might use the identifier "CRTCE" and a CRTC decision in French might use the identifier "CRTCF".

Two Tribunal Identifiers:

Two or more identifiers will be used when courts regularly render decisions in two or more official languages and when the court wishes to use different acronyms for decisions in each language (unlike the CRTC, for instance). For example, the identifiers for the Supreme Court of Canada are SCC and CSC. When two or more identifiers exist, use the identifier which corresponds to the language in which you are writing.

3.10.2.4 Core of the Citation—Ordinal Number

- The ordinal number is assigned by the court. This number returns to "1" on January 1st of each year.
- For oral decisions published after judgment was rendered, the court should assign the next available ordinal number for the year in which that oral decision was rendered. This will allow the year of the neutral citation to correctly reflect the year in which the oral decision was rendered.

3.10.2.5 Optional Elements (Pinpoint)

- A pinpoint is only made to the first reporter cited. Therefore, include a pinpoint *only* if the decision has not been published in a printed reporter and the neutral citation is standing on its own.
- Reference to a paragraph in a decision is expressed by using the character ¶ or the term "para." (plural ¶ or "paras.").
- Reference to footnotes or endnotes in a decision is expressed by using the term "note".

3.11 CITATION TO ELECTRONIC SERVICES

- Use the following abbreviations when citing to electronic services:

Australian Legal Information Institute	AustLII
Azimut (produced by SOQUIJ)	Azimut
British and Irish Legal Information Institute	BILII
Butterworths Services	Butterworths
Canadian Legal Information Institute	CanLII
*e*Carswell	eC
Jurifrance	JF
Lawnet	Lawnet
Legifrance	Legifrance
LexisNexis	Lexis
LexUM	LexUM
Quicklaw	QL
Westlaw	WL

- Electronic services reproduce judgments printed in paper reporters. They also provide access to judgments that are not reported in paper reporters.

3.11.1 Judgments Published in Printed Reporters

3.11.1.1 No Quote or Pinpoint Used

If you do not quote from the judgment or provide a pinpoint, simply cite the case as you would cite it to the printed reporter without referring to the electronic service. A parallel citation may be given to other printed reporters, and to the neutral citation if one is available.

3.11.1.2 Quote or Pinpoint Used

- Traditional citations are not neutral. If you cite to the S.C.R., readers will assume that the printed reporter was the actual source for your pinpoint or quotation. If you cite to the S.C.R. and pinpoint a paragraph, and then provide a parallel citation to the D.L.R., readers will assume that one of the two printed reporters is the source for all future pinpoints. Therefore if your source is actually an electronic service, you need to identify either the electronic service or provide a neutral citation.

3.11.1.2.1 If a neutral citation is available

* Provide the traditional citation followed by the neutral citation. Never refer to an electronic service if a neutral citation exists.

3.11.1.2.2 If no neutral citation is available

Provide the traditional citation, as described above, and either

* *Option One:*
  * Indicate that the case is available on an electronic service by placing the name of the service in parentheses.
  * If the document cannot be readily found on the service without knowing the database within the electronic service, indicate the database in which the document can be found (*e.g.* "(QL, O.J.)").
  * This form of citation should be used only for electronic services that require a subscription, or for Internet sites that are similarly organized with comprehensive indexes, search tools, professional editors, and recognizable abbreviations. Citation to government Internet sites should include the full Internet address (see *Option Two*).
  * Include a paragraph number as a pinpoint reference, if available. If a paragraph number is not available and the page numbering of a printed source is reproduced in the electronic source, pinpoint to those page numbers. Do not pinpoint to the electronic service's screen number or page number, as these are specific to the service used and can vary in different formats (*e.g.* text, html).
  * If possible, do not cite to an electronic service to which the majority of readers will not have access. For example, do not cite to Azimut when writing for an audience outside of Quebec.

* or *Option Two:*
  * If the case is accessed through the Internet, introduce the citation by "online:" preceded by a comma. Provide the name of the site followed by the full URL of the document within "< >".
  * Cite the full Web address of the document you are citing unless the address is specific to one Web session. In this instance, cite the home page of the Web site.
  * Internet sources differ in their reliability. Judgment must be exercised when citing to these sources.
  * Many online articles expire after a short period of time. Cite to online sources only if the source provides an archive of material for a reasonable period of time, preferably several years.

3—Jurisprudence

- Include a paragraph number as a pinpoint reference, if available. If the page numbering of a printed source is reproduced in the electronic source, reference may be made to those page numbers.

N.B. If you verify your pinpoint or quotation in the printed reporter, you need not mention the electronic service as a source, and can simply give the traditional citation, although you would still need to provide the neutral citation, if one is available.

Examples

Vanderburgh v. ScotiaMcLeod Inc., [1992] 6 W.W.R. 673 at 675 (Alta.Q.B.) **(eC)** [*Vanderburgh*].

Nixon v. United States, 506 U.S. 224 (1993) **(WL)** [*Nixon*].

Er Joo Nguang v. Public Prosecutor, [2000] 2 Sing. L.R. 645 (H.C.) **(Lawnet)**.

Premakumar v. Air Canada (4 February 2002) CHRT D.T. 03/02 at para. 89, **online: CHRT <http://www.chrt-tcdp.gc.ca/decisions/docs/ premakumar-e.htm>.**

3.11.1.2.3 Pinpoint

- Pinpoint either to paragraph numbers or to the page numbering of a printed reporter within the on-screen text. Do not pinpoint to screen-page numbers identified by the electronic service.

3.11.1.2.4 Parallel Citations

Example

Vanderburgh v. ScotiaMcLeod Inc. (1992), 4 Alta. L.R. (3d) 138 at 140, **[1992] 6 W.W.R. 673 at 675 (Q.B.) (eC).**

- Where possible, include at least one parallel citation to a printed source.
- Always include a parallel citation to the neutral citation, if one is available.

3.11.2 Judgments Not Available in Printed Reporters

For judgments not available in paper reporters, electronic database services provide either a neutral citation, their own case identifiers, or only docket numbers.

3.11.2.1 Electronic Services That Provide a Neutral Citation

- Never cite to the database's identifier if a neutral citation is available. A neutral citation is preferred to a database's particular case identifier because the neutral citation is more universal.

- If the judgment is published in a printed reporter and a neutral citation is also available, list the printed reporter, followed by the neutral citation.

Example	
Decision not published in printed reporter; neutral citation available	*R. v. Benjafield*, 2002 UKHL 2.

3.11.2.2 Electronic Services That Provide Their Own Case Identifiers

Examples					
	Style of cause,	identifier given by service	pinpoint	(jurisdiction and/or court) (if applicable)	(electronic service).
eCarswell	*Underwood v. Underwood*,	1995 CarswellOnt 88		(Ont. Gen. Div.)	(eC).
Lexis	*Davies v. M.N.R.*,	[1997] Can. Tax Ct. LEXIS 5874	at 5		(Lexis).
Quicklaw	*Fuentes v. Canada (Minister of Employment and Immigration)*,	[1995] F.C.J. No. 206	at para. 10	(T.D.)	(QL).
Westlaw	*Fincher v. Baker*,	[1997] WL 675447	at 2	(Ala. Civ. App.)	(WL).

- Provide the identifier given by the service after the style of cause. This identifier usually includes the year of the decision and a sequential number. It serves to identify the decision within the database service.
- Pinpoint either to paragraph numbers or to the page numbering of a printed reporter within the on-screen text. Do not pinpoint to screen-page numbers identified by the electronic service.
- *e*Carswell: If the only identifier listed is an *e*CARSWELL identifier (*i.e.* there is no reference to a paper reporter), the judgment is otherwise unreported.
- **Lexis**: The year included within the LEXIS identifier must be placed in brackets. If the only identifier listed is the one given by Lexis, the judgment is otherwise unreported.
- **Quicklaw**: The Quicklaw identifier can be found on the screen below the style of cause. If the only identifier listed is a Quicklaw identifier (*i.e.* there is no reference to a paper reporter), the judgment may otherwise not be reported. Use the database

QUICKCITE, which lists all the sources for any particular judgment, to confirm that the judgment is not reported elsewhere.

- **Westlaw**: The year included in the WESTLAW identifier must be placed within brackets. If the identifier contains "WL" only, the judgment is otherwise unreported.

3.11.2.2.1 Lawnet

Example					
Style of cause,	database identifier given by service	date	(jurisdiction and/or court),	pinpoint	(electronic service)
Beryl Claire Clarke and Others v. Silkair (Singpore) Pte. Ltd.,	Suit Nos. 1746, 1748-1752 of 1999,	24 October 2001,	(Sing. H.C.),	at para. 10	(Lawnet).

3.11.2.3 Electronic Services That Provide Only Docket Numbers for a Case

Examples		
Traditional citation for judgments not reported in paper format,	electronic service	<URL > (if applicable).
Caisse populaire de Trois-Pistoles c. April (31 January 2002), Kamouraska 250-22-001090-013 (C.Q. civ.)	(Azimut).	
R. v. Logan (15 December 1995), Port Hardy 9317 (B.C. Prov. Ct.),	online: Electronic Frontier Canada	<http://www.efc.ca/pages/legal.html#court>.

- Provide the citation as if it was an unreported judgment. See section 3.2.12.

4

GOVERNMENT DOCUMENTS

4.1 CANADA

4.1.1 Debates

Examples						
Jurisdiction,	legislature,	*title,*	number	(date)	pinpoint	(speaker).
		House of Commons Debates,	064	(17 May 2001)	at 4175	(Hon. Elinor Caplan).
Ontario,	Legislative Assembly,	*Official Report of Debates (Hansard),*	53	(18 October 2001)	at 2819	(Julia Munro).
Yukon,	Legislative Assembly,	*Hansard,*	18	(22 November 2000)	at 552	(Mr. Jenkins).

- Indicate the jurisdiction for provincial legislatures, unless it is mentioned in the title of the debates. Do not include the jurisdiction for the House of Commons or Senate.
- Indicate the name of the legislature, unless it is mentioned in the title of the debates.
- Cite the title, in italics, as it appears on the title page of the document.

- Place the volume and/or document number, if any, after the title, preceded by a comma.
- Include the full date in parentheses followed by the pinpoint.
- Include the name of the speaker in parentheses at the end of the citation.

4.1.1.1 Minutes

Example					
Jurisdiction,	legislature,	*title*,	legislature,	volume number	(date).
Quebec,	National Assembly,	*Procès-verbaux*,	35th Leg.,	No. 5	(5 December 1994).

- Indicate the jurisdiction for provincial legislatures, unless it is mentioned in the title.
- Indicate the name of the legislature, unless it is mentioned in the title.
- Cite the title, in italics, as it appears on the title page of the document.
- Indicate the number of the legislature.
- Place the volume and/or document number, if any, after the number of the legislature, preceded by a comma.

4.1.2 Parliamentary and Non-parliamentary Documents

These documents include reports and studies written by committees, commissions, ministers, and individual authors, for legislative assemblies or governmental bodies.

If the document is found in the publication of a parliamentary body, such as a committee report published in the journals of debates, cite it as a parliamentary paper, according to the rules at section 4.1.2.1.

If the document is published under a separate cover, and does not emanate directly from a legislative body, cite it according to the rules for non-parliamentary papers, at section 4.1.2.2.

4.1.2.1 *Parliamentary Papers*

4.1.2.1.1 Published in Debates

Example								
Jurisdiction,	legislature,	issuing body,	"title of report"	in	*title*,	Number	(date)	pinpoint.
Ontario,	Legislative Assembly,	Standing Committee on regulations and private bills,	"Election of Chair"	in	*Official Reports of Debates (Hansard)*,	No. T-6	(26 September 2001)	at 41.

- Indicate the jurisdiction only if citing provincial papers.
- For debates, follow the rules from section 4.1.1. After the name of the legislature, add the name of issuing body and the title of the report.
- The title of the report is placed in quotation marks.
- Place the number of the paper, if any, after the title, preceded by a comma.

4.1.2.1.2 Sessional Papers

Examples									
Jurisdiction,	legislature,	"title of report"	by	author	in	*title*,	sessional paper number	(year)	pinpoint.
Canada,	Parliament,	"Report of the Chief Inspector of Dominion Lands Agencies"	by	H.G. Cuttle	in	*Sessional Papers*,	No. 25	(1920)	at 3.
Ontario,	Legislative Assembly,	"Report on Workmen's Compensation for Injuries"	by	James Mavor	in	*Sessional Papers*,	No. 40	(1900)	at 6-7.

- Indicate the jurisdiction only if citing provincial papers.
- Indicate the issuing body and the title of the report.
- If an author is given, place the name after the title of report.
- If the sessional paper is numbered, cite the number after the title, preceded by a comma.

N.B. Most jurisdictions stopped publishing sessional papers by 1940.

4.1.2.2 Non-parliamentary Papers

4.1.2.2.1 General Form

Examples						
Jurisdic-tion,	issuing body,	*Title,*	volume	(publi-cation inform-ation)	pinpoint	(additional information) (optional).
Canada,	Royal Commiss-ion on Electoral Reform and Party Financing,	*Reforming Electoral Democracy,*	vol. 4	(Ottawa: Communi-cation Group, 1991)	at 99	(Chair: Pierre Lortie).
		Report of the Parliament-ary Ad Hoc Committee on AIDS		(Ottawa: Ad Hoc Committee on AIDS, 1990)	at 5.	
Quebec,	Ministère de la justice,	*Comment-aires du ministre de la justice,*	vol. 1	(Quebec: Publicat-ions du Québec, 1993)	at 705.	

- Include the jurisdiction unless it is provided in another element of the citation.
- Indicate the issuing body unless it is named in the title of the report.
- If there is a volume, cite it after the title.
- Publication information is provided according to the rules with respect to books at sections 6.2.7-6.2.9.
- The name of the commissioner or chairperson may be included in parentheses at the end of the citation.

4.1.2.2.2 Interpretation Bulletins

Examples					
Depart-ment,	Interpretation Bulletin	IT-number,	"title"	(date)	pinpoint.
M.N.R.,	Interpretation Bulletin	IT-459,	"Income Tax Act Adventure or Concern in the Nature of Trade"	(8 September 1980).	
M.N.R.,	Interpretation Bulletin	IT-525R,	"Performing Artists"	(17 August 1995).	
M.N.R.,	Interpretation Bulletin	IT-244R3,	"Gifts by Individuals of Life Insurance Policies as Charitable Donations"	(6 September 1991)	at para. 4.

- If the bulletin has been revised insert "R" after the IT number. The number of revisions is indicated by the number following the "R" (*e.g.* "R3").
- As Interpretation Bulletins are divided into paragraphs, pinpoint to a paragraph.

4.1.2.2.3 Parliamentary Inquiry

Example				
Jurisdiction,	Parliamentary Inquiry,	*title*	(publication information)	pinpoint.
Alberta,	Parliamentary Inquiry,	Report on Comity and Parliamentary Practice in Municipal Bodies in Alberta	(Edmonton: Queen's Printer, 1993)	at 2.

- If the document is a parliamentary inquiry, include this information before the title.

4.1.2.2.4   Reports Published in Different Volumes

4.1.2.2.4.1   Volumes with a Single Title

Example			
Jurisdiction,	*title,*	volume	(publication information).
Ontario,	*Report of the Royal Commission on Certain Sectors of the Building Industry,*	vol. 1, 2	(Toronto: Queen's Printer, 1974).

- When a publication with a single title is published in separate volumes, include the volume number after the title. To distinguish the subdivisions, indicate "vol." or any other appellation used in the report.

4.1.2.2.4.2   Volumes with Different Titles

Example		
Citation for volume 1	;	citation for volume 2
Canada, *Report of the Royal Commission on Aboriginal Peoples: Looking Forward, Looking Back,* **vol. 1** (Ottawa: Supply and Services Canada, 1996) at 8	;	Canada, *Report of the Royal Commission on Aboriginal Peoples: Restructuring the Relationship,* **vol. 2** (Ottawa: Supply and Services Canada, 1996) at 14.

- When citing subdivisions with different titles, include a full citation for each subdivision separated by a semicolon. Treat the title of the subdivision as a subtitle of the entire work.

4.1.2.2.5   Nature of the Publication

Example					
Issuing body,	*title*	(nature of publication)	author (if applicable)	(publication information)	pinpoint.
Statistics Canada,	*Market Research Handbook*	(Socio-economic guide)		(Ottawa: Small Business and Special Surveys Division, 2001)	at 167.

- If an indication of the nature of the publication appears on the title page, include this information within parentheses immediately after the title.

4.1.2.2.6   Individual Authors

Example				
Issuing body,	*title*	by	author	(publication information).
Agriculture and Agri-Food Canada,	*The Health of Our Water: Toward Sustainable Agriculture in Canada*	by	D.R. Coote & L.J. Gregorich, eds.	(Ottawa: Minister of Public Works and Government Services Canada, 2000).

- If there is an individual author of the paper, include the author's name after the title.

4.1.3 Public Papers of Inter-governmental Conferences

Examples				
Name of conference or committee,	*title,*	document number	(location of the conference:	date of conference).
Meeting of the Continuing Committee of Ministers on the Constitution,	*The Canadian Charter of Rights and Freedoms— Discussion Draft, July 4, 1980,*	Doc. 830-81/027	(Ottawa:	8-12 September 1980).
Federal-Provincial-Territorial Meeting of Ministers Responsible for Justice,	*Dealing with Impaired Driving in Prince Edward Island: A Summary 1986-1997,*	Doc. 830-600/021	(Montreal:	4-5 December 1997).

- Indicate the name of the conference or committee in full, followed by the title of the paper, and the document number.
- Provide the location and full date of the conference in parentheses.

4.2   UNITED KINGDOM

Indicate that you are citing a government document of the United Kingdom by placing "U.K." at the beginning of the citation.

4.2.1 Debates

4.2.1.1 Before 1803

Example						
U.K.,	house,	*Parliamentary History of England,*	volume,	column	(date)	(speaker) (optional).
U.K.,	H.C.,	*Parliamentary History of England,*	vol. 12,	col. 1327	(27 May 1774).	

- For debates prior to 1803, cite to the *Parliamentary History of England*.
- Abbreviate the house as "H.C." for House of Commons and "H.L." for House of Lords.
- The speaker may be indicated in parentheses at the end of the citation.

4.2.1.2 1803 and After

Examples								
U.K.,	house,	*title,*	series,	volume,	column	pinpoint	(date)	(speaker) (optional).
U.K.,	H.L.,	*Parliamentary Debates,*	5th ser.,	vol. 442,	col. 3	at col. 6	(3 May 1983)	(Baroness Masham of Ilton).
U.K.,	S.P.,	*Official Report,*	session 1 (2000),	vol. 7, No. 6,	col. 634		(22 June 2000)	(Peter Peacock).
U.K.,	N.I.A.,	*Official Report*				at 500	(24 October 2000).	
U.K.,	N.A.W.,	*Official Record*				at 27	(19 July 2001).	

• The speaker may be indicated in parentheses at the end of the citation.
• After "U.K.", indicate the house using the following abbreviations:

House of Lords	H.L.
House of Commons	H.C.
Scottish Parliament	S.P.
Northern Ireland Assembly	N.I.A.
National Assembly for Wales	N.A.W.

4.2.2 Journals

Examples				
U.K.,	*journal,*	volume	(date)	pinpoint.
U.K.,	Journal of the House of Commons,	vol. 234	(9 December 1977)	at 95.
U.K.,	*Journal of the House of Lords,*	vol. 22	(10 January 1995)	at 89.

• Do not repeat the reference to the house, since it is included in the title of the journal.

4.2.3 Parliamentary Papers

Examples									
U.K.,	house,	"title",	sessional or command paper number	in *Sessional Papers,*	vol.	(year)	first page	Pin-point	(president) (if any).
U.K.,	H.C.,	"Report of the Committee on the Law Relating to Rights of Light",	Cmnd 473	in *Sessional Papers,*	vol. 17	(1957-58)	955		(President: C.E. Harman).
U.K.,	H.C.,	"Monopolies and Mergers Commission Report on the Supply in the U.K. of the Services of Administering Performing Rights and Film Synchronisation Rights",	Cm 3147	in *Sessional Papers*		1995-96	1.		

- Indicate the title as it appears on the title page of the report.
- Place the sessional number or command paper number after the title of the paper.
- The name of the president may be included in parentheses at the end of the citation.
- Cite to the House of Commons' bound *Sessional Papers* unless the paper only appears in the House of Lords' *Sessional Papers*.
- The proper abbreviation of "Command" is essential for identifying the document. Note that the proper abbreviation is indicated on the title page of each *Command Paper*:

1833-1869	1st series (1-4222)	c.
1870-1899	2d series (1-9550)	C.
1900-1918	3d series (1-9239)	Cd
1919-1956	4th series (1-9889)	Cmd
1957-1986	5th series (1-9927)	Cmnd
1986-present	6th series (1-)	Cm

- Indicate the first page of the paper after the date.
- Cite to the internal pagination of the paper for a pinpoint.

- The name of the president may be included as parenthetical information at the end of the citation.

4.2.4 Non-parliamentary Papers

Examples					
U.K.,	issuing body,	*title*	(nature of paper) (if applicable)	authors (if applicable)	(publication information).
U.K.,	Royal Commission on Criminal Procedure,	*Police Interrogation: The Psychological Approach*			(London: Her Majesty's Stationery Office, 1980).
U.K.,	Royal Commission of the Press,	*Studies on the Press*	(Working Paper No. 3)	by Oliver Boyd-Barrett, Dr. Colin Seymour-Ure & Professor Jeremy Turnstall	(London: Her Majesty's Stationery Office, 1978).

- Cite non-parliamentary papers in the same manner as Canadian non-parliamentary papers, according to the rules at section 4.1.2.2.

4.3 UNITED STATES

Indicate that you are citing a government document of the United States by placing "U.S." at the beginning of the citation.

4.3.1 Debates

Examples							
U.S.,	*Cong. Rec.*,	edition,	volume,	part,	pinpoint	(date)	(speaker) (optional).
U.S.,	*Cong. Rec.*,		vol. 125,	15,	at 18691	(1979)	
U.S.,	*Cong. Rec.*,	daily ed.,	vol. 143,	69,	at H3176	(22 May 1977)	(Rep. Portman).

- Cite congressional debates after 1873 to the *Congressional Record.*
- For information on how to cite earlier congressional debates, consult *The Bluebook: A Uniform System of Citation*, 17th ed. (Cambridge, Mass., Harvard Law Review Association, 2000).

4.3.2 Committee Hearings

4.3.2.1 Federal

Examples					
U.S.,	*title,*	Congress number	(publication information)	pinpoint	(speaker) (optional).
U.S.,	*Federal Property Campaign Fundraising Reform Act of 2000: Hearing on H.R. 4845 Before the House Committee of the Judiciary,*	106th Cong.	(2000)	at 2-3.	
U.S.,	*Assisted Suicide: Legal, Medical, Ethical and Social Issues: Hearing Before the Subcommittee on Health and Environment of the House Committee on Commerce,*	105th Cong.	(Washington, D.C.: United States Government Printing Office, 1997)	at 2	(Dr. C. Everett Koop).

- Always cite the year; provide further publication information, if available.

4.3.2.2 State

Example							
U.S.,	*Title,*	number of the legislative body (or, if not numbered, the year),	Legisla-ture number or designat-ion,	state	(public-ation inform-ation)	Pin-point	(speaker) (optional).
U.S.,	*Rico Litigation: Hearing on S. 1197 Before the Senate Comm. On Commerce and Econ. Dev.,*	41st Legis.,	1st Reg. Sess. 5,	Ariz.	(1993)		(statement of Barry Wong, policy analyst).

- Abbreviate the state according to the list in Appendix B.
- Always cite the year; provide further publication information, if available.

4.3.3 Reports and Documents

4.3.3.1 Federal

4.3.3.1.1   Numbered Documents and Reports

Example					
U.S.,	issuing body,	*title*	(number)	(publication information)	pinpoint.
U.S.,	Commission on Protecting and Reducing Government Secrecy,	*Secrecy: Report of the Commission on Protecting and Reducing Government Secrecy: Pursuant to Public Law 236, 103rd Congress*	(S. Doc. No. 105-2)	(Washington, D.C.: United States Government Printing Office, 1997)	at 3.

* Always cite the year of publication. Provide further publication information if available.
* Use the following abbreviations with the document number:

Documents	Reports
H.R. Doc. No.	H.R. Rep. No.
H.R. Misc. Doc. No.	H.R. Conf. Rep. No.
S. Doc. No.	S. Rep. No.
S. Exec. Doc. No.	

4.3.3.1.2   Unnumbered Documents and Committee Prints

Examples					
U.S.,	issuing body,	*title,*	Committee Print (if relevant)	(publication information)	pinpoint.
U.S.,	Staff of House Committee on Veterans' Affairs, 105th Cong.,	*Persian Gulf Illnesses: An Overview,*	Committee Print	(1998)	at 15.
U.S.,	National Commission on Children,	*Beyond Rhetoric: A New American Agenda for Children and Families*		(Washington, D.C.: The Commission, 1991)	at 41.

- Include the Congress number with the issuing body, if relevant.
- Always cite the yearof publication. Provide further publication information, if available.

4.3.3.2   *State*

Examples						
	U.S.,	issuing body,	*title*	(number) (if applicable)	(publication information)	pinpoint.
Numbered Documents and Reports	U.S.,	California Energy Commission	*Existing Renewable Resources Account, vol. 1*	(500-01-014V1)	(2001).	
Unnumbered Documents	U.S.,	Washington State Transport Commission,	*Washington's Transportation Plan 2003-2022*		(Washington State Department of Transportation, 2002).	

- Provide the document number, if available.
- Always cite the year of publication. Provide further publication information if available.

4.4   FRANCE

Indicate that you are citing a government document of France by placing "France" at the beginning of the citation.

4.4.1   Debates

4.4.1.1   From 1787 to 1860

Example						
France,	*Archives parlementaires,*	series,	tome,	date,	pinpoint,	(speaker) (optional).
France,	*Archives parlementaires,*	1st series,	t. 83,	5 January 1794,	s. 3.	

- Cite to Archives parlementaires: recueil complet des débats législatifs et politiques des chambres françaises, using the short title "Archives parlementaires".
- Indicate the series after the title. The first series covers 1787-1799, the second 1800-1860.
- Pinpoints should refer to sections.
- The name of the speaker may be added in parentheses at the end of the citation.

4.4.1.2   1871 to the Present

Examples							
France,	*journal,*	house,	Débats parlementaires,	division,	number and date,	pinpoint,	(speaker) (optional).
France,	*J.O.,*	Assemblée nationale,	Débats parlementaires,	Compte rendu intégral,	1st session of 23 January 2001,	at 635	(Gilbert Maurel).
France,	*J.O.,*	Sénat,	Débats parlementaires,	Compte rendu intégral,	Session of 3 April 2001.		

- From 1871 to the present, parliamentary debates are published in *Journal officiel de la République française*, abbreviated "*J.O.*"
- Indicate the house, followed by "Débats parlementaires". The following periods are exceptions to this rule:
    - 1871-1880: omit both the house and "Débats parlementaires".
    - 1943-1945, 1945-1946, 1947-1958: indicate only "Débats de [name of house]".
- The names of the houses have changed in different periods:

1881-1940	Chambre des députés		1880-1940	Sénat
1943-1945	Assemblée consultative provisoire		1946-1958	Conseil de la République
1945-1946	Assemblée constituante		1958-	Sénat
1947-1958	Assemblée de l'Union française			
1958-	Assemblée nationale			

- Indicate the division only from 1980 to the present for the Assemblée nationale, and from 1983 to the present for the Sénat. The divisions are "Compte rendu intégral" and "Questions écrites remises à la Présidence de l'Assemblée nationale et réponses des ministres" for the Assemblee nationale, and "Compte rendu intégral" and "Questions remises à la Présidence du Sénat et réponses des ministres aux questions écrites" for the Sénat.
- Indicate the number (if any) and the date of the session followed by the pinpoint.
- The name of the speaker may be added in parentheses at the end of the citation.

4.4.2 Earlier Versions of the *Journal officiel*

Example				
France,	*title*,	year,	tome or volume,	pinpoint.
France,	*Journal officiel de l'Empire français*,	1868,	t. 1,	at 14.

- Before 1871, parliamentary debates, parliamentary documents, and non-parliamentary documents were generally published in the various precursors to the *Journal officiel de la République française*:

1787-1810	*Gazette nationale* or *Moniteur universel*
1811-1848	*Moniteur universel*
1848-1852	*Moniteur universel, Journal officiel de la République*
1852-1870	*Journal officiel de l'Empire français*

- The citation form varies according to the organization of the journal. In general, the citation should include at least the title, the year in question or the date of publication, the tome or volume (if any), and the pinpoint.

4.4.3 Parliamentary Documents

4.4.3.1 *Travaux et réunions parlementaires*

Examples						
France,	house,	issuing body,	"title",	Compte rendu or *Bulletin*	(date)	(President) (optional).
France,	Assemblée nationale,	Délégation aux droits des femmes,	"Auditions sur le suivi de l'application des lois relatives à l'IVG et à la contraception",	Compte rendu No. 4	(6 November 2001)	(President: Martine Lignières-Cassou).
France,	Sénat,	Commission des affaires culturelles,	"Auditions de M. Jack Lang, ministre de l'éducation nationale",	*Bulletin du 11 juin 2001*	(13 June 2001)	(President: Adrien Gouteyron).

- Indicate the title of the *travaux*, then the number of the corresponding Comte rendu (for *travaux* of the Assemblée nationale) or the date of the Bulletin (for *travaux* of the Sénat). "*Bulletin*" should be in italics.
- The name of the president may be added in parentheses at the end of the citation.

4.4.3.2 *Rapports d'information (Reports)*

Example							
France,	house,	issuing body,	*title*,	by author(s),	Report number	(date)	pinpoint.
France,	Sénat,	Commiss-ion des affaires étrangères,	*La réforme de la coopération à l'épreuve des réalités : un premier bilan 1998-2001*,	by Guy Penne, André Dulait & Paulette Brisepierre,	Report No. 46	(30 October 2001)	at 7.

4.4.4 Non-parliamentary Documents

Examples						
France,	issuing body,	*title*,	Report number or volume,	publication information	pinpoint	(additional information) (optional).
France,		*Commission d'enquête sur la sécurité du transport maritime des produits dangereux ou polluants*,	Report No. 2535, vol. 1,			(5 July 2000; President: Daniel Paul).
France,	Conseil économique et social,	*La conjoncture économique et sociale à la fin de l'an 2000: embellie et danger*,		Avis et rapports du Conseil économique et social, *J.O.*, No. 2000-17	At II-4	(20 December 2000; report by Dominique Taddei).
France,	Ministère de la justice,	*Bulletin officiel*,	No. 82		at 3	(from 1 April to 30 June 2001).

• Follow the rules for Canadian non-parliamentary documents in section 4.1.2.2.

4.5   AUSTRALIA

Indicate that you are citing a government document of Australia by placing "Austl." at the beginning of the citation.

4.5.1   Debates

Examples						
Austl.,	jurisdiction,	house,	*Parliamentary Debates*	(date)	pinpoint	(speaker) (optional).
Austl.,	Commonwealth,	House of Representatives,	*Parliamentary Debates*	(17 September 2001)	at 30739	(Mr. Howard, Prime Minister).
Austl.,	Victoria,	Legislative Assembly,	*Parliamentary Debates*	(23 October 1968)	at 1197.	

- After "Austl.", indicate the jurisdiction. See Appendix C for details.
- Always indicate the reporter as *"Parliamentary Debates"*.
- The name and title of the speaker may be indicated in parentheses at the end of the citation.

4.5.2   Parliamentary Papers

Example					
Austl.,	jurisdiction,	*title,*	number	(year)	pinpoint.
Austl.,	Commonwealth,	*Department of Foreign Affairs Annual Report 1975,*	Parl. Paper No. 142	(1976)	at 5.

- The number is preceded by "Parl. Paper No."

4.5.3 Non-parliamentary Papers

Examples							
Austl.,	Jurisdiction,	issuing body,	*title*	(nature of paper)	by author(s) (if applicable)	(publication information)	pinpoint
Austl.,	Common-wealth,	Royal Commission into Aboriginal Deaths in Custody,	*Report of the Inquiry into the Death of Stanley John Gollan*		by Commissioner Elliott Johnston, Q.C.	(Canberra: Australian Government Publishing Service, 1990)	at 31.
Austl.,	Common-wealth,	Law Reform Commission,	*Annual Report 1998*	(Report No. 49)		(Canberra: Australian Government Publishing Service, 1988).	

- Cite Australian non-parliamentary papers in the same manner as Canadian non-parliamentary papers, according to the rules set out in section 4.1.2.2.

4.5.4 Ministerial Documents

Example						
Author,	Jurisdiction,	*title*,	Document Service,	number	(date)	pinpoint.
Paul Keating,	Common-wealth (Austl.),	*Opening of the Global Cultural Diversity Conference,*	Ministerial Document Service,	No. 172/94-95	(27 April 1995)	at 5977.

- If additional information is required to identify the jurisdiction as within Australia include "Austl." in parentheses following the jurisdiction named and before the comma preceding the title.

4.6   NEW ZEALAND

Indicate that you are citing a government document of New Zealand by placing "N.Z." at the beginning of the citation.

4.6.1   Debates

Example					
N.Z.,	*Hansard,*	stage: subject	(question number)	date	(speaker) (optional).
N.Z.,	*Hansard,*	Questions To Ministers: Biosecurity Risk-Motor Vehicle and Equipment Imports	(No. 3)	1 March 2000	(Ian Ewen-Street).

- *Hansard* provides the type of stage. It often will be one of the following: Questions to Ministers, Debate-General, Report of [a named] Committee or Miscellaneous.
- Subject is the title of the debate, *e.g.* Labour, Associate Minister-Accountability.
- The question number may be indicated in parentheses after the "stage: subject".
- The speaker may be indicated in parentheses at the end of the citation.

4.6.2   Parliamentary Papers

N.Z.,	"title",	date,	session	(chair)	shoulder number.
N.Z.,	"Report of the Government Administration Committee, Inquiry into New Zealand's Adoption Laws",	August 2001,	46th Parliament	(Dianne Yates, Chair).	
N.Z.	"Report of the Game Bird Habitat Trust Board for the year ended 31 August 1999",	February 2000,			C.22.

- The name of the chair may be indicated in parentheses after the session.
- The prefix of the shoulder number indicates the subject group, as follows:

Subject groups
A. Political and Foreign Affairs
B. Finance and Revenue
C. Environment and Primary Production
D. Energy and Works
E. Welfare and Justice
F. Communications
G. General
H. Commissions, "Royal Commissions"

4.7 SINGAPORE

Indicate that you are citing a government document of Singapore by placing "Sing." at the beginning of the citation.

4.7.1 Parliamentary Debates

Example						
Sing.,	*Parliamentary Debates,*	vol.,	column	column pinpoint	(date)	(speaker) (optional).
Sing.	*Parliamentary Debates,*	vol. 73,	col. 2436	at 2437	(15 October 2001)	(Professor S. Jayakumar).

4.8   INTERNET SITES

Example			
Full citation,	online:	name of Web site	<URL>.
U.S., Commission on Security and Cooperation in Europe, *Presidential Elections and Independence Referendums in the Baltic States, the Soviet Union and Successor States* (Washington, D.C.: The Commission, 1992) at 53,	online:	Commission on Security and Cooperation in Europe	<http://www.csce.gov/reports.cfm>.

- Provide the full traditional citation, followed a comma, "online:", the name of the Web page, and the URL.
- Cite the full Web address of the document you are citing unless the address is specific to one Web session. In this instance, cite the home page of the Web site.
- Internet sources differ in their reliability. Judgment must be exercised when citing to these sources.
- Many online documents expire after a short period of time. Cite to online sources only if the source provides an archive of material for a reasonable period of time, preferably several years.
- Include a paragraph number as a pinpoint reference, if available. If the page numbering of a printed source is reproduced in the electronic source, reference may be made to those page numbers.

5

INTERNATIONAL MATERIALS

5.1   INTERNATIONAL DOCUMENTS

5.1.1   Treaties and Other International Agreements

Examples					
Title,	parties (if applicable),	date of signature,	treaty series reference,	parallel citation	other information (optional).
Treaty relating to Boundary Waters and Questions Arising with Canada,	United States and United Kingdom,	11 January 1909,	36 U.S. Stat. 2448,	U.K.T.S. 1910 No. 23	
Convention for the Protection of Human Rights and Fundamental Freedoms,		4 November 1950,	213 U.N.T.S. 221 at 223,	Eur. T.S. 5	[*ECHR*].

International Covenant on Civil and Political Rights,		19 December 1966,	999 U.N.T.S. 171, arts. 9-14,	Can. T.S. 1976 No. 47, 6 I.L.M. 368	(entered into force 23 March 1976, accession by Canada 19 May 1976) [*ICCPR*].
North American Free Trade Agreement Between the Government of Canada, the Government of Mexico and the Government of the United States,		17 December 1992,	Can. T.S. 1994 No. 2,	32 I.L.M. 289	(entered into force 1 January 1994) [*NAFTA*].
General Agreement on Tariffs and Trade,		30 October 1947,	58 U.N.T.S. 187,	Can. T.S. 1947 No. 27	(entered into force 1 January 1948) [*GATT 1947*].

- Begin with the complete title of the treaty. When the names of the signatories appear in the title of a treaty, shorten them to reflect common usage (*e.g.* "United Kingdom", not "United Kingdom of Great Britain and Northern Ireland"), but do not abbreviate them (*e.g.* U.K.).
- If the names of the parties to a bilateral treaty are not mentioned in the title, include the shortened names of the parties after the title, between commas. The names of the parties to a multilateral treaty may be included at the end of the citation.
- Provide the date when the treaty was signed or opened for signature.
- Provide the treaty series citation after the date. It is preferable to provide a parallel citation for treaties. Refer to treaty series in the following order of preference: (1) *United Nations Treaty Series* (U.N.T.S.) or *League of Nations Treaty Series* (L.N.T.S.); (2) Official treaty series of a state involved (*e.g. Canada Treaty Series* (Can. T.S.), *United Kingdom Treaty Series* (U.K.T.S.)); (3) Other sources of international treaties (*e.g. International Legal Materials* (I.L.M.)).
- Additional information may be provided at the end of the citation, *e.g.* the names of the parties to a multilateral treaty, the date of entry into force, the number of ratifications, and the status of particular countries.

Here is a list of treaty series and their abbreviations:

Air and Aviation Treaties of the World	A.A.T.W.
Australian Treaty Series	A.T.S.
Canada Treaty Series	Can. T.S.
Consolidated Treaty Series	Cons. T.S.
Documents juridiques internationaux	*D.J.I.*
European Treaty Series	Eur. T.S.
International Legal Materials	I.L.M.
Journal Officiel	J.O.
League of Nations Treaty Series	L.N.T.S.
Organization of American States Treaty Series	O.A.S.T.S.
Recueil des traités du Canada	R.T. Can.
Recueil des traités et accords de la France	R.T.A.F.
Recueil des traités des Nations Unies	R.T.N.U.
Recueil des traités de la Société des Nations	R.T.S.N.
Recueil général des traités de la France	Rec. G.T.F.
Recueil des traités d'alliance, de paix, de trêve, de neutralité, de commerce, de limites, d'échange, et plusieurs autres actes à la connaissance des relations étrangères des puissances et États de l'Europe	Rec. T.A.
Série des traités et conventions européennes	S.T.E.
United States Statutes at Large	U.S. Stat.
Treaties and other International Agreements of the United States of America 1776-1949	T.I. Agree (formerly U.S.B.S.)
United States Treaties and Other International Acts Series	T.I.A.S.
British and Foreign State Papers	U.K.F.S.
United Kingdom Treaty Series	U.K.T.S.
United Nations Treaty Series	U.N.T.S.
United States Treaties and Other International Agreements	U.S.T.

5—International Materials

5.1.2   United Nations Documents

The UN document being cited may not always contain all the elements found in the examples below. Adapt the citation and provide the information necessary to identify the document clearly.

In citing documents of the United Nations, abbreviate the following commonly used words and phrases as follows:

Decision	Dec.
Document	Doc.
Emergency	Emer.
Meeting	Mtg.
Mimeograph(ed)	Mimeo.
Number	No.
Official Records	OR
Plenary	Plen.
Recommendation	Rec.
Regular	Reg.
Resolution	Res.
Session	Sess.
Special	Spec.
Supplement	Supp.

5.1.2.1   Charter of the United Nations

The *Charter of the United Nations* does not require a citation. It may, however, be cited as: *Charter of the United Nations*, 26 June 1945, Can. T.S. 1945 No. 7.

5.1.2.2   Official Records

Official records published by UN organizations contain three parts: meetings, supplements, and annexes. The official records are identified by the particular body's acronym followed by "OR". Provide the full names of UN bodies that have no official acronym. Official acronyms of the principal United Nations bodies are:

Economic and Social Council	ESC
First Committee, Second Committee, etc.	C1, C2, etc.
General Assembly	GA
Security Council	SC
Trade and Development Board	TDB
Trusteeship Council	TC
United Nations Conference on Trade and Development	UNCTAD

5.1.2.2.1   Meetings

Examples							
UN body's acronym and "OR",	session number or number of years since the body's inception,	meeting,	UN Doc. No. (and sales no. if applicable)	(year of document) (if applicable)	Pinpoint	[provisional].
UNCTAD TDBOR,	23d Sess.,	565th Mtg.,	UN Doc. TD/B/ SR.565	(1981).		
UN SCOR,	53d Year,	3849th Mtg.,	UN Doc. S/PV.3849	(1998)		[provisional].
UN ESCOR,	1984,	23d Plen. Mtg.,	UN Doc. E/1984/ SR.23.			

- Begin by indicating "UN" (unless "UN" is part of the body's acronym) followed by the UN body's acronym and "OR" (Official records).
- Provide the session number after the name of the body. If the session number is not available, give the year of the body since its inception. If neither the session number nor the year of the body is available, provide the calendar year.
- Provide the meeting number after the sessional information.
- Provide the UN document number after the meeting number. If a document has more than one document number, indicate them all, separating them with a hyphen. The

sales document number may also be given after the document number in parentheses ("Sales No. #").

- Provide the calendar year in parentheses after the UN document number, unless it has been cited previously.
- Provide the pinpoint. If the pinpoint follows the UN document number, place a comma after the UN document number.
- Indicate provisional documents by placing "[provisional]" at the end of the citation.

5.1.2.2.2   Supplements

UN Resolutions, decisions, and reports appear as supplements to documents published in the Official records.

Examples									
	Author (if applicable),	*title,*	UN body Res. or Dec. number,	UN body's acronym and "OR",	Session number or calendar year,	Supp. No.,	UN doc. number	(calendar year) (if applicable)	1st page and pinpoint.
Resolution		*Universal Declaration of Human Rights,*	GA Res. 217(III),	UN GAOR,	3d Sess.,	Supp. No. 13,	UN Doc. A/810	(1948)	71.
Decision		*Protection of the heritage of indigenous people,*	ESC Dec. 1998/ 277,	UN ESCOR,	1998,	Supp. No. 1,	UN Doc. E/1998/ 98,		113.
Reports	Commission on Crime Prevention and Criminal Justice,	*Report on the Ninth Session,*		UN ESCOR,	2000,	Supp. No. 10,	UN Doc. E/2000/ 30.		
		Report of the UN Commissioner for Refugees,		UN GAOR,	15th Sess.,	Supp. No. 11,	UN Doc. A/4378/ Rev.1	(1960).	

- Begin by providing the title in italics. For reports, cite the author if not mentioned in the title.
- For decisions and resolutions, provide the decision or resolution number after the title.
- For decisions and resolutions, provide the UN body's acronym and "OR" (Official records) after the decision or resolution number, *e.g.* UN ESCOR. For reports, provide the UN body's official records acronym after the report's title.
- Provide the session number after the UN body's official records acronym. If the session number is not available, give the year of the body since its inception. If neither the session number nor the year of the body is available, provide the calendar year.
- Provide the supplement number and the UN document number after the sessional information.
- Provide the calendar year in parentheses after the UN document number, unless the year has been cited previously.
- Conclude the citation with the first page number and pinpoint. A comma precedes the page number when these immediately follow the UN document number.

5.1.2.2.3   Annexes

Examples						
Title,	UN body's acronym and "OR",	session number or number of years since the body's inception,	annex, agenda item no.,	UN doc. number	(year) (if applicable)	1st page and/or pinpoint.
Protectionism and structural adjustment,	UNCTAD TDBOR,	32d Sess.,	Annex, Agenda Item 6,	UN Doc. TD/B/ 1081	(1986)	at 23.
USSR: Draft Resolution,	UN ESCOR,	3d year, 7th Sess.,	Annex, Agenda Item 7,	UN Doc. E/884/ Rev.1	(1948)	at para. 3

- Begin by providing the title of the document in italics.
- Provide the UN body's acronym and "OR" (Official records) after the title.
- Provide the session number after the UN body's acronym. If the session number is not available, give the year of the body since its inception. If neither the session number nor the year of the body is available, provide the calendar year.
- Indicate "Annex" and the agenda item number, followed by the UN document number.
- Provide the calendar year in parentheses after the UN document number, unless the year has been cited previously.

- Conclude the citation with the first page number and pinpoint. A comma precedes the page number when these immediately follow the UN document number.

5.1.2.3 Mimeographs

Example
UN SC, Disarmament Commission, *Questions About Arms Manufacturing in Eastern Iraq*, UN Doc. S/CN.10/L.666 (July 1993) [mimeo. restricted].

- If the UN document is only available in mimeograph form, cite it using the rules for supplements, at section 5.1.2.2.2. Abbreviate "mimeograph" as "mimeo." and place it in brackets at the end of the citation. If applicable, include "provisional", "limited", or "restricted" in the same brackets.

5.1.2.4 Periodicals

Example
C.P. Romulo, "External Debt in Central America" (1987) CEPAL Review No. 32 (UN, Economic Commission for Latin America and the Caribbean).

- When citing periodical articles published by the UN, follow the rules for citing articles provided at section 6.1. If it is unclear from the title of the periodical that the UN is the publisher, include "UN" and the particular body responsible for the publication in parentheses at the end of the citation.

5.1.2.5 Yearbooks

Example
"Report of the Commission to the General Assembly on the work of its thirty-ninth Session" (UN Doc. A/42/10) in *Yearbook of the International Law Commission 1987*, vol. 2, part 2 (New York: UN, 1989) at 50 (UNDOC. A/CN 4/SER. A/1987/Add. 1).

- Cite UN yearbooks using the same rules as for collections of essays, at section 6.3. Give the UN document number of the article cited and of the yearbook, if available.

5.1.2.6 Sales Publications

Example
UN, *Recommendations on the Transport of Dangerous Goods*, 9th ed. (New York: UN, 1995) at 18.

- Cite sales publications using the rules for books, at section 6.2.

5.1.3 European Communities

European Communities regulations, directives, decisions, debates, and other documents are published in the *Official Journal of the European Communities*. The *Official Journal* is published every working day in all eleven official languages of the European Union (EU). It consists of two related series (the L series for legislation and the C series for information and notices) and a supplement (the S series for public tenders).

5.1.3.1 Regulations, Directives, and Decisions

Legislation from the European Communities includes instruments referred to as regulations, directives, and decisions. They are published in the *Official Journal of the European Communities: Legislation* (O.J. L.).

Examples					
	EC,	*title,*	[year of reporter]	official journal and vol. no./1st page	pinpoint.
Regulations	EC,	*Commission Regulation 1149/99 of 31 May 1999 opening individual invitations to tender for the sale for export of vinous alcohol,*	[1999]	O.J. L. 137/31	at 39.
Directives	EC,	*Council Directive 99/59 of 17 June 1999 ending Directive 77/388/EEC as regards the value added tax arrangements applicable to telecommunications services,*	[1999]	O.J. L. 162/63.	

Decisions	EC,	*Commission Decision 98/85 of 16 December 1998 concerning certain protective measures with regard to live birds coming from, or originating in Hong Kong and China,*	[1998]	O.J. L. 15/45	at 46.

- Begin with "EC", then provide the full title of the instrument in italics. The instrument number is included in the title. In the case of directives and decisions, it consists of the last two digits of the year and a sequential number (*e.g.* 98/85). In the case of regulations, it consists of a sequential number followed by the last two digits of the year (*e.g.* 1149/99).
- Cite EC legislation to the *Official Journal of the European Communities: Legislation* (O.J. L.). Indicate the O.J. L. volume number and the first page of the instrument, separated by a slash.

5.1.3.2   Debates of the European Parliament

Example					
EC,	*date of sitting or title,*	[year]	official journal and vol. no./first page	pinpoint.	
EC,	*Sitting of Wednesday, 5 May 1999,*	[1999]	O.J. D. 4-539/144	at 152.	

- Begin with "EC". Provide the title of the document or the date of the sitting.
- Provide the year the sitting was reported in brackets, followed by the abbreviation of the *Official Journal of the European Communities: Debates of the European Parliament* (O.J. D.) and the volume number. Note that volume numbers have two components (*e.g.* 4-539). A slash separates the volume number from the first page (*e.g.* 4-539/144).

5.1.3.3   Other Documents

Examples	
Information and Notices	EC, *Application of Article 94 of Council Regulation (EEC)*, No. 574/72, [1991] O.J. C. 77/3.
General publications	EC, Commission, *Report from the Commission to the Council and the European Parliament* (Luxembourg: EC, 1995).
Periodicals	EC, *External Trade: Monthly Statistics* (1994) No. 1 at 16.

- Indicate "EC" as the author of all EC documents. If available, provide a more precise authoring body.
- Refer to the *Official Journal of the European Communities: Information and Notices* (O.J. C.) in the same manner as other sections of the official journal.
- For general publications, apply the appropriate rules from Chapter 6.
- When citing periodicals, italicize the title of the periodical and indicate the issue number after the year.

5.1.4 Council of Europe

Documents from the Council of Europe can be found in its official publications:

Documents: Working Papers	Documents
Information Bulletin on Legal Affairs	Inf. Bull.
Official Report of Debates	Debates
Orders of the Day and Minutes of Proceedings	Orders
Texts Adopted by the Assembly	Texts Adopted

Examples							
	Council of Europe,	body,	sessional informa-tion,	*title* (if applicable),	official publica-tion,	(year)	pinpoint.
Debates	Council of Europe,	P.A.,	2001 Ordinary Sess. (First Part)		Debates, vol. 1	(2001)	at 67.
Texts Adopted	Council of Europe,	C.A.,	21st Sess., Part 3,		Texts Adopted, Rec. 585	(1970)	at 1.
Orders and minutes	Council of Europe,	C.A., Part 2,	21st Sess.,		Orders, 10th Sitting	(1969)	at 20.

Working Papers	Council of Europe,	P.A.,	2000 Ordinary Sess. (Third Part)	*Situation of lesbians and gays in Council of Europe member states,*	Docum- ents, vol. 5, Doc. 8755	(2000)	at 1.
Series	Council of Europe,	Com- mittee of Mini- sters,		*Recom- mendation R(82)1*	(1980) 12 Inf. Bull. 58.		

- Begin the citation with "Council of Europe", followed by the particular body responsible for the instrument. Abbreviate "Parliamentary Assembly" to "P.A.", and "Consultative Assembly" to "C.A."
- Provide the sessional information followed by the title of the document, if applicable.
- Indicate the official publication.
- Indicate the year of publication in parentheses after the official publication.
- Note that citing periodicals (*e.g.* Inf. Bull.) should be done according to rules for citing periodicals presented at section 6.1.

5.1.5 Organization of American States

Examples							
OAS,	issuing organ,	session no. (if applicable),	*title,*	OAS document no.	(year)	pinpoint.	
OAS,	General Assembly,	2d Sess.,	*Draft Standards Regarding the Formulation of Reservations to Multilateral Treaties,*	OR OEA/ Ser.P/AG/ Doc.202	(1972).		
OAS,	Inter- American Commissi on on Human Rights,		*Draft of the Inter- American Declaration on the Rights of Indigenous Peoples,*	OR OEA/ Ser.L/V/II .90/Doc.1 4, rev. 1	(1995)	at 1.	

- Begin the citation with "OAS" and give the full name of any issuing body. The OAS and issuing bodies are the authors of all OAS documents.
- Where applicable, put the session or meeting number after the name of the issuing body.
- Cite the official title of the document.
- Place "OR" before the OAS document number. The document number begins with the letters "OEA" (Organización de los Estados Americanos) and not "OAS".
- Conclude the citation by indicating the year of the document in parentheses. The year may be followed by a pinpoint reference, where applicable.

5.1.6 World Trade Organization and the General Agreement on Tariffs and Trade

Examples						
	GATT or WTO,	*title,*	Dec., Rec., or Doc. number	Session number,	B.I.S.D.	online.
Decisions and recommend- ations		*Accession of Guatemala,*	GATT C.P. Dec. L/6824,	47th Sess.,	38th Supp. B.I.S.D. (1991) 16.	
		Freedom of Contract in Transport Insurance,	GATT C.P. Rec. of 27 May 1959,	15th Sess.,	8th Supp. B.I.S.D. (1960) 26.	
Reports	GATT,	*Report of the Panel adopted by the Committee on Anti- Dumping Practices on 30 October 1995,*	GATT Doc. ADP/ 137,		42d Supp. B.I.S.D. (1995) 17.	

5—International Materials

	WTO,	*Report of the Working Party on the Accession of Bulgaria,*	WTO Doc. WT/AC C/BGR/ 5 (1996),			online: WTO <http://docs-online.wto. org>.
Meetings	WTO, General Council,	*Minutes of Meeting* (held on 22 November 2000),	WTO Doc. WT/GC /M/60,			online: WTO <http://docs-online.wto. org>.

- Decisions and recommendations do not have an author. GATT and WTO are the authors of all reports. Include the particular issuing body, if one exists, unless it is clear from the title of the report.
- Give the decision, recommendation, or document number. If none, give the full date of the decision or recommendation. Abbreviate "Contracting Parties" to "C.P.", "Decision" to "Dec.", and "Recommendation" to "Rec."
- Where possible, cite GATT Documents to the *Basic Instruments and Selected Documents* (B.I.S.D.), followed by the year in parentheses and the first page of the document.
- If a report is printed independently with no document number, cite it using the rules for books, at section 6.2, *e.g.* GATT, *The International Markets for Meat: 1990/91* (Geneva: GATT, 1991).

5.1.7 Organisation of Economic Co-operation and Development

Examples						
	OECD, authoring body (if applicable),	*title,*	series title,	Working Paper number,	document number	(public-ation inform-ation or year).
Series	OECD, Develop-ment Assistance Committee,	*Japan (No. 34),*	Develop-ment Co-operation Review Series			(Paris: OECD, 1999).

Working Papers	OECD, Economics Department,	*Encouraging Environmen-ally Sustainable Growth in Australia,*		Working Paper No. 309,	Doc. No. ECO/ WKP (2001)35	(2001).
Periodical	OECD,	*Agricultural Policies, Markets and Trade in OECD Countries: Monitoring and Evaluation 1996*				(1996).

- Indicate "OECD" and the authoring body, followed by the title in italics.
- If the document is a work in a series, provide the series title.
- If the document is a working paper, provide the working paper number, if applicable, and the OECD document number. Note that the document number begins with "OCDE", in French or English.
- Provide the publication information in parentheses at the end of the citation. For periodicals, provide the month of publication, if applicable.

5.2   CASES

See Appendices E and G for a list of abbreviations of international organizations and their reporters.

5.2.1   Permanent Court of International Justice (1922-1940)

Cite acts and rules of the P.C.I.J. by title, volume number, and name of publication, followed by the first page or document number, *e.g. Revised Rules of the Court* (1926), P.C.I.J. 33 (Ser. D) No. 1.

5—International Materials

5.2.1.1 Judgments, Orders, and Advisory Opinions

Examples						
	Style of cause (names of parties)	*(year),*	type of decision,	reporter	case no.	pin-point.
Judgments	*Panevezys-Saldutiskis Railway Case (Estonia v. Lithuania)*	(1939),		P.C.I.J. (Ser. A/B)	No. 76	at 16.
Orders	*Panevezys-Saldutiskis Railway Case (Estonia v. Lithuania),*		Order of 30 June 1938,	P.C.I.J. (Ser. A/B)	No. 75	at 8.
Advisory Opinions	*Case of the Customs Régime Between Germany and Austria*	(1931),	Advisory Opinion,	P.C.I.J. (Ser. A/B)	No. 41	at 3.

- Begin with the style of cause and the names of the parties involved. Names of parties are not provided for advisory opinions as they are requested by international organizations and do not directly settle inter-state disputes.
- For judgments and advisory opinions, provide the year in parentheses after the style of cause.
- Specify if the document is an order or an advisory opinion. If referring to an order, provide the full date.
- Provide the P.C.I.J. series followed by the case number. Judgments of the P.C.I.J. are published in *Series A: Collection of Judgments* (P.C.I.J. (Ser. A)) and in *Series A/B: Judgments, Orders and Advisory Opinions* (Ser. A/B)). Orders and advisory opinions are published in *Series B: Collection of Advisory Opinions* (P.C.I.J. (Ser. B)) and in *Series A/B: Judgments, Orders and Advisory Opinions* (P.C.I.J. (Ser. A/B)).

5.2.1.2 Pleadings, Oral Arguments, and Documents

Examples						
Style of cause (names of parties),	"title of document"	(date),	reporter	case no.,	first page	pin-point.
Lighthouses Case Between France and Greece (France v. Greece),	"Oral argument of Professor Basdevant"	(5 February 1934),	P.C.I.J. (Ser. C)	No. 74,	222	at 227.
Pajzs, Csáky, Esterházy Case (Hungary v. Yugoslavia),	"Application Instituting Proceedings"	(1 December 1935),	P.C.I.J. (Ser. C)	No. 79,	10	at 12.

- Begin with the style of cause and, in parentheses, the names of the parties involved.
- Provide the official title of the document, followed by the full date.
- Indicate the P.C.I.J. Series and the case number. Pleadings, oral arguments, and other documents are published in *Series C: Pleadings, Oral Arguments and Documents* (P.C.I.J. (Ser. C)).
- Place a comma between the case number and the first page of the document. Include a pinpoint, if necessary.

5.2.2 International Court of Justice (1945-present)

Cite acts and rules of the I.C.J. by title, volume number, and name of publication, followed by the first page or document number, *e.g. Travel and Subsistence Regulations of the International Court of Justice,* [1947] I.C.J. Acts & Doc. 94.

5.2.2.1 Judgments, Orders, and Advisory Opinions

I.C.J. judgments, opinions, or orders not yet printed may be cited to the I.C.J. website in conformity with the online citing rules.

5—International Materials

Examples						
	Style of cause (names of parties),	type of decision,	[year of reporter]	reporter	first page	pinpoint.
Judgments	*Case concerning East Timor (Portugal v. Australia),*		[1995]	I.C.J. Rep.	90	at 103.
Orders	*Fisheries Jurisdiction Case (Spain v. Canada),*	Order of 8 May 1996,	[1996]	I.C.J. Rep.	58.	
Advisory Opinions	*Legality of the Threat or Use of Nuclear Weapons Case,*	Advisory Opinion,	[1996]	I.C.J. Rep.	226	at 230.

- Begin with the style of cause and the names of the parties involved. Although the I.C.J. Reports sometimes separates the parties' names with a slash (*e.g. El Salvador/Honduras*), always separate them with a "*v.*" Names of the parties are not provided for advisory opinions.
- Specify if the document is an order or an advisory opinion. If referring to an order, provide the full date.
- Provide the year of the reporter in brackets, followed by the reporter and the first page. Judgments, orders, and advisory opinions of the I.C.J. are published in the court's official reporter: *Reports of Judgments, Advisory Opinions and Orders* (I.C.J. Rep.).
- Include a pinpoint, if necessary.

5.2.2.2 *Pleadings, Oral Arguments, and Documents*

Examples						
Style of cause (names of parties),	"title of document"	(date),	[year of reporter]	reporter (vol. no.)	first page	pinpoint.
Case concerning Right of Passage over Indian Territory (Portugal v. India),	"Oral argument of Shri M.C. Setalvad"	(23 September 1957),	[1960]	I.C.J. Pleadings (Vol. 4)	14	at 23.
Fisheries Jurisdiction Case (Spain v. Canada),	"Application Instituting Proceedings Submitted by Spain"	(28 March 1995),		I.C.J. Pleadings	3.	

- Begin with the style of cause and, in parentheses, the names of the parties.
- After the style of cause, provide the title of the document as indicated in the reporter, followed by the date in parentheses.
- Cite the reporter and the first page of the document. The I.C.J. publishes pleadings and other documents in *Pleadings, Oral Arguments and Documents* (I.C.J. Pleadings). If there is a volume number, cite it in Arabic numerals before the number of the first page.
- Note that after 1981, I.C.J. Pleadings give no indication as to the date of publication of the reporter. The I.C.J. Pleadings are identified by the title of decision. Pleadings are available on the ICJ Web site: <www.icj-cij.org>.

5.2.3 Court of Justice of the European Communities and European Court of First Instance

Examples							
	Style of cause,	case no.,	[year of reporter]	reporter	first page	pinpoint,	parallel citation.
E.C.J.	*Commission v. Luxembourg,*	C-26/99,	[1999]	E.C.R.	I-8987	at I-8995.	
C.F.I.	*Kesko v. Commission,*	T-22/97,	[1999]	E.C.R.	II-3775	at II-3822.	

5—International Materials

- Begin with the style of cause. Abbreviate the names of institutions (*e.g.* "Council" rather than "Council of the European Communities").
- Indicate the case number. "C-" indicates a decision of the Court of Justice of the European Communities (E.C.J.). "T-" indicates a decision of the European Court of First Instance (C.F.I.).
- Refer to the reporter and indicate the first page of the case. Decisions of the E.C.J. and the C.F.I. are published in the courts' official reporter *Reports of Cases before the Court of Justice and the Court of First Instance*. Refer to it as the European Court Reports (E.C.R.).
- Page numbers are preceded by a "I" for E.C.J. decisions and a "II" for C.F.I. decisions.
- If possible, provide a parallel citation to the *Common Market Law Reports* (C.M.L.R.) or to the *Common Market Reporter* (C.M.R.).

5.2.4 European Court of Human Rights and European Commission of Human Rights

Examples					
Style of cause	(year of judgment),	vol. no.	reporter	first page,	parallel citation.
Kurt v. Turkey	(1998),	74	Eur. Ct. H.R. (Ser. A)	1152,	27 E.H.R.R. 373.
Larkos v. Cyprus	(1999),	I	Eur. Ct. H.R. (Ser. A)	557,	30 E.H.R.R. 597.
Spencer v. United Kingdom	(1998),	92A	Eur. Comm. H.R.D.R.	56,	41 Y.B. Eur. Conv. H.R. 72.

- Begin with the style of cause followed by the year of the decision in parentheses.
- Provide the volume number of the official reporter before the name of the reporter, followed by the name of the reporter and the first page of the judgment. Cite to the official reporters of the Court and Commission: *European Court of Human Rights, Series A: Judgments and Decisions* (Eur. Ct. H.R. (Ser. A)); *Collection of Decisions of the European Commission of Human Rights* (Eur. Comm. H.R. C.D. (1960-1974)); *Decisions and Reports of the European Commission of Human Rights* (Eur. Comm. H.R. D.R. (1975-1999)).
- If possible, provide a parallel citation to the *Yearbook of the European Convention on Human Rights* (Y.B. Eur. Conv. H.R.) or to the *European Human Rights Reports* (E.H.R.R.).

5.2.5 Inter-American Court of Human Rights

5.2.5.1 Judgments and Advisory Opinions

Examples								
	Style of cause (name of state concerned)	*(year of judg-ment),*	*type of decision and no.,*	*reporter*	*case or report no.,*	*pin-point,*	parallel citation.
Judgments	*Neira Alegría Case (Peru)*	(1996),		Inter-Am. Ct. H.R. (Ser. C)	No. 29,	at para. 55,	*Annual Report of the Inter-American Court of Human Rights: 1996,* OEA/Ser.L/V/III.1 9/doc.4 (1997) 179.
Advisory Opinions	*Reports of the Inter-American Commission on Human Rights (Art. 51 of the American Convention on Human Rights) (Chile)*	(1997),	Advis-ory Opinion OC-15/97,	Inter-Am. Ct. H.R. (Ser. A),	No. 15,	at para. 53,	*Annual Report of the Inter-American Commission on Human Rights: 1997,* OEA/Ser.L/VIII.3 9/doc.5 (1998) 307.

- Begin with the style of cause. If the case involves an individual state, include the name of that state in parentheses.
- Provide the date of the decision in parentheses.
- Specify if the document is an advisory opinion and provide the advisory opinion number.
- Provide the reporter and case number. The Inter-American Court of Human Rights publishes judgments in *Inter-American Court of Human Rights, Series C: Decisions and Judgments* and advisory opinions in *Inter-American Court of Human Rights, Series A: Judgments and Opinions*.
- Provide a parallel citation to the annual report of the court or to *International Legal Materials* (I.L.M.) or the *Inter-American Yearbook on Human Rights*.

5—International Materials

5.2.5.2 *Pleadings, Oral Arguments, and Documents*

Example					
Style of cause (*name of the state concerned*),	type of decision and no.,	"title of document"	(date of document),	reporter and (series)	first page and pinpoint.
Proposed Amendments to the Naturalization Provisions of the Constitution of Costa Rica,	Advisory Opinion OC-4/84,	"Verbatim Record of Public Hearing"	(7 September 1983),	Inter-Am. Ct. H.R. (Ser. B)	23.

- Begin with the style of cause.
- Specify if an advisory opinion. If so, give the advisory opinion number.
- Include the title of the document in quotation marks, followed by the full date in parentheses.
- Provide the reporter and first page. The Inter-American Court of Human Rights published pleadings, oral arguments, and other documents in *Inter-American Court of Human Rights, Series B: Pleadings, Oral Arguments and Documents.*

5.2.6 Inter-American Commission on Human Rights

Example						
Style of cause	(year of judgment),	Inter-Am. Comm. H.R.	case or report no.,	pinpoint,	annual report,	document number (year of document).
Sánchez v. Mexico	(1992),	Inter-Am. Comm. H.R.	No.27/92,		*Annual Report of the Inter-American Commission on Human Rights: 1992-93,*	OEA/Ser.L/V/II.83/doc.14 104.

- Begin with the style of cause followed by the year of decision in parentheses.
- Indicate "Inter-Am. Comm. H.R." followed by the case or report number.
- Decisions of the Inter-American Commission on Human Rights are published in the commission's annual reports. Cite the commission's annual report and the document number. The document number starts with the letters OEA (not OAS) whatever the language of the document.

5.2.7   International Criminal Tribunal for Yugoslavia

Example				
Style of cause	(year of judgment),	case no.	(tribunal),	parallel citation.
Prosecutor v. Delalic	(2001),	Case No. IT-96-21-A	(International Criminal Tribunal for the Former Yugoslavia, Appeals Chamber),	online: United Nations <http://www.un.org/icty/judgement.htm>.

- Begin with the style of cause, followed by the year of the decision, the case number, the name of the international tribunal, and the court level in parentheses. Internet parallel citations may be made by following the rules of section 3.11.

5.2.8   International Criminal Tribunal for Rwanda

Example				
Style of cause	(year of judgment),	case no.	(tribunal),	parallel citation.
Prosecutor v. Ruggiu	(2000),	Case No. ICTR-97-32-I	(International Criminal Tribunal for Rwanda, Trial Chamber I),	online: United Nations <http://www.ictr.org/>.

- Begin with the style of cause, followed by the year of the decision, the case number, the name of the international tribunal, and the court level in parentheses. Internet parallel citations may be made by following the rules of section 3.11.

5—International Materials

5.2.9 GATT 1947 Panel Reports

Examples					
Style of cause (complainant)	(year of decision),	GATT doc. no.,	B.I.S.D. vol. and (year)	first page and pinpoint,	parallel citation.
Republic of Korea— Restrictions on Imports of Beef (Complaint by New Zealand)	(1989),	GATT Doc. L/6505,	36th Supp. B.I.S.D. (1990)	234,	online: WTO<http:// www.wto.org/ english/tratop_e /dispu_e/ gt47ds_e.htm>.
United States— Counterveiling Duties on Fresh, Chilled and Frozen Pork from Canada (Complaint by Canada)	(1991),	GATT Doc. DS7/R,	38th Supp. B.I.S.D. (1990-91)	30,	online: WTO<http:// www.wto.org/ english/tratop_e /dispu_e/ gt47ds_e.htm>.

- Begin with the style of cause followed by the name of the complainant(s) in parentheses.
- Provide the year of the decision in parentheses followed by a comma and the GATT document number.
- Refer to the GATT's B.I.S.D. (*Basic Instruments and Selected Documents*) by providing the supplement number, followed by B.I.S.D., the year in parentheses, and the initial page of the document.
- Where applicable, include pinpoint paragraph references immediately after the document reference.
- Internet parallel citation should follow the rules set out in section 3.11.

5.2.10 WTO Panel and Appellate Body Reports

Examples						
	Style of cause (complainant)	(year of decision),	WTO doc. no.	pin-point	(type of report),	parallel citation.
Panel Report	United States— Sections 301-310 of The Trade Act of 1974 (Complaint by the European Communities)	(1999),	WTO Doc. WT/DS152 /R	at para. 3.1	(Panel Report),	online: WTO <http://docs-online.wto. org/gen_ search/asp>.
Appellate Body Report	India—Patent Protection for Pharmaceut-ical and Agricultural Chemical Products (Complaint by the United States)	(1997),	WTO Doc. WT/DS50/ AB/R		(Appellate Body Report),	online: WTO <http://docs-online.wto. org/gen_ search/asp>.

- Provide the style of cause, followed by the names of the complainants. If the complaints are treated as one in the report, provide the names of all complainants after the style of cause. If there are many complainants, however, and each complaint is treated separately, provide only the name of the complainant to which the report is destined. If there are more than three complainants, provide the name of one complainant followed by "*et al.*"
- Provide the year of the decision in parentheses, followed by the WTO doc. number. A report can have more than one document number (*e.g.* "WT/DS 8, 10, 11/AB/R"). In the document number, "WT/DS" indicates World Trade Dispute Settlement, "AB" indicates an Appellate Body, and "R" indicates report. If the case involves more than one complainant, different reports may be addressed to particular complainants. In such cases, the last element of the document number will indicate the name of the particular complainant to which the report is destined (*e.g.* "WT/DS27/R/USA").
- Following the WTO document number, specify in parentheses whether it is a Panel Report or an Appellate Body Report.
- Internet parallel citation should follow the rules set out in section 3.11.

5.2.11 Canada-United States Free Trade Agreement Panels

Examples						
	Style of cause	(year of decision),	decision no.,	reporter	(type of panel),	parallel citation.
Published	*Re Red Raspberries from Canada*	(1990),	USA-89-1904-01,	3 T.C.T. 8175	(Ch. 19 Panel),	online: NAFTA Secretariat <http://www. nafta-sec-alena.org/ english/index. htm>.
Unpublished	*Re Fresh, Chilled or Frozen Pork from Canada*	(1991),	ECC-91-1904-01USA		(Ex. Chall. Ctee),	online: NAFTA Secretariat <http://www. nafta-sec-alena.org/ english/index. htm>.

- After the style of cause, provide the date of the decision in parentheses, followed by the document number. Indicate a reporter reference, if available.
- Abbreviate the various panels as follows: "Ch. 18 Panel" (Canada-United States Trade Commission Panel under Chapter 18), "Ch. 19 Panel" (Canada-United States Binational Panel under Chapter 19), and "Ex. Chall. Ctee" (Extraordinary Challenge Committee).
- Internet parallel citation should follow the rules set out in section 3.11.

5.2.12 North American Free Trade Agreement Binational Panels

Examples					
	Style of cause (names of parties)	(year of decision),	decision no.	(type of panel),	parallel citation.
Review of Canadian Agency Final Determination	*Re Synthetic Baler Twine With a Knot Strength of 200 LBS or Less, Originating in or Exported from the United States of America* (*United States v. Canada*)	(1995),	CDA-94-1904-02	(Ch. 19 Panel),	online: NAFTA Secretariat <http://www. nafta-sec-alena.org/ english/index. htm>.
Review of Mexican Agency Final Determination	*Re Polystyrene and Impact Crystal from the United States of America* (*United States v. Mexico*)	(1995),	MEX-94-1904-03	(Ch. 19 Panel),	online: NAFTA Secretariat <http://www. nafta-sec-alena.org/ english/index. htm>.
Review of Canadian Measures	*Re Tariffs Applied by Canada to Certain U.S.-Origin Agricultural Products* (*United States v. Canada*)	(1996),	CDA-95-2008-01	(Ch. 20 Panel),	online: NAFTA Secretariat <http://www. nafta-sec-alena.org/ english/index. htm>.

- Begin with the style of cause, followed by the names of the parties involved in parentheses.
- Provide the year of the decision in parentheses. Include the document number and refer to a reporter, if possible.
- Provide information of the chapter under which the complaint was brought. "Chapter 19 Binational Panel" is abbreviated to "Ch. 19 Panel". "Chapter 20: Arbitral Panel" is abbreviated to "Ch. 20 Panel".
- Internet parallel citation should follow the rules set out in section 3.11.

5.2.13 International Arbitration Cases

Examples					
	Style of cause or case no.	(year of decision),	reporter and pinpoint	(framework),	(names of arbitrators) (optional).
Names of parties available	*Southern Pacific Properties v. Egypt*	(1992),	32 I.L.M. 933 at 1008,	(International Centre for Settlement of Investment Disputes),	(Arbitrators: Dr. Eduardo Jiménez de Aréchaga, Mohamed Amin El Mahdi, Robert F. Pietrowski Jr.).
Names of parties not revealed	Case No. 6248	(1990),	19 Y.B. Comm. Arb. 124 at 129	(International Chamber of Commerce).	

- Provide the style of cause including the parties' names, if available. In the case of arbitration awards where parties are anonymously reported, provide the case number.
- Indicate the year of the decision in parentheses, followed by a reference to a reporter.
- In parentheses at the end of the cite, specify, if possible, which organization is responsible for providing the arbitration framework or mechanism.
- Names of arbitrators may also be provided in parentheses at the end of the citation.

5.2.14 International Law Cases Decided before National Courts

Examples			
Style of cause,	domestic reporter,	international reporter	(country and court).
Re Noble and Wolf,	[1949] 4 D.L.R. 375,	[1948] Ann. Dig. I.L.C. 302	(Can., Ont. C.A.).
Lindon v. Commonwealth of Australia (No. 2)	(1996), 136 A.L.R. 251,	118 I.L.R. 338	(Austl., H.C.).
Institute of Chartered Accountants in England and Wales v. Commissioners of Customs and Excise,	[1999] 2 All E.R. 449,	[1999] 2 C.M.L.R. 1333	(U.K., H.L.).

- When a national court decides an international case, a reference may be provided to a national reporter. Considering the nature of the case, however, provide a reference to an internationally available reporter such as the *Annual Digest and Reports of Public International Law Cases* (Ann. Dig. I.L.C.), the *International Law Reports* (I.L.R.), the *Common Market Law Reports* (C.M.L.R.), or the *Common Market Reporter* (C.M.R.). Note that after 1950, the Ann. Dig. I.L.C. became the I.L.R.
- Indicate the country and the jurisdiction where the case was held and specify the court that made the decision.

5.3   INTERNET SITES

Example			
Traditional citation,	online:	name of Web site	<URL>.
U.S., Commission on Security and Cooperation in Europe, *Presidential Elections and Independence Referendums in the Baltic States, the Soviet Union and Successor States*, (Washington, D.C.: The Commission, 1992) at 53,	online:	Commission on Security and Cooperation in Europe	<http://www.csce.gov/reports.cfm>.

- Provide the full traditional citation, followed by a comma, "online:", the name of the Web page, and the URL.
- Cite the full Web address of the document you are citing unless the address is specific to one Web session. In this instance, cite the home page of the Web site.
- Internet sources differ in their reliability. Judgment must be exercised when citing to these sources.
- Many online documents expire after a short period of time. Cite to online sources only if the source provides an archive of material for a reasonable period of time, preferably several years.
- Include a paragraph number as a pinpoint reference, if available. If the page numbering of a printed source is reproduced in the electronic source, reference may be made to those page numbers.

6

SECONDARY SOURCES AND OTHER MATERIALS

6.1 PERIODICALS

6.1.1 General Form

Example								
Author,	"title of article"	(year)	volume	abbreviation of journal	page	pin-point	(electronic service) (if applicable).
John Borrows,	"Domesticating Doctrines: Aboriginal Peoples after the Royal Commission"	(2001)	46	McGill L.J.	615	¶ 5	(QL).

6.1.2 Author

6.1.2.1 Single Author

Example
Reva B. Siegel, "She the People: The Nineteenth Amendment, Sex Equality, Federalism, and the Family" (2002) 115 Harvard L. Rev. 947.

- Indicate the author's name as it appears in the article. Include all names and initials used, but note that there is no space between two initials. Do not substitute names where initials are used, and do not substitute initials when names are used. If the author's name, as it appears at the top or bottom of the article, includes titles such as "The Honourable", "Madam Justice", "Rabbi", "Professor", or "Lord", include these titles. However, do not do not include authors' degrees or other credentials.

6.1.2.2 Joint Authors

Example
Arjun P. Aggarwal & Madhu M. Gupta, "Same-Sex Sexual Harassment: Is It Sex Discrimination? A Review of Canadian and American Law" (2000) 27 Man. L.J. 333.

- Include up to three authors only.
- Separate the last two authors' names with an ampersand ("&").
- If there are more than three authors, provide only the first author's name followed by "*et al.*"

6.1.3 Title of Article

Examples
Robert Chambers, **"Resulting Trusts in Canada"** (2000) 38 Alta. L.R. 378.
Lee Kiat Seng, **"*Ubi Jus Ubi Remedium*? Insurer's Duty to Disclose: Time for Another Look?"** [1997] S.J.L.S. 185.

- Place the title of the article in quotation marks.
- Do not put a comma after the title.
- A colon separates a title from a subtitle.
- Capitalize the title according to the conventions of the language in which the title is written.
- For further rules on titles, see section 6.2.3 below.

6.1.4 Year of Publication

Examples	
Journal organized by volumes	David M. Brown, "Freedom From or Freedom For?: Religion As a Case Study in Defining the Content of Charter Rights" **(2000)** 33 U.B.C. L. Rev. 551.
Journal organized by year	Frédéric Pollaud-Dulian, "À propos de la sécurité juridique" **[2001]** R.T.D. civ. 487.

- If a journal is identified by volume numbers, indicate the year of publication in parentheses.
- If a journal is not organized by volume numbers, provide the year (shown on the spine of the volume) in brackets.

6.1.5 Volume

Examples	
Paginated consecutively	David Lametti, "Publish *and* Profit?: Justifying the Ownership of Copyright in the Academic Setting" (2001) **26** Queen's L.J. 497.
Not paginated consecutively	Bryan Schwartz, "How Possible Increases in the Scope of the Agreement on Internal Trade Would Affect the Health and Social Services Sectors" (1998) **7:2** Health L. Rev. 3.

- Place the volume number between the year of publication and the name of the journal.
- Where issues of a volume are not consecutively paginated (*i.e.* where each issue starts with page 1), place the issue number immediately after the volume number, separated by a colon.

6.1.6 Title of Journal

Examples
Dennis Klimchuk, "Causation, Thin Skulls and Equality" (1998) 11 **Can. J. L. & Jur.** 115.
Joan Sangster, "Criminalizing the Colonized: Ontario Native Women Confront the Criminal Justice System, 1920-60" (1999) 80 **Canadian Historical Review** 32.

- Abbreviate the title of the periodical according to the list of abbreviations in Appendix H. If no abbreviation can be found in this *Guide* or other guides to legal abbreviation, write the name of the journal in full.
- Do not italicize the title or the abbreviation.

6.1.6.1 France

Example		
Author,	"title"	publication information.
Fabrice Leduc,	"La détermination du prix, une exigence exceptionnelle?"	J.C.P. 1992.I.3631.

- Cite the author and title of articles published in French general reporters using the same form as other articles, as set out in sections 6.1.2-6.1.3.
- Cite the reporter as set out in sections 3.5.4-3.5.9.

Abbreviate the reporter as follows:

Actualité juridique de droit administratif	A.J.D.A.
Bulletin de la Cour de cassation, section civile	Bull. civ.
Gazette du Palais	Gaz. Pal.
Recueil Dalloz and *Recueil Dalloz et Sirey* (1945-present)	D.
Recueil des décisions du Conseil d'État or *Recueil Lebon*	Rec.
Semaine Juridique (1937-present)	J.C.P.

6.1.7 First Page of Article

Example
Joseph Eliot Magnet, "National Minorities and the Multinational State" (2001) 26 Queen's L.J. **397**.

- Indicate the first page of the article after the title of the journal.

6.1.7.1 Article Published in Parts

Examples	
Publication in two separate volumes	R.A. Macdonald, "Enforcing Rights in Corporeal Moveables: Revendication and Its Surrogates" (1986) 31 McGill L.J. 573 **&** (1986) 32 McGill L.J. 1.
Publication in two separate parts of the same volume	Edward W. Keyserlingk, "The Unborn Child's Right to Prenatal Care" (1982) 3 Health L. Can. **10 & 31**.

- If parts of the article are published in different volumes, provide the author and the title as usual, then include both full citations, separated by an ampersand.
- If the article is published in parts of one volume, include both first page numbers, separated by an ampersand.

6.1.8 Pinpoint

Example
Bradley J. Freedman & Robert J.C. Deane, "Trade-marks and the Internet: A Canadian Perspective" (2001) 34 U.B.C. L. Rev. 345 **at 399**.

- Place the pinpoint reference after the publication information.
- Paragraph pinpoints are preferred to page pinpoints. Begin a page or paragraph pinpoint with "at" unless using ¶. Refer to paragraphs by using "para.", "paras.", or ¶. Do not include "p." to indicate the page number.
- Separate consecutive page or paragraph references by a hyphen, and retain at least the last two digits at all times (*e.g.* "32-35", not "32-5").
- Non-sequential page numbers are separated by a comma.
- To indicate a general section of the text without referring to specific pages or paragraphs, use "ff" following the page or paragraph number(s). It is preferable, however, to cite a specific set of pages or paragraphs.
- To pinpoint to a specific footnote, abbreviate "footnote" to "n." (*e.g.* at 99, n. 140) and "footnotes" to "nn." (*e.g.* at 142, nn. 73-75). If pages numbers are not available because the article is online, simply cite to the note number (*e.g.* at n. 140).
- All numbers (page, paragraph, or other) are given in Arabic numerals, regardless of how they appear in the text.

6.2   BOOKS

6.2.1   General Form

Examples								
Author,	*title*,	edition	other ele- ments	(place of publica- tion:	publisher,	year of public- ation)	pin- point	(elect- ronic service) (if applic- able).
Peter W. Hogg,	*Constitu- tional Law of Canada*,	5th ed.		(Toronto:	Carswell,	1998)	at 20.	
Margaret Somerville,	*Death Talk: The Case against Euthanasia and Physician- Assisted Suicide*			(Montreal and Kingston:	McGill- Queen's University Press,	2001)	at 78.	
J. Anthony VanDuzer,	*The Law of Partnerships and Corporations*			(Toronto:	Irwin Law,	1997)	c. 2 (B) (3)	(QL).

- Other elements should be provided as necessary following the format given below. Their order is: name of editor or compiler; name of translator; total number of volumes or number of cited volume; volume title; series title and volume number within series (if necessary); looseleaf.

6.2.2 Author

6.2.2.1 Single Author

Examples
Ellen Anderson, *Judging Bertha Wilson: Law as Large as Life* (Toronto: University of Toronto Press for The Osgoode Society for Canadian Legal History, 2001).
Rt. Hon. Lord Denning, *What Next in the Law* (London: Butterworths, 1982).
H. Patrick Glenn, *Legal Traditions of the World* (Oxford: Oxford University Press, 2000).
Grant Purves, *War Criminals: The Deschênes Commission*, rev. ed. (Current Issue Review) (Ottawa: Canada Communication Group, 1996).

- Indicate the author's name as it is presented on the title page of the book. Include all names and initials used, but note that there is no space between two initials. Do not substitute names when initials are used, and do not substitute initials when names are used. If the author's name, as it appears on the title page, includes titles such as "The Honourable", "Madam Justice", "Rabbi", "Professor", or "Lord", include these titles. However, do not do not include authors' degrees or other credentials.

6.2.2.2 Joint Authors

Examples
Ronald C.C. Cuming & Roderick J. Wood, *British Columbia Personal Property Security Handbook*, 4th ed. (Toronto: Carswell, 1998).
P. Macklem *et al.*, *Canadian Constitutional Law*, 2d ed. (Toronto: Emond Montgomery, 1997).

- Include up to three authors only, separating the last two authors' names with an ampersand.
- If there are more than three authors, include only the first author's name and "*et al.*"
- Place a comma after *et al.*
- For collaboration less than full joint authorship (*e.g.* with), follow the usage on the title page.

6.2.2.3 *Editor of a Collection*

Example
Christine Boyle & David R. Percy, eds., *Contracts: Cases and Commentaries*, 6th ed. (Toronto: Carswell, 1999).

- Indicate the editor's name before the title of the collection.
- List up to three editors; if there are more than three, indicate the first followed by "*et al.*"
- Abbreviate "editor" to "ed." and "editors" to "eds.", followed by a comma.
- For authors of essays within a collection, see section 6.3.

6.2.2.4 *Editor or Reviser of the Text of Another*

6.2.2.4.1   Author's Name as Part of Title

Example				
Editor,	ed.,	*title,*	edition	(publication information).
Ruth Sullivan,	ed.,	*Driedger on the Construction of Statutes,*	3d ed.	(London: Butterworths, 1994).

- If the author's name has become part of the title, treat the editor as author, followed by "ed."

6.2.2.4.2   Author's Name is Not Part of the Title

Example				
Author,	*title,*	edition by	editor	(publication information).
S.A. De Smith,	*Judicial Review of Administrative Action,*	4th ed. by	J.M. Evans	(London: Stevens & Sons, 1980).

- If the author's name has not become part of the title, indicate the editor after the edition.
- Precede the editor's name with "ed. by". If there is a numbered edition, mention it (*e.g.* "5th ed. by").

- Provide the full identifying information for both the author and the editor as their names appear in the publication.

6.2.2.5 Translator

N.B. Languages likely to be unfamiliar to readers should be translated. If desired, the original language may also be provided in a footnote.

6.2.2.5.1   Published Translation

Example				
Author,	*title,*	trans. by	name of translator	(publication information).
Hans Kelsen,	*Introduction to the Problems of Legal Theory,*	trans. by	Bonnie Litschewski Paulson & Stanley L. Paulson	(Oxford: Clarendon Press, 1992).

- For published translations, include the translator's name, preceded by "trans.", before the publication information.
- If it is necessary to modify the translation, indicate this with "[modified by author]" after the publication information.

6.2.2.5.2   Translation by the Author of the Text in which the Work is Cited

Example				
Author,	title	(publication information)	pinpoint	[translated by author].
Pierre-Gabriel Jobin,	*La vente dans le Code civil du Québec*	(Cowansville, Qc.: Yvon Blais, 1993)	at 15	[translated by author].

- If using a work in a language other than English and providing a translation for ease of understanding, cite to the work and insert "translated by author" in brackets after the citation. In the above example, the translation is not provided by P.G. Jobin, but by the person who is citing Jobin's publication.

6.2.3 Title

Examples
Allan Manson, Patrick Healy & Gary J. Trotter, *Sentencing and Penal Policy in Canada: Cases, Materials, and Commentary* (Toronto: Emond Montgomery, 2000). Jean-Louis Baudouin, *La responsabilité civile délictuelle*, 4th ed. (Cowansville, Qc.: Yvon Blais, 1994).

- Indicate the title in full, in italics. Follow the orthography and punctuation of the published title, with the following exceptions:
  - Subtitles are preceded by a colon;
  - Place a comma before dates included at the end of the title;
  - Do not use abbreviations unless they appear in the published title.
- Capitalize the title according to the conventions of the language in which the title is written.
- If a title of a work is in a language other than English, French, or a language with which readers will be familiar, use either of the following rules:
  - Provide the title in the original language followed by a translation of the title into English. Place the translation in Roman font and in brackets with no punctuation between the original title and translation. When including the original title, it may be preferable to Romanize languages not written in Latin characters, such as Chinese and Hebrew.
  - Provide a translation of the title in English in italics followed by, *e.g.* "(in German)", to indicate the language of the original text. There should be no punctuation between the translation of the title and the parentheses.

6.2.3.1 *Published Proceedings of Conferences or Symposia*

Example
Georges Erasmus, "Towards a National Agenda" in Frank Cassidy, ed., *Aboriginal Self-Determination. Proceedings of a Conference Held September 30 - October 3, 1990* (Lantzville, B.C.: Oolichan Books, 1991).

- Information about the conference or symposium should be treated as part of the title. Place this information in italics after a period.

6.2.4 Volume Number

6.2.4.1 Books in English

6.2.4.1.1 Volumes Published under Separate Titles

Example				
Author,	*title*,	volume	(publication information)	pinpoint.
Anne F. Bayefsky,	*Canada's Constitutional Act 1982 & Amendments: A Documentary History*,	vol. 2	(Toronto: McGraw-Hill, 1989)	at 669.

- Place the volume before the publication information.
- Provide the volume number in Arabic numerals, even if the book itself uses Roman numerals.
- Insert a comma between the title and the volume number.

6.2.4.1.2 Volumes Published under a Single Title

Example						
Author,	*title*,	editor (if applicable)	translator (if applicable)	(publication information)	volume	pin-point.
Karl Marx,	*Capital: A Critical Analysis of Capitalist Production*,	ed. by Friedrich Engels,	trans. by Samuel Moore & Edward B. Aveling	(London: Swan Sonnenschein, 1908)	vol. 1	at 15.

- If the volumes are subdivisions of a single book, insert the volume after the publication information.
- Do not put a comma between the publication information and the volume.
- Provide the volume number in Arabic numerals, even if the book itself uses Roman numerals.

6—Secondary Sources and Other Materials

6.2.4.2 Books in French

Examples					
Author,	*title,*	tome and/or volume,	edition	editor (if applicable)	(publication information).
Jean Carbonnier,	*Droit civil : les obligations,*	t. 4,	22d ed.		(Paris: Presses Universitaires de France, 2000).
Henri Mazeaud *et al.,*	*Leçons de droit civil,*	t. 3, vol. 1,	7th ed.	by Yves Picod	(Paris: Montchrestien, 1999).

- French legal writing may be divided into "tomes", with each "tome" further subdivided into "volumes".
- Abbreviate "tome" to "t." and abbreviate "volume" to "vol."
- Use only Arabic numerals for tome and volume numbers.
- Tome and volume information appears after the title.

6.2.5 Edition

Examples
John G. Fleming, *The Law of Torts,* **9th ed.** (Sydney: Law Book, 1998).
Carlos L. Israels & Egon Guttman, *Modern Securities Transfer,* rev. ed. (Boston: Warren, Gorham & Lamont, 1971).

- If the work has appeared in several editions, place the number of the edition (*e.g.* "8th ed.") after the title.
- Abbreviate "edition" to "ed."
- Note that the ordinal suffix is not superscript.
- If the work has been revised but no edition number is given, insert "rev. ed." after the title.

6.2.6   Books in Looseleaf Form

Example			
Author,	*title*,	looseleaf	(publication information).
Georges Audet *et al.*,	*Le congédiement en droit québécois en matière de contrat individuel de travail*,	looseleaf	(Cowansville, Qc.: Yvon Blais, 1991).

- Cite looseleaf manuals in the same manner as books, with the following exceptions:
  - following the title, indicate that the source is in looseleaf format;
  - use the publication date that appears on the copyright page, even if it differs from a date that appears elsewhere in the looseleaf manual;
  - where available, use paragraph numbers to pinpoint; otherwise, use page numbers.

6.2.7   Place of Publication

Examples
Bruce MacDougall, *Queer Judgments: Homosexuality, Expression, and the Courts in Canada* (**Toronto**: University of Toronto Press, 2000).
George Grant, *English-Speaking Justice* (**Concord, Ont.**: Auausi Press, 1998).

- Indicate the place of publication as it appears on the title page or on the verso of the title page. Use an English form of a name if it exists (*e.g.* Munich not München, Prague not Praha).
- If more than one place of publication is listed, include the first name only.
- If no place of publication is listed, use "N.p."
- If additional information is required to identify the place of publication (*e.g.* the province, state, or country) include that information, in abbreviated form, after the place of publication.

6.2.8 Publisher

Examples	
	H. Patrick Glenn & Pierre-Gabriel Jobin, eds., *Contemporary Law 1994 Droit contemporain* (Cowansville, Qc.: **Yvon Blais**, 1994).
NOT	H. Patrick Glenn & Pierre-Gabriel Jobin, eds., *Contemporary Law 1994 Droit contemporain* (Cowansville, Qc.: **Les Éditions Yvon Blais inc.**, 1994).
BUT	Chris Madsen, *Another Kind of Justice:Canadian Military Law from Confederation to Somalia* (Vancouver: **University of British Columbia Press**, 1999).
	Ellen Anderson, *Judging Bertha Wilson: Law as Large as Life* (Toronto: **University of Toronto Press for The Osgoode Society for Canadian Legal History**, 2001).

- Cite the publisher's name as it appears on the title page.
- The publisher's name should not be abbreviated (*e.g.* "University Press" and not "UP").
- Omit the definite article even if it is the first word of the name.
- Omit terms that identify corporate status.
- Omit the words "Publishing" or "Publishers".
- For French books, omit "Éditions" unless it is part of an indivisible whole (*e.g.* "Éditions de l'Homme"). This rule applies as well to other languages (*e.g.* Verlag).
- Include "Press" in English and "Presses" in French.
- For copublishers, provide the place of publication and the name for each, separated by a colon, and followed by the year.
- Where a publisher is working for an organization indicate this by "for".
- If no publisher is listed, use "n.p." A Single "N.p." (capitalized) should be used where neither a place of publication nor a publisher appears.

6.2.9 Year of Publication

Example
Patrick J. Monahan, Michael J. Bryant & Nancy C. Côté, *Coming to Terms with Plan B: Ten Principles Governing Secession* (Toronto: C.D. Howe Institute, **1996**).

- Indicate the year of the current edition, not of the first edition. Generally, use the most recent copyright date, unless a year of publication is given explicitly.
- Do not refer to the year of printing.
- If no year is listed, use "n.d." If the year is known or can be inferred, but does not appear in the book, place the year in brackets, with a question mark, if necessary.

6.2.10 Pinpoint

Examples
Allen M. Linden & Lewis N. Klar, eds., *Canadian Tort Law*, 11th ed. (Toronto: Butterworths, 1999) **at 206-09, 258-61**.
Ronald Joseph Delisle & Don Stuart, eds., *Evidence: Principles and Problems*, 6th ed. (Toronto: Carswell, 2001) **c. 4 at 450ff**.
Kent Roach, *Constitutional Remedies in Canada* (Aurora, Ont.: Canada Law Book, 1994) ¶ **12.30**.
Donald Bloxham, *Genocide on Trial: War Crimes Trials and the Formation of Holocaust History and Memory* (Oxford: Oxford University Press, 2001) **at 43, n. 139**.

- Place the pinpoint reference after the publication information.
- Paragraph pinpoints are preferred to page pinpoints. Begin a page or paragraph pinpoint with "at para.", "at paras.", or ¶. Do not include "p." to indicate the page number.
- Separate consecutive page or paragraph references by a hyphen, and retain at least the last two digits at all times (*e.g.* "32-35", not "32-5").
- Non-sequential page numbers are separated by a comma.
- To indicate a general section of the text use "ff" following the page or paragraph number(s). It is preferable, however, to cite a specific set of pages or paragraphs.
- Abbreviate "chapter" and "chapters" to "c."
- To pinpoint to a specific footnote, abbreviate "footnote" to "n." (*e.g.* at 43, n. 139) and "footnotes" to "nn." (*e.g.* at 43, nn. 139-41). If pages numbers are not available because the book is online, simply cite to the note number (*e.g.* at n. 140).
- Cite numbers (page, paragraph, or other) as they appear in the text (*e.g.* 5-6, v-vi).

6.3   COLLECTIONS OF ESSAYS

Examples							
Author of essay,	"title of essay"	in	editor (if applic-able),	ed.,	*title of book*	(publication information)	first page of essay	pin-point.
Bruce Chapman,	"Sex Discrimination and the Equal Good of Pensions"	in	Peter Newman,	ed.,	*The New Palgrave Dictionary of Economics and the Law*	(London: MacMillan Press, 1998)	451	at 453.
Madeleine Cantin Cumyn,	"L'origine de la fiducie québécoise"	in			*Mélanges Paul-André Crépeau*	(Cowansville, Qc.: Yvon Blais, 1997)	199	at 203.
Abdullahi Ahmed An-Na'im,	"Conclusion"	in	Abdul-lahi Ahmed An-Na'im,	ed.,	*Human Rights in Cross-Cultural Perspectives: A Quest for Consensus*	(Philadelphia: University of Pennsylvania Press, 1992)	427.	

- The name of the author and the title of the essay are placed before the reference to the collection.
- The citation to the collection is introduced by "in".
- The name of the editor of the collection is followed by "ed.", placed between commas. Note that some collections have no named editor. In such cases, none should be given in the citation.
- Provide the title of the collection in italics, followed by the publication information.
- Indicate the first page of the essay and any applicable pinpoint references after the publication information.
- If in a book, cite the work as though it were an entry in a collection of essays, using "Foreword", "Preface", "Introduction", or "Conclusion", as appropriate.

6.4 DICTIONARIES

6.4.1 General Dictionaries

Examples			
Title,	edition,	*s.v.*	"keyword".
The Oxford English Dictionary,	2d ed.,	*s.v.*	"law".
Black's Law Dictionary,	7th ed.,	*s.v.*	"promissory estoppel".

- Provide the title of the dictionary in italics.
- Indicate the edition or year.
- Abbreviate *"sub verbo"* to *"s.v."*, which is Latin for "under the word".

6.4.2 Specialized Dictionaries

Examples						
Editor or author,	ed. (if applicable),	*title,*	edition (if applicable)	(publication information)	*s.v.*	"keyword".
Paul-A. Crépeau,	ed.,	*Private Law Dictionary and Bilingual Lexicons,*	2d ed.	(Cowansville, Qc.: Yvon Blais, 1991)	*s.v.*	"code".
Hubert Reid,		*Dictionnaire de droit québécois et canadien,*		(Montreal: Wilson & Lafleur, 1994)	*s.v.*	"hypothèque".

- Cite the specialized dictionary as if it were a book. See section 6.2.
- Abbreviate *"sub verbo"* to *"s.v."*, which is Latin for "under the word".

6—Secondary Sources and Other Materials

6.5   ENCYCLOPEDIC DIGESTS

6.5.1   Common Law

Examples
Halsbury's Laws of England, 4th ed., vol. 34 (London: Butterworths, 1980) at 60, para. 71.
American Jurisprudence, 2d ed., vol. 17A (Rochester, N.Y.: Lawyer's Cooperative, 1991) "Contracts", § 97.

- Follow the rules for books at section 6.2, but do not include the author's name.
- Where available, cite to paragraph or section numbers in preference to page numbers.
- If the section in question has a title, it may be included.

6.5.2   France

6.5.2.1   General Form

Examples					
Title of collection,	edition (if applicable),	subject heading	by	author of the section of the encyclopedia,	pinpoint.
Juris-classeur civil,		art. 3, fasc. N	by	Phillipe Malaurie,	No. 38.
Encyclopédie juridique Dalloz: Répertoire de droit civil,	2d ed.,	"Publicité foncière"	by	Marc Donnier,	No. 528.

- Whenever possible, refer to the *Juris-classeur civil.*
- Provide the full title of the collection in italics.
- If more than one edition of the encyclopedia has been published, include the number of the edition.
- Do not provide parallel citations, even when a section is published in multiple collections of the *Juris-classeur.*
- Establish a short form by using the abbreviated title of the encyclopedia.

The abbreviations of the principal encyclopedias are:

Encyclopédie juridique Dalloz: Répertoire de droit administratif	*Rép. admin.*
Encyclopédie juridique Dalloz: Répertoire de droit civil	*Rép. civ.*
Encyclopédie juridique Dalloz: Répertoire de droit commercial	*Rép. com.*
Juris-classeur administratif	*J.-cl. admin.*
Juris-classeur civil	*J.-cl. civ.*
Juris-classeur civil annexe	*J.-cl. civ. annexe*
Juris-classeur commercial	*J.-cl. com.*
Juris-classeur commercial: Banque et crédit	*J.-cl. com. B.C.*
Juris-classeur répertoire notarial	*J.-cl. rép. not.*
Juris-classeur responsabilité civile	*J.-cl. resp. civ.*

6.5.2.2 Subject Headings

Examples	
Organized alpha-betically	*Encyclopédie juridique Dalloz: Répertoire de droit civil*, **"Parenté-alliance"** by Janine Revel. *Juris-classeur civil annexe*, **"Associations" fasc. 1-A**, by Robert Brichet.
Organized by articles of a code	*Juris-classeur civil*, **app. art. 3, fasc. 4** by Yves Luchaire. *Juris-classeur civil*, **art. 1354 to 1356, fasc. 20** by Daniel Veaux.
Organized by system	*Juris-classeur commercial: Concurrence consommation*, **vol. 1, fasc. 360** by Véronique Sélinsky.

- **Organized alphabetically**: Include the keyword indicating the section in quotation marks. If there is a fascicule number corresponding to the section, insert "fasc." followed by the number.
- **Organized by articles of a code**: Provide the article number under which the section is classified. Use the same form as is used in the collection. If applicable, indicate "fasc." followed by the number.
- **Organized by system**: Provide the number of the volume in which the section is found. If applicable, indicate "fasc." followed by the number.
- Regardless of the system of classification of the subject headings, indicate the number of the fascicule after the volume number, separated by a comma.

6—Secondary Sources and Other Materials

- Do not refer to the date of the revision of the fascicule.

6.6   BOOK REVIEWS

Examples						
Author of book review,	"title of book review" (if applicable),	Book Review of	*title of book reviewed*	by	author of book reviewed	citation information.
H. Patrick Glenn,	"A Review of Kevin Y.L. Tan, *The Singapore Legal System*",	Book Review				(2000) 45 McGill L.J. 339.
John D. Whyte,		Book Review of	*The Moral Foundations of Canadian Federalism: Paradigms, Achievements and Tragedies of Nationhood*	by	Samuel V. La Selva	(1997) 42 McGill L.J. 189.
J. Anthony Van Duzer,		Book Review of	*The Ontario Personal Property Act: Commentary and Analysis*	by	Jacob S. Ziegel & David L. Denomme	(2000/2001) 32 Ottawa L. Rev. 307.

- If the review has a title, include it after the author of the review.
- Insert "Book Review of" before the title of the book reviewed.
- After the title of the book reviewed, indicate the name of the author of the book introduced with "by".
- If the title of the review includes both the title of the book reviewed and its author, do not repeat this information.

6.7   CASE COMMENTS AND COMMENTS ON LEGISLATION

Examples						
	Author,	"title" (if applicable),	type of comment	on	*style of cause* or *title of law or bill* (if applicable)	publication information.
Case Comment	Dianne L. Martin,	*"R. v. White and Côté: A Case Comment"*,	Case Comment			(1997) 42 McGill L.J. 459.
Legislative Comment	C.E.S. Franks,	"Parlia-mentary Control of Security Activities",	Legislative Comment	on	*An Act to Establish the Canadian Security Intelligence Service,* Bill C-157	(1984) 29 McGill L.J. 326.

- Indicate the title of the comment (if available) in quotation marks.
- For case comments, indicate "Case Comment on". Also include the style of cause, unless it is in the title.
- For legislative comments, indicate "Legislative Comment on". Also include the title of the law or bill, unless it is in the title.

6.7.1   France

6.7.1.1   *Annotation*

Example							
Author,	Annotation of	court,	date of decision,	reporter.	year of publication.	section.	first page.
Danielle Corrignan-Carsin,	Annotation of	Cass. soc.,	10 mai 1999,	J.C.P.	1999.	II.	1425.

- There is a space between the reporter and the year (J.C.P. 1999). However, there is no space between the year and the section; nor is there a space between the section and the page number (1999.II.1425).
- Introduce the case citation with "Annotation of".

- See section 3.5 for the rules on citing French jurisprudence.

6.7.1.2 Comments Published in General Reporters

Examples						
Author,	"title"	reporter.	year of publication.	section.	first page	pinpoint.
Bertrand Mathieu & Michel Verpeaux,	"Jurisprudence constitutionnelle"	J.C.P.	2000.	I.	2178	at 2180.
Xavier Labbée,	"Esquisse d'une définition civiliste de l'espèce humaine"	D.	1999.	Chron.	437	at 440.

- There is a space between the reporter and the year (D. 1999). However there is no space between the year and the section; nor is there a space between the section and the page number (1999.Chron.437).
- After the title, indicate the reporter information according to the rules at section 3.5.4.

6.8   COMMENTS, REMARKS, AND NOTES

Examples			
Author (if applicable),	"title" (if applicable),	style of document	publication information.
Monroe Leigh,		Editorial Comment	(1996) 90 A.J.I.L. 235.
	" 'Round and 'Round the Bramble Bush: From Legal Realism to Critical Legal Scholarship",	Note	(1982) 95 Harv. L. Rev. 1669.

- Include the style of document (*e.g.* Note) before the publication information. Do not enclose "Comments", "Remarks", or "Note" in quotation marks. If the note has a title, however, place the title in quotation marks.

6.9   HISTORICAL LEGAL MATERIALS

6.9.1   Roman Law

Collection	Abbreviation	Example
Laws of the Twelve Tables	XII. Tab.	XII. Tab. 8.2
Institutes of Gaius	G.	G. 3.220
Code of Theodosius	Cod. Th.	Cod. Th. 8.14.1
Institutes of Justinian	Inst.	Inst. 4.4 pr. (trans. Birks & McLeod)
Digest of Justinian	Dig.	Dig. 47.10.1 (Ulpian)
Codex of Justinian	Cod.	Cod. 6.42.16
Novels	Nov.	Nov. 22.3

- Cite to the traditional divisions of the work (generally book, title, section), not to the page number of the particular edition or translation. Note that there are no spaces between the numbers of the different divisions.
  - The abbreviation "pr." means "*principium*" or "beginning" and refers to the unnumbered material before the first section of a title. It is preceded by a space.
  - For Justinian's *Digest*, the author of the passage in question can be indicated parenthetically after the reference.
- Use Arabic numerals, separated by periods, to indicate the divisions, regardless of the usage of the edition or translation used.
- The particular edition or translation used may be indicated in parentheses at the end of the reference.

6.9.2 Canon Law

Collection	*Abbreviation*	*Example*
Decretum of Gratian	Decr. [optional]	Part 1: D.50 c.11 Part 2: C.30 q.4 c.5 Part 2, De poenitentia: De poen. D.1 c.75 Part 3: De cons. D.1 c.5
Decretals of Gregory IX (*Liber extra*)	X	X 5.38.12
Decretals of Boniface VIII (*Liber sextus*)	VI	VI 5.2.16
Constitutions of Clement V (*Clementinae*)	Clem.	Clem. 3.7.2
Extravagants of John XXII (*Extravagantes Johannis XXII*)	Extrav. Jo. XII	Extrav. Jo. XII 14.2
Common Extravagants (*Extravagantes communes*)	Extrav. Com.	Extrav. Com. 3.2.9
Codex Iuris Canonici (1917)	1917 Code	1917 Code c.88, § 2
Codex Iuris Canonici (1983)	1983 Code	1983 Code c.221, § 1

- Cite to the traditional divisions of the work, not the page number of the particular edition or translation.
- Use Arabic numerals to indicate the divisions, regardless of the usage of the edition or translation.
- The particular edition or translation used may be indicated in parentheses at the end of the reference.

6.10 UNPUBLISHED MANUSCRIPTS

6.10.1 General Form

Example					
Author,	*title*	(date of creation)	[unpublished,	archived at	location].
I. Cotler,	*Canadian Charter of Rights and Freedoms*	(1998)	[unpublished,	archived at	McGill University Faculty of Law Library].

- Include the title according to the genre. If it is an article, place the title in quotation marks. If it is a book, place the title in italics.
- Include the date of creation in parentheses after the title.
- Indicate that the manuscript was unpublished by enclosing "unpublished, archived at" and the location of the manuscript in brackets.

6.10.2 Forthcoming Manuscripts

Example				
Author,	title	publication information	[forthcoming in	projected date of publication].
M. Milde,	"Legal Ethics: Why Aristotle Might Be Hepful"	J. Soc. Philo.	[forthcoming in	2001].

- Indicate the title according to the type of manuscript. If the manuscript is an article, place the title in quotation marks. If the manuscript is a book, place the title in italics.
- Include the publication information according to the classification of the document, but do not indicate the year of publication.
- Indicate that the manuscript has not yet been published by enclosing in brackets "forthcoming in", with the projected date of publication, if available.

6.10.3 Theses and Dissertations

Example					
Author,	title	(degree,	institution,	year)	[unpublished].
Mark Dockstator,	*Towards Understanding of First Nations Self-Government*	(D. Jur. Thesis,	Osgoode Hall Law School,	1994)	[unpublished].

- After the author's name and the title of the thesis or dissertation, indicate the degree for which it was written, the institution, and the year in parentheses. If it is unclear which degree it was written for or institution it was submitted to, include the field of study (*e.g.* law, political science, economics).
- At the end of the citation include "unpublished" in brackets.
- If the thesis has been published, cite to the published source, if possible.
- Theses issued by microform services (*e.g.* University Microfilms International) should be cited in the same manner as published books, with the service as publisher.

6.11 ADDRESSES AND PAPERS DELIVERED AT CONFERENCES

Example					
Speaker,	"title" (if available) or Address	(Lecture, Paper, or other publication information)	conference or venue,	date)	publication information or [unpublished].
Jane Beach,	"A Comprehensive System of Child Care"	(Paper presented to the	National Child Care Conference and Lobby,	October 1992)	[unpublished].

- If the address has a title, provide the title. If it has no title, indicate "Address".
- Include the lecture series in which the address was delivered, if available.
- Indicate the location or institution where the address was delivered.
- Provide the publication information if the address has been published.
- If unpublished, insert "[unpublished]" at the end of the citation. Indicate, if available, where a transcript of the unpublished address is available.

- If published as a collection, cite in the same manner as a collection of essays. See section 6.3, above.

6.12 MAGAZINES

Examples								
Author (if available),	"title of article"	*Magazine*	vol. no.: issue no.	(date)	first page of article	pin-point	electronic source (if applicable).
Beverley Spencer,	"Life of Reilly"	*Canadian Lawyer*	24:9	(September 2000)	30	at 34.	
Barbara Amiel,	"Silly New Security Rules"	*Maclean's*		(6 November 2001)	21,		online: Macleans.ca <http://www.macleans.ca.>
Charles Platt,	"You've Got Smell!"	*Wired*	7:11	(November 1999)	257,		online: Wired <http://www.wired.com/wired/archive/7.11/digiscent.html>.

- Include the name of the author of the article, if available, followed by the title of the article in quotation marks.
- Provide the name of the magazine in italics. Enclose any other optional identifying information, such as the place of publication, in brackets and italics immediately following the name of the newspaper, newswire, or other source.
- Include the volume number and/or issue number, separated by a colon.
- Insert the full date in parentheses. If the date is a time-span (*e.g.* 22-28 November) rather than a precise date, indicate the first day of coverage (*e.g.* 22 November).
- Indicate the first page of the article.
- Do not include the page number of the printed source if citing to an online source.
- Many online articles expire after a short period of time. Cite to online sources only if the source provides an archive of material for a reasonable period of time, preferably several years. For further information on citing to electronic sources, see section 6.17 below.

6.13 NEWSPAPERS, NEWSWIRES, AND OTHER NEWS SOURCES

Examples					
Author	"title of article"	*Newspaper*	(date)	page.	electronic source (if applicable).
Caroline Davies	"War crimes suspect 'has fled to Britain'"	*The Daily Telegraph*	(28 December 1999),		online: The Telegraph Group <http://www.telegraph.co.uk.>
	"Chief justice says Alta courts jammed as people appear as their own lawyers"	*Canadian Press*	(26 January 2002)		(QL).
	"Paralysed woman given right to die"	*BBC News*	(22 March 2002),		online: BBC News <http://news.bbc.co.uk/hi/english/health/newsid_ 1887000/1887281.stm>.
	"U.S. Taxes Canada's Softwood Industry"	*Los Angeles Times*	(1 November 2001)	B3.	

- Provide the name of the author, if available, followed by the title of the article in quotation marks.
- Provide the name of the newspaper, newswire, or other source in italics.
- If geographic information is required to identify the source, indicate it within brackets in the title (*e.g.* "*Business Times [of Singapore]*" or "*The [Montreal] Gazette*").

- Newspapers
    - If geographic information is required to identify a newspaper, indicate the city within brackets in the title.
    - If pages are numbered by section, provide the sections identifier (*e.g.* A4).
    - If the article is contained on a single page, do not repeat that page for a pinpoint.

- Newswires
  - Replace the newspaper name in italics with the newswire name in italics
  - For further information on citing to electronic sources, see section 6.17.

- Other Sources
  - Many online articles expire after a short period of time. Cite to online sources only if the source provides an archive of material for a reasonable period of time, preferably several years.
  - Do not include the page number of the printed source if citing to an online source.
  - For further information on citing to electronic sources, see section 6.17 below.

6.13.1 Editorials and Letter to the Editor

Examples				
Author of letter (if applicable) or title of editorial (if applicable),	style of document	*Newspaper*	(date)	page.
"Russian Justice,"	Editorial,	*The Globe and Mail*	(20 March 2002)	A18.
Gary Bridgeman,	Letter to the Editor,	*The [Montreal] Gazette*	(3 May 1997)	B4.
Ray McFeteridge,	Letter to the Editor,	*The Calgary Herald*	(28 February 2002)	A18.

- Indicate "Letter to the Editor" after the author of a letter to the editor.
- Indicate "Editorial" after the title of an editorial.
- Italicize the name of the newspaper, magazine, or other source. Enclose any other optional identifying information, such as the place of publication, in brackets and italics (*e.g. "Business Times [of Singapore]"* or *"The [Montreal] Gazette"*).

6.14 NEWS RELEASES

Example					
Issuing body,	type of document	document number,	"title" (optional)	(date)	electronic source (if applicable).
Canadian Security Intelligence Service,	News Release/ Communiqué,		"Special Allocation of Funds to Security and Intelligence Organizations"	(19 October 2001).	

- Indicate the type of document as it appears at the top of the page (*e.g.* "News Release").
- If the document is numbered, provide the number immediately after indicating the type of document.

6.15 LETTERS, MEMORANDA, AND INTERVIEWS

Examples			
Letter or Interview	persons involved	(date)	further information.
Letter from	Sir Robert Wilmot to Lord George Sackville	(16 November 1753)	in James Walton, ed., *"The King's Business": Letters on the Administration of Ireland 1740-1761, from the Papers of Sir Robert Wilmot* (New York: AMS Press, 1996).
Interview of	Edward Beauvais by Douglas Sanderson	(29 May 1948)	on *This Week*, CBC Radio, Toronto, CBC Radio Archives.
	P.E. Moore, Acting Superintendent of Medical Services, Indian Affairs Branch, to E.L. Fairclough, Minister of Citizenship	[n.d. 1959?]	Hull, Indian and Northern Affairs Canada (6-24-3, vol. 2).

- Include the parties names, followed by the date the letter was written. If there is no date available, place "[n.d.]" or, for example, [n.d. 1959?] to indicate a probable date.
- Indicate an interview or memorandum by placing "Interview of" or "Memorandum from" and the parties' names at the beginning of the citation.
- If the position of a person involved is not obvious or is not mentioned in the text, include as much detail on the position as is necessary, preceded by a comma.
- If the author was the interviewer, it is not necessary to identify the interviewer.
- If the author was not the interviewer, include the name of the interviewer.
- If the letter, memorandum, or interview is published, appears online, or is held in an archive, include the appropriate citation for such sources.

6.16 ARCHIVAL MATERIALS

Title of document and other information,	location of archive,	name of archive	(classification number).
Daniel Tracey v. Jean Baptiste Bourtron dit Larochelle (23 December 1830),	Montreal,	Archives Nationales du Québec	(files of the Court of Quarter Sessions).
Chief Andrew Paull to T.A. Crerar (22 June 1944),	Ottawa,	National Archives of Canada	(RG 10, vol. 6826, file 496-3-2, pt. 1).

- If a document is located in an archive, provide as much information on the document as possible using the traditional citation rules, followed by the archival information.

6.17 ELECTRONIC SOURCES

6.17.1 Electronic Services

Examples	
Traditional citation,	(electronic service and database).
Hilliard Aronovitch, "Critical Note: A Liberal Reading of the American Constitution" (1997) Can. J. L. & Jur. 521	(Lexis).
Joseph Eliot Magnet, *Constitutional Law of Canada: Cases, Notes and Materials*, 8th ed. (Kingston: Quicklaw, 2001)	(QL).

- Provide the full citation, followed by the electronic service in parentheses.

- If the document cannot be readily found on the service without knowing the database within the electronic service, indicate the database in which the document can be found (*e.g.* "(QL, MCGL)").
- If a publisher is not listed, or if the text is not published elsewhere than in the electronic service, cite the online service as the publisher (*e.g.* "(Kingston: Quicklaw, 2001)").
- This form of citation should be used only for electronic services that require a subscription, or for Internet sites that are similarly organized with comprehensive indexes, search tools, and professional editors and that have a recognizable abbreviation.
- Include a paragraph number as a pinpoint reference, if available. If the page numbering of a printed source is reproduced in the electronic source, reference may be made to those page numbers. Do not pinpoint to the electronic service's screen number or page number, as these are specific to the service used and can vary in different formats (*e.g.* text, html).
- Do not cite to an electronic service to which the majority of readers will not have access. For example, do not cite to Lawnet (Singapore) when writing for a Canadian audience.

The following is a list of abbreviations of acceptable electronic services:

Australian Legal Information Institute	AustLII
Azimut (produced by SOQUIJ)	Azimut
British and Irish Legal Information Institute	BILII
Butterworths Services	Butterworths
Canadian Legal Information Institute	CanLII
*e*Carswell	eC
Jurifrance	JF
Lawnet	Lawnet
LexisNexis	Lexis
LexUM	LexUM
Quicklaw	QL
Westlaw	WL

6.17.2 Internet Sites

Examples			
Traditional citation,	online:	name of Web site	<URL>.
Joshua Rozenberg, "Professor who puts the world to rights" *The Daily Telegraph* (6 December 2001),	online:	The Telegraph Group	<http://www.telegraph.co.uk>.
Gillian Kelly, "Post-traumatic Stress Disorder: a Recognizable Psychiatric Illness,"	online:	Legal Analysis Papers	<http://www.telecoms.net/law>.

- Provide the full traditional citation, followed a comma, "online:", the name of the Web page, and the URL.
- Cite the full Web address of the document you are citing unless the address is specific to one Web session. In this instance, cite the home page of the Web site.
- Internet sources differ in their reliability. Judgment must be exercised when citing to these sources.
- Many online articles expire after a short period of time. Cite to online sources only if the source provides an archive of material for a reasonable period of time, preferably several years.
- Include a paragraph number as a pinpoint reference, if available. If the page numbering of a printed source is reproduced in the electronic source, reference may be made to those page numbers.

6.17.3 CD-ROM and DVD

Examples				
Traditional citation,	CD-ROM or DVD:	*title of the disc if different*	update (if applicable)	(publication information).
Peter W. Hogg & Mary Ellen Turpel, "Implementing Aboriginal Self-Government: Constitutional and Jurisdictional Issues",	CD-ROM:	*For Seven Generations: An Information Legacy of the Royal Commission on Aboriginal Peoples*		(Ottawa: Libraxus, 1997).
Brian Laghi, "Gay Seeks Rights-Code Protection" *The Globe and Mail* (4 November 1997) A4,	CD-ROM:	*The Globe and Mail on CD-ROM,*		(Outremont: CEDROM-SNI, 1998).

- Provide the traditional citation for the document being cited, followed by a comma.
- Indicate that the document is available on disc by placing "CD-ROM:" or "DVD:" after the comma.
- Indicate the title of the disc in italics, followed by a comma.
- Include the edition or update information after the title, if applicable.
- In parentheses, provide the publication information for the disc. Include the place of publication, the publisher, and the year of publication.

INDEX

McGill Law Journal
Revue de droit de McGill

Préface

Ce *Manuel* bilingue de la référence juridique est une compilation réunissant les efforts de tous les rédacteurs de la *Revue de droit de McGill*, tous étudiants à la faculté de droit de l'Université McGill. Depuis sa première publication en 1986, le *Manuel* s'est révélé être un outil de référence essentiel pour le milieu juridique canadien, tant pour les juges et les avocats que pour les professeurs et les étudiants. En plus d'être utilisé dans plusieurs programmes de méthodologie à travers le pays, environ trente revues, au Canada ct à Singapour, ont officiellement adopté les règles de référence. Les éditions de 1987, 1992 et 1998 ont assuré la mise à jour du *Manuel* conformément aux modifications de la forme de référence et ont ainsi permis aux rédacteurs d'ajouter des directives de référence pour certaines juridictions et divers documents.

Le *Manuel* a été révisé au cours d'une même année académique en plus du travail régulier de publier quatre numéros. Pendant l'été 2001, certains membres du volume 47 commencèrent la recherche et révisèrent la version électronique du *Manuel* afin de s'assurer qu'elle correspondait à la version imprimée du quatrième édition. La révision de la cinquième édition a débuté à l'automne lorsque les membres du volume 47 ont mis à jour les exemples du *Manuel* et ont cherché la forme adéquate de référence pour les juridictions et les sections qui n'étaient pas incluses à la quatrième édition. La révision des modifications apportées à l'automne et la recherche additionnelle afin de finaliser les nouvelles parties s'est déroulé pendant la session d'hiver. Entre-temps, un travail minutieux sur l'appendice, l'introduction, les sections de Singapour, les sections sur la référence aux sources électroniques et sur la référence neutre se poursuivait. La première version du *Manuel*, prête en mars, exigea d'autre travail de correction et de révision, travail qui avait toujours lieu une semaine avant les examens.

Le travail de la cinquième édition représentait un défi important, car il nous fallait tisser les directives de nouvelles juridictions et de nouveaux documents dans la toile préexistante des compromis des années précédentes afin de respecter les formes et les pratiques des deux langues et des différentes traditions culturelles et juridiques. Il s'est avéré difficile d'atteindre le juste-milieu entre le maintien de la stabilité des références de notre système de référence actuel et la mise à jour des documents pour rendre la référence juridique plus efficace et pragmatique. Lorsqu'une règle servait un objectif précis et était en grande partie acceptée, ou lorsque des modifications auraient provoqué maintes confusions, nous avons cru bon de ne pas modifier la règle pour garder une constance et une efficacité des règles de référence ; nous y avons cependant ajouté des explications. Toutefois, si une règle était désuète à cause de nouveaux développements dans la pratique des références, nous y avons apporté les changements nécessaires. Lorsqu'il n'y avait pas de consensus dans la pratique, nous avons opté pour la règle la plus efficace et la plus cohérente avec le reste du *Manuel*.

Nous tenons à exprimer tout particulièrement notre gratitude aux Professeurs Gary F. Bell, Michael Hor et Victor V. Ramraj de la faculté de droit de l'Université nationale de Singapour qui ont généreusement partagé les fruits de leur recherche pour toutes les sections de Singapour. Incorporer les pratiques de références de Singapour au système de référence du *Manuel* fut une tâche complexe. Nous les remercions grandement pour leur aide et leurs nombreuses suggestions. Le *Manuel* a fortement profité de leurs contributions.

Nous aimerions également remercier Me Daniel Boyer (Bibliothécaire de droit civil Wainwright) et Professeur René Provost (Vice-doyen à l'enseignement, faculté de droit de l'Université McGill) pour avoir accepté de réviser quelques sections du *Manuel* ainsi que Professeur John Swan (faculté de droit de l'Université McGill) et Janet Moss (Bibliothécaire administrative, *Gerard V. La Forest Law Library, University of New Brunswick*) pour leurs suggestions. De plus, le chapitre sur les documents gouvernementaux n'aurait pu être aussi exhaustif sans l'aide des bibliothécaires de la Bibliothèque McLennan de l'Université McGill, notamment Phyllis Rudin. La nouvelle édition n'aurait certainement pas été possible sans l'aide précieuse et la patience sans borne de notre assistante de production, Nicole Leger, qui a passé d'innombrables heures à incorporer les changements à la quatrième édition. Nous tenons à souligner la contribution de la Bibliothèque de droit Nahum de l'Université McGill, de la Bibliothèque de droit de l'Université de York et de la Grande Bibliothèque du Barreau du Haut-Canada. Les employés dévoués du Centre d'administration informatique de droit à McGill ont été d'une assistance technique inestimable.

Nous sommes reconnaissants pour toutes les suggestions apportées par les membres des années précédentes, car leurs commentaires serviront de fondation à cette nouvelle édition. Nous aimerions également souligner notre vive gratitude pour le dévouement de tous ceux et celles qui ont participé à la première, deuxième, troisième et quatrième éditions du *Manuel*. Cette cinquième édition est le fruit de ces années d'efforts et de coopération entre les membres de la *Revue* et les nombreux collaborateurs – les juges, les conseillers juridiques, les directeurs de recherche, les professeurs, les bibliothécaires, les éditeurs, les avocats et les étudiants – qui ont si généreusement répondu à nos questions et qui ont fait nombre de commentaires constructifs aux versions préliminaires du *Manuel*. Nous nous réjouissons de constater que le nombre de publications académiques ayant adopté ce *Manuel* a doublé depuis la dernière édition. Nous les remercions, ainsi que les institutions judiciaires, pour avoir accepté de s'associer à ce projet.

Les mots de la fin s'adressent à tous mes collègues de la Revue. Ce projet n'aurait pu avoir lieu sans leur dévouement exceptionnel, leur travail méticuleux, leur esprit d'équipe et leur enthousiasme.

Timothy Reibetanz
Rédacteur du manuel des références
Revue de droit de McGill, vol. 47

COMMENTAIRES :

Pour tout commentaire ou toute suggestion, n'hésitez pas à nous contacter :

Revue de droit de McGill
3644, rue Peel
Montréal, (Qc) H3A 1W9 Canada
Téléphone : (514) 398-7397
Télécopieur : (514) 398-7360
Courriel : journal.law@mcgill.ca
http://www.journal.law.mcgill.ca

NOUVEAU À LA CINQUIÈME ÉDITION

CHANGEMENTS IMPORTANTS

Référence neutre. Une innovation récente dans la citation de la jurisprudence, la référence neutre, est inclus. La référence neutre, contrairement à la référence traditionnelle, est publiée directement par les cours. Elle est indépendante des services électroniques et des recueils imprimés. L'incorporation de la référence neutre est expliqué dans le chapitre 3. Voir la section 3.1 pour déterminer quelle source de la jurisprudence il faut citer.

Noms des auteurs. Les prénoms des auteurs sont maintenant inclus dans la référence tels qu'ils paraissent dans la source à laquelle on renvoie. L'ancienne approche ne permettait pas d'identifier l'auteur et faisait fi de la pluralité culturelle de certaines pratiques d'indentification. Voir le chapitre 6.

L'intitulé. Le «c.» doit être mis en italique dans l'intitulé. Ce changement reflète la pratique de citation moderne. Voir la section 3.2.2.

L'usage du "ci-après". Mettre le titre abrégé entre crochets à la fin de la référence, soit avant le signe de ponctuation final, sans le mot «ci-après». Voir la section 1.4.1.

Média électronique. Le chapitre traitant le média électronique a été simplifié et intégré dans les autres chapitres.

NOUVEAU

Nouvelles sections. L'introduction contient plus d'information sur les bibliographies ainsi que des renseignements détaillés sur la forme de la référence dans un texte. Des sections informent sur la forme de référence pour documents gouvernementaux américains. Les récents changements dans la distribution des pourvois législatifs du Royaume-Uni sont reflétés par des nouvelles parties sur la législation de l'Irlande du Nord et de l'Écosse. Des nouvelles sections ont été ajoutés pour l'Australie, la Nouvelle-Zélande, Singapour, et l'Afrique du Sud. Plus de documents sont traités par le chapitre 6, «Doctrine et autres documents».

Appendices. Les appendices ont été généreusement élargi afin d'inclure plus de périodiques, d'annuaires, d'abréviations géographiques et de cours. De plus, la liste des recueils de jurisprudence s'est accru pour comprendre l'indication géographique ainsi que l'année de chacun des recueils.

Table des matières

1

INTRODUCTION

Les règles de ce *Manuel* s'appliquent aux notes de bas de page, aux références dans le texte et aux bibliographies. Utiliser les règles de la partie française lorsque vous écrivez en français, et ce, même lorsque la source originale est dans une autre langue. N'utiliser les règles de la partie anglaise que lorsque vous écrivez en anglais. Si l'exemple utilise une virgule, faire de même ; si la règle impose des parenthèses, ne pas les remplacer par des crochets. Selon un usage bien établi, le soulignement peut toujours remplacer l'italique. S'il est toujours préférable de fournir des références parallèles à la jurisprudence, elles ont toutefois été omises dans les exemples du *Manuel* afin de simplifier la présentation. Dans ce *Manuel*, les caractères gras qui figurent dans les références mettent les exemples en évidence : ne pas les reproduire.

1.1 BIBLIOGRAPHIES

Exemples

LÉGISLATION
Barristers and Solicitors Act, R.S.B.C. 1979, c. 26.
Loi antiterroriste, L.C. 2001, c. 41.
Loi de 1991 sur les sages-femmes, L.O. 1991, c. 31.
Loi sur les sociétés et fiducies du Québec, L.R.Q. c. S-29.0.

JURISPRUDENCE
Delgamuukw c. Colombie-Britannique, [1997] 3 R.C.S. 1010, 153 D.L.R. (4e) 193.
Kendle v. Melsom, 1998 HCA 13.
Cass. civ. 1re, 26 juin 2001, D. 2001.Jur.2593 (note V. Avena-Robardet).
Létourneau c. Laflèche Auto ltée, [1986] R.J.Q. 1956 (C.S.).

DOCTRINE : MONOGRAPHIES

Lafond, Pierre-Claude. *Précis de droit des biens*, Montréal, Thémis, 1999.

Médina, Annie. *Abus de biens sociaux : prévention, détection, poursuite*, Paris, Dalloz, 2001.

Nadeau, Alain-Robert. *Vie privée et droits fondamentaux*, Cowansville (Qc), Yvon Blais, 2000.

Tan, Cheng Han. *Matrimonial Law in Singapore and Malaysia*, Singapore, Butterworths Asia, 1994.

DOCTRINE : ARTICLES

Lamontagne, Denys-Claude. «L'imbrication du possessoire et du pétitoire», (1995) 55 R. du B. 661.

———. «L'influence du droit public sur le droit immobilier», [1986] R.D.I. 401.

Turp, Daniel. «Le droit au Québec à l'autodétermination et à l'indépendance : la loi sur la *clarté* du Canada et la loi sur les *droits fondamentaux* du Québec en collision» dans Marie-Françoise Labouz, dir., *Intégrations et identités nord-américaines : vues de Montréal*, Bruxelles, Bruylant, 2001, 137.

Wang Sheng Chang. «Combination of Arbitration with Conciliation and Remittance of Awards – with Special Reference to the Asia-Oceana Region» (2002) 19 J. Int. Arb. 51.

Généralement, les bibliographies et les listes d'autorités de textes juridiques sont divisées en sections (par ex. législation, jurisprudence et doctrine). Dans chaque section, les sources sont en ordre alphabétique. Si certaines sources ne correspondent pas à une de ces catégories, une section résiduelle intitulée «autres sources» peut être ajoutée. Il peut être utile de diviser la section contenant la doctrine en sous-sections (par ex. monographies, périodiques et ouvrages collectifs). Diviser les sources entre celles qui sont internes et celles qui sont étrangères au pays peut également s'avérer efficace.

Même si les références bibliographiques à la législation et à la jurisprudence devront être faite telles qu'indiquées dans ce *Manuel*, la présentation des références à la doctrine sera différente dans les bibliographies de celle des notes de bas de page.

Pour la doctrine comprise dans une bibliographie, le nom de famille de l'auteur est inscrit en premier. Il importe de constater qu'un nom de famille peut paraître avant, après ou entre les prénoms, selon les traditions culturelles. Afin de déterminer lequel il faut mettre en premier dans une bibliographie, consulter les données cataloguées à l'arrière de la première page d'une monographie ou d'autres références à l'auteur (par ex. dans l'introduction d'un livre, dans les catalogues disponibles à la bibliothèque ou dans tout autre document renvoyant à l'auteur). Si ce nom n'apparaît pas normalement en premier dans le nom de l'auteur, mettre une virgule après ce nom, suivi du prénom et des initiales comprises dans le nom, s'il y en a, tel que le tout figure sur l'édition.

À l'exception du nom de l'auteur (ou du directeur d'un ouvrage collectif), toute autre information contenue dans une référence à la doctrine doit être organisée selon les directives du *Manuel*. Si la référence est directement précédée par une référence à un autre document du même auteur, remplacer le nom de l'auteur ainsi que ses initiales par un triple tiret, soit l'équivalent de six traits d'union. La référence à une œuvre par un seul auteur précède une œuvre par cet auteur et d'autres auteurs. Chaque référence devrait avoir un retrait de 0,63 cm (mettre en retrait toutes les lignes sauf la première).

1.2   RÉFÉRENCES DANS LE TEXTE

Les références dans le texte sont une alternative aux notes de bas de page. Il est possible de renvoyer aux sources entre parenthèses dans le texte ou de faire référence à toutes les sources utilisées à la fin du paragraphe, auquel cas il faut mettre en retrait les marges de gauche et de droite et utiliser une plus petite police de caractère. Il n'est pas nécessaire de créer un titre abrégé si aucun autre renvoi à la cause n'est fait dans les paragraphes subséquents (voir l'exemple de *Robitaille* ci-dessous). Le *supra* utilisé dans les références subséquentes renvoie à la page à laquelle la référence a été faite par ex, *supra* à la p. 7.

Exemples

En plus des conditions pour «méfait donnant ouverture à un droit d'action» indépendamment de la violation pour laquelle on poursuit, les dommages-intérêts punitifs seront accordés lorsque la conduite du défendeur est si «malveillante, opprimante et abusive qu'elle choque le sens de dignité de la cour» (*Hill c. Église de scientologie de Toronto*, [1995] 2 R.C.S. 1130 au para. 196, 186 N.R. 1, juge Cory, [*Hill*]). Une telle conduite comprend la diffamation (*Hill*), l'omission de fournir des soins médicaux (*Robitaille v. Vancouver Hockey Club* (1981), 124 D.L.R. (3e) 228 (B.C.C.A.)) et, exceptionnellement, les comportements abusifs des compagnies d'assurance (*Whiten c. Pilot Insurance*, 2002 CSC 18 [*Whiten*]).

En plus des conditions pour «méfait donnant ouverture à un droit d'action» indépendamment de la violation pour laquelle on poursuit, les dommages-intérêts punitifs seront accordés lorsque la conduite du défendeur est si «malveillante, opprimante et abusive qu'elle choque le sens de dignité de la cour» (*Hill*). Une telle conduite comprend la diffamation (*Hill*), l'omission de fournir des soins médicaux et exceptionnellement, les comportements abusifs des compagnies d'assurance (*Whiten*).

Hill c. Église de scientologie de Toronto, [1995] 2 R.C.S. 1130 au para. 196, 184 N.R. 1, juge Cory [*Hill*].
Robitaille v. Vancouver Hockey Club (1981), 124 D.L.R. (3e) 228 (B.C.C.A.).
Whiten c. Pilot Insurance, 2002 CSC 18 [*Whiten*].

1.3   RÈGLES GÉNÉRALES CONCERNANT LES NOTES DE BAS DE PAGE

Dans les textes juridiques, les notes de bas de page ont plusieurs fonctions, les plus fréquentes étant les *notes discursives* et les *notes de référence*. Les *notes discursives* comprennent des commentaires pertinents sur le sujet dont traite le texte mais également assez périphériques pour que leur inclusion dans le texte diminue l'effet de l'argument principal. Les *notes de référence*, par contre, indiquent de quelles sources proviennent les arguments ou les citations auxquels elles renvoient. Les notes de référence et les notes discursives peuvent être combinées dans une même note.

1.3.1   La création des notes de bas de page

Créer des notes uniquement dans les cas suivants : (1) la première fois que l'on renvoie à la source en question ; (2) chaque référence ou allusion à un passage particulier de la source ; (3) chaque citation ultérieure tirée de la source. Fournir la référence complète dans la première référence à la source.

1.3.2   L'indication des notes de bas de page dans les textes

Dans les textes juridiques, les notes de bas de page sont indiquées par des numéros en exposant. La numérotation des notes commence à 1 et continue de façon consécutive, par entiers positifs. Les appels de notes tels que «*», «†» et «‡» ne sont pas utilisés. De préférence, mettre le numéro de la note de bas de page à la fin d'une phrase avant la ponctuation[1]. Il n'y a pas d'espace entre le texte cité et le numéro de la note. Lorsqu'on renvoie à un seul mot, placer le numéro de la note[2] immédiatement après le mot en question. Toutefois, si le mot est suivi d'un signe de ponctuation, le numéro précède la ponctuation. S'il s'agit d'une citation placée «entre guillemets»[3], le numéro suit les guillemets et avant la ponctuation. Cet ordre est contraire à celui qui s'impose aux textes anglais où le numéro suit la ponctuation.

1.3.3   L'emplacement des notes de bas de page

Les notes de bas de page figurent au bas de la page, sous le texte (elles devraient, si possible, figurer sur la même page que le texte auquel elles correspondent). Les notes de bas de page devraient être distinguées du texte d'une manière ou d'une autre, par ex. elles ont souvent une plus petite police de caractère que celle du texte et sont séparées du texte par une ligne horizontale.

1.3.4   La combinaison des notes de bas de page

Ne jamais mettre plus d'un numéro de note à n'importe quel endroit dans le texte. Essayer de combiner les références en une note de bas de page. Lorsque plusieurs références figurent dans une même note, elles sont séparées par un point-virgule et la note se termine par un point. Les références à plusieurs documents peuvent généralement se combiner en une note dont le numéro est placé à la fin du paragraphe, si cela n'entraîne aucune confusion. Éviter de combiner les notes renvoyant à plusieurs citations de différentes sources.

1.3.5 Les références aux sources non françaises

Exemples
[27] David Kairys, dir., *The Politics of Law : A Progressive Critique*, 3e éd., New York, Basic Books, 1998 à la p. 76.   [60] *Credit Union Act*, S.N.S. 1994, c. 4.

Si vous écrivez en français, respectez les règles de référence française, quelle que soit la langue dans laquelle la source est rédigée. Tout titre reste dans la langue d'origine, mais tout autre élément de la référence respecte les règles françaises, particulièrement l'usage de la ponctuation.

1.3.6 Formules introductives

Exemples
Voir *Egan c. Canada*, [1995] 2 R.C.S. 513. **Voir généralement** *McKinney c. University of Guelph*, [1990] 3 R.C.S. 229. **Voir toutefois** *Miron c. Trudel*, [1995] 2 R.C.S. 418.

Les formules introductives permettent d'expliquer le lien logique entre la source à laquelle renvoie la note et l'idée énoncée dans le texte. Seul *contra* est en italique (c'est le seul mot de langue étrangère faisant partie de la liste) ; toutes les autres formules devraient être dans une police romaine. Sans être exhaustive, la liste suivante présente quelques formules :

1—Introduction

Exemples	
Egan	Il n'y a pas de formule introductive lorsque l'autorité en question est citée dans le texte ou est explicitement mentionnée dans le texte.
Voir *Egan*	L'autorité en question appuie l'idée exprimée dans le texte.
Voir notamment *Egan*	L'autorité en question est la plus concluante parmi plusieurs références qui soutiennent l'idée exprimée dans le texte. Utiliser cette formule lorsque seules les meilleures sources ont été choisies.
Voir par ex. *Egan*	L'autorité en question est l'une parmi plusieurs appuyant l'idée exprimée dans le texte.
Voir généralement *Egan*	L'autorité en question fournit des renseignements généraux sur le sujet.
Voir aussi *Egan*	L'autorité en question s'ajoute à d'autres qui appuient l'idée exprimée dans le texte, mais elle n'est pas la plus concluante et n'est pas entièrement à propos.
En accord avec *Egan*	Ainsi qu'avec la formule «voir aussi», l'autorité en question s'ajoute à d'autres qui appuient l'idée exprimée dans le texte. Toutefois, dans ce cas-ci, l'autorité appuie directement l'idée exprimée dans le texte et a autant de poids que la première autorité. Le terme «accord» est également utilisé pour indiquer que la loi d'une indication géographique correspond avec la loi d'une autre indication géographique.
Comparer *Egan*	L'autorité en question offre une comparaison intéressante servant à illustrer l'idée exprimée dans le texte.
Voir toutefois *Egan*	L'autorité en question est en désaccord partiel avec l'idée exprimée dans le texte, mais elle ne la contredit pas directement.
Contra *Egan*	L'autorité en question contredit directement l'idée exprimée dans le texte.

1.3.7 Information entre parenthèses

Exemples
Roncarelli c. Duplessis, [1959] R.S.C. 121, 16 D.L.R. (2ᵉ) 689, juge Rand (une décision discrétionnaire «[must] be based upon a weighing of considerations pertinent to the object of the administration» à la p. 140) ; *Oakwood Development Ltd. c. St. François Xavier (Municipalité)*, [1985] 2 R.C.S. 164, 20 D.L.R. (4ᵉ) 641, juge Wilson («l'omission d'un organe de décision administrative de tenir compte d'un élément très important constitue une erreur au même titre que la prise en considération inappropriée d'un facteur étranger à l'affaire» à la p. 174).
Voir *Protection de la jeunesse – 631*, [1993] R.D.F. 535 (le parent a obtenu l'accès au journal intime de son adolescent) ; *Droit de la famille – 2206*, [1995] R.J.Q. 1419 (C.S.) [*D.D.F. 2206*] (le parent a enregistré la conversation téléphonique entre l'enfant et son père).

- En plus des indicateurs, il peut être utile de fournir une brève description entre parenthèses après la référence à la jurisprudence, particulièrement si l'idée affirmée ou infirmée par une cause manque de clarté. Une citation courte de la cause peut également être incluse entre parenthèses.
- L'information entre parenthèses renvoie à la référence qui la précède. Ainsi, placer l'information entre parenthèses après la décision à laquelle l'information renvoie. Par exemple, *R. c. Robillard* (2000), [2001] R.J.Q. 1, 151 C.C.C. (3ᵉ) 296 (C.A.) (le juge de la Cour supérieure a erré en déclarant que la réception en preuve des communications non confidentielles était susceptible de déconsidérer l'administration de la justice), infirmant [1999] J.Q. n° 5583 (C.S.).
- Toute information entre parenthèses se met après la référence aux services électroniques.

1.4 RÉFÉRENCES ULTÉRIEURES ET ANTÉRIEURES

Il arrive souvent qu'une source soit mentionnée plusieurs fois. La référence complète n'apparaît qu'une seule fois, soit dans la note qui accompagne la première mention. Les références ultérieures renvoient à cette première référence.

1—Introduction

1.4.1   Créer un titre abrégé

1.4.1.1 *Modèle de base*

Exemples

---

[4] *Lamborghini (Canada) inc. c. Automobili Lamborghini S.P.A.* (1996), [1997] R.J.Q. 58 (C.A.) [***Lamborghini***].

[21] *Lamborghini, supra* note 4 à la p. 66.

- Si le titre d'une source est court, le titre complet peut être utilisé dans toutes les références ultérieures. Si le titre d'une source est long, un titre abrégé devrait être créé et utilisé dans toutes les références ultérieures.
- Mettre le titre abrégé entre crochets à la fin de la référence, soit avant le signe de ponctuation final. Ne pas mettre les crochets en italique.
- Le titre abrégé suit les références aux services électroniques (par ex. (QL)) mais devrait précéder l'information entre parenthèses (voir *D.D.F. 2206* à la section 1.3.7).
- Toutes les références ultérieures utilisent les symboles de renvoi appropriés (par ex. *supra* ou *ibid.*) ainsi que le titre abrégé de la source pour guider le lecteur à la note de la référence complète.

1.4.1.2 *Législation*

Exemples

---

[3] ***Code criminel***, L.R.C. 1985, c. C-46.

[12] *Charte des droits et libertés de la personne*, L.R.Q. c. C-12 [***Charte québécoise***].

[34] *Loi sur la Gendarmerie royale du Canada*, L.R.C. 1985 (2e supp.), c. 8 [***Loi sur la G.R.C.***].

[37] *Charte canadienne des droits et libertés*, partie I de la *Loi constitutionnelle de 1982*, constituant l'annexe B de la *Loi de 1982 sur le Canada* (R.-U.), 1982, c. 11 [***Charte canadienne***].

- Si une loi a un titre abrégé officiel, il devrait toujours être fourni dans la première référence. Si ce titre abrégé officiel est suffisamment court, il peut être utilisé pour les références ultérieures (par ex. *Code criminel*).
- Si une loi n'a pas de titre abrégé officiel ou que celui-ci est trop long pour les références ultérieures, il peut être abrégé par un titre distinctif indiqué entre crochets à la fin de la référence.

1.4.1.3 Jurisprudence

Exemples
[3] *R. c. Van der Peet*, [1996] 2 R.C.S. 507, 137 D.L.R. (4e) 289 **[*Van der Peet* avec renvois aux R.C.S.]**. [7] *Van der Peet*, *supra* note 3 à la p. 512.

- Choisir une partie distincte de l'intitulé ou le nom de l'une des parties pour créer un titre abrégé.
- Si la référence originale comporte une référence parallèle, indiquer le recueil utilisé pour les références précises subséquentes à l'aide de la mention «avec renvois aux», suivie de l'abréviation du recueil.

1.4.1.4 Doctrine

Exemples
[3] Aline Grenon, «La protection du consommateur et les sûretés mobilières au Québec et en Ontario : "solutions" distinctes ?» (2001) R. du B. can. 917 **[Grenon, «Protection»]**. [6]   Marie-Thérèse Chicha, *L'équité salariale : mise en œuvre et enjeux*, 2e éd., Cowansville (Qc), Yvon Blais, 2000. [9] Aline Grenon, «Le crédit-bail et la vente à tempérament dans le *Code civil du Québec*» (1994) 25 R.G.D. 217 **[Grenon, «Crédit-bail»]**. [12] **Chicha**, *supra* note 6 à la p. 183. [26]   Louise Rolland, «La simulation dans le droit civil des obligations : le mensonge révélateur» dans Nicholas Kasirer, *Le faux en droit privé*, Montréal, Thémis, 2000, 93. [43] **Grenon, «Protection»**, *supra* note 3 à la p. 923. [86] Philippe Jestaz, «Faux et détournement d'institution en droit français de la famille» dans Kasirer, *supra* note 26, 1 à la p. 13.

- La doctrine peut être citée en renvoyant au nom de l'auteur (par ex. notes 6 et 12).
- Lorsqu'on renvoie à plusieurs ouvrages d'un même auteur, utiliser le nom de famille de l'auteur et un titre abrégé (de un ou deux mots). Le titre abrégé utilisé devra respecter la forme typographique du titre du document, soit l'utilisation d'italique pour les livres ou l'utilisation des guillemets pour les articles (voir par ex. la note 43).
- Lorsqu'on renvoie à un deuxième article d'un ouvrage collectif, renvoyer à la référence du premier article en mentionnant le nom du directeur de l'ouvrage collectif (voir par ex. la note 86).

1—Introduction

1.4.2 *Ibid.*

Exemples
[12] Voir *Lapointe c. Hôpital le Gardeur*, [1989] R.J.Q. 2619 (C.A.) [*Lapointe*].
[13] *Ibid.* à la p. 2629. Voir aussi *Laferrière c. Lawson*, [1991] 1 R.C.S. 541 à la p. 592 [*Laferrière*].
[14] *Laferrière*, *ibid.* à la p. 595.
[15] *Ibid.*
[16] *Ibid.* à la p. 605.
[98] Voir aussi *Pelletier c. Roberge*, [1991] R.R.A. 726 (C.A. Qué.), pour une application de la théorie de la perte de chance en droit québécois (voir *ibid.* à la p. 737).
[138] Voir la *Loi sur les compagnies*, L.R.Q. c. C-38, art. 77 ; Paul Martel avec Luc Martel, *Les conventions entre actionnaires*, 7ᵉ éd., Montréal, Wilson & Lafleur, Martel, 1999.
[139] Voir la *Loi sur les compagnies*, *ibid.*, art. 79.

- *Ibid.* est l'abréviation du latin *ibidem* : «au même endroit».
- Utiliser *ibid.* pour renvoyer à la référence précédente. Ne pas indiquer le numéro de la note à laquelle on renvoie.
- On peut utiliser *ibid.* après une référence complète (par ex. note 13) ou même après un autre *ibid.* (par ex. note 16). Identifier la source avec un titre abrégé lorsque plusieurs sources figurent dans la référence précédente (par ex. note 14).
- Lorsque *ibid.* est utilisé sans référence précise, *ibid.* renvoie à la même référence précise que celle de la note précédente (par ex. note 15).
- Pour renvoyer à la même source plusieurs fois dans une même note, utiliser *ibid.* entre parenthèses (par ex. note 98).

1.4.3 *Supra*

Exemples
[17] *Canada (P.G.) c. Biorex inc.*, [1996] R.D.J. 548 (C.A.) [*Biorex*] ; voir aussi *Loi sur les jeunes contrevenants*, L.R.C. 1985, c. R-1.
[72] *Biorex*, *supra* note 17 à la p. 551.
[73] *Ibid.* aux pp. 552-54. Voir aussi *Loi sur les jeunes contrevenants*, *supra* note 17, art. 5.
[77] *Supra* note 43 à la p. 120.
[94] Voir aussi *supra* **note 24 et texte correspondant**.

- *Supra* est le mot latin pour «ci-dessus».

- Utiliser *supra* et le titre abrégé pour renvoyer à une référence précédente contenant la référence complète. *Supra* doit toujours renvoyer à la référence complète et non à un autre *supra* ou *ibid*.
- Si la source est identifiée clairement dans le texte, il n'est pas nécessaire de l'identifier dans la note (par ex. note 77).
- Pour renvoyer à la note et au texte, utiliser la formule suivante : «*supra* note 24 et texte correspondant».
- Pour ne renvoyer qu'au texte, utiliser «ci-dessus» (voir la section 1.4.5).

1.4.4 *Infra*

Exemples

[16] Pour un autre exemple de restrictions imposées au bail, voir ***infra*** note 76.

[76] Le *Code civil du Québec* établit un régime spécifique pour les baux résidentiels à l'art. 1892 et s. Ce régime protège beaucoup plus les locataires que le système normal du bail d'un logement en droit québécois, et est administré par une bureaucratie spéciale.

- *Infra* est le mot latin pour «ci-dessous».
- Utiliser *infra* pour renvoyer à une note ultérieure.
- L'utilisation d'*infra* devrait être évitée. Il est préférable de fournir la référence au complet dès la première référence.
- Pour ne renvoyer qu'au texte, utiliser «ci-dessous» (voir la section 1.4.5).

1.4.5 Ci-dessus et ci-dessous

Exemples

[21] Voir la partie III.A, **ci-dessus,** pour l'analyse de cette question.

[52] Voir la discussion plus approfondie de cette cause aux pp. 164-70, **ci-dessous**.

[70] Voir l'analyse de la décision dans l'arrêt *Oakes* au **texte correspondant à la note** 41.

- Utiliser les expressions «ci-dessus» et «ci-dessous» pour renvoyer le lecteur à une partie du texte et non aux notes de bas de page.
- Si le texte n'est pas divisé en parties ou en paragraphes facilement identifiables (sous-titres ou numéros de paragraphes, par exemple) ou si la pagination finale du texte n'est pas claire au moment de la rédaction, utiliser la formule «voir texte correspondant à la note».

1.5   RENVOIS AUX SOURCES CITANT OU REPRODUISANT LA SOURCE ORIGINALE

Exemples	
Tel que cité dans	*Papers Relating to the Commission appointed to enquire into the state and condition of the Indians of the North-West Coast of British Columbia*, British Columbia Sessional Papers, 1888 aux pp. 432-33, **tel que cité dans** Hamar Foster, «Honouring the Queen's Flag : A Legal and Historical Perspective on the Nisga'a Treaty» (1998) 120 B.C. Studies 11 à la p. 13.
Reproduit(e) dans	George R. au Gouverneur Arthur Phillip, Instruction royale, 25 avril 1787 (27 Geo. III), **reproduite dans** *Historical Documents of New South Wales*, t. 1, 2ᵉ partie, Sydney, Government Printer, 1892-1901 à la p. 67.
	Pacte international relatif aux droits civils et politiques, 19 décembre 1966, 999 R.T.N.U. 171, R.T. Can. 1976 nᵒ 47.
	NON Pacte international relatif aux droits civils et politiques, 19 décembre 1966, 999 R.T.N.U. 171, R.T. Can. 1976 nᵒ 47, reproduit dans Hugh M. Kindred et al., dir., International Law Chiefly as Interpreted and Applied in Canada : Documentary Supplement, n.p., Emond Montgomery, 2000, 87.

De préférence renvoyer à la source originale. Si une source originale est citée en partie dans une source secondaire, consulter autant que possible la source originale afin de vérifier le contexte et l'exactitude de la citation. Cependant, il peut arriver que la source originale soit difficile à trouver ou qu'elle ait été détruite. Le cas échéant, on peut renvoyer à la source primaire telle que citée dans la source secondaire en fournissant le plus d'information sur la source primaire, suivie de «tel que cité dans» et la référence à la source secondaire.

Dans certains cas, renvoyer à un document entièrement réimprimé dans un ouvrage collectif tel que dans les collections reproduisant les débats, les lettres ou les manuscrits qui seraient autrement disponibles dans les archives. Fournir le plus d'information sur le document original, suivi de «reproduit dans» et de la référence à la source secondaire. Ne pas renvoyer aux éditions reproduisant des extraits de sources originales facilement disponibles, par ex. des manuels.

1.6   RÈGLES GÉNÉRALES CONCERNANT LES CITATIONS

Exemples

«[**L**]'objection identitaire s'avère en définitive bien fondée»[32], et représente ainsi un élément important du débat.

Donc, «[c]ette dichotomie découle tout naturellement de *l'impossibilité des juges de se dégager de leurs principes nationaux*» [**nos italiques**][53].

- Ces règles s'appliquent autant au texte qu'aux notes de bas de page.
- Les citations courtes (de quatre lignes ou moins) s'insèrent dans le texte entre guillemets. Les citations plus longues (de plus de quatre lignes) sont mises en retrait des marges, à simple interligne et sans guillemets. Les dispositions législatives peuvent également être citées en retrait des marges, bien qu'elles aient moins de quatre lignes.
- L'orthographe, la mise en majuscules et la ponctuation d'une citation doivent être identiques à la source originale ; toute modification doit être clairement indiquée entre crochets. Si une citation est insérée dans une phrase du texte et que la citation commence par une majuscule, celle-ci devient une minuscule ; si la citation est placée au début de la phrase et qu'elle commence par une minuscule, mettre une majuscule. Indiquer ces modifications entre crochets. Utiliser une ellipse entre crochets ([...]) pour désigner qu'une partie d'un passage a été supprimée. Cette règle diffère de celle utilisée en anglais.
- Lorsque la source originale contient une faute, inclure la correction entre crochets. Ne pas utiliser «[*sic*]», à moins d'avoir une raison particulière de vouloir signaler l'erreur.
- Pour mettre l'accent sur une partie d'une citation, la mettre en italique et ajouter «[nos italiques]» après la citation. Lorsqu'on cite un texte sans inclure ses notes de bas de page, ajouter «[notes omises]» après la citation. (Noter que cette règle est contraire aux règles de la partie anglaise, selon lesquelles ces expressions sont placées à la fin de la référence et non de la citation.) Toutefois, ces expressions doivent suivre le titre abrégé du document (par ex. *Banville c. Hydro-Québec*, [2001] A.Q. n° 4063 ¶ 10 (QL) [*Banville*] [nos italiques]).

1.6.1   Citation d'une source d'une autre langue

Exemple

Comme l'indique Robin, «les faits de l'espèce ne permettent pas de conclure à la mauvaise foi» [**notre traduction**][79].

- Si possible, utiliser une version française de la source lorsqu'on écrit en français et une version anglaise lorsqu'on écrit en anglais.

1—Introduction

- Noter que ce ne sont que certaines juridictions canadiennes qui adoptent des lois en français et en anglais, notamment le Canada, le Québec, le Manitoba, le Nouveau-Brunswick, l'Ontario, les Territoires du Nord-Ouest et le Territoire du Yukon. De plus, il se peut qu'avant une certaine date, celles-ci n'existent qu'en version anglaise.
- Il n'est pas nécessaire de traduire un passage tiré d'une source étrangère lorsqu'on rédige un texte juridique. Toutefois, si l'on désire le traduire, il faut s'assurer que la référence indique clairement qui a traduit la citation. Si la traduction a été faite par un professionnel, cela devrait être indiqué selon les règles énoncées à la section 6.2.2.3.7. Si la traduction a été faite par l'auteur, indiquer «notre traduction» entre crochets après la citation.

2

LÉGISLATION

2.1 CANADA

2.1.1 Lois

2.1.1.1 Modèle de base

Exemples						
Titre,	recueil	législature	année	(session ou supplément),	chapitre,	référence précise.
Code criminel,	L.R.	C.	1985,		c. C-46,	art. 745.
Loi de l'impôt sur le revenu,	L.R.	C.	1985	(5ᵉ supp.),	c. 1,	art. 18(1)(m)(iv)(c).
Charte des droits et libertés de la personne,	L.R.	Q.			c. C-12,	art. 10.

- Il n'y a pas d'espace entre les indications du recueil et de la législature.
- Au moment de la publication du *Manuel*, les gouvernements fédéral et provincial considèrent non officielles les copies électroniques des lois et des règlements. Elles servent à faciliter l'accès lors de la recherche. Afin d'indiquer l'utilisation d'une version électronique non officielle, suivre les directives à la section 2.9.

2.1.1.2 Titre

Exemples

Loi de 2000 sur la cour d'appel, L.S. 2000, c. C-42.1, art. 11.

Health Care Protection Act, S.A. 2000, c. H-3.3.

- Indiquer le titre de la loi en italique et mettre une virgule non italique après le titre.
- Utiliser le titre abrégé officiel de la loi. Si la loi n'a pas de titre abrégé officiel, indiquer le titre qui se trouve au début de la loi. N'indiquer l'article défini (par ex. «le», «la») que s'il fait partie du titre.
- Si le titre de la loi est indiqué dans le texte, ne pas le répéter dans la référence.
- Ne mettre en majuscules que les mots qui sont en majuscules dans la loi.
- Si l'année fait partie du titre de la loi, elle doit être indiquée comme telle en italique.

N.B. Remplacer «*Ordinance*» par «*Act*» lorsqu'on inscrit le titre de la législation des Territoires du Nord-Ouest ou du Territoire du Yukon qui a été adoptée sous forme d'ordonnance.

N.B. Les lois sont adoptées en français et en anglais dans les juridictions suivantes : Canada, Manitoba, Nouveau-Brunswick, Ontario, Québec, Nunavut, les Territoires du Nord-Ouest et le Territoire du Yukon. Toutefois, il se peut que des lois adoptées avant une certaine date n'existent qu'en anglais.

2.1.1.3 Recueil

- Les lois fédérales paraissent dans des recueils reliés de lois révisées ou sessionnelles. Les recueils à feuilles mobiles contiennent les lois dans leur forme la plus à jour, jusqu'à la date indiquée au bas des feuilles mobiles (c'est-à-dire les lois révisées y compris les modifications ultérieures à la révision). Voir la section 2.1.1.3.1.
- Pour les lois du Québec, renvoyer aux recueils à feuilles mobiles. Voir la section 2.1.1.3.2.
- Pour les juridictions de *common law*, renvoyer aux lois révisées (et aux lois réadoptées au Manitoba) de préférence. Ne renvoyer aux recueils sessionnels que lorsqu'on fait référence à une section qui a été ajoutée ou modifiée depuis la date de révision ou si l'on fait référence à une loi qui n'a pas été révisée ou réadoptée (par ex. si elle a été adoptée depuis que la dernière révision a été publiée).

2.1.1.3.1   Lois révisées et recueils sessionnels

Exemples	
Lois révisées	*Code des droits de la personne*, **L.R.**O. 1990, c. H.19. *Loi sur les compagnies,* **L.R.**Q. c. C-38, art. 29.
Recueils sessionnels	*Protected Areas of British Columbia Act,* **S.**B.C. 2000, c. 17.

- Abréger «Lois révisées», «Lois refondues» et «Lois réadoptées» par «L.R.». Abréger «Lois» et «Statuts» par «L.» pour les références aux volumes sessionnels. Abréger «*Statutes*» par «S.».
- Utiliser «L.» pour «Lois» (non pas «O.» pour «Ordinances») lorsqu'on renvoie à un recueil de lois des Territoires du Nord-Ouest ou du Territoire du Yukon.

N.B. Lorsqu'on ne trouve pas une loi dans les recueils actuels des lois révisées, il ne faut pas présumer que la loi n'existe pas ou qu'elle n'est plus pertinente. Par exemple, la *Loi sur les corporations canadiennes* a été remplacée par la *Loi sur les sociétés par actions* pour les sociétés à but lucratif, mais elle reste en vigueur pour les sociétés à but non lucratif. La *Loi sur les corporations canadiennes* n'a pas été rapportée dans la révision de 1985 des *Lois révisées du Canada*, mais elle se trouve dans la révision de 1970. Cette version, telle que modifiée, a toujours force de loi.

2.1.1.3.2   Recueils à feuilles mobiles

- Renvoyer aux recueils à feuilles mobiles des juridictions indiquées dans le tableau ci-dessous.
- Ne pas mettre de virgule entre le recueil et le numéro de chapitre lorsqu'on renvoie aux recueils à feuilles mobiles du Québec (L.R.Q.) ou du Manitoba (C.P.L.M.).
- Ne pas renvoyer aux recueils à feuilles mobiles des lois fédérales, de l'Alberta, de la Colombie-Britannique, de l'Île-du-Prince-Édouard ou de la Saskatchewan. Ces recueils ne sont pas officiels.
- Les lois de Terre-Neuve et Labrador, des Territoires du Nord-Ouest, du Nunavut, de l'Ontario et du Territoire du Yukon n'existent pas en recueil à feuilles mobiles.
- Voir généralement Mary Jane T. Sinclair, *Updating Statutes and Regulations for all Canadian Jurisdictions*, Toronto, Carswell, 1995 et consulter l'*Acte d'interprétation* des différentes juridictions.

Exemples	
Manitoba	*Code des droits de la personne*, L.M. 1987-88, c. 45, **C.P.L.M. c. H175**, art. 8.
	La référence aux feuilles mobiles est facultative. Si elle est utilisée, elle doit être précédée par la référence aux recueils reliés sessionnels. La référence précise est indiquée à la fin de la référence.
	Indiquer «C.P.L.M.» pour faire référence à la *Codification permanente des lois du Manitoba*, suivi du numéro de chapitre, sans indiquer l'année.
	Les lois qui sont comprises dans les lois réadoptées sont désignées par le même numéro de chapitre dans la C.P.L.M. que dans les lois réadoptées.
Nouveau-Brunswick	La consolidation présentée en feuilles mobiles est un document officiel. Toutefois, lorsqu'on renvoie à une loi promulguée depuis la dernière version reliée des *Lois révisées du Nouveau-Brunswick* (actuellement 1973), faire référence au volume annuel, par ex.. *Loi hospitalière*, L.N.-B. 1992, H-6.1 (dans la plupart des cas, ne pas consulter le volume annuel parce que la consolidation en feuilles mobiles est officielle). Lorsqu'on renvoie généralement à une loi incluse dans un recueil relié des *Lois révisées*, mais qui a été depuis modifiée, renvoyer au «L.R.N.-B. 1973», considéré comme la version modifiée de la *Loi*. Si toutefois la modification est pertinente à l'idée exprimée dans le texte, faire d'abord référence à la loi originale dans un recueil relié des *Lois révisées*, suivie de «mod. par» et de la référence à la nouvelle loi dans le volume annuel.
Nouvelle-Écosse	La consolidation présentée en feuilles mobiles est un document officiel. Toutefois, lorsqu'on renvoie à une loi promulguée depuis la dernière version reliée des *Revised Statutes of Nova Scotia* (actuellement 1989), faire référence au volume annuel, par ex.. *Fisheries and Coastal Resources Act* S.N.S. 1996, c. 25, art. 11 (dans la plupart des cas, ne pas consulter le volume annuel parce que la consolidation en feuilles mobiles est officielle). Lorsqu'on renvoie généralement à une loi incluse dans un recueil relié des *Revised Statutes*, mais qui a été depuis modifiée, renvoyer au «R.S.N.S. 1989», considéré comme la version modifiée de la *Loi*. Si toutefois la modification est pertinente à l'idée exprimée dans le texte, faire d'abord référence à la loi originale dans un recueil relié des *Revised Statutes*, suivie de «mod. par» et de la référence à la nouvelle loi dans le volume annuel.

Québec	*Loi sur la conservation de la faune*, **L.R.Q. c. C-61**, art. 89.
	Si possible, renvoyer aux recueils à feuilles mobiles des lois du Québec.
	Lorsqu'on renvoie aux recueils à feuilles mobiles, utiliser «L.R.Q.», suivi du numéro de chapitre et sans indiquer l'année.
	La référence «L.R.Q. 1977», suivie du numéro de chapitre, renvoie aux recueils reliés des lois révisées.

2.1.1.4 Indication géographique

Exemples
Loi sur les agences de voyages, **L.R.O.** 1990, T.19.
Workers Compensation Act, **S.P.E.I.** 1994, c. 67.

- Inscrire l'indication géographique immédiatement après l'indication du recueil.
- Certaines indications géographiques sont abrégées différemment dans les références à des instruments législatifs que dans d'autres contextes (par ex. «M.» plutôt que «Man.» pour «Manitoba»).
- Certaines juridictions étant unilingues anglophones, abréger leur nom uniquement en anglais dans les références aux lois.

Abréviations des indications géographiques dans les références législatives :

Alberta	A.
Bas-Canada	B.-C.
Canada	C.
Colombie-Britannique	B.C.
Haut-Canada	U.C.
Île-du-Prince-Édouard	P.E.I.
Manitoba	M.
Nouveau-Brunswick	N.-B.
Nouvelle-Écosse	N.S.
Nunavut (1er avril 1999 et après)	Nu.
Ontario	O.
Province du Canada	Prov. C.
Québec	Q.
Saskatchewan	S.

2—Législation

Terre-Neuve (Lois – avant le 6 décembre 2001 / Règlements avant le 13 décembre 2001 / Gazette avant le 21 décembre 2001)	N.
Terre-Neuve et Labrador (Lois – le 6 décembre 2001 et après / Règlements le 13 décembre 2001 et après / Gazette le 21 décembre et après)	N.L.
Territoires du Nord-Ouest	T.N.-O.
Territoire du Yukon	Y.

2.1.1.5 Année, session et supplément

Exemples	
Année	*Loi de 1998 sur l'Adoption internationale*, L.O. **1998**, c. 29.
Session qui s'étend sur plus d'une année	*Hospital Act*, L.Y. 1989-90, c. 13.
Plus d'une session dans une même année	*An Act to Amend the Labour Act*, S.P.E.I. **2000 (1re sess.)**, c. 7.
Supplément	*Loi sur les Douanes*, L.R.C. **1985 (2e supp.)**, c. 1.
Année du règne	*An Act respecting the Civilization and Enfranchisement of certain Indians*, S.Prov. C. 1859 (**22 Vict.**), c. 9.

- Indiquer l'année après l'indication géographique. Mettre une virgule après l'année, à moins qu'un numéro de session ou de supplément ne suive l'année, auquel cas la virgule suit l'indication de la session ou du supplément.
- Indiquer l'année du règne entre parenthèses, suivie de l'année civile pour les lois fédérales adoptées avant 1867 ainsi que pour les lois provinciales adoptées avant que la province ne joigne la confédération.
- Ne pas indiquer l'année lorsqu'on renvoie aux recueils à feuilles mobiles du Québec (L.R.Q.) ou du Manitoba (C.P.L.M.) et ne pas mettre de virgule entre le recueil et le numéro de chapitre. Voir la section 2.1.1.3.2.
- Lorsqu'une session s'étend sur plus d'une année, renvoyer à toutes les années sur lesquelles s'étend le recueil.
- Si un recueil contient les lois de plusieurs sessions, les chapitres étant numérotés indépendamment pour chaque session, indiquer, entre parenthèses, le numéro de la session (par ex. «1re», «2e») ainsi que l'abréviation «sess.» après l'année.
- Faire référence au supplément pour les lois et modifications qui ont été adoptées pendant l'année d'une révision ou d'une refonte des lois mais qui n'ont pas été comprises dans la refonte. Indiquer le numéro de supplément entre parenthèses, après la date (par ex. «1er», «2e»). Le mot «supplément» est abrégé par «supp.».

2.1.1.6 Chapitre

Exemples
Chester Trails Act, R.S.N.S. 2001, **c. 21**.
Loi sur les tribunaux judiciaires, L.R.Q. **c. T-16**.
Landlord and Tenant (Residential Tenancies) Act, 1973, S.N. 1973, **n° 18**.

- Inclure la désignation numérique ou alphanumérique du chapitre telle qu'indiquée dans le recueil.
- Abréger «chapitre» par «c.».
- *N.B.* Entre 1934 et 1975-76, les lois dans les recueils sessionnels de Terre-Neuve sont désignées par un numéro. Abréger «numéro» par «n°».

2.1.1.7 Référence précise

Exemples
Citizens' Representative Act, S.N. 2001, C-14.1, **art. 41, 46-48**.
Dangerous Goods Transportation and Handling Act, S.A. 1998, c. D-3, **art. 3(a)-(d), 6(1)(a), (b)**.
Loi de 1999 sur les services gouvernementaux, L.C. 1999, c. 13, **art. 2(1), al. 4**.
Loi sur les aspects civils de l'enlèvement international et interprovincial d'enfants, L.R.Q. c. A-23.01, **préambule**.
Loi sur l'assurance-emploi, L.C. 1996, c. 23, **ann. II**.

- Lorsqu'on renvoie à un article particulier d'une loi, indiquer la référence précise après l'indication du chapitre et après une virgule, sans utiliser «à l'art.».
- Abréger «article(s)» par «art.» dans les notes de bas de page et non dans le corps du texte. À l'exception des alinéas non numérotés ou sans désignation alphabétique, les subdivisions plus précises que les articles (par ex. les paragraphes ou sous-paragraphes) sont aussi abrégées par «art.».
- Après le numéro de l'article, indiquer les alinéas numérotés ou désignés par une lettre, entre parenthèses (par ex. «art. 92(1)(a)»).
- Faire référence à un paragraphe non numéroté ou sans désignation alphabétique comme un «alinéa», abrégé «al.».
- Ne jamais abréger le mot «préambule».
- Abréger «annexe» par «ann.».
- Séparer les articles consécutifs par un trait d'union. Si les articles ne sont pas consécutifs, ils sont séparés par une virgule.

2.1.1.8 Modifications, abrogations et remises en vigueur

Exemples	
Modification sous-entendue	*Loi sur les représentations théâtrales*, L.R.Q. 1977, c. R-25.
Modification mentionnée	*Loi sur les mesures d'urgence*, L.M. 1987, c. 11, **mod. par. L.M. 1997, c. 28**. *Municipal Taxation Act*, R.S.A. 1980, c. M-31, art. 24(1)(b), **mod. par** *School Act*, **S.A. 1988, c. S-3.1, art. 249(a)**.
Abrogation	*Loi sur les prestations familiales*, L.R.O. 1990, c. F-2, **abr. par** *Loi de 1997 sur la réforme de l'aide sociale*, **L.O. 1997, c. 25, art. 4(1)**.
Loi modifiant une loi antérieure	*Loi modifiant la Loi sur les normes du travail*, L.T.N.-O. 1999, c. 18, **modifiant L.R.T.N.-O. 1988, c. L-1**.
Loi abrogeant une loi antérieure	*Loi sur la Société de développement autochtone de la Baie James*, L.R.Q. 2000, c. S-9.1, **abrogeant** *Loi constituant la Société de développement autochtone de la Baie James*, **L.Q. 1978, c. 96**.

- Il est sous-entendu que les références renvoient à la loi telle que modifiée.
- Indiquer que la loi a été modifiée uniquement si cette mention est pertinente à la question traitée dans le texte. Lorsqu'on indique une modification, renvoyer d'abord à la loi originale, suivie de «mod. par» et de la référence à la nouvelle loi.
- Lorsqu'on fait référence à une loi qui a été abrogée, renvoyer à la loi abrogative. Abréger «abrogée par» par «abr. par».
- Indiquer «modifiant» lorsqu'on fait référence à une loi qui modifie une loi antérieure et indiquer «abrogeant» lorsqu'on fait référence à une loi qui abroge une loi antérieure.
- Dans tous les cas, le titre de la deuxième loi (qu'il s'agisse d'une loi modifiée ou abrogée, ou d'une loi modifiant ou abrogeant) n'est indiqué que s'il est différent du titre de la première loi ou s'il n'est pas compris dans le titre de celle-ci.
- Si une loi ou une partie d'une loi a été abrogée et remplacée par une autre, renvoyer à la loi originale en premier suivie de «rem. en vigueur par» puis de la référence complète de la nouvelle partie. N'utiliser cette terminologie que lorsque les dispositions abrogées et remplacées se trouvent dans le même article.

2.1.1.9 Appendices

Exemple
Déclaration canadienne des droits, L.C. 1960, c. 44, **reproduite dans L.R.C. 1985, app. III**.

- Pour les lois qui paraissent dans un appendice, ne pas seulement faire référence à l'appendice.
- Toujours renvoyer à la référence officielle, suivie de «reproduite dans» pour introduire la référence à l'appendice.
- Indiquer la révision ou le volume dont fait partie l'appendice, suivi d'une virgule et du numéro de l'appendice.
- Abréger «appendice» par «app.».

2.1.1.10 Loi contenue dans une autre loi

Exemple
Loi sur la Société d'expansion du Cap-Breton, art. 27, **constituant la partie II de la *Loi organique de 1987 sur le Canada atlantique*, L.C. 1988, c. 50**.

- Renvoyer au titre de la loi contenue dans la loi principale en premier lieu, suivi d'une virgule et de la référence complète de la partie pertinente de la loi principale introduite par «constituant».
- Les références précises à la loi contenue sont indiquées avant la référence à la loi principale.

2.1.2 Lois constitutionnelles

Exemples	
Loi constitutionnelle de 1867	*Loi constitutionnelle de 1867* (R.-U.), 30 & 31 Vict., c. 3, reproduite dans L.R.C. 1985, app. II, n° 5.
Loi de 1982 sur le Canada	*Loi de 1982 sur le Canada* (R.-U.), 1982, c. 11.
Loi constitutionnelle de 1982	*Loi constitutionnelle de 1982*, constituant l'annexe B de la *Loi de 1982 sur le Canada* (R.-U.), 1982, c. 11.
Charte	*Charte canadienne des droits et libertés*, partie I de la *Loi constitutionnelle de 1982*, constituant l'annexe B de la *Loi de 1982 sur le Canada* (R.-U.), 1982, c. 11.
Autres lois constitutionnelles	*Acte de Québec de 1774* (R.-U.), 14 Geo. III, c. 83, art. 3, reproduit dans L.R.C. 1985, app. II, n° 2.

La plupart des lois constitutionnelles ont été adoptées sous des noms différents de ceux couramment utilisés ; il faut utiliser le nouveau titre. Consulter l'annexe de la *Loi constitutionnelle de 1982* pour trouver le nouveau titre de la loi. Si la mention de l'ancien titre est pertinente à l'argument élaboré dans le texte, l'indiquer entre parenthèses à la fin de la référence.

- Puisque la *Loi de 1982 sur le Canada* est une loi du Royaume-Uni, sa référence suit les règles concernant les lois du Royaume-Uni, à la section 2.2.1.
- Puisque la *Charte* n'a pas été promulguée indépendamment, renvoyer à la partie I de la *Loi constitutionnelle de 1982*.
- Au besoin, inclure un renvoi à l'appendice II des L.R.C. 1985 après la référence officielle. (La plupart des lois constitutionnelles canadiennes se trouvent à l'appendice II.)

2.1.2.1 Référence précise

Exemples	
Loi constitutionnelle de 1867	Loi constitutionnelle de 1867 (R.-U.), 30 & 31 Vict., c. 3, **art. 91**, reproduit dans L.R.C. 1985, app. II, n° 5.
Loi de 1982 sur le Canada	Loi de 1982 sur le Canada (R.-U.), 1982, c. 11, **art. 1.**
Loi constitutionnelle de 1982	Loi constitutionnelle de 1982, **art. 35,** constituant l'annexe B de la Loi de 1982 sur le Canada (R.-U.), 1982, c. 11.
Charte	Charte canadienne des droits et libertés, **art. 7,** partie I de la Loi constitutionnelle de 1982, constituant l'annexe B de la Loi de 1982 sur le Canada (R.-U.), 1982, c. 11.
Autres lois constitutionnelles	Acte de Québec de 1774 (R.-U.), 14 Geo. III, c. 83, **art. 3,** reproduit dans L.R.C. 1985, app. II, n° 2.

- Les références précises aux articles de la Charte et de la Loi constitutionnelle de 1982 sont indiquées immédiatement après le titre.
- Indiquer les références précises à la Loi de 1982 sur le Canada et aux autres lois constitutionnelles après le numéro du chapitre.

2.1.3 Codes du Québec

Exemples	
Code civil du Québec	Art. 1457 **C.c.Q.**
Code civil du Québec (1980)	Art. 441 **C.c.Q. (1980)**.
Code civil du Bas Canada	Art. 838 **C.c.B.-C.**
Code de procédure civile	Art. 20 **C.p.c.**
Code de procédure pénale	Art. 104 **C.p.p.**

- Ne jamais fournir la référence complète lorsqu'on renvoie à un code ; on y fait référence tel qu'indiqué.

N.B. Pour renvoyer aux commentaires du ministre, voir la section 4.1.2.2.1.

N.B. Le «C.c.Q. (1980)» renvoie à une série de dispositions concernant le droit de la famille qui furent promulguées en 1980 : *Loi instituant un nouveau Code civil et portant réforme du droit de la famille*, L.Q. 1980, c. 39. Il ne faut pas confondre cette loi avec le *Code civil du Québec*, L.Q. 1991, c. 64 («C.c.Q.»), en vigueur depuis le 1ᵉʳ janvier 1994 et qui a remplacé le *Code civil du Bas-Canada* de 1866.

2.1.4 Nunavut

Au moment de la publication du *Manuel*, un Imprimeur de la Reine territorial du Nunavut n'existe pas encore. Il n'y a donc pas de publication officielle des lois du Nunavut. Pour obtenir des copies officielles des lois du Nunavut, il est possible de contacter par téléphone l'Assemblée législative du Nunavut au (877) 334-7266. Des versions non officielles des lois sont disponibles sur le site Internet de la cour de justice du Nunavut <http://www.nunavutcourtofjustice.ca/library/legislation.htm>, sur Quicklaw, sur Legis <http://www.legis.ca> et sur <http://www.lex-nu.ca>.

2.1.4.1 *Lois adoptées par le Nunavut*

Exemple
Loi sur le drapeau du Nunavut, L.Nu. 1999, c. 1.

- Pour les lois adoptées par le Nunavut après le 1ᵉʳ avril 1999, fournir la référence traditionnelle telle qu'indiquée à la section 2.1.1.

2.1.4.2 *Lois adoptées par les Territoires du Nord-Ouest pour le Nunavut*

Exemple
Nunavut Judicial System Implementation Act, L.T.N.-O. 1998, c. 34, telle qu'adoptée pour le Nunavut, conformément à la *Loi sur le Nunavut*, L.C. 1993, c. 28.

- Pour les lois adoptées par les Territoires du Nord-Ouest pour le Nunavut avant le 1ᵉʳ avril 1999 et qui ne s'appliquent qu'au Nunavut, fournir la référence traditionnelle, suivie de «tel qu'adopté pour le Nunavut, conformément à la *Loi sur le Nunavut*, L.C. 1993, c. 28».

2.1.4.3 Lois reproduites par le Canada pour le Nunavut

Exemple
Loi sur les langues officielles, L.R.T.N.-O. 1998, c. O-1, reproduite pour le Nunavut par art. 29 de la *Loi sur le Nunavut*, L.C. 1993, c. 28.

- En vertu de l'article 29 de la *Loi sur le Nunavut*, L.C. 1993, c. 28, les lois des Territoires du Nord-Ouest ont été reproduites pour le Nunavut et sont entrées en vigueur le 1er avril 1999 dans la mesure où elles s'appliquent au Nunavut.
- Fournir la référence traditionnelle suivie de «reproduite pour le Nunavut par art. 29 de la *Loi sur le Nunavut*, L.C. 1993, c. 28».

2.1.5 Projets de loi

Exemples								
	Numéro,	*titre,*	session,	législature,	indication géographique,	année,	référence précise	(renseignements supplémentaires) (facultatif).
Canada	P.L. C-7,	*Loi concernant le système de justice pénale pour les adolescents, et modifiant et abrogeant certaines lois en conséquence,*	1re sess.,	37e Parl.,		2001,	art. 2	(adopté par la Chambre des communes le 29 mai 2001).
	P.L. S-33,	*Loi modifiant la Loi sur le transport aérien,*	1re sess.,	37e Parl.,		2001,	art. 42(1)(h)	(adopté par le sénat le 6 novembre 2001).
Provinces et territoires	P.L. 161,	*Loi concernant le cadre juridique des technologies de l'information,*	2e sess.,	36e lég.,	Québec,	2001		(sanctionné le 21 juin 2001), L.Q. 2001, c. 32.

2—Législation

- Le numéro des projets de loi de la Chambre des communes est précédé par «C-», celui des projets de loi du Sénat par «S-».
- Toujours indiquer le titre non abrégé du projet de loi. Mettre le titre en italique et respecter l'utilisation des majuscules.
- Lorsqu'on renvoie à un projet de loi provincial, mentionner l'indication géographique.
- Ne pas indiquer l'année du règne.
- Diviser les projets de loi en «articles» dont l'abréviation est «art.»
- Les renseignements supplémentaires (par ex. la date d'une des lectures ou l'étape franchie dans l'adoption du projet de loi) sont indiqués entre parenthèses à la fin de la référence, s'il y a lieu.
- Si possible, indiquer le numéro de chapitre de la future loi.

2.1.6 Règlements

Indication géographique	Non refondue	Refondue ou réadoptée
Canada	D.O.R.S./2000-111, art. 4.	C.R.C., c. 1180, art. 3 (1978).
Alberta	Alta. Reg. 184/2001, art. 2.	
Colombie-Britannique	B.C. Reg. 362/2000, art. 4.	
Île-du-Prince-Édouard	P.E.I. Reg. EC1999-598, art. 3.	
Manitoba	Règl. du Man. 155/2001, art. 3.	Règl. du Man. 368/97R, art. 2.
Nouveau-Brunswick	Règl. du N.-B. 2000-8, art. 11.	
Nouvelle-Écosse	N.S. Reg. 24/2000, art. 8.	
Nunavut	Nu. Reg. 045-99, art. 2.	
Ontario	Règl. de l'Ont. 426/00, art. 2.	R.R.O. 1990, Reg. 1015, art. 3.
Québec	D. 1240-2000, 25 octobre 2000, G.O.Q. 2000.II.6817, art. 2.	R.R.Q. 1981, c. C-11, r. 9, art. 10
Saskatchewan	S. Reg. 67/2001, art. 3.	R.R.S. 2000, c. C-50.2, Reg. 21, O.C. 359/2000, art. 6.
Terre-Neuve	Nfld. Reg. 78/99, art. 4.	

Indication géographique	Non refondue	Refondue ou réadoptée
Terre-Neuve et Labrador	N.L.R. 08/02, art. 2.	
Territoires du Nord-Ouest	T.N.-O. Reg. 253-77, art. 3.	R.R.T.N.-O. 1990, c. E-27, art. 16.
Yukon	Y.D. 2000/130, art. 9.	

2.1.6.1 Règlements fédéraux

2.1.6.1.1 Règlements refondus

Exemple				
Titre,	C.R.C.,	chapitre,	référence précise	(année) (facultatif).
Règlement sur le fil de fer barbelé,	C.R.C.,	c. 1180,	art. 3	(1978).

- Lorsqu'on renvoie aux règlements refondus, abréger *Codification des règlements du Canada* par «C.R.C.».
- L'indication de l'année de la révision des règlements est facultative ; à moins qu'une année ne soit spécifiée, il est sous-entendu que les références renvoient à la dernière révision.

2.1.6.1.2 Règlements non refondus

Exemple			
Titre,	D.O.R.S./	année-numéro du règlement,	référence précise.
Règlement canadien sur la sûreté aérienne	D.O.R.S./	2000-111,	art. 4.

- Les règlements fédéraux promulgués après la codification se trouvent dans la partie II de la *Gazette du Canada*. Il n'est pas nécessaire de renvoyer à la Gazette.
- Abréger «Décrets, ordonnances et règlements» par «D.O.R.S.».
- L'indication du titre est facultative.

2—Législation

2.1.6.2 Règlements provinciaux et territoriaux

- Le titre de tout règlement peut être inclus au début de toute référence. Il est en italique suivi d'une virgule.

N.B. L'Alberta, la Colombie-Britannique, l'Île-du-Prince-Édouard, le Nouveau-Brunswick, Terre-Neuve et Labrador, le Nunavut, la Nouvelle-Écosse et le Territoire du Yukon ne publient pas de versions révisées de leurs règlements.

2.1.6.2.1 Alberta

Exemple			
Indication géographique	Reg.	numéro/année,	référence précise.
Alta.	Reg.	184/2001,	art. 2.

2.1.6.2.2 Colombie-Britannique

Exemple			
Indication géographique	Reg.	numéro/année,	référence précise.
B.C.	Reg.	362/2000,	art. 4.

- Renvoyer à la consolidation à feuilles mobiles de la Colombie-Britannique de la même façon qu'aux règlements non révisés.

2.1.6.2.3 Île-du-Prince-Édouard

Exemple			
Indication géographique	Reg.	ECannée-numéro,	référence précise.
P.E.I.	Reg.	EC1999-598,	art. 3.

- Dans le numéro du règlement, «EC» est l'abréviation de *Executive Council.*

2.1.6.2.4   Manitoba

Exemples				
	Règl. du	indication géographique	numéro/année,	référence précise.
Non réadopté	Règl. du	Man.	155/2001,	art. 3.
Réadopté	Règl. du	Man.	468/97R,	art. 2.

• La plupart des règlements manitobains ont été réadoptés en anglais et en français en 1987 et 1988.
• Pour les règlements manitobains réadoptés, ajouter un «R» immédiatement après les deux derniers chiffres de l'année.

2.1.6.2.5   Nouveau-Brunswick

Exemple			
Règl. du	indication géographique	année-numéro,	référence précise.
Règl. du	N.-B.	2000-8,	art. 11.

• Les règlements du Nouveau-Brunswick ont été refondus en 1963.
• Le recueil à feuilles mobiles des règlements du Nouveau-Brunswick n'est pas une refonte officielle.

2.1.6.2.6   Nouvelle-Écosse

Exemple			
Indication géographique	Reg.	numéro/année,	référence précise
N.S.	Reg.	24/2000,	art. 8.

2.1.6.2.7   Nunavut

Exemple			
Règl. du	indication géographique	numéro-année,	référence précise.
Règl. du	Nu.	045-99,	art. 2.

- La *Gazette du Nunavut* doit être consultée pour tous les règlements à partir du 1er avril 1999.
- Pour tous les règlements avant le 1er avril 1999, consulter les *Règlements révisés des Territoires du Nord-Ouest,* (1990) ainsi que la *Gazette des Territoires du Nord-Ouest,* IIe partie.
- Aucune version révisée des règlements du Nunavut n'a été publiée.

2.1.6.2.8   Ontario

2.1.6.2.8.1   Non refondus

Exemple			
Règl. de	indication géographique	numéro/année,	référence précise.
Règl. de	l'Ont.	426/00,	art. 2.

2.1.6.2.8.2   Refondus

Exemple				
R.R.O.	année de refonte,	Reg.	numéro,	référence précise.
R.R.O.	1990,	Reg.	1015,	art. 3.

2.1.6.2.9 Québec

2.1.6.2.9.1 Non refondus

Exemple				
D.	numéro-année,	date,	référence à la Gazette,	référence précise.
D.	1240-2000,	25 octobre 2000,	G.O.Q. 2000.II.6817,	art. 2.

• Pour les références à la *Gazette officielle du Québec*, voir la section 2.1.7.1.

2.1.6.2.9.2 Refondus

Exemple			
R.R.Q. 1981,	chapitre,	numéro du règlement,	référence précise.
R.R.Q. 1981,	c. C-11,	r. 9,	art. 10.

2.1.6.2.10 Saskatchewan

2.1.6.2.10.1 Non refondus

Exemple			
Indication géographique	Reg.	numéro/année,	référence précise.
S.	Reg.	67/2001,	art. 3.

2.1.6.2.10.2 Refondus

Exemple					
R.R.S.	année de refonte,	chapitre,	numéro,	O.C. numéro/année (s'il y a lieu),	référence précise.
R.R.S.	2000,	c. C-50.2,	Reg. 21,	O.C. 359/2000,	art. 6.

2.1.6.2.11 Terre-Neuve et Labrador

Exemples				
	Indication géographique	Reg. ou R.	numéro/année,	référence précise.
Avant le 13 décembre 2001	Nfld.	Reg.	78/99,	art. 4.
13 décembre 2001 à aujourd'hui	N.L.	R.	8/02,	art. 2.

2.1.6.2.12 Territoires du Nord-Ouest

2.1.6.2.12.1 Non refondus

Exemple			
Règl. des	indication géographique	numéro-année,	référence précise.
Règl. des	T.N.-O.	253-77,	art. 3.

2.1.6.2.12.2 Refondus

Exemple			
R.T.N.-O.	année de refonte,	chapitre,	référence précise.
R.R.T.N.-O.	1990,	c. E-27,	art. 16.

2.1.6.2.13 Territoire du Yukon

Exemple			
Indication géographique	D.	année/numéro,	référence précise.
Y.	D.	2000/130,	art. 9.

• Abréger «Decret» par «D.».

2.1.7   Autres informations publiées dans les gazettes

2.1.7.1   *Modèle de base*

Exemples					
Titre,	abréviation de la gazette	année.	partie de la gazette.	page	(renseignements supplémentaires) (facultatif).
Ministerial Order 36/91,	A. Gaz.	1991.	I.	1609.	
Avis (Banque du Canada),	Gaz. C.	1995.	I.	4412.	
D.309/2001,	A. Gaz.	2001.	I.	1752	(*Provincial Parks Act*).

- *N.B.* Il y a un espace entre l'abréviation de la gazette et l'année (par ex. «A. Gaz. 1991»). Cependant, il n'y a pas d'espace entre l'année, la partie de la gazette et la page (par ex. «1995.I.4412»).
- En général, le titre du document est indiqué. Si le document est numéroté, inclure le numéro avec le titre, tel qu'indiqué dans la gazette. Ce numéro peut comprendre l'année ou les deux derniers chiffres de l'année. Avec le titre, inclure le numéro du texte réglementaire («T.R.») s'il y en a un. Le nom de la personne ou de la partie concernée par un avis peut être inclus entre paranthèses après le titre.
- Indiquer la partie de la gazette suivie de l'année. Si la gazette n'est pas publiée en plusieurs parties, indiquer la page immédiatement après l'année (par ex. «1991.74»).
- On peut inclure des renseignements supplémentaires que l'on estime nécessaires, tels que le nom de la loi en vertu de laquelle un décret est promulgué (voir l'exemple *Provincial Parks Act* ci-dessus).

Abréger les gazettes de la manière suivante :

The Alberta Gazette	A. Gaz.
The British Columbia Gazette	B.C. Gaz.
La Gazette de l'Ontario	Gaz. O.
Gazette des Territoires du Nord-Ouest	Gaz. T.N.-O.
Gazette du Canada	Gaz. C.
Gazette du Manitoba	Gaz. M.
Nouveau-Brunswick : *Gazette royale*	Gaz. N.-B.
La Gazette du Yukon	Gaz. Y.
Gazette officielle du Québec	G.O.Q.
The Newfoundland Gazette (avant le 21 décembre 2001)	N. Gaz.
The Newfoundland and Labrador Gazette (le 21 décembre 2001 à aujourd'hui)	N.L. Gaz.
Nouvelle-Écosse : *Royal Gazette*	N.S. Gaz.
Gazette du Nunavut	Gaz. Nu.
Île-du-Prince-Édouard : *Royal Gazette*	P.E.I. Gaz.
The Saskatchewan Gazette	S. Gaz.

2.1.7.2 Décrets

2.1.7.2.1   Fédéral

Exemples		
Titre (s'il y a lieu),	C.P. année-numéro ou numéro du texte réglementaire,	référence à la gazette.
	C.P. 1997-627,	Gaz. C. 1997.II.1381.
Décret refusant d'annuler ou de renvoyer au CRTC une décision concernant CFJO-FM,	T.R./97-51,	Gaz. C. 1997.II.1523.

• Inclure le titre en italique s'il y en a un.

- Abréger «Conseil Privé» par «C.P.».
- Inscrire le numéro du texte réglementaire («T.R.»), s'il y a lieu.
- On peut inclure des renseignements supplémentaires à la fin de la référence entre parenthèses, tel le titre de la loi en vertu de laquelle le décret a été promulgué.

2.1.7.2.2   Provincial et territorial

Exemples			
Titre (s'il y a lieu),	numéro du décret,	référence à la gazette	(renseignements supplémetaires) (facultatif).
	D. 1989/19,	Gaz. Y. 1989.II.57.	
Town of Paradise Order,	O.C. 99-529,	N. Gaz. 1999.II.451	(*Municipalities Act*).
Règlement sur la levée de la suspension et sur l'application de l'article 41.1 de la Loi sur les normes du travail à l'égard de certains salariés,	D.570-93,	G.O.Q. 1993.II.3309	(*Loi sur les normes du travail à l'égard de certains salariés*).

- Inclure le titre en italique s'il y en a un.
- Utiliser l'abréviation pour *Order in Council* telle qu'elle paraît dans la gazette. Utiliser «D.» pour «Décret».
- Fournir le numéro tel qu'il paraît dans la gazette. Ce numéro comprend parfois l'année ou les deux derniers chiffres de l'année.
- On peut inclure des renseignements supplémentaires entre parenthèses à la fin de la référence, tel le titre de la loi en vertu de laquelle le décret est promulgué.

2.1.7.3 *Proclamations et instructions royales*

Exemples				
Référence à la loi entrée en vigueur ou à l'émetteur de la Proclamation ou de l'Instruction,	type du document,	date,	numéro du texte réglementaire,	référence.
Loi sur l'Agence spatiale canadienne, L.C. 1990, c. 13,		entrée en vigueur le 14 décembre 1990,	T.R./91-5,	Gaz. C. 1991.I.74.
	Proclamation,	1ᵉʳ avril 1991,		S. Gaz. 1991.I.1174.
George R.,	Proclamation,	7 octobre 1763 (3 Geo. III),		reproduite dans L.R.C. 1985, app. II, n° 1.
George R. au Gouverneur Arthur Phillip,	Instruction royale,	25 avril 1787 (27 Geo. III),		reproduite dans *Historical Documents of New South Wales*, t. 1, 2ᵉ partie, Sydney, Government Printer, 1892-1901 à la p. 67.

- Pour renvoyer à des proclamations, utiliser «Proclamation» et «Instruction royale» comme titre si le contexte l'exige.
- Indiquer la date, suivie de la gazette ou autre référence.
- Pour les proclamations fédérales de 1972 à aujourd'hui, indiquer le numéro du texte réglementaire («T.R.»).

2.1.8 Règlements municipaux

Exemples						
	Ville,	Règlement	numéro,	*titre*	(date),	référence précise.
Non refondus	Ville de Blainville,	Règlement	nº 955-43,	*Règlement de zonage*	(10 janvier 1994),	art. 2.3.6.6.
Refondus	Ville de Montréal,	Règlement refondu	c. S-0.1.1,	*Règlement sur les Services de collecte,*		art. 5.

• Indiquer le numéro du règlement municipal et le titre complet s'il n'existe pas de titre abrégé.

2.1.9 Règles de pratique

Exemples		
Indication géographique,	*titre,*	référence précise.
	Règles de la Cour suprême du Canada,	r. 16.
Terre-Neuve et Labrador,	*Rules of the Supreme Court,*	r. 16.01(2).

• Mettre l'indication géographique, à moins qu'elle ne fasse partie du titre des règles.
• Ne pas inclure la mention «Canada» pour les règles de la Cour suprême du Canada ni pour celles de la Cour fédérale.
• Abréger «règle» par «r.».
• Pour renvoyer au *Code de procédure civile* ou au *Code de procédure pénale* du Québec, voir la section 2.1.3.

2.2 ROYAUME-UNI

À l'exception des différences notées ci-dessous, renvoyer à la législation du Royaume-Uni de la même manière qu'à celle du Canada.

2—Législation

2.2.1 Lois

Exemples	
Avant 1963	*Statute of Westminster, 1931* (R.-U.), 22 & 23 Geo. V., c. 4, art. 2.
1ᵉʳ janvier 1963 à aujourd'hui	*Terrorism Act 2000* (R.-U.), 2000, c. 11, art. 129.

- Mettre «(R.-U.)» après le titre de la loi pour indiquer son origine.
- **Avant 1963 :** Lorsque le titre comprend l'année, mettre une virgule avant l'année. Renvoyer à l'année de règne en chiffres arabes. Le nombre suivant l'abréviation du monarque est en chiffres romains (par ex. «Geo. V»).
- **1ᵉʳ janvier 1963 à aujourd'hui :** Lorsque le titre comprend l'année, ne pas mettre une virgule avant l'année. Renvoyer à l'année civile après «R.-U.» précédée par une virgule.

2.2.1.1 Irlande du Nord

2.2.1.1.1 Lois adoptées par le Royaume-Uni

Exemples	
Avant 1963	*Public Health (Ireland) Act, 1878* (R.-U.), 41 & 42 Vict., c. 52.
1ᵉʳ janvier 1963 à aujourd'hui	*Northern Ireland Act 1998* (R.-U.), 1998, c. 47, art. 5.

- Renvoyer à la législation de l'Irlande du Nord adoptée par le Royaume-Uni de la même manière qu'à celle du Royaume-Uni.

2.2.1.1.2 Lois adoptées par l'Irlande du Nord

Exemples	
1921-1972	*Criminal Law Amendment (Northern Ireland) Act*, R.S.N.I. 1923, c. 8.
	National Insurance Act, N.I. Pub. Gen. Acts 1946, c. 23, art. 7.
1999 à aujourd'hui	*Family Law Act (Northern Ireland) 2001*, (I.N.), 2001, c. 12.

- Abréger «*Northern Ireland Public General Acts*» par «N.I. Pub. Gen. Acts».
- Abréger «*Statutes Revised, Northern Ireland*» par «R.S.N.I.».
- Le Royaume-Uni a adopté des lois pour l'Irlande du Nord de 1972 à 1999. L'Assemblée de l'Irlande du Nord, établie le 19 novembre 1998, a adopté ses propres lois à partir du 2 décembre 1999. Pour les lois adoptées par l'Assemblée après 1999, mettre «(I.N.)» après le titre de la loi pour indiquer son origine. À l'exception des différences notées, renvoyer aux lois de l'Irlande du Nord de la même manière qu'à celles du Royaume-Uni. Le Royaume-Uni peut à ce jour adopter des lois qui s'appliquent en Irlande du Nord.

2.2.1.2 Écosse

Exemples	
Avant 1998	*Contract (Scotland) Act 1997* (R.-U.), 1997, c. 34.
	Scotland Act 1998 (R.-U.), 1998, c. 46, art. 4.
1998 à aujourd'hui	*Standards in Scotland's Schools etc. Act*, A.S.P. 2000, c. 6, art. 2.

- Avant 1998, faire référence à la législation de l'Écosse de la même manière qu'à celle du Royaume Uni.
- Les *Acts* adoptés par le Royaume-Uni s'appliquent à l'Écosse si ces lois se rapportent à une question réservée ou non transmise.
- Abréger «*Acts of Scottish Parliament*» par «A.S.P.» pour les *Acts* du 19 novembre 1998 à aujourd'hui.

2.2.1.3 Pays de Galles

Exemple
Government of Wales Act 1998 (R.-U.), 1998, c. 38, art. 3.

- Le Royaume-Uni adopte la législation relative au Pays de Galles. Les références aux lois du Pays de Galles suivent le même modèle de référence des lois du Royaume-Uni.

2.2.2 Projets de loi

2.2.2.1 Royaume-Uni

Exemples					
Numéro du projet de loi,	*titre,*	session,	année,	référence précise	(renseignements supplémentaires) (facultatif).
Bill 49,	*Anti-terrorism, Crime and Security,*	sess. 2001-2002,	2001		(1re lecture 19 novembre 2001).
Bill 40,	*British Overseas Territories Bill [HL],*	sess. 2001-2002,	2001,	art. 2.	

- Inclure «[HL]» dans le titre pour les projets de loi qui proviennent de la Chambre des lords.

2.2.2.2 Irlande du Nord

Exemple					
Numéro,	*titre,*	session,	année,	référence précise	(renseignements supplémentaires) (facultatif).
NIA Bill 15/00,	*A bill to amend the Game Preservation (Northern Ireland) Act 1928,*	sess. 2001-2002,	2001,	art. 2	(Committee Stage 29 octobre 2001).

2.2.2.3 Écosse

Exemple					
Numéro,	*titre,*	session,	année,	référence précise	(renseignements supplémentaires) (facultatif).
SP Bill 36,	*Freedom of Information (Scotland) Bill,*	1re sess.,	2001,	art. 16.	

2.2.3 Règlements

2.2.3.1 Royaume-Uni

Exemples			
	Titre (facultatif),	S.R. & O. ou S.I.	année/numéro.
Avant 1948	*Public Health (Prevention of Tuberculosis) Regulations 1925,*	S.R. & O.	1927/757.
1948 à aujourd'hui	*The Community Legal Service (Costs) Regulations 2000,*	S.I.	2000/441.

- L'indication du titre du règlement est facultative.
- Abréger *Statutory Rules & Orders* (avant 1948) par «S.R. & O.» et *Statutory Instruments* (après 1948) par «S.I.».

2.2.3.2 Irlande du Nord

Exemples			
Titre (facultatif),	S.R. & O. ou S.I.	année/ numéro	(N.I. numéro).
The Proceeds of Crime (Northern Ireland) Order 1996,	S.I.	1996/1299	(N.I. 9).
Tax Credits (Miscellaneous Amendments No. 8) (Northern Ireland) Regulations,	S.I.	2001/3086.	
Cheese Regulations (N.I.) 1970,	S.R. & O.	1970/14.	

- L'indication du titre du règlement est facultative.
- Si le règlement ou l'ordre a été adopté par le Royaume-Uni, il est compris dans le *Statutory Instruments.*
- Certains des règlements adoptés par l'Assemblée de l'Irlande du Nord sont également inclus dans le *Statutory Instruments.* Ces règlements comprennent «(N.I.)» et un numéro à la fin du titre du règlement.
- Si l'Assemblée de l'Irlande du Nord a adopté un règlement, l'abréger «S.R.» pour «*Statutory Rule*».
- Les règlements de l'Irlande du Nord sont inclus dans le *Statutory Regulations and Orders* (abréger «S.R. & O.») à partir de 1922.
- S'il y a un numéro d'ordre de l'Irlande du Nord, l'inclure après «année/numéro» pour indiquer que l'ordre a été promulgué par l'Assemblée de l'Irlande du Nord.

2.2.3.3 Écosse

Renvoyer aux règlements de l'Écosse de la même manière qu'à ceux du Royaume-Uni.

2.2.3.3.1   Règlements adoptés par le Royaume-Uni

Exemple		
Titre (facultatif),	S.R. & O. ou S.I.	année/numéro.
Employment Tribunals (Constitution and Rules of Procedure) (Scotland),	S.I.	2001/1170.

2.2.3.3.2   Règlements adoptés par l'Écosse

Exemple		
Titre (facultatif),	Scot. S.I.	année/numéro.
National Health Service (General Ophthalmic Services) (Scotland) Amendment Regulations,	Scot. S.I.	2001/62.

• Abréger «Scottish Statutory Instruments» par «Scot. S.I.».

2.2.3.4 Pays de Galles

Exemple			
Titre (facultatif),	S.R. & O. ou S.I.	année/numéro	(W. numéro).
Children's Homes Amendment (Wales) Regulations 2001,	S.I.	2001/140	(W. 6).

• Après «année/numéro», inclure le numéro du règlement du Pays de Galles pour indiquer qu'il a été promulgué par l'Assemblée du Pays de Galles.

2.3   ÉTATS-UNIS

N.B. Tous les éléments de référence à la législation des États-Unis sont en anglais à l'exception des mentions telles que «codifié à».

2.3.1 Constitution fédérale et constitutions des États

Exemples
U.S. Const. art. II, § 2, cl. 1.
U.S. Const. amend. XVIII, § 1.
Fla. Const., Part V, § 3(b)(4).

- Abréger «article» par «art.», «section» par «§» et «sections» par «§§».
- Un paragraphe qui fait partie d'une section est une «clause», abrégée «cl.» (au singulier comme au pluriel).
- Abréger «amendement» par «amend.».
- Abréger «préambule» par «pmbl.».
- Indiquer les numéros d'article et de modification en chiffres romains majuscules. Les numéros de section et de clause sont indiqués en chiffres arabes.

Voir l'annexe B pour la liste des abréviations des États.

2.3.2 Lois

En ordre de préférence, renvoyer à :

1. Un code officiel ;
2. Un code non officiel ;
3. Un recueil officiel de lois sessionnelles ;
4. Un recueil non officiel de lois sessionnelles ;
5. Un service à feuilles mobiles.

2.3.2.1 Codes

Un code aux États-Unis constitue le regroupement et la codification par sujet des lois générales et permanentes des États-Unis. Pour déterminer si un code étatique est officiel ou non, consulter *The Bluebook : A Uniform System of Citation*, 17ᵉ éd., Cambridge (Mass.), Harvard Law Review Association, 2000.

Un code officiel est un code des lois des États-Unis organisé en 50 titres, rédigé sous la surveillance d'une autorité gouvernementale appropriée (par ex. le département de la Justice fédérale). Le *United States Code* («U.S.C.») est le code officiel du gouvernement fédéral.

Un code non officiel est un code des lois des États-Unis préparé par une maison d'édition. Il existe deux codes non officiels pour les lois fédérales : le *United States Code Service* («U.S.C.S.») et le *United States Code Annotated* («U.S.C.A.»).

Exemples								
	Titre (exceptionnellement),	partie du code (s'il y a lieu)	titre abrégé du code	numéro du titre (s'il y a lieu)	article	(éditeur	supplément (s'il y a lieu)	année).
Codes officiels	*Clayton Act,*	15	U.S.C.		§ 3			(1993).
			Minn. Stat.		§ 169.947			(1990).
			I.R.C.		§ 61			(1994).
Codes non officiels		18	U.S.C.A.		§ 351	(West		1997).
			Pa. Stat. Ann.	tit. 63	§ 425.3	(West	Supp.	1986).
			Wis. Stat. Ann.		§ 939.645	(West	Supp.	1992).

- Ne pas renvoyer au titre original d'une loi codifiée. N'indiquer le titre que pour des raisons particulières (par ex. si la loi est normalement connue sous ce nom). Mettre le titre en italique.
- Si le code est classé par titres, chapitres ou volumes distincts et numérotés, indiquer le numéro de cette division. Lorsqu'on fait référence au code fédéral, indiquer la division avant l'abréviation du code. Lorsqu'on renvoie au code d'un État, consulter *The Bluebook: A Uniform System of Citation*, 17ᵉ éd., Cambridge (Mass.), Harvard Law Review Association, 2000.
- Ne pas mettre le titre abrégé du code en italique. Les références au *Internal Revenue Code* peuvent remplacer «26 U.S.C.» par «I.R.C.».
- À moins que le code ne soit publié par un éditeur officiel, indiquer le nom de l'éditeur avant l'année ou avant «Supp.», selon le cas.
- Lorsqu'on renvoie à un supplément inséré dans une pochette, indiquer «Supp.» avant la mention de l'année qui paraît sur la page titre du supplément.
- Indiquer l'année de publication du code entre parenthèses à la fin de la référence. Lorsqu'on renvoie à un recueil relié, fournir l'année qui paraît sur la reliure. Lorsqu'on renvoie à un supplément, fournir l'année qui figure sur la page titre du supplément.

2.3.2.2 Lois sessionnelles

Les lois sessionnelles sont les lois promulguées par une session congressionnelle, reliées et organisées chronologiquement. Les lois sessionnelles font le suivi chronologique d'une loi.

Exemples								
Titre (ou date de promul- gation),	numéro de la loi ou du chapitre,	partie (s'il y a lieu),	référence au recueil des lois sessionnelles	première page de la loi	référence précise au recueil	(année) (si elle n'est pas dans le titre)	(référence au code) (facultative).
The Deficit Reduction Act of 1984,	Pub. L. No. 98-369,		98 Stat.	494			(codifié tel que modifié au 26 U.S.C. § 1-9504 (1988)).
Coastal Zone Protection Act of 1996,	Pub. L. No. 104-150,	§ 7(2),	110 Stat.	1380	à la p. 1382	(1997).	
Act of 25 April 1978,	c. 515,	§ 3,	1978 Ala. Acts	569	à la p. 569.		

- Indiquer le titre de la loi en italique. Si la loi n'a pas de titre, l'identifier par la date de sa promulgation (par ex. Act of 25 April 1978). S'il manque la date de promulgation, identifier la loi par sa date de mise en vigueur (par ex. «Act en vigueur [date]»).
- Indiquer le numéro de la loi (*Public law number*), introduit par l'abréviation «Pub. L. No.» ou le numéro du chapitre. Le numéro devant le trait d'union est le numéro de session, celui après est son numéro de référence.
- Pour renvoyer à une partie particulière, indiquer le numéro de la partie après le numéro de la loi ou le numéro du chapitre, selon le cas. Lorsqu'on renvoie à une partie précise, indiquer la référence précise au recueil.
- Pour les lois fédérales, le recueil officiel des lois sessionnelles est le *Statutes at Large*, abrégé par «Stat.». L'abréviation du recueil est précédée par le numéro de volume et suivie de la première page de la loi. Pour déterminer si un recueil de lois sessionnelles étatiques est officiel ou non, consulter *The Bluebook : A Uniform System of Citation*, 17ᵉ éd., Cambridge (Mass.), Harvard Law Review Association, 2000.
- Indiquer la référence précise au recueil de lois sessionnelles après la référence à la première page. Lorsqu'on fournit une référence précise au recueil, inclure une référence précise à la partie après le numéro de la loi ou du chapitre.
- Indiquer l'année de publication entre parenthèses à la fin de la référence, à moins que l'année ne fasse partie du titre de la loi. Si l'année du titre ne coïncide pas avec l'année de publication de la loi, les deux années doivent être indiquées. Voir l'exemple du *Coastal Zone Protection Act of 1996* ci-dessus.
- Fournir des renseignements concernant la codification de la loi, si possible. Les parties des lois sont souvent classées par titres d'un code. Le cas échéant, fournir ces renseignements entre parenthèses à la fin de la référence (par ex. «codifié tel que modifié dans plusieurs sections du 26 U.S.C.» et suivi du nom du code).

2—Législation

2.3.2.3 *Recueil non officiel de lois sessionnelles*

Exemple					
Titre,	numéro de la loi,	[volume]	U.S.C.C.A.N.	référence précise,	référence au *Statutes at Large.*
Veteran's Benefits Improvements Act of 1996,	Pub. L. No. 104-275,	[1996]	U.S.C.C.A.N.	3762,	110 Stat. 3322.

*   Le recueil de lois sessionnelles fédérales le plus important est le *United States Code Congressional and Administrative News*, abrégé «U.S.C.C.A.N.».
*   Lorsqu'on renvoie au U.S.C.C.A.N., indiquer la référence au *Statutes at Large* («Stat.»), recueil officiel dans lequel paraîtra la loi.

2.3.3 *Uniform Codes, Uniform Acts* et *Restatements*

Les *Uniform Codes* et *Uniform Acts* sont des propositions législatives publiées par la *National Conference of Commissioners of Uniform State Laws*, qui visent l'adoption par tous les congrès d'États, les districts et les protectorats. Les *Restatements* sont des rapports sur l'état de la *common law* américaine qui porte sur tel sujet ou telle interprétation des lois publiques publiées par le *American Law Institute*.

Exemples		
Titre	partie	(année d'adoption).
U.C.C.	§ 2-012	(1995).
Uniform Adoption Act	§ 10	(1971).
Restatement of Contracts	§ 88	(1932).
Restatement (Second) of the Law of Property	§ 15	(1977).

*   Indiquer le titre en italique, à moins que ce ne soit un code.
*   Ne pas mettre de virgule après le titre d'un code ou d'un *Restatement*.
*   Lorsqu'il existe plus d'un *Restatement*, indiquer son numéro entre parenthèses.
*   Indiquer l'année d'adoption, de promulgation ou de la plus récente modification entre parenthèses à la fin de la référence.

2.3.4   Projets de loi et résolutions

2.3.4.1   Projets de loi fédéraux

Exemples								
É.-U.,	Bill	chambre	numéro,	*titre,*	numéro du Congrès,	année,	référence précise	(État, si promulgué).
É.-U.,	Bill	H.R.	6,	*Higher Education Amendments of 1988,*	105ᵉ Cong.,	1997		(promulgué).
É.-U.,	Bill	S.	7,	*Educational Excellence for All Learners Act of 2001,*	107ᵉ Cong.,	2001,	art. 103.	

- Utiliser «H.R.» pour «*House of Representatives*» et «S.» pour «*Senate*».

2.3.4.2   Résolutions fédérales

Exemples						
É.-U.,	résolution	numéro,	*titre,*	numéro du Congrès,	année	(État, si promulgué).
É.-U.,	H.R. Con. Res.	6,	*Expressing the Sense of the Congress Regarding the Need to Pass Legislation to Increase Penalties on Perpetrators of Hate Crimes,*	107ᵉ Cong.,	2001.	
É.-U.,	H.R. Res.	31,	*Designating Minority Membership on Certain Standing Committees of the House,*	104ᵉ Cong.,	1995	(promulgué).

Liste des abréviations employées pour les résolutions :

House Concurrent Resolutions	H.R. Con. Res.
House Resolutions	H.R. Res.
House Joint Resolutions	H.R.J. Res.
Senate Concurrent Resolutions	S. Con. Res.
Senate Resolutions	S. Res.
Senate Joint Resolutions	S.J. Res.

2.3.4.3 *États*

Exemples									
É.-U.,	type of bill or resolut-ion	numéro,	*titre,*	année ou numéro de la législa-ture,	numéro ou désignation de la session législative,	État,	année,	référence précise	(État, si promu-lgué).
É.-U.,	A.B.	31,	*An Act to Add Section 51885 to the Education Code, Relating to Educational Technology,*	1997-98,	Reg. Sess.,	Cal.,	1996,	art. 1.	
É.-U.,	S.R.	10,	*Calling for the Establishme nt of a Delaware State Police Community Relations Task Force,*	141ᵉ Gen. Assem.,	Reg. Sess.,	Del.,	2001		(promu-lgué).

- Les législateurs étatiques peuvent tenir des *Regular Sessions* ainsi que des *First, Second* et *Third Sessions*. Abréger ces expressions par «1st Extra Sess.», «2d Extra. Sess.» et «3d Extra. Sess.». Abréger «*Special Sessions*» par «Spec. Sess.»
- Voir la liste des abréviations concernant les États à l'annexe B.

2.3.5 Règles et règlements

2.3.5.1 Code of Federal Regulations

Le *Code of Federal Regulations* regroupe les règlements codifiés des États-Unis et est classé par les 50 mêmes titres que le *United States Code*.

Exemples				
Titre (exceptionellement),	volume	recueil	référence précise	(année).
EPA Effluent Limitations Guidelines,	40	C.F.R.	§ 405.53	(1980).
	47	C.F.R.	§ 73.609	(1994).

- Indiquer le titre de la règle ou du règlement lorsqu'ils sont normalement connus ainsi. Pour les règles et les règlements fédéraux, renvoyer à la compilation officielle du gouvernement, si possible.
- Le *Code of Federal Regulations*, abrégé par «C.F.R.», est la compilation officielle du gouvernement fédéral.

N.B. Pour identifier les compilations étatiques officielles, voir *The Bluebook : A Uniform System of Citation*, 17e éd., Cambridge (Mass.), Harvard Law Review Association, 2000.

2.3.5.2 *Registres administratifs*

Les registres administratifs comprennent entre autres les règlements administratifs mis en application par les autorités gouvernementales.

Exemple						
Titre (s'il y a lieu),	volume	Fed. Reg.	page	(année)	(information de codification	référence précise).
	44	Fed. Reg.	41,629	(1980)	(à être codifié à 12 C.F.R.	§ 201.51-201.53).

- Lorsque des règles ou des règlements n'ont pas encore été codifiés, renvoyer aux registres administratifs.
- Au niveau fédéral, renvoyer au *Federal Register* («Fed. Reg.»).
- Indiquer le numéro du volume, l'abréviation du registre, le numéro de page et l'année.
- Si possible, indiquer à quel endroit la règle ou le règlement paraîtra dans le C.F.R. ou autre compilation officielle à la fin de la référence.

N.B. Pour identifier les registres administratifs étatiques, voir *The Bluebook : A Uniform System of Citation*, 17ᵉ éd., Cambridge (Mass.), Harvard Law Review Association, 2000.

2.4   FRANCE

2.4.1   Lois et autres instruments législatifs

Exemples					
Titre,	J.O.,	date de publication,	(N.C.) (s'il y a lieu),	page,	référence parallèle.
Loi nᵒ 99-493 du 15 juin 1999,	J.O.,	16 juin 1999,		8759,	D. 1999.Lég.3.7.
Ordonnance nᵒ 2001-766 du 29 août 2001,	J.O.,	31 août 2001,		13946,	D. 2001.Lég.2564.
Décret du 5 décembre 1978 portant classement d'un site pittoresque,	J.O.,	6 décembre 1978	(N.C.),	9250.	

- Si l'instrument législatif est numéroté, l'inclusion du titre descriptif est facultative. S'il n'est pas numéroté, l'inclusion du titre est nécessaire.
- Toujours faire référence au *Journal officiel de la République française* en premier lieu, abrégé «J.O.», suivi de la date de publication et du numéro de page. Pour une liste des titres des anciens journaux officiels, voir la section 4.4.2. Pour les suppléments du J.O., indiquer «(N.C.)», pour «numéro complémentaire», après la date de publication.
- Si possible, indiquer une référence parallèle à un recueil général français, selon les règles à la section 3.5.4.

2.4.2 Codes

Code civil des Français **(1804-1807)**	Art. 9 **C.c.F.**
Code Napoléon **(1807-1814)**	Art. 9 **C.N.**
Code civil **(1815-)**	Art. 2203 **C. civ.**
Code pénal	Art. 56 **C. pén.**
Code de propriété intellectuelle	Art. 123(8) **C.P.I.**
Nouveau Code de procédure civile	Art. 1435 **N.C. proc. Civ.**
Code de procédure pénale	Art. 144(2) **C. proc. pén.**

- Ne jamais fournir la référence complète lorsqu'on renvoie à un code ; on y renvoie tel qu'indiqué.

5 AUSTRALIE

5.1 Lois

xemples		
tre	(indication géographique),	référence précise.
orporations Act 2001	(Cth.).	
lectricity Reform Act 2000	(N.T.).	
Marine Pollution Act 1987	(N.S.W.),	art. 53(1)(d).

Renvoyer aux lois par leur titre abrégé officiel en italique. Inclure l'année de la loi au titre. Indiquer l'abréviation de l'indication géographique immédiatement après le titre.

Abréger les indications géographiques de la manière suivante :

Commonwealth	Cth.
Territoire de la Capitale Australienne	A.C.T.
Nouvelle Galles du Sud	N.S.W.
Territoire du Nord	N.T.
Queensland	Qld.
Australie-Méridionale	S.A.
Tasmanie	Tas.
Victoria	Vic.
Australie-occidentale	W.A.

La législation se retrouve dans les compilations statutaires suivantes :

Acts of Parliament of the Commonwealth of Australia
Laws of the Australian Capital Territory, Acts
Statutes of New South Wales
Northern Territory of Australia Laws
Laws of the Northern Territory of Australia
Queensland Acts
Queensland Statutes
South Australia Statutes
Tasmanian Statutes
Acts of the Victorian Parliament
Victorian Statutes
Statutes of Western Australia

2.5.2   Législation déléguée (règlements)

Exemples		
Titre	(indication géographique),	référence précise.
Admiralty Rules 1998	(Cth.),	art. 5(b).
Income Tax Regulations (Amendment) 1996	(Cth.).	
Supreme Court Rules (Amendment) 1996	(A.C.T.),	art. 2.

- Les références aux règlements et aux règles suivent le même modèle de référence que celui qui prévaut pour les lois.

Les règlements se retrouvent dans les compilations suivantes :

Commonwealth Statutory Rules
Laws of the Australian Capital Territory, Subordinate Legislation
New South Wales Rules, Regulations, and By-Laws
Queensland Subordinate Legislation
Tasmanian Statutory Rules
Victorian Statutory Rules, Regulations, and By-Laws
Western Australia Subsidiary Legislation

2.6   NOUVELLE-ZÉLANDE

À l'exception des différences notées ci-dessous, faire référence à la législation de la Nouvelle-Zélande de la même manière qu'à celle du Canada.

2—Législation

2.6.1 Lois

Exemples				
Titre	(N.-Z.),	année/numéro,	RS	première page.
Abolition of the Death Penalty Act 1989	(N.-Z.),	1989/119,	41 RS	1.
Kiwifruit Industry Restructuring Act 1999	(N.-Z.),	1999/95.		

- Mettre «(N.-Z.)» après le titre de la loi pour indiquer son lieu d'origine.

2.6.2 Législation déléguée (règlements)

Exemples					
Titre	(N.-Z.),	année/numéro ou Gazette année,	page de la gazette	RS	première page.
Kiwifruit Export Regulations 1999	(N.-Z.),	1999/310.			
Ticketing of Meat Notice 1979	(N.-Z.),	Gazette 1979,	2030.		
High Court Amendment Rules (No 2) 1987	(N.-Z.),	1987/169,		40 RS	904.

- Mettre «(N.-Z.)» après le titre de la loi pour indiquer son origine.
- Fournir le numéro du volume suivi de «RS» (l'abréviation de *Reprint Series*).

2.7   SINGAPOUR

2.7.1 Documents constitutionnels

Constitution of the Republic of Singapore (1999 Rev. Ed.), art. 12(1).
Independence of Singapore Agreement 1965 (1985 Rev. Ed.).
Republic of Singapore Independence Act (1985 Rev. Ed.), n° 7 de 1965, art. 2.

- Faire référence aux modifications constitutionnelles de la même manière qu'à toute autre forme de législation.
- Abréger «*Revised Edition*» par «Rev. Ed.».

2.7.2 Législation

Exemples	
Lois incluses dans l'édition refondue	*Penal Code* (Cap. 224, 1985 Rev. Ed. Sing.), art. 34.
Lois qui n'ont pas encore un chapitre assigné dans l'édition refondue	*United Nations Act 2001* (n° 44 de 2001, Sing.), art. 2.

- Abréger l'édition refondue des lois de la République de Singapour par «Rev. Ed. Sing.».
- Abréger chapitre par «Cap.».
- Pour les lois récentes qui n'ont pas un chapitre assigné dans l'édition refondue, utiliser le numéro de la loi tel qu'indiqué dans l'exemple ci-dessus. Ne pas confondre le numéro de la loi avec le numéro du supplément de la loi («*Acts Supplement*») qui est un numéro attribué à chaque supplément de la *Government Gazette* publiant les récentes adaptations législatives.
- Pour la législation avant le 15 août 1945, incorporer au titre de la loi les abréviations suivantes :
  - Pour la législation de la période de *Straits Settlements* (1er avril 1867 au 15 février 1942) utiliser «S.S.»
  - Pour la législation publiée sous l'administration militaire japonaise lors de l'occupation de Singapour (15 février 1942 au 15 août 1945), utiliser «J.M.A.» pour *Japanese Military Administration*
- Pour la législation après le 15 août 1945, utiliser «Sing.» pour renvoyer à la législation promulguée pendant les périodes suivantes :
  Administration militaire britannique (*British Military Administration*)
  Colonie de Singapour (*Colony of Singapore*)
  - État de Singapour (*State of Singapore*) tant avant que pendant la fédération avec la Malaisie
  - République de Singapour (*Republic of Singapore*)

2.7.3 Modifications et abrogations

Exemple
Penal Code (Cap. 224, 1985 Rev. Ed. Sing.), art. 73, mod. par *Penal Code (Amendment) Act*, n° 18 de 1998, art. 2.

- Pour plus de détails, voir la section 2.1.1.8.

2.7.4   Lois anglaises applicables à Singapour

Exemple
Misrepresentation Act (Cap. 390, 1994 Rev. Ed. Sing.), art. 2.

- Renvoyer aux lois anglaises applicables à Singapour en vertu de *Application of English Law Act* (Cap. 7A, 1994 Rev. Ed. Sing.) en utilisant l'édition refondue de Singapour de la même manière que les lois promulguées par Singapour.

2.7.5   Législation auxiliaire (règlements)

Exemples		
Titre	(Rev. Ed. ou S. n°),	numéro du règlement.
Housing and Development Conveyancing Fees Rules	(1999 Rev. Ed. Sing.),	art. 2.
United Nations (Anti-Terrorism Measures) Regulations 2001	(S. 561/2001 Sing.),	art. 3.

- Les éditions refondues de la législation auxiliaire ne sont pas numérotées.
- Abréger «*Revised Edition*» par «Rev. Ed.»

2.8   AFRIQUE DU SUD

2.8.1   Lois

Exemples			
Titre,	numéro	de année,	référence précise.
Constitution of the Republic of South Africa 1996,	n° 108	de 1996.	
National Environmental Management Act, 1998,	n° 107	de 1998,	art. 3.

2.8.2   Projets de loi

Exemples					
Numéro,	*titre,*	session,	parlement,	année,	référence précise.
B50-2000,	*Conventional Arms Control Bill,*	2e sess.,	2e parl.,	2001.	
B03-2001,	*Unemployment Insurance Bill,*	2e sess.,	2e parl.,	2001,	art. 2.

- Renvoyer aux projets de loi de l'Afrique du Sud de la même manière qu'à ceux du Canada.
- Ajouter tout renseignement supplémentaire entre parenthèses à la fin de la référence.

2.9   LÉGISLATION DISPONIBLE SUR SERVICE ÉLECTRONIQUE

Noter que les lois reproduites sur support électronique sont considérées comme des copies non officielles pour fins de recherche. La copie officielle sur support papier demeure l'autorité d'un texte législatif.

2.9.1   Services électroniques

Exemples	
Référence complète à la législation	(service électronique et banque de données (facultatif)).
Crown Liability Act, R.S.C. 1985, c. C-38	(QL, L.R.Q.).
Americans with Disabilities Act, 42 U.S.C. § 12101 (1990)	(Lexis).
United Nations Act 2001 (No. 44 of 2001, Sing.) s. 2	(Lawnet).

- Fournir la référence complète, suivie du service électronique entre parenthèses.
- Si le document ne peut être facilement trouvé sur le service sans connaître la banque de données du service électronique, indiquer la banque de données dans laquelle le document a été trouvé (par ex. «(QL, L.R.Q.)»).
- Cette forme de référence ne devrait être utilisée que pour les services électroniques qui exigent un abonnement ou pour les sites Internet qui ont une table des matières, des engins de recherche, des rédacteurs professionnels et une abréviation reconnue. Les renvois aux sites Internet gouvernementaux doivent inclure l'adresse Internet au complet (voir la section 2.9.2).

2—Législation

- Inclure le numéro de paragraphe comme référence précise, si possible. Si la pagination d'une source sur support papier est reproduite sur le service électronique, renvoyer aux numéros de pages de la source sur support papier. Ne pas renvoyer à la référence précise des numéros de l'écran ou des pages du service électronique car ces numéros sont propres au service électronique utilisé et la forme peut changer d'un format électronique à un autre (texte, html).

Si possible, ne pas renvoyer à un service électronique auquel la majorité des lecteurs ne pourra accéder. Par exemple, ne pas renvoyer à Azimut lorsque l'auditoire ciblé n'est pas au Québec.

Voici une liste des abréviations de services électroniques courants :

Australian Legal Information Institute	AustLII
Azimut (produit par SOQUIJ)	Azimut
British and Irish Legal Information Institute	BILII
Butterworths Services	Butterworths
Institut canadien d'information juridique	IIJCan
*e*Carswell	eC
Lawnet	Lawnet
Legifrance	Legifrance
LexisNexis	Lexis
LexUM	LexUM
Quicklaw	QL
Westlaw	WL

2.9.2 Sites Internet

Exemple			
Référence traditionnelle,	en ligne :	nom du site	<adresse universelle>.
Loi sur la protection des renseignements personnels dans le secteur privé, L.R.Q. c. P-39.1, art. 11,	en ligne :	Publications du Québec	<http://www.publication sduquebec.gouv.qc.ca>.

- Fournir la référence traditionnelle, suivie d'une virgule, de «en ligne :», du nom du site Internet et de l'adresse universelle (URL).
- Renvoyer à l'adresse universelle du document à moins que cette adresse ne soit propre à une session Internet, auquel cas renvoyer à la page d'accueil.
- Toutes les sources Internet ne sont pas fiables, il faut donc porter une attention particulière lorsqu'on renvoie à de telles sources.
- Plusieurs textes en ligne disparaissent après un certain temps. Renvoyer à une source en ligne si cette source fournit des documents archivés remontant à quelques années.
- Inclure un numéro de paragraphe comme référence précise si possible. Si la pagination d'une source imprimée est reproduite dans une source électronique, renvoyer à la pagination utilisée par la source imprimée.

3

JURISPRUDENCE

Ce chapitre renvoie à la référence neutre à plusieurs reprises. Une référence neutre permet l'identification permanente d'une cause indépendant du service électronique ou du recueil imprimé dans lequel elle est publiée. Pour plus de renseignements sur la référence neutre et le renvoi aux services électroniques, voir les sections 3.10 et 3.11.

3.1   À QUELLE SOURCE RENVOYER

Exemples	
Référence neutre disponible mais pas encore publiée dans un recueil imprimé : renvoyer à la référence neutre seulement (ne pas faire référence à un service électronique).	*Whiten c. Pilot Insurance*, 2002 CSC 18.
Référence neutre disponible, publiée dans au moins un recueil imprimé : renvoyer au(x) recueil(s) imprimé(s) et inclure la référence neutre comme référence parallèle.	*R. c. Latimer*, [2001] 1 R.C.S. 3, 193 D.L.R. (4ᵉ) 577, 2001 CSC 1 [*Latimer* avec renvois au R.C.S.).
Pas de référence neutre disponible, publiée à la fois dans un recueil officiel et dans un autre recueil, renvoyer au recueil officiel. Utiliser l'autre recueil pour la référence parallèle de préférence.	*Baker c. Canada (Ministre de la Citoyenneté et de l'Immigration)*, [1999] 2 R.C.S. 817 à la p. 820, 174 D.L.R. (4ᵉ) 193, juge L'Heureux-Dubé [*Baker* avec renvois au R.C.S.).

Pas de référence neutre disponible, pas publiée dans un recueil officiel : renvoyer à un recueil semi-officiel ou non officiel en fournissant une référence parallèle si possible.	*Wigle v. Allstate Insurance Co. of Canada* (1984), 49 O.R. (2ᵉ) 101 (C.S.).
Pas de référence neutre disponible, publiée dans un recueil imprimé sur un service électronique ou l'Internet : identifier le service électronique ou l'adresse universelle (URL) après la référence traditionnelle.	*Lachine General Hospital c. Québec (P.G)*, [1996] R.J.Q. 2804 à la p. 2809, 142 D.L.R. (4ᵉ) 659, juge Robert (QL) [*Lachine* avec renvois au R.J.Q.].
Pas de référence neutre disponible, pas publiée dans un recueil imprimé, accédée par service électronique ou Internet : renvoyer au numéro tel qu'indiqué sur le service électronique.	*R. v. Leimanis*, [1992] B.C.J. n° 2280 (Prov. Ct.) (QL).
Pas de référence neutre disponible, décision ni publiée ni accédée par service électronique : suivre les règles pour les décisions non publiées.	*Commission des droits de la personne du Québec c. Brasserie O'Keefe* (13 septembre 1990), Montréal 500-05-005826-873 (C.S.).

3.2   CANADA – RÉFÉRENCES AUX RECUEILS IMPRIMÉS

3.2.1 Modèle de base

Exemples							
Intitulé	(année de la décision),	[année du recueil]	volume	recueil	série (s'il y a lieu)	page	(indication géographique et/ou cour) (si nécessaire).
Bazley c. Curry,		[1999]	2	R.C.S.		534.	
R. c. Ewanchuk,		[1999]	1	R.C.S.		330.	
R. v. Laliberté	(2001),		31	C.R.	(5ᵉ)	1	(Sask. C.A.).
Bailey c. Chagnon,		[1996]	14	R.D.J.		566	(C.S. Qué.).

Exemple				
Première référence	référence précise,	référence parallèle,	juge (facultatif)	[introduction du titre abrégé].
R. c. Sharpe, [2001] 1 R.C.S. 45	à la p. 97,	194 D.L.R. (4ᵉ) 1, 2001 CSC 2,	juge en chef McLachlin	[*Sharpe* avec renvois aux R.C.S.].

3.2.2 Intitulé

- Ne pas répéter l'intitulé dans la note s'il est déjà mentionné dans le texte.
- Mettre en italique le nom des parties et le «c.» ou «v.» qui sépare le nom des parties.
- Afin de refléter les règles de la référence neutre, le «c.» et le «v.» dans l'intitulé indiquent la langue dans laquelle la décision est rendue. Si la décision est rendue en anglais, utiliser «v.». Si la décision est rendue en français, utiliser «c.». Pour les décisions bilingues, utiliser «c.» si vous écrivez en français et «v.» si vous écrivez en anglais. Si vous écrivez dans une autre langue, utiliser l'un ou l'autre.

Exemples		
	Si vous écrivez en français	Si vous écrivez en anglais
Décision rendue en français	*Traverse Trois-Pistoles Escoumins ltée c. Québec (Commission des Transports)*	*Traverse Trois-Pistoles Escoumins ltée c. Quebec (Commission des Transports)*
Décision rendue en anglais	*Pacific Developments Ltd. v. Calgary (Ville de)*	*Pacific Developments Ltd. v. Calgary (City of)*
Décision bilingue	*Comité pour le traitement égal des actionnaires minoritaires de la Société Asbestos ltée c. Ontario (Commission des valeurs mobilières)*	*Committee for the Equal Treatment of Asbestos Minority Shareholders v. Ontario (Securities Commission)*

- Mettre en majuscule la première lettre du premier mot figurant de chaque côté du «c.», ainsi que la première lettre des noms propres. Ne pas mettre en majuscule les prépositions, les conjonctions et les autres mots faisant partie des expressions procédurales.
- Traduire les descriptions telles que «Ville de» mais ne traduire ni les mots qui font partie du nom d'une partie tels que «Université» ni les abréviations telles que «ltée» ou «s.r.l.».

- Omettre «Le», «La», «L'», «Les» ou «The» lorsque l'article défini est le premier mot d'un nom d'une partie, même s'il fait partie du nom d'une raison sociale. Toutefois, indiquer l'article défini s'il fait partie du nom d'une chose poursuivie *in rem* (un navire ou un avion, par ex. *Le Mihalis Angelos*).

3.2.2.1 Nom des parties

Exemples	
	Blackburn-Moreault c. **Moreault** **Marcil** c. **Hétu**
NON	*Rolande Blackburn-Moreault c. Henri Moreault* *Marcil c. Hétu et Hurtubise*

- N'utiliser que les noms de famille. Omettre les prénoms et les initiales.
- Lorsqu'il y a jonction de plusieurs instances, ne mentionner que la première instance.
- Omettre toute expression, telle que «*et al.*», qui indique qu'il y a plusieurs parties.

3.2.2.2 Personne représentée par un tuteur

Exemple
Dobson (**tuteur à l'instance**) *c. Dobson*

3.2.2.3 Noms corporatifs et de sociétés

Exemples	
	Pelletier c. **Madawaska Co. ltée** **J.J. Joubert ltée** *c. Lapierre* *KPMG* **s.r.l.** *c. Lachance* *Lemieux c.* **Société** *Radio-Canada*
NON	*Pelletier c. Madawaska Co.* *Joubert ltée c. Lapierre* *Lemieux c. Radio-Canada*
Société	**Astier, Favrot** *c. Mendelsohn*

- Toujours inclure «Ltd.», «ltée», «s.r.l.» ou «LLP». Ne pas traduire ces expressions ou abréviations.

- Si le nom de la compagnie indique clairement son statut corporatif, omettre les expressions telles que «inc.» mais si le nom n'indique pas ce statut ou si les termes ne sont pas à la fin du nom de l'entreprise, utiliser ces expressions pour identifier le statut corporatif des parties.
- Indiquer les prénoms et les initiales qui font partie du nom d'une raison sociale.
- Indiquer les noms de tous les partenaires d'une société.
- Quand une compagnie a un nom bilingue, utiliser le nom de la compagnie dans la langue de la décision à laquelle vous renvoyez. Si la décision est bilingue, utiliser le nom dans la langue dans laquelle vous écrivez. Si vous écrivez dans une autre langue que le français ou l'anglais, utilisez le nom qui vous convient.

3.2.2.4 Pays, unités fédérales, provinces et municipalités

Exemples	
Pays	*États-Unis v. Shulman*
NON	*Les États-Unis d'Amérique v. Shulman*
Province, État	*Québec (P.G.) c. Auger.*
Municipalités	*Laurentide Motels Ltd. c. **Beauport (Ville de)***
	***Charlesbourg-Est (Municipalité de)** c. Asselin*
	*Vigi Santé ltée c. Montréal **(Communauté urbaine de)***

- Indiquer le nom français du pays communément utilisé et non son nom officiel ou son abréviation.
- Omettre «Province de», «État de», «Peuple de» ou tout autre identificateur du même genre.
- Placer les identificateurs, tels que «Ville de», «Communauté urbaine de», «Comté de», «District de » ou «Municipalité de» entre parenthèses après le nom du lieu.

3.2.2.5 Testaments et successions

Exemples	
Nom de la succession	*Tremblay c. **Trudel, succession***
Nom de la succession si ni le demandeur ni le défendeur ne sont inclus	*Re Succession Eurig*

- Ne pas indiquer le nom des exécuteurs testamentaires.

3.2.2.6   Faillites et mises sous séquestre

Exemples
*Chablis Textiles (**Syndic de**) c. London Life Insurance*
*Lasalle Land Co. (**Liquidateur de**) c. Alepin*

- Indiquer le nom du failli ou de la compagnie mise sous séquestre par «syndic de», «séquestre de» ou «liquidateur de».

3.2.2.7   Titres de la loi

Exemples	
Si le nom de la loi indique clairement l'indication géographique	*Re Code canadien du travail*
Si l'indication géographique ne peut être inférée par le nom de la loi	*Renvoi relatif à la Loi sur l'Instruction publique (Québec)*

3.2.2.8   La Couronne – affaires pénales

Exemple
***R.** c. Blondin*

- Utiliser «R.» pour identifier la Couronne dans les causes pénales et pour remplacer les expressions telles que «La Reine», «Régina», «La Couronne», «La Reine du chef de» ou tout terme semblable qui sert à identifier la Couronne.

3.2.2.9 La Couronne – affaires civiles

Exemples	
P.G.	Schreiber c. Canada (**P.G.**)
M.R.N.	Savard c. **M.R.N.**
Autres organismes gouvernementaux	Chagnon c. Québec (**Commission d'accès à l'information**)
Ne pas répéter le nom de l'indication géographique	Banque Laurentienne du Canada c. Canada (**Commission des droits de la personne**) **NON** : Banque Laurentienne du Canada c. Canada (**Commission canadienne des droits de la personne**)
Ne pas inclure le nom d'un individu représentant un organisme gouvernemental	Canada (**Ministre de l'Emploi et de l'Immigration**) c. Jiminez-Perez **NON** : Jean Boisvert (Directeur du centre d'Immigration Canada de Winnipeg) c. Jiminez-Perez

- Dans les affaires civiles, utiliser le nom de l'identification.
- Abréger «Ministre du Revenu national» par «M.R.N.» et «Sous-ministre du Revenu national» par «Sous-M.R.N.»
- Utiliser l'abréviation «P.G.» pour désigner «Procureur général».
- Utiliser le nom de l'indication géographique, suivi du nom de l'organisme gouvernemental (tel que la Commission, le Ministère) entre parenthèses.
  - Lorsqu'on fait référence à un tribunal administratif fédéral ou provincial, suivre les règles énoncées à l'annexe F.
  - Ne pas inclure le nom d'un individu représentant un organisme gouvernemental.

3.2.2.10 Sociétés d'État

Exemple
Westaim Corp. c. **Monnaie royale canadienne**

- Ne pas indiquer le nom de l'indication géographique avant le nom de la société d'État.

3.2.2.11 Commissions et conseils des affaires municipales

Exemple
Québec (P.G.) c. Montréal (Communauté urbaine) **Service de police**

3.2.2.12 Conseils scolaires

Exemples	
	Ross c. **District nᵒ 15 du Nouveau-Brunswick**
NON	*Ross c.* **Conseil scolaire du district nᵒ 15 du Nouveau-Brunswick**

- Omettre les termes tels que «Conseil scolaire» et «Conseil d'administration» ; n'indiquer que le nom de l'institution.

3.2.2.13 Syndicats

Exemple	
	Lavigne c. **Syndicat des employés de la Fonction publique de l'Ontario**
NON	*Lavigne c. S.E.F.P.O.*

- Ne pas abréger le nom des syndicats car de telles abréviations varient d'une fois à l'autre.

3.2.2.14 Agences d'aide sociale

Exemples
Doe c. **Metropolitan Toronto Child and Family Services**
*Manitoba (**Directeur de la protection de l'enfance**) c. Y*

- Inclure le nom de la communauté d'où l'agence provient sauf si le nom de la communauté fait partie du nom de l'agence, par exemple, *Doe c. Metropolitan Toronto Child and Family Services*.

3.2.2.15 Nom des parties protégées

Exemples
D.P. c. C.S. *Droit de la famille —1763*

- Si le nom des parties n'est pas divulgué, utiliser les initiales disponibles ou le titre et la description numérique fournis dans le recueil.

3.2.2.16 Intitulés différents pour une même cause – l'emploi de sub nom.

Exemple
Compagnie des chemins de fer nationaux du Canada c. Canada (Commission canadienne des droits de la personne), [1987] 1 R.C.S. 1114, **(sub nom. Action Travail des Femmes c. Canadian National Railways Co.)** 40 D.L.R. (4ᵉ) 193.

- La référence commence par le nom des parties tels qu'il paraît dans le premier recueil.
- Si la référence parallèle renvoie aux mêmes parties sous des noms différents, indiquer cet intitulé entre parenthèses, devancé par la mention «*sub nom.*», immédiatement avant la référence parallèle.
- *Sub nom.* est l'abréviation de *sub nomine*, soit «sous le nom de» en latin.

3.2.2.17 Tierce partie agissant pour une des parties – l'emploi de ex rel.

Exemple
Ryel c. Québec (P.G.) ***ex rel. Société immobilière du Québec***

- Dans une action, utiliser l'expression «*ex rel.*» pour indiquer qu'une tierce partie agit au nom d'une autre partie.
- *Ex rel.* est l'abréviation de *ex relatione*, qui signifie «à cause de la relation ou de l'information» en latin.

3—Jurisprudence

3.2.2.18 Expressions procédurales et renvois constitutionnels

Exemples	
Constitutionnel	**Renvoi relatif à** la Loi sur les armes à feu
Autre	**Re** Denis **Ex parte** Royal Dress Co. : **Re** Hudson Fashion Shoppe Ltd.

- L'expression «*Renvoi relatif à*» n'est utilisée que pour les renvois constitutionnels ; dans tout autre cas, utiliser «*Re*».
- Remplacer «*In re*», «Dans l'affaire de» et «*In the matter of*» par «*Re*».
- Écrire «*Ex parte*» au long. La mention «*ex parte*», dans l'intitulé d'une décision, signifie que la partie nommée après la mention a demandé l'action.

3.2.3 Année

3.2.3.1 Année de la décision

Règle générale :	*fournir l'année de la décision entre parenthèses*	R. v. Borden (**1993**), 24 C.R. (4ᵉ) 184 (N.S.C.A.).
L'année du recueil et l'année de la décision sont différentes :	*fournir les deux années*	Joyal c. Hôpital du Christ-Roi (**1996**), [1997] R.J.Q. 38 (C.A.).
L'année du recueil et l'année de la décision est la même :	*ne pas fournir l'année de la décision*	Raymond v. Adrema Ltd., [**1962**] O.R. 677 (H.C.J.). *NON* Raymond v. Adrema Ltd. (1962), [**1962**] O.R. 677 (H.C.J.).

- Fournir l'année de la décision entre parenthèses après l'intitulé et suivie d'une virgule.
- Si l'année de la décision est la même que l'année du recueil, fournir l'année de la décision n'est pas nécessaire. Seulement fournir l'année du recueil entre crochets.

3.2.3.2 Année du recueil

Recueil classé par année. Un volume publié par année.	*Raymond v. Adrema Ltd.*, **[1962]** O.R. 677 (H.C.J.).
Recueil classé par année. Plusieurs volumes publiés par année.	*Renvoi relatif à la sécession du Québec*, **[1998]** 2 R.C.S. 217.
Recueil dont les volumes sont classés par série. Ne pas fournir l'année du recueil.	*R. v. Borden* (1993), 24 C.R. (4ᵉ) 184 (N.S.C.A.).

- Les recueils sont publiés en volumes classés par série (par ex. D.L.R., C.C.C.) ou en volumes classés par année de parution (par ex. R.C.S., R.J.Q.).
- Si les volumes sont classés par série, ne pas indiquer l'année pour identifier le volume.
- Si les volumes sont classés par année de parution, l'année est nécessaire à l'identification du volume. Fournir l'année du recueil entre crochets.
- Noter que certains recueils ont changé leur mode de classification. Par exemple, le *Receuil de la Cour Suprême du Canada* est classé par série de 1877-1923 (par ex. 27 R.C.S.), par année de 1923-1974 (par ex. [1950] R.C.S.), et par année avec plusieurs volumes par année depuis 1975 (par ex. [1982] 2 R.C.S.). Aussi, les *Ontario Reports* sont classés par année de parution avant 1974 (par ex. [1973] O.R.) et en série depuis 1974 (par ex. 20 O.R.).

3.2.4 Recueil

Exemple
Forbes c. Desaulniers (1991), [1992] **R.L.** 250 (C.A.).

Indiquer l'abréviation du nom du recueil selon la liste des abréviations de recueils à l'annexe G.

3.2.4.1 Recueils officiels

- Les recueils officiels sont publiés par l'Imprimeur de la Reine.
- Si la décision a été publiée dans un recueil officiel, renvoyer au recueil officiel en premier lieu.
- Lorsqu'il existe des différences entre deux versions du même jugement, la version publiée dans les recueils officiels a préséance.

La liste suivante indique les recueils officiels :

Recueils de la Cour suprême (1970-présent) *Canada Law Reports : Supreme Court of Canada* (1923-1969) *Canada Supreme Court Reports* (1876-1922)	R.C.S.
Recueils de la Cour fédérale (1971-présent)	C.F.
Recueils de jurisprudence de la Cour de l'Échiquier (1923-1970) *Exchequer Court of Canada Reports* (1875-1922)	R .C. de l'É

3.2.4.2 Recueils semi-officiels

- Renvoyer aux recueils semi-officiels en premier lieu si le jugement n'a pas été publié dans un recueil officiel.
- Les recueils semi-officiels sont publiés sous l'égide du barreau d'une province ou d'un territoire.

La liste suivante indique les recueils semi-officiels publiés en 2002 :

Alberta	*Alberta Reports* (1976-présent) *N.B.* : Alberta Law Reports (3e) (Alta. L.R. (3e)) — est non officiel.	A.R.
Colombie-Britannique	Aucun recueil semi-officiel publié en 2002.	
Manitoba	Aucun recueil semi-officiel publié en 2002.	
Nouveau-Brunswick	*New Brunswick Reports* (2e) (1968-présent)	N.B.R. (2e)
Nouvelle-Écosse	*Nova Scotia Reports* (2e) (1969-présent)	N.S.R. (2e)
Nunavut	Aucun recueil semi-officiel publié en 2002.	
Ontario	*Ontario Reports* (3e) (1991-présent)	O.R.
Québec	*Recueils de jurisprudence du Québec* (1986-présent)	R.J.Q.
Saskatchewan	Aucun recueil semi-officiel publié en 2002.	
Terre-Neuve et Île-du-Prince-Édouard	Newfoundland & Prince Edward Island Reports (1971-présent)	Nfld. & P.E.I.R.
Territoires du Nord-Ouest	Aucun recueil semi-officiel publié en 2002.	N.W.T.R.
Territoire du Yukon	Aucun recueil semi-officiel publié en 2002.	

Pour une liste complète des recueils semi-officiels (incluant ceux qui ne sont plus publiés en 2002), voir l'annexe G.

3.2.4.3 Recueils non officiels

- Lorsque la cause n'est pas publiée dans les recueils officiels ou semi-officiels, renvoyer à tout autre recueil.
- Respecter si possible les directives suivantes :
  - les recueils généraux (par ex. les *Western Weekly Reports*) sont préférés aux recueils spécialisés (par ex. le *Canadian Criminal Cases*) ;
  - les recueils couvrant un grand territoire géographique (par ex. les *Dominion Law Reports*) sont préférés aux recueils couvrant un territoire géographique plus petit (par ex. les *Saskatchewan Reports*) ;
  - généralement, les recueils facilement disponibles sont préférés (par ex. les *Dominion Law Reports*).

Une liste des recueils non officiels se trouve à l'annexe G.

3.2.5 Série

Exemples	
Numéro de série	*Newell v. Royal Bank of Canada* (1997), 156 N.S.R. (**2ᵉ**) 347 (C.A.).
Nouvelle série	*Re Cameron* (1974), 18 C.B.R. (**n.s.**) 99 (C.S. Qué).

- Si le recueil a été publié en plusieurs séries, indiquer la série entre parenthèses, entre l'abréviation du recueil et la première page du jugement.
- Remplacer «Nouvelle série» ou «*New Series*» par «n.s.».
- Indiquer le numéro de série en français (par ex. «(4ᵉ)» non pas «(4th)»).

3.2.6 Première page

Exemple
Ford c. Québec (P.G.), [1988] 2 R.C.S. **712**.

- Indiquer le numéro de la première page du jugement.

3.2.7   Référence précise

Exemples
R. c. Latimer, [2001] 1 R.C.S. 3, 2001 CSC 1 **au para. 27**.
Bagagerie S.A. c. Bagagerie Willy (1992), 45 C.P.R. (3ᵉ) 503 **à la p. 507** (C.A.F.).
Québec (P.G.) c. Germain, [1995] R.J.Q. 2313 **à la p. 2320 et s.** (C.A.).
Canadien Pacifique c. Bande indienne de Matsqui, [1995] 1 R.C.S. 3 **aux pp. 40, 49**, 122 D.L.R. (4ᵉ) 129.
Madden c. Demers (1920), 29 B.R. 505 **aux pp. 510-12**.

- Indiquer la référence précise après la première page du jugement.
- Indiquer la page ou le paragraphe. Lorsque les paragraphes sont numérotés, y renvoyer à l'aide de «au n°», «au para» ou ¶. Pour renvoyer à une page, utiliser «à la p.» et pour renvoyer à plusieurs pages, utiliser «aux pp.» Ne pas mettre de virgule avant la référence précise.
- La référence précise se fait au premier recueil mentionné.
- Pour indiquer une partie générale indiquer «et s.» (abréviation de «et suivantes») immédiatement après le numéro. Il est toutefois préférable de renvoyer aux pages ou aux paragraphes précis.
- Les pages ou les paragraphes consécutifs sont séparés par un trait d'union. Retenir au moins les deux derniers chiffres des nombres (par ex. «aux pp. 32-35» et non «aux pp. 32-5»).
- Les pages ou les paragraphes non consécutifs sont séparés par une virgule (par ex. «aux pp. 40, 49»).

3.2.8   Références parallèles

Exemples
Université du Québec à Trois-Rivières c. Larocque, [1993] 1 R.C.S. 471 à la p. 473, **101 D.L.R. (4ᵉ) 494** [*Larocque* avec renvois aux R.C.S.].
Bracklow v. Bracklow (1999), 181 D.L.R. (4ᵉ) 522, **[2000] 3 W.W.R. 633** (B.C.S.C.).
Delgamuukw v. British Columbia (1991), 79 D.L.R. (4ᵉ) 185, **[1991] 3 W.W.R. 97** (B.C.S.C.) [*Delgamuukw* **avec renvois aux D.L.R.**].

- Si possible, fournir au moins une référence parallèle.
- Séparer les références parallèles par des virgules.
- Indiquer à quel recueil renvoient les références ultérieures (par ex. «[*Delgamuukw* **avec renvois aux D.L.R.**]») ; de préférence, renvoyer au premier recueil, soit le plus officiel. Si l'on renvoie à des paragraphes numérotés, il n'est pas nécessaire d'indiquer

à quel recueil les références ultérieures appartiennent. Ainsi, il ne sera pas nécessaire d'indiquer que les prochaines références renvoient à la référence neutre.

- Indiquer l'année du volume du recueil de la référence parallèle même si elle répète l'année dans laquelle la décision a été rendue. Voir l'exemple *Delgamuukw*.
- Omettre les références précises aux recueils des références parallèles.

3.2.9   Indication géographique et cour

Exemples
Beauchemin c. Blainville (Ville de) (2001), 202 D.L.R. (4ᵉ) 147 **(C.S. Qué)**.
Re McEachern (1996), 147 Nfld. & P.E.I.R. 146 **(P.E.I.S.C. (T.D.))**.
Rempel v. Reynolds (1991), 94 **Sask. R.** 299 **(Q.B.)**.
Air Canada c. Joyal, [1982] **C.A.** 39 **(Qué)**.
Miller c. Monit International, [2001] 1 **R.C.S.** 432, 2001 CSC 13.

- Fournir l'indication géographique et la cour entre parenthèses après le numéro de page ou la référence précise, s'il y a lieu à moins qu'il n'y ait des références parallèles. L'indication géographique et la cour devraient suivre toutes les références parallèles, sauf si c'est une référence neutre.
- Omettre l'indication géographique si elle est évidente d'après le nom du recueil auquel on fait référence et n'indiquer que le niveau de la cour. Omettre le niveau de la cour si celui-ci est évident d'après le nom du recueil.
- La référence neutre indique clairement la cour et l'indication géographique. Lorsqu'on utilise une référence neutre seule ou en référence parallèle, ne jamais inclure une autre abréviation de la cour et de l'indication géographique autre que celle de la référence neutre.
- Utiliser les abréviations françaises des indications géographiques et des cours lorsque le lieu en question est bilingue (par ex. «B.R. Man.» plutôt que «Man. Q.B.» au Manitoba) ; si la cour n'émet que des jugements en anglais, utiliser l'abréviation anglaise (par ex. «Sask. Q.B.» en Saskatchewan).
- Il n'y a pas d'espace entre les abréviations des cours qui sont fermées de majuscules. Laisser un espace quant l'abréviation formée de majuscules est placée à côté d'une abréviation formée de majuscules et de miniscules (par ex. C.Q., B.C.C.A, Div. gén. Ont., C.Q.).

Voir les abréviations aux annexes.

3.2.10 Juge

Exemples
R. c. Sharpe, [2001] 1 R.C.S. 4 à la p. 61, 2001 CSC 2, **juge en chef McLachlin**.   *Gosselin c. Québec (P.G.)*, [1999] R.J.Q. 1033 (C.A.), **juge Robert, dissident**.

- Indiquer le nom du juge à la fin de la référence s'il est pertinent à l'idée exprimée.

3.2.11 Étapes successives d'une cause

3.2.11.1 Étapes antérieures

Exemples	
Décision confirmée	*Law c. Canada (Ministre de l'Emploi et de l'Immigration)*, [1999] 1 R.C.S. 497, **confirmant (1996), 135 D.L.R. (4ᵉ) 293 (C.F.A.).**
Décision infirmée	*Wilson & Lafleur ltée c. Société québécoise d'information juridique*, [2000] R.J.Q. 1086 (C.A.), **infirmant [1998] R.J.Q. 2489 (C.S.).**

- Indiquer les étapes antérieures d'une cause si celles-ci sont pertinentes à l'idée énoncée.
- Les étapes antérieures d'une cause paraissent à la fin de la référence.
- Les décisions sont séparées par une virgule.
- Les expressions «confirmant» et «infirmant» renvoient à la première référence.
- Si la décision confirme ou infirme une décision antérieure pour des motifs autres que ceux discutés, utiliser «confirmant pour d'autres motifs» ou «infirmant pour d'autres motifs».
- Des références parallèles peuvent être ajoutées aux décisions antérieures.

3.2.11.2 Étapes postérieures

Exemples	
Décision confirmée	*Granovsky c. Canada (Ministre de l'Emploi et de l'Immigration)*, [1998] 3 F.C. 175 (C.A.), **conf. par [2000] 1 R.C.S. 703, 2000 CSC 28**.
Décision infirmée	*Ontario English Catholic Teachers' Association c. Ontario (P.G.)* (1998), 162 D.L.R. (4ᵉ) 257 (Div. gén. Ont.), **inf. par (1999), 172 D.L.R. (4ᵉ) 193 (C.A. Ont.), inf. par [2001] 1 R.C.S. 470, 2001 CSC 15**.

- Indiquer les étapes postérieures d'une cause si celle-ci a été jugée postérieurement par d'autres cours.

- Les étapes postérieures d'une cause figurent à la fin de la référence.
- Les différentes décisions sont séparées par des virgules.
- Utiliser «conf. par» pour abréger «confirmé par» et «inf. par» pour abréger «infirmé par».
- Si la décision a été confirmée ou infirmée pour des motifs autres que ceux discutés, utiliser «conf. pour d'autres motifs par» ou «inf. pour d'autres motifs par».
- Les expressions «conf. par» et «inf. par» renvoient à la première référence. Ainsi, dans l'exemple *Ontario English Catholic Teachers' Association*, l'expression «inf. par» qui précède la décision de la Cour suprême indique que la Cour suprême infirma la décision de la Division Générale d'Ontario. Elle n'a pas infirmé la décision de la Cour d'appel d'Ontario.
- Des références parallèles peuvent être ajoutées aux décisions des diverses instances.

3.2.11.3 *Étapes antérieures et postérieures*

Exemples	
Décision confirmée	*Ardoch Algonquin First Nation v. Ontario* (1997), 148 D.L.R. (4ᵉ) 126 (C.A. Ont.), **infirmant [1997] 1 C.N.L.R. 66 (Div. gén. Ont.), conf. par [2000] 1 R.C.S. 950, 2000 CSC 37**.
Décision infirmée	*Canada c. Canderel ltée*, [1995] 2 C.F. 232 (C.A.), **infirmant [1994] 1 C.T.C. 2336 (C.C.I.), inf. par [1998] 1 R.C.S. 147**.

- Suivre les règles pour les étapes antérieures et postérieures des sections ci-dessus.
- Toute décision confirmative ou infirmative renvoie à la première référence. Ainsi, dans l'exemple *Canderel ltée*, la Cour fédérale d'appel a infirmé la décision de la Cour canadienne de l'impôt, mais sa propre décision a été infirmée par la Cour suprême du Canada (c'est-à-dire que la Cour suprême du Canada a confirmé la décision de la cour de l'impôt).
- Indiquer les étapes antérieures avant les étapes postérieures.

3.2.11.4 Autorisation de pourvoi

Exemples			
	Référence à la décision dont l'autorisation de pourvoi est demandée,	**cour**	**référence à la décision envers le pourvoi.**
Pourvoi demandé	*White Resource Management Ltd. v. Durish* (1992), 131 A.R. 273 (C.A.),	autorisation de pourvoi à la C.S.C. demandée.	
Pourvoi autorisée	*Westec Aerospace v. Raytheon Aircraft* (1999), 173 D.L.R. (4ᵉ) 498 (B.C.C.A.),	autorisation de pourvoi à la C.S.C. autorisée,	[2000] 1 R.C.S. xxii.
Pourvoi refusé	*Sinclair v. Law Society of Manitoba* (1997), 124 Man. R. (2ᵉ) 145 (C.A.),	autorisation de pourvoi à la C.S.C refusée,	[1998] 3 R.C.S. vii.
Pourvoi de plein droit	*Whiten v. Pilot Insurance* (1996), 132 D.L.R. (4ᵉ) 568 (Div. gén. Ont.),	pourvoi de plein droit à la C.A.	

- Inclure la référence à la décision dont l'autorisation de pourvoi est demandée.
- Indiquer la cour devant laquelle on désire faire une demande de pourvoi. Si possible, indiquer si le pourvoi a été autorisé ou refusé et renvoyer à cette décision.

3.2.12 Jugements non publiés

3.2.12.1 Common law

Exemple				
Intitulé	(date),	district judiciaire	numéro de greffe	(indication géographique et cour).
R. c. Crète	(18 avril 1991),	Ottawa	97/03674	(Ont. C.P.).

- Pour les causes provenant des provinces de *common law*, indiquer l'intitulé, la date de la décision entre parenthèses, suivie d'une virgule, du district judiciaire et du numéro de greffe, ainsi que l'indication géographique et la cour entre parenthèses.

3.2.12.2 Québec

Exemple					
Intitulé	(date),	district judiciaire	numéro de greffe,	référence à *Jurisprudence Express* (s'il y a lieu)	(indication géographique et cour).
Commission des normes du travail c. Mercier	(13 novembre 2000),	Québec	200-22-010758-993,	J.E. 2000-2257	(C.Q.).

- Pour les causes provenant du Québec, indiquer l'intitulé, la date entre parenthèses, suivie du district judiciaire et du numéro de greffe, ainsi que l'indication géographique et la cour entre parenthèses. Si possible, fournir la référence à *Jurisprudence Express* après le numéro de greffe.

3.2.13 Organes et tribunaux administratifs

3.2.13.1 Références aux recueils imprimés

Exemples	
Contradictoire	*Médecins (Ordre professionnel des) c. Latulippe (C.D. Méd.)*, [1997] D.D.O.P. 89 (TP).
Non contradictoire	*Re Citric Acid and Sodium Citrate* (1985), 10 C.E.R. 88 (Tribunal canadien des importations).

- Indiquer l'intitulé de la décision tel qu'il paraît au recueil, que le processus soit contradictoire ou non. Lorsqu'il n'y a pas d'intitulé, indiquer le numéro de la décision.
- Indiquer l'abréviation de l'organe ou du tribunal administratif entre parenthèses à la fin de la référence, si on ne peut le déduire du titre du recueil (utiliser le nom si aucune abréviation n'est trouvée). Utiliser l'abréviation employée par l'organe administratif. Noter que ces acronymes sont composés de lettres simples identifiant chaque mot important du nom et ne prennent normalement pas de points. Utiliser la plus courte abréviation pour les provinces et les territoires (par ex. Commission des valeurs mobilières du Québec : CVMQ ; Commission des valeurs mobilières de l'Ontario : CMVO ; *Newfoundland and Labrador Human Rights Commission* : NLHRC). Toutefois, les abréviations d'un recueil imprimé (par ex. O.S.C. Bull.) peuvent être différentes de celles d'un organisme administratif (par ex. OSC).
- Inclure au moins une citation parallèle si possible.

3.2.13.2 Décisions en ligne

Exemples
Plus grande accessibilité aux médias substituts par les personnes aveugles (8 mars 2002), Décision de télécom CRTC 2002-13, en ligne : CRTC <http://www.crtc.gc.ca/archive/FRN/Decisions/2002/dt2002-13.htm>.
Canada (Commissaire de la concurrence) v. Quebecor (15 janvier 2001), 2000 Trib. conc. 1, en ligne : Trib. conc. <http://www.ct-tc.gc.ca/francais/cas/ct-2000-005/0009.pdf>.
Re Bourse de Montréal (30 novembre 2001), CVMQ Décision 2001-C-0553, *Bulletin hebdomadaire* 33:12 (29 mars 2002), en ligne : CVMQ <http://www.cvmq.com/fr/decision/membre.asp>.
Re 2950995 Canada inc. (9 mai 2000), CVMO Décision, en ligne : CVMO <http://www.osc.gov.on.ca/en/Enforcement/Decisions/decisions_list.html#2001decisions>.
Re Foresight Capital Corporation (22 août 2001), 2001 BCSECCOM 848, en ligne : BCSC <http://www.bcsc.bc.ca/Enforcement/default.asp>.

- Indiquer la date de la décision, le plus précisément possible, entre parenthèses, après l'intitulé et suivie d'une virgule.
- Indiquer le numéro de la décision et l'abréviation utilisés par le tribunal ou l'agence. Noter que ces acronymes sont composés de lettres simples identifiant chaque mot important du nom et ne prennent normalement pas de points. Utiliser les plus courtes abréviations pour les provinces et les territoires (par ex. Commission des valeurs mobilières du Québec : CVMQ ; Commission des valeurs mobilières de l'Ontario : CVMO ; *Newfoundland and Labrador Human Rights Commission* : NLHRC).

3.2.14 Plaidoiries et documents à l'audience

Exemples	
Mémoire	*Renvoi relatif à la sécession du Québec*, [1998] 2 R.C.S. 217 (**mémoire de l'appelant au para. 16**).
Plaidoiries orales	*Vriend c. Alberta*, [1998] 1 R.C.S. 493 (**plaidoirie orale de l'appelant**).
Règlement hors cour	*Mulroney c. Canada (P.G.)* [**Règlement hors cour**], [1997] A.Q. n° 45 (C.S. Qué.) (QL).
Éléments de preuve	*R. c. Swain*, [1991] 1 R.C.S. 933 (**preuve, recommandation du Dr Fleming de remettre l'appelant en liberté**).

- Lors d'une référence à un mémoire, indiquer la référence complète de la cause, suivie du nom des parties et du numéro de la page ou du paragraphe, entre parenthèses. Utiliser les références complètes pour les parties. On peut créer un titre abrégé lors de la première référence au document (par ex. Mémoire de l'appelant au para. 16 [M.A.]).
- Lorsqu'on renvoie à une plaidoirie orale, indiquer la référence complète de la décision, suivie de «plaidoirie orale» et du nom de la partie, entre parenthèses.
- Lorsqu'on renvoie au règlement public hors cours, fournir l'intitulé, suivi de «Règlement hors cour» entre crochets avant les autres éléments de la référence. Si le règlement a été annoncé dans une communiqué de presse, voir la section 6.14.
- Lorsqu'on renvoie à un élément de preuve, indiquer la référence complète de la décision, suivie de «preuve» et d'une brève description de l'élément entre parenthèses.
- Lorsqu'on renvoie à une transcription, suivre les règles des jugements non publiés, à la section 3.2.12.

3.3   ROYAUME-UNI – RÉFÉRENCES AUX RECUEILS IMPRIMÉS

3.3.1 Modèle de base

Exemples						
Intitulé	(année de la décision),	[année du recueil]	volume	recueil	page	(cour).
R. v. Woollin	(1998),	[1999]		A.C.	82	(H.L.).
Burgess v. Home Office	(2000),	[2001]	1	W.L.R.	93	(C.A.).

- Les causes du Royaume-Uni suivent les mêmes règles que les jugements canadiens.
- Les *Law Reports* ont préséance sur les *Weekly Law Reports* (W.L.R.) et sur les *All England Law Reports* (All. E.R.).
- Renvoyer à un recueil général de préférence à un recueil spécialisé.
- Inclure des références parallèles si possible.

Voir la liste des recueils de jurisprudence du Royaume-Uni et leurs abréviations à l'annexe G et la liste des cours et de leurs abréviations, à l'annexe F.

3.3.2 Recueil

3.3.2.1 Law Reports

- Les *Law Reports* sont organisés en séries. Renvoyer à la série et non au *Law Reports*.

• Il n'y a pas de recueil distinct pour la Cour d'appel. Inclure l'abréviation «C.A.» pour «*Court of Appeal*» à la fin de chaque référence à une cause rendue dans cette cour.

Abréger les séries de *Law Reports* comme suit :

Appeal Cases (*House of Lords* et *Judicial Committee of the Privy Council*)	A.C.
Chancery (*Chancery Division* et décisions en appel de la *Court of Appeal*)	Ch.
Queen's (King's) Bench (Division du Banc de la Reine (du Roi) et décisions en appel de la *Court of Appeal*)	Q.B. (K.B.)
Probate (1891-1971) (*Family Division*, *Probate*, *Divorce* et *Admiralty Division*, décisions en appel et *Ecclesiastical Courts*)	P.
Family (1972 à aujourd'hui)	Fam.
Industrial Courts Reports (1972-1974) and *Industrial Cases Reports* (1975 à aujourd'hui)	I.C.R.
Law Reports Restrictive Practices (1957-1972) (*National Industrial Relations Court and Restrictive Practices Court*, décisions en appel de cette cour et les décisions de la *High Court* pertinentes aux relations industrielles)	L.R. R.P.

3.3.2.2 Modèle d'une cause de 1875 à 1890

Exemple
Bird v. Jones (1845), 7 **Q.B.D.** 742 (C.A.) [*Bird*].

• Indiquer «D.», l'abréviation de «*Division*», après l'abréviation du titre du recueil, afin de distinguer la collection des recueils datant de 1875 à 1890 de la collection plus récente qui porte le même nom.

3.3.2.3 Modèle d'une cause de 1865 à 1875

Exemple
Currie v. Misa (1875), **L.R. 10 Ex.** 153.

• Indiquer «L.R.», l'abréviation de «*Law Reports*», avant le volume, afin de distinguer cette collection de recueils de la collection plus récente qui porte le même nom.

3.3.2.4 *Modèle d'une cause de 1537 à 1865*

Exemple
Lord Byron v. Johnston (1816), 2 Mer. 28, 35 E.R. 851 (Ch.).

- Si possible, renvoyer au recueil nommé (*nominate reporter*) et fournir une référence parallèle aux *English Reports* si disponible.
- Les English Reports et les All England Reports Reprints sont des réimpressions.

3.3.2.5 Yearbooks

Exemple							
Intitulé	(année),	*yearbook*	trimestre	année du règne	monarque,	numéro du plaidoyer (*plea*),	numéro du feuillet (*folio*).
Doige's Case	(1422),	Y.B.	Trin.	20	Hen. VI,	pl. 4,	fol. 34.

- Utiliser les abréviations de trimestres suivantes : «Mich.» pour «Michaelmas», «Hil.» pour «Hilary», «Pach.» pour «Easter» et «Trin.» pour «Trinity».
- Indiquer l'année du règne en chiffres arabes.
- Référer au monarque en utilisant des chiffres romains.
- Abréger «plea» par «pl.».
- Abréger «folio» par «fol.».

3.3.2.6 *Réimpressions*

Exemple		
Référence au *yearbook*	reproduit dans	référence à la réimpression.
Beauver v. Abbot of St. Albans (1312), Y.B. Mich. 6 Edw. II,	reproduit dans	(1921) 38 Selden Soc. 32.

- Lorsqu'on renvoie à une réimpression, fournir autant de renseignements que possible concernant l'entrée originale du *yearbook*. Renvoyer à la source dans laquelle se trouve la réimpression.

3.3.3 Écosse, Irlande jusqu'à 1924 et Irlande du Nord

Exemples	
Écosse	*M'Courtney v. HM Advocate*, [1977] J.C. 68 (H.C.J. **Scot.**).
Irlande	*Hardman v. Maffet* (1884), 13 **L.R. Ir.** 499 (Ch.D.).
Irlande du Nord	*R. v. Crooks*, [1999] **N.I.** 226 (C.A.).

- Lorsque le titre du recueil n'indique pas l'indication géographique, indiquer «Scot.» pour «*Scotland*», «Ir.» pour «*Ireland*», et «N.I.» pour «*Northern Ireland*», entre parenthèses à la fin de la référence.
- Indiquer le nom de la cour, car chaque volume est divisé en parties selon la cour et chaque partie est paginée séparément.
- Voir Annexe F pour les abréviations des tribunaux et l'annexe G pour celles des recueils.

3.3.4 Juge

Abréviations des titres principaux des juges :

Lord Justice	L.J.
Lord Justices	L.JJ.
Master of the Rolls	M.R.
Lord Chancellor	L.C.
Vice Chancellor	V.C.
Baron	B.
Chief Baron	C.B.

N.B. Pour plus d'information sur les références à la jurisprudence du Royaume-Uni, consulter Donald Raistrick, *Index to Legal Citations and Abbreviations*, 2e éd., Londres, Bowker-Saur, 1993.

3.4   ÉTATS-UNIS – RÉFÉRENCES AUX RECUEILS IMPRIMÉS

3.4.1   Modèle de base

Exemples								
Intitulé,	vol.	recueil	série	page	référence précise	(indication géographique et/ou cour	année).	(autre information) (s'il y a lieu).
People v. Kevorkian,	527	N.W.	2d	714		(Mich.	1994).	
Roche Holding Ltd.,	113	F.T.C.		1086	aux pp. 1087-90		(1990).	
Headquarters Space & Missile,	103	Lab. Arb. (BNA)		1198			(1995)	(McCurdy, Arb.).

- Les références aux décisions administratives et à l'arbitrage suivent le même modèle que celui qui prévaut pour les jugements.
- Pour l'arbitrage, fournir le nom de l'arbitre suivi d'une virgule et de «Arb.» entre parenthèses à la fin de la référence.

3.4.2   Intitulé

Exemples	
	California v. United States
	Larez v. Los Angeles (City of)
NON	*State of California v. United States of America*
	Larez v. L.A.

- Indiquer l'intitulé selon les règles des jugements canadiens.
- Lorsqu'une des parties est un état ou un pays, utiliser le nom couramment utilisé plutôt que la forme descriptive ou que l'abréviation.
- Si une des parties est une ville dont le nom pourrait se confondre avec celui d'un État, indiquer les renseignements permettant de l'identifier entre parenthèses en anglais : «New York (City of)» ou «Washington (D.C.)».

3.4.3 Recueil et série

Exemples
Lotus Development v. Borland International, 140 **F.3d** 70 (1ᵉʳ Cir. 1998) [*Lotus*].   *Scott v. Sanford*, 60 **U.S.** (19 How.) 393 (1857).

- Après l'intitulé, indiquer le numéro du volume, l'abréviation du recueil, le numéro de la série et la première page de l'arrêt. Il n'y a pas d'espace entre l'abréviation du recueil et le numéro de la série.
- Avant 1875, les *U.S. Reports* sont aussi numérotés en ordre consécutif selon chaque éditeur. Indiquer ce numéro ainsi que le nom de l'éditeur entre parenthèses après «U.S.».
- À l'exception de Cranch et Black, le nom du rédacteur est abrégé de la manière suivante :

Wallace	Wall.
Black	Black
Howard	How.
Peters	Pet.
Wheaton	Wheat.
Cranch	Cranch
Dallas	Dal.

Les recueils principaux sont abrégés de la manière suivante :

Atlantic Reporter	A.
California Reporter	Cal.
Federal Reporter	F.
Federal Supplement	F. Supp.
Lawyers' Edition	L. Ed. 2d
New York Supplement	N.Y.S.
North Eastern Reporter	N.E.
North Western Reporter	N.W.
Pacific Reporter	P.

South Eastern Reporter	S.E.
South Western Reporter	S.W.
Southern Reporter	So.
Supreme Court Reporter	S. Ct.
United States Reports	U.S.
United States Law Week	U.S.L.W.

- Pour la Cour suprême des États Unis, faire référence aux recueils dans l'ordre de préférence suivant : «U.S., S. Ct., L. Ed. 2d, U.S.L.W.»
- Pour les cours fédérales, renvoyer à F. ou F. Supp.
- Pour les cours d'États, renvoyer au recueil régional plutôt qu'au recueil de l'État.

Pour une liste plus étoffée des recueils et leurs abréviations, voir l'annexe G.

3.4.4   Référence précise

Exemples
United States v. McVeigh, 153 F.3d 1166 **à la p. 1170** (10ᵉ Cir. 1998).
McVeigh, *supra* note 1 **à la p. 1173**.

- Indiquer «à la p.» avant la référence précise.

3.4.5   Cour

3.4.5.1   *Cours fédérales*

Exemples	
Cour suprême des États-Unis	*Roe v. Wade*, 410 **U.S.** 113 (1973). *AT&T v. Iowa Utilities Board*, 66 U.S.L.W. 3387 (**U.S.** 17 novembre 1997).
Cours d'appel	*Microsystems v. Microsoft*, 188 F.3d 1115 (**9ᵉ Cir.** 1999).
Cours de district	*Yniguez v. Mofford*, 730 F. Supp. 309 (**D. Ariz.** 1990).

- Lorsqu'on fait référence à un arrêt de la Cour suprême des États-Unis dans un recueil autre que le *United States Law Week* (U.S.L.W.), aucune mention de la Cour n'est nécessaire. Toutefois, si l'on renvoie au U.S.L.W., indiquer «U.S.», la cour et la date entre parenthèses à la fin de la référence.

- Abréger les cours d'appel de chaque circuit en précisant le numéro du circuit.
- Utiliser «D.C. Cir.» pour désigner la Cour d'appel du circuit du *District of Columbia* et «Fed. Cir.» pour désigner la Cour du circuit fédéral.
- Pour les cours de district, fournir l'abréviation du nom du district.

3.4.5.2 Cours d'États

Exemples
Peevyhouse v. Garland Coal & Mining, 382 P.2d 109 (**Okla. Sup. Ct.** 1963).
Truman v. Thomas, 165 **Cal.** Rptr. 308 (**Sup. Ct.** 1980).
Hinterlong v. Baldwin, 308 **Ill. App.** 3d 441 (1999).

- Indiquer le nom de la cour et l'indication géographique entre parenthèses, en utilisant les abréviations des annexes B et F.
- Omettre le nom de l'État si celui-ci fait partie du titre du recueil.
- Omettre le nom de la cour s'il s'agit du plus haut tribunal de l'État.

3.4.6 Année de la décision

- Fournir l'année de décision entre parenthèses à la fin de la référence, même s'il y a des références parallèles.

N.B. Pour plus d'information sur les références à la jurisprudence américaine, consulter *The Bluebook : A Uniform System of Citation*, 17ᵉ éd., Cambridge (Mass.), Harvard Law Review Association, 2000.

3.5   FRANCE – RÉFERENCÉS AUX RECUEILS IMPRIMÉS

3.5.1 Modèle de base

Exemples

	Tribunal ou chambre (s'il y a lieu)	ville (s'il y a lieu),	date,	*intitulé* (s'il y a lieu,	recueil.	année du recueil.	partie du recueil. (s'il y a lieu)	page et/ou numéro de la décision	(note) (s'il y a lieu).
Cour de cassation	Cass. civ. 2ᵉ,		14 juin 2001,		D.	2001.	Jur.	3075	(note Didier Cholet).
Cour d'appel		Paris,	12 janvier 2000,		J.C.P.	2000.	II.	10433	(note Philippe Pierre).
Cour de première instance	Trib. gr. inst.	Mans,	7 septembre 1999,		J.C.P.	2000.	II.	10258	(note Colette Saujot).

N.B. Il n'y a pas d'espace entre les mentions de l'année, de la partie du recueil et de la page (par ex. «2000.II.10258»).

3.5.2 Cour

3.5.2.1 *Tribunaux de première instance*

Exemples

Tribunal	ville,	date,	*intitulé* (s'il y a lieu),	recueil	année de publication du recueil.	semestre (s'il y a lieu)	partie du recueil.	page	(note) (s'il y a lieu).
Trib. admin.	Nantes,	27 novembre 1981,	*Mme Robin*,	Rec.	1981.			544.	
Trib. gr. inst.	Paris,	10 septembre 1998,		Gaz. Pal.	1999.	1ᵉʳ sem.	Jur.	37.	

- Indiquer la ville où le tribunal siège.
- Lorsqu'on renvoie à la *Gazette du Palais* (Gaz. Pal.), les espaces entre le recueil, l'année, le semestre, la partie et la page doivent être comme suit : «Gaz. Pal. 1983. 2ᵉ sem. Jur.623».

Abréger le nom des tribunaux comme suit :

Tribunal administratif	Trib. admin.
Tribunal civil ou Tribunal de première instance (tribunal civil de droit commun avant 1958)	Trib. civ.
Tribunal commercial	Trib. com.
Tribunal correctionnel	Trib. corr.
Tribunal de grande instance (tribunal civil de droit commun après 1958)	Trib. gr. inst.
Tribunal d'instance (tribunal civil de droit commun pour les petites créances après 1958)	Trib. inst.

Pour une liste plus complète des cours et tribunaux, voir Annexe F.

3.5.2.2 Cour d'appel

Exemple							
Ville,	date,	recueil	année de publication du recueil.	semestre. (s'il y a lieu)	partie du recueil	page	(note).
Orléans,	23 octobre 1997,	Gaz. Pal.	1999.	1er sem.	Jur.	217	(note Benoît de Roque- feuil).

- Omettre le nom de la cour.
- Indiquer seulement la ville où siège le tribunal.

3.5.2.3 Cour de cassation

Exemple						
Chambre,	date,	recueil	année de publication du recueil.	partie du recueil.	page,	numéro de la décision (s'il y a lieu).
Cass. Civ. 1re,	30 mars 1999,	Bull. Civ.	1999.	I.	77,	n° 118.

Abréger le nom des cours et des chambres de la façon suivante :

Chambre civile, selon qu'il s'agit de la première, la deuxième ou la troisième chambre (après 1952)	Cass. civ. 1re, Cass. civ. 2e, Cass. civ. 3^e
Chambre commerciale	Cass. com.
Chambre sociale	Cass. soc.
Chambre criminelle	Cass. crim.
Chambre des requêtes	Cass. req.
Chambres réunies (avant1967)	Cass. Ch. réun.
Assemblée plénière (après1967)	Cass. Ass. plén.
Chambre mixte	Cass. mixte

3.5.2.4   *Conseil d'État*

Exemple					
Cour,	date,	*intitulé,*	recueil	année.	page.
Cons. d'État,	27 janvier 1984,	*Ordre des avocats de la Polynésie française,*	Rec.	1984.	20.

• Abréger «Conseil d'État» par «Cons. d'État».

3.5.2.5   *Conseil constitutionnel*

Exemple						
Cour,	date,	*intitulé,*	recueil	année.	page,	numéro de la décision.
Cons. constitutionnel,	25 juin 1986,	*Privatisations,*	Rec.	1986.	61,	86-207 DC.

• Abréger «Conseil constitutionnel» par «Cons. constitutionnel».
• Indiquer le numéro de la décision à la fin de la référence.

3.5.3 Intitulé

Exemple
Cass. com., 22 janvier 1991, ***Ouest Abri***, D. 1991.Jur.175.

- Normalement, l'intitulé des causes françaises n'est pas indiqué.
- L'intitulé devrait être indiqué dans les circonstances suivantes :
  - lorsqu'on renvoie à une décision d'un tribunal administratif ou du Conseil d'État ;
  - lorsqu'on renvoie à un jugement non publié ou à un jugement résumé dans la partie «Sommaire» d'un recueil ;
  - pour éviter la confusion (par ex. lorsqu'un tribunal a rendu deux décisions un même jour) ;
  - lorsque la cause est mieux connue sous le nom des parties que selon les renseignements habituels.
- L'intitulé est indiqué en italique, entre virgules, après la date à laquelle la décision a été rendue.

3.5.4 Recueil

Exemples						
Cour,	date,	recueil	année de publication du recueil.	semestre (s'il y a lieu).	partie du recueil.	page et/ou numéro de décision.
Cass. Civ. 3e,	23 juin 1999,	J.C.P.	2000.		II.	10333.
Cass Soc.,	3 février 1998,	Gaz. Pal.	1998.	1er sem.	Jur.	176.

- Il y a un espace entre le recueil et l'année (par ex. «J.C.P. 1993.»). Par contre, il n'y a pas d'espace entre l'année, le semestre, la partie et la page (par ex. «1993.II.22063»).

Voici une liste non exhaustive des recueils :

Recueil Dalloz et *Recueil Dalloz et Sirey* (1945-présent)	D.
Gazette du Palais	Gaz. Pal.
Bulletin de la Cour de cassation, section civile	Bull. civ.
Semaine Juridique (1937-présent)	J.C.P.

| Recueil des décisions du Conseil d'État ou Recueil Lebon | R.C.E. ou Rec. |
| Actualité juridique de droit administratif | A.J.D.A. |

Voir l'annexe G pour une liste plus complète des abréviations des titres des recueils.

3.5.5 Année

| Exemple |
| Paris, 5 février 1999, Gaz. Pal. **1999**. 2e sem. Jur.452. |

- Indiquer l'année de publication du volume après l'abréviation du recueil.

3.5.6 Semestre

- Indiquer le numéro du semestre après l'année de publication lorsqu'on renvoie à la *Gazette du Palais* (Gaz. Pal.).

3.5.7 Partie du recueil

- Quand la partie du recueil est numérotée, indiquer le numéro de la partie en chiffres romains après l'année de publication.
- Quand la partie du recueil n'est pas numérotée, indiquer l'abréviation du titre de la partie.
- Exception : ne pas inclure la partie du recueil dans le cas du *Recueil Lebon* (Rec.) ou de l'*Actualité juridique de droit administratif* (A.J.D.A.).

Abréviation des titres des parties des recueils :

Assemblée plénière	Ass. plén.
Chambre mixte	Ch. mixte
Chambres des requêtes	Req.
Chambres réunies	Ch. réun.
Chroniques	Chron.
Doctrine	Doctr.
Informations rapides	Inf.
Jurisprudence	Jur.
Législation, Lois et décrets, Textes de lois, etc.	Lég.

Panorama de jurisprudence	Pan.
Sommaire	Somm.

3.5.8 Page et numéro de la décision

Exemples	
Semaine juridique	Ass. plén., 6 novembre 1998, J.C.P., 1999.II.**10000 bis**.
Bulletin de la Cour de cassation	Cass. civ. 2ᵉ, 7 juin 2001, Bull. civ. 2001, II.**75, nº 110**.

- Indiquer la première page de la décision après la partie du recueil ou son année de publication.
- Pour la *Semaine juridique*, indiquer le numéro de la décision (par ex. «10000 bis»).
- Pour les *Bulletin de la Cour de cassation*, mentionner le numéro de page et le numéro de la décision, séparés par une virgule.

3.5.9 Référence précise

Exemple
Trib. gr. inst. Narbonne, 12 mars 1999, Gaz. Pal. 1999. 1ᵉʳ sem. Jur.405 **à la p. 406**.

- Étant donné la concision de la plupart des jugements, les références précises ne sont guère employées. S'il faut en mettre une, elle se place après le numéro de la première page, introduite par «à la p.».

3.5.10 Référence parallèle

Exemple	
Première référence,	référence parallèle.
Cass. civ. 1ʳᵉ, 26 mai 1999, Bull. civ. 1999.I.115, nº 175.	J.C.P. 1999.II.10112.

- On peut indiquer une ou plusieurs références parallèles.

3.5.11 Notes, rapports et conclusions

Exemple
Cass. civ. 1re, 6 juillet 1999, J.C.P. 1999.II.10217 **(note Thierry Garé)**.

- Mentionner si la décision est suivie d'une note, d'un rapport ou d'une conclusion à la fin de la référence.
- Inscrire entre parenthèses «note», «rapport» ou «concl.», suivi du nom de l'auteur.

3.6   AUSTRALIE – RÉFÉRENCES AUX RECUEILS IMPRIMÉS

3.6.1   Modèle de base

Exemples						
Intitulé	(année du décision),	[année du recueil]	volume	recueil	page	(indication géographiqu e et/ou cour) (s'il y a lieu).
CDJ v. VAJ	(1998),		197	C.L.R.	172	(H.C.A.).
Standard Portland Cement Company Pty. Ltd. v. Good	(1983),		57	A.L.J.R.	151	(P.C.).
Thwaites v. Ryan	(1983),	[1984]		V.R.	65	(S.C.).
Bentley v. Furlan,		[1999]	3	V.R.	63	(S.C.).

- Les références aux jugements australiens suivent le même modèle de référence que celui qui prévaut pour les jugements canadiens.
- Renvoyer à un recueil général plutôt qu'à un recueil spécialisé.

3.6.2 Recueil

3.6.2.1 Law Reports

Abréger les recueils comme suit :

Commonwealth Law Reports (1903-présent) — Officiel	C.L.R.
Australian Law Reports (1973-présent)	A.L.R.
Federal Court Reports (1984-présent) — Officiel	F.C.R.
Australian Law Journal Reports (1958-présent)	A.L.J.R.
Federal Law Reports (1956-présent)	F.L.R.
New South Wales Law Reports (1971-présent) — Officiel	N.S.W.L.R.
Queensland State Reports (1902-1957) — Officiel	Qd. S.R.
Queensland Reports (1958-présent) — Officiel	Qd. R.
South Australia State Reports (1922-présent) — Officiel	S.A.S.R.
Tasmanian Law Reports (1896-1940) — Officiel	Tas. L.R.
Tasmanian State Reports (1941-1978)	Tas. R.
Tasmanian Reports (1979-présent) — Officiel	Tas. R.
Victorian Law Reports (1886-1956)	V.L.R.
Victorian Reports (1957-présent) — Officiel	V.R.
Western Australia Law Reports (1899-1959)	W.A.L.R.
Western Australia Law Reports (1960-présent) — Officiel	W.A.R.
Australian Capital Territory Reports (1973-présent)	A.C.T.R.
Northern Territory Reports (1978-présent)	N.T.R.
Northern Territory Law Reports (1992-présent)	N.T.L.R.

- Pour les décisions du *Privy Council* (P.C.) et de la *High Court of Australia* (H.C.A.), faire référence aux C.L.R., A.L.R. et au A.A.L.R. selon cet ordre de préférence.
- Pour les autres décisions de cours générales, renvoyer au F.C.R. de préférence.
- Pour les États et territoires australiens, renvoyer au recueil étatique ou territorial officiel si possible, sinon utiliser un des recueils non officiels.

3.6.3 Cour

Inclure le nom de la cour fédérale, étatique ou territoriale entre parenthèses à la fin de la référence de la façon suivante :

Privy Council (Australia)	P.C.
High Court of Australia	H.C.A.
Federal Court of Australia	F.C.A.
Supreme Court of Queensland — Court of Appeal	Qld. C.A.
Supreme Court of Queensland	Qld. S.C.
Supreme Court of the Australian Capital Territory	A.C.T.S.C.
Supreme Court of New South Wales	N.S.W.S.C.
Supreme Court of New South Wales — Court of Appeal	N.S.W.C.A.
Supreme Court of Tasmania	Tas. S.C.
Supreme Court of Victoria — Court of Appeal	Vic. S.C.A.
Supreme Court of Victoria	Vic. S.C.
Supreme Court of Southern Australia	S.A.S.C.
District Court of Southern Australia	S.A.D.C.
Supreme Court of Western Australia	W.A.S.C.
Supreme Court of Western Australia — Court of Appeal	W.A.S.C.A.
Supreme Court of the Northern Territory	N.T.S.C.

- Si l'indication géographique des tribunaux étatiques et territoriaux est évidente, n'indiquer que l'instance de la cour.

3.7   NOUVELLE-ZÉLANDE – RÉFÉRENCES AUX RECUEILS IMPRIMÉS

3.7.1 Modèle de base

Exemples						
Intitulé	(année de la décision),	[année du recueil]	volume	recueil	page	(indication géographique et/ou cour) (s'il y a lieu).
Erbium Ltd. v. Gregory,		[1998]		D.C.R.	1119.	
Ryde Holdings Ltd. v. Sorenson,		[1988]	2	N.Z.L.R.	157	(H.C.).

- Les références aux jugements de la Nouvelle-Zélande suivent le même modèle de référence que celui qui prévaut pour les jugements canadiens.
- Renvoyer à un recueil général de préférence à un recueil spécialisé.

3.7.2 Recueils

3.7.2.1 Law Reports

- Les *Law Reports* sont divisés en séries. Renvoyer aux séries plutôt qu'aux *Law Reports*.
- Puisqu'il n'y a pas de recueil particulier pour le *Judicial Committee of the Privy Council* (post-1932), la *Court of Appeal* ou la *High Court*, inclure «P.C.», «C.A.», ou «H.C.» à la fin de chaque référence à une décision de cette cour.

Abréger les séries *Law Reports* comme suit :

New Zealand Law Reports (1883-présent) (Privy Council, Court of Appeal, High Court)	N.Z.L.R.
New Zealand Privy Council Cases (1840-1932)	N.Z.P.C.C.
Gazette Law Reports (1898-1953) (Court of Appeal, Supreme Court (High Court), Court of Arbitration)	G.L.R.
District Court Reports (1980-présent)	N.Z.D.C.R.
Magistrates' Court Reports (1939-1979)	M.C.D.

Magistrates' Court Reports (1906-1953)	M.C.R.
Book of Awards (1894-1991) (Arbitration Court, Court of Appeal)	B.A.
Employment Reports of New Zealand (1991-présent) (Court of Appeal, Labour Court, Aircrew Industrial Tribunal)	E.R.N.Z.
New Zealand Industrial Law Reports (1987-1990) (Labour Court, Court of Appeal, Aircrew Industrial Tribunal)	N.Z.I.L.R.
Judgments of the Arbitration Court of New Zealand (1979-1986) (Arbitration Court, Court of Appeal)	N.Z.A.C.
New Zealand Family Law Reports (1981-présent) (Privy Council, Court of Appeal, High Court, Family Court, Youth Court, District Court)	N.Z.F.L.R.
Criminal Reports of New Zealand (1993-présent) (Court of Appeal, High Court)	C.R.N.Z.

3.7.3 Cour

Privy Council (Nouvelle-Zélande)	P.C.
New Zealand Court of Appeal	N.Z.C.A.
New Zealand High Court	N.Z.H.C.
District Court of New Zealand	D.C.N.Z.
Magistrates' Court of New Zealand	Mag. Ct. N.Z.
Coroners Court	Cor. Ct.
New Zealand Employment Court	N.Z. Empl. Ct.
Environment Court	Env. Ct.
Family Court of New Zealand	Fam. Ct. N.Z.
Maori Land Court / Te Kooti Whenua Maori	Maori Land Ct.
Maori Appellate Court	Maori A.C.
New Zealand Youth Court	N.Z.Y.C.
Waitangi Tribunal / Te Rōpū Whakamana i te Tiriti o Waitangi	Waitangi Trib.

3.8   SINGAPOUR – RÉFÉRENCES AUX RECUEILS IMPRIMÉS

3.8.1   Modèle de base

Exemples						
Intitulé	(année de la décision),	[année du recueil]	volume	recueil	page	(indication géographique et/ou cour) (s'il y a lieu).
Er Joo Nguang v. Public Prosecutor,		[2000]	2	Sing. L.R.	645	(H.C.).
Jeyaretnam Joshua Benjamin v. Lee Kuan Yew,		[1991]	2	M.L.J.	135	(Sing. C.A.).
Re Ong Yew Teck	(1960),		26	M.L.J.	67	(Sing. H.C.).

• Indiquer le nom au complet des parties afin d'identifier la pluralité des pratiques culturelles gouvernantes à Singapour.
• Inclure l'abréviation «Sing.» sauf s'il s'agit d'une référence au *Singapore Law Reports*.

3.8.2   Décisions non publiées

Exemple			
Intitulé	(date),	numéro de la décision	(indication géographique et/ou cour) (s'il y a lieu).
Public Prosecutor v. Loh Chai Huat	(31 mai 2001),	D.A.C. No. 36923 de 2000	(Sing. Dist. Ct.).

3.8.3   Recueils législatifs

Les recueils principaux sont abrégés de la manière suivante :

Singapore Law Reports	Sing. L.R.
Malayan Law Journal	M.L.J.
Criminal Law Aid Scheme News	C.L.A.S.N.
Straits Settlements Law Reports	S.S.L.R.

3.8.4   Cours

Le nom des cours s'abrège comme suit :

Court of Appeal	C.A.
High Court	H.C.
District Court	Dist. Ct.
Magistrates' Court	Mag. Ct.

• Il n'existe pas de subdivision pour les cours de district à Singapour.

3.9   AFRIQUE DU SUD – RÉFÉRENCES AUX RECUEILS IMPRIMÉS

3.9.1   Modèle de base

Exemples						
Intitulé	(année de la décision),	[année du recueil]	volume	recueil	page	(indication géographique et/ou cour) (s'il y a lieu).
Oosthuizen v. Stanley,		[1938]		A.D.	322	(S. Afr. S.C.).
Messina Associated Carriers v. Kleinhaus,		[2001]	3	S. Afr. L.R.	868	(S.C.A.).

- Les références aux jugements de l'Afrique de Sud suivent le même modèle de référence des jugements canadiens.
- Renvoyer aux *South African Law Reports* ou *Butterworths Constitutional Law Reports* si possible.

3.9.2 Recueil

Abréger les recueils principaux de la manière suivante :

Butterworths Constitutional Law Reports	B. Const. L.R.
South African Law Reports, Appellate Division (1910-1946)	A.D.
South African Law Reports (1947-présent)	S. Afr. L.R.

Pour une liste complète des recueils, voir l'annexe G.

3.9.3 Tribunal

Abréger le nom des tribunaux comme suit :

Bophuthatswana High Court	Boph. H.C.
Cape Provincial Division	Cape Prov. Div.
Ciskei High Court	Ciskei H.C.
Constitutional Court of South Africa	S. Afr. Const. Ct.
Durban and Coast Local Division	D&C Local Div.
Eastern Cape Division	E. Cape Div.
Labour Court of South Africa	S. Afr. Labour Ct.
Labour Court of Appeal of South Africa	S. Afr. Labour C.A.
Land Claims Court of South Africa	S. Afr. Land Claims Ct.
Natal Provincial Division	Natal Prov. Div.
Northern Cape Division	N. Cape Div.
Orange Free State Provincial Division	O.F.S. Prov. Div.
South-Eastern Cape Division	S-E. Cape Div.
Supreme Court of Appeal of South Africa	S. Afr. S.C.
Transkei High Court	Transkei H.C.
Transvaal Provincial Division	Transv. Prov. Div.
Witwatersrand Local Division	Wit. Local Div.
Venda High Court	Venda H.C.

3.10 LA RÉFÉRENCE NEUTRE

3.10.1 Relation avec la référence des recueils imprimés

Une référence neutre permet l'identification permanente d'une cause indépendante de la banque de données électronique ou du recueil imprimé dans lesquels elle est publiée. La cour assigne la référence neutre lorsqu'une décision est rendue. Puisque les références neutres émanent directement de la Cour, on ne peut renvoyer à une décision par la référence neutre si aucune référence neutre n'est introduite par la décision.

Le Comité canadien de la référence, qui a créé le système de référence neutre au Canada, a suggéré qu'il serait approprié pour les usagers d'inclure la référence neutre comme référence parallèle suivant une référence traditionnelle à un recueil imprimé une fois la décision publiée dans un recueil imprimé. Le Comité a suggéré que la référence neutre n'apparaisse seule que lorsque la décision à laquelle elle renvoie a déjà été publiée dans un recueil imprimé.

On compte deux désavantages principaux à la proposition du Comité. Premièrement, une fois la décision publiée, les auteurs devront ajouter une référence neutre parallèle à la suite des références traditionnelles à la décision dans un recueil imprimé. Cette étape supplémentaire n'était pas nécessaire avant l'introduction de la référence neutre. Deuxièmement, un autre bien-fondé de la référence neutre identifié par le Comité est celui de fournir une identification permanente et universelle d'une décision. Exiger que la référence neutre soit utilisée comme référence parallèle une fois la décision publiée dans un recueil imprimé insinue d'une part que la méthode d'identification la plus permanente est la référence traditionnelle au recueil imprimé, d'autre part que la référence neutre sert principalement de remplacement pour la référence aux sources électroniques.

Quoi qu'il en soit, le net avantage d'utiliser la référence neutre comme référence parallèle, plutôt que comme seule référence, est qu'il est plus facile pour les lecteurs de trouver des décisions dans des recueils imprimés lorsqu'ils possèdent une référence directe à l'ouvrage spécifique et à la page du recueil imprimé. En contrepartie, un lecteur qui n'a qu'une référence neutre devra chercher dans les index du recueil imprimé pour trouver la décision. Ces index, jusqu'à présent, ne cataloguent pas les décisions par référence neutre.

Par conséquent, nous trouvons plus efficace de suivre la proposition du Comité jusqu'à ce que la recherche d'une décision par l'utilisation d'une référence neutre dans les recueils imprimés soit facilitée.

N.B. Lorsqu'une référence neutre est disponible pour une décision, elle doit paraître comme référence parallèle quand la décision à laquelle elle renvoie est publiée dans un recueil imprimé (qu'il soit officiel, semi-officiel ou non officiel). Une référence neutre ne doit être insérée seule que si, au moment de l'écriture, la décision à laquelle elle renvoie n'a pas été publiée dans un recueil imprimé.

3.10.2 Modèle de base

Exemples						
		Corps de la référence neutre			renseignements facultatifs	
Intitulé,	référence traditionnelle si publiée,	année	code de désignation du tribunal	numéro de séquence de la décision	numéro de paragraphe	note.
R. c. Law,		2002	CSC	10	¶ 22.	
R. v. Sangha	(2001), 288 A.R. 170,	2001	ABQB	373	para. 8.	
R. v. Rezvi		2002	UKHL	3.		
Ordre des arpenteurs-géomètres du Québec c. Tremblay		2001	QCTP	24		note 14.
Preston v. Chow,		2002	MBCA	34	¶ 29-30, 33.	

- Le corps de la référence est assigné par la cour et ne peut être changé.
- Il n'y a pas de points dans une référence neutre (excepté suivant le c. dans le type de la cause et à la fin de la référence).
- L'indication géographique et le niveau de la cour sont toujours identifiés dans une référence neutre. Qu'une référence neutre soit présentée seule ou soit incluse comme référence parallèle, ne jamais inclure d'autres abréviations d'indications géographiques et de cours.
- Quand la référence neutre est utilisée à titre de référence parallèle, elle doit succéder à toutes autres références parallèles aux recueils imprimés.
- Renvoyer aux références neutres des cours d'autres pays de la même manière.
- Quand une référence neutre est disponible, ne jamais inclure un service électronique (par ex. QL).

3.10.2.1 Corps de la référence – intitulé

L'intitulé est le même que celui utilisé dans la référence aux recueils imprimés (voir la section 3.2.2).

3.10.2.2 Corps de la référence – année

L'année est l'année pendant laquelle la décision a été rendue par la cour. Si la date de la décision est fixée plus tard, l'année peut être l'année de l'entrée de la cause dans le registre de la cour.

3.10.2.3 Corps de la référence – code de désignation du tribunal

Le code de désignation du tribunal est assigné par la cour et peut contenir jusqu'à huit caractères. Le code de désignation débute par un préfixe de deux caractères qui, à l'exception des Territoires du Nord-Ouest, correspond au code de l'indication géographique traditionnelle de deux lettres (celles-ci sont les mêmes en anglais et en français).

Alberta	AB
Colombie-Britannique	BC
Île-du-Prince-Édouard	PE
Manitoba	MB
Nouveau-Brunswick	NB
Nouvelle-Écosse	NS
Nunavut	NU
Ontario	ON
Québec	QC
Saskatchewan	SK
Terre-Neuve et Labrador	NF (NL?)
Territoires du Nord-Ouest	NWT or NT
Yukon	YK

- L'acronyme naturel du tribunal de la cour suit ce préfixe, mais doit omettre la réintroduction de toute lettre représentant l'indication géographique. Par exemple, Le Tribunal des professions du Québec est «QCTP» et non «QCTPQ».
- Au moment de la publication du *Manuel*, le préfixe de deux lettres pour Terre-Neuve et Labrador est «NF». Le nom de la province ayant changé en 2001, le préfixe pourrait devenir «NL».

Un code de désignation du tribunal:
Un code de désignation sera utilisé quand :

- un tribunal rend habituellement les décisions dans une seule langue officielle,

- un tribunal n'est pas bilingue, ou
- si un tribunal est bilingue, il utilise le même acronyme pour les décisions en anglais et en français. Dans ce cas, un code suffixe peut être ajouté au code de désignation du tribunal indiquant la langue de la décision. Par exemple, une décision du CRTC en anglais peut utiliser le code de désignation «CRTCE» et une décision en français peut utiliser le code de désignation «CRTCF».

Deux codes de désignation du tribunal :

Deux codes de désignation du tribunal ou plus seront utilisés quand les cours rendent régulièrement des décisions dans deux langues officielles ou plus et quand la cour souhaite utiliser différents acronymes pour les décisions dans chaque langue (contrairement au CRTC, par exemple). À titre d'exemple, les codes de désignation de la Cour suprême du Canada sont SCC et CSC. Quand il existe deux codes de désignation ou plus, utiliser le code qui correspond à la langue dans laquelle vous écrivez.

3.10.2.4 Corps de la référence – numéro de séquence de la décision

- Le numéro de séquence est assigné par la cour. Ce numéro revient à «1» le 1er janvier de chaque année.
- Pour une décision orale publiée après que le jugement a été rendu, on devra simplement lui assigner le prochain numéro de séquence disponible pour l'année durant laquelle la décision orale a été rendue. L'année reflétera ainsi l'année précise pendant laquelle la décision orale a été rendue.
- Pour les décisions orales publiées après qu'un jugement a été rendu, la cour assigne le prochain numéro de séquence disponible pour l'année pendant laquelle la décision a été rendue. Ainsi, l'année de la référence neutre signifiera l'année pendant laquelle la décision orale a été rendue.

3.10.2.5 Renseignements facultatifs (référence précise)

- Une référence précise n'est faite qu'au premier recueil. Par conséquent, n'inclure une référence précise que si la décision n'a pas été publiée dans un recueil imprimé et que si la référence neutre paraît seule.
- La référence à un paragraphe dans une décision est signifiée par l'utilisation du caractère ¶ ou du terme «para.».
- Dans une décision, la référence aux notes de bas de page ou aux notes en fin de texte est signifiée par l'utilisation du terme «note».

3.11 RÉFÉRENCE AUX SERVICES ÉLECTRONIQUES

Utiliser les abréviations suivantes pour faire référence à un service électronique :

Australian Legal Information Institute	AustLII
Azimut (produit par SOQUIJ)	Azimut
British and Irish Legal Information Institute	BILII
Butterworths Services	Butterworths
Institut canadien d'information juridique	IIJCan
*e*Carswell	eC
Lawnet	Lawnet
Legifrance	Legifrance
LexisNexis	Lexis
LexUM	LexUM
Quicklaw	QL
Westlaw	WL

- Les services électroniques reproduisent des jugements imprimés sur support papier. On peut également avoir accès aux jugements non disponibles sur support papier.

3.11.1 Jugements publiés dans les recueils imprimés

3.11.1.1 Aucune citation ou référence précise utilisée

Si aucune citation à un jugement ou aucune référence précise n'est fournie, renvoyer à la décision de la même manière que lorsqu'on renvoie à un recueil imprimé sans faire référence à un service électronique.

Exemple
Vanderburgh v. ScotiaMcLeod Inc. (1992), 4 Alta. L.R. (3e) 138 at 140, [1992] 6 W.W.R. 673 à la p. 675 (Q.B.).

3.11.1.2 Citation d'un jugement ou référence précise

- Les références traditionnelles ne sont pas des références précises. Lorsqu'on renvoie au R.C.S., par exemple, les lecteurs présupposeront que le recueil imprimé était la source de la citation ou de la référence précise. Lorsqu'on renvoie au R.C.S. et fait référence à un paragraphe précis, puis qu'on renvoie à une référence parallèle (par ex. D.L.R.), les lecteurs présupposeront que l'un des deux recueils imprimés est la source pour toutes références précises ultérieures. Par conséquent, si la source utilisée est un service électronique, il faut indiquer le service électronique ou fournir la référence neutre.

3.11.1.2.1 Référence neutre disponible

- Fournir la référence traditionnelle suivie de la référence neutre. Ne jamais renvoyer à un service électronique si la référence neutre existe.

3.11.1.2.2 Référence neutre non disponible

Fournir la référence traditionnelle de la façon décrite ci-dessus en plus de
Première option :
- Indiquer que la décision est disponible sur un service électronique en fournissant le nom du service entre parenthèses.
- Si le document ne peut être facilement trouvé sur le services sans connaître la banque de données du service électronique, indiquer la banque de données dans laquelle le document a été trouvé (par ex. «(QL, A.Q.)»).
- Cette forme de référence ne devrait être utilisée que pour les services électroniques qui exigent un abonnement ou pour les sites Internet qui ont une table des matières claire, des engins de recherche, des rédacteurs professionnels et une abréviation reconnue. Les renvois aux sites Internet gouvernementaux doivent inclure l'adresse Internet au complet (voir la deuxième option).
- Inclure le numéro de paragraphe comme référence précise, si possible. Si la numérotation de la page d'une source sur support papier est reproduite sur le service électronique, renvoyer aux numéros de pages de la source sur support papier. Ne pas renvoyer à la référence précise des numéros de l'écran ou des pages du service électronique car ces numéros sont propres au service électronique utilisé et la forme peut changer d'un format électronique à un autre (texte, html).
- Si possible, ne pas renvoyer à un service électronique auquel la majorité des lecteurs ne pourra accéder. Par exemple, ne pas renvoyer à Azimut lorsque l'auditoire ciblé n'est pas au Québec.

ou deuxième option :
- Si la décision est accédée par Internet, fournir la référence traditionnelle, suivie d'une virgule, de «en ligne :», du nom du site Internet et de l'adresse universelle (URL) entre chevrons simples (<et>).
- Renvoyer à l'adresse universelle du document à moins que cette adresse ne soit propre à une session Internet, auquel cas renvoyer à la page d'accueil.
- Toutes les sources Internet ne sont pas fiables ; il faut donc porter une attention particulière lorsqu'on renvoie à de telles sources.

- Plusieurs textes en ligne disparaissent après un certain temps. Renvoyer à une source en ligne si cette source fournit des documents archivés remontant à quelques années.
- Inclure un numéro de paragraphe comme référence précise si possible. Si la pagination d'une source imprimée est reproduite dans une source électronique, renvoyer à la pagination utilisée par la source imprimée.

N.B. Lorsqu'on vérifie la référence précise ou la citation dans un recueil imprimé, ne pas indiquer le service électronique comme source. Fournir la référence traditionnelle et si possible, la référence neutre.

Exemples
Vanderburgh c. ScotiaMcLeod inc., [1992] 6 W.W.R. 673 à la p. 675 (Alta.Q.B.) **(QL)** [*Vanderburgh*].
Nixon c. United States, 506 U.S. 224 (1993) **(WL)** [*Nixon*].
Zündel c. Canada (Minister of Citizenship and Immigration) (1996), 138 D.L.R. (4ᵉ) 12 (F.C.T.D.) **(Lexis)**.
Er Joo Nguang c. Public Prosecutor, [2000] 2 Sing. L.R. 645 (H.C.) **(Lawnet)**.
Premakumar c. Air Canada (février 2002) TCDP D.T. 03/02, **en ligne : TCDP <http://www.chrt-tcdp.gc.ca/decisions/docs/premakumar-f.htm)**.

3.11.1.2.3 Référence précise

- Préciser le paragraphe ou la page du recueil imprimé se trouvant sur la version électronique. Ne pas inscrire les numéros de pages du document électronique.

3.11.1.2.4 Références parallèles

Exemple
Vanderburgh c. ScotiaMcLeod inc. (1992), 4 Alta. L.R. (3ᵉ) 138 à la p. 140, **[1992] 6 W.W.R. 673 à la p. 675 (Q.B.) (QL).**

- Dans la mesure du possible, inclure au moins une référence parallèle à un recueil sur support papier.
- Toujours fournir une référence parallèle à la référence neutre, si possible.

3.11.2 Jugement non disponible dans les recueils imprimés

Pour les jugements non publiés sur support papier, les services de banque de données donnent, soit une référence neutre, soit leur propre code de désignation de décision, soit seulement le numéro de greffe de la décision.

3.11.2.1 Services de banques de données fournissant une référence neutre

- Ne jamais renvoyer au code de désignation si la référence neutre est disponible. Préférer la référence neutre, qui est plus universelle, au code de désignation de la base de données.
- Si le jugement est publié sur support papier et qu'une référence neutre est disponible, inscrire la référence du recueil sur support papier d'abord, suivie de la référence neutre.

Exemple	
Décision non publiée dans un recueil imprimé ; référence neutre disponible	*R. c. Benjafield*, 2002 UKHL 2.

3.11.2.2 Services électroniques fournissant leurs propres codes de désignation

	Intitulé,	code de désignation de la banque de données fourni par le service	référence précise	Indication géographique et/ou cour (si possible),	(nom du service).
*e*Carswell	*Underwood v. Underwood,*	1995 CarswellOnt 88		(Ont. Gen. Div.)	(eC).
Lexis	*Davies v. M.N.R.,*	[1997] Can. Tax Ct. LEXIS 5874	at 5		(Lexis).
Quicklaw	*Fuentes v. Canada (Minister of Employment and Immigration),*	[1995] F.C.J. n° 206	au para. 10	(T.D.)	(QL).
Westlaw	*Fincher v. Baker,*	[1997] WL 675447	at 2	(Ala. Civ. App.)	(WL).

- Mettre l'code de désignation fourni par le service après l'intitulé de la cause. Ce code inclut généralement la date de la décision et le numéro séquentiel. Il sert à identifier la décision au sein de la banque de données.
- Renvoyer aux numéros de paragraphes ou aux pages se rapportant au recueil sur support papier indiqués sur la base de données ; ne pas utiliser les pages-écrans identifiées par les banques de données.
- *e*Carswell : Le code de désignation de *e*CARSWELL se situe sous l'intitulé. Si la seule référence inscrite est le code de désignation eCARSWELL (c'est-à-dire, s'il n'y a pas de référence à un recueil sur support papier), le jugement n'a pas été publié ailleurs.
- **Lexis** : La date comprise dans le code de désignation LEXIS doit être mise entre crochets. Le code de désignation LEXIS se situe sous l'intitulé et la mention de la cour. Si le seul code de désignation reconnu est celui fourni par Lexis, le jugement n'est pas publié.
- **Quicklaw** : À l'écran, le code de désignation QUICKLAW se trouve sous l'intitulé. Si aucune autre référence n'est fournie (que seul le code de désignation de QUICKLAW est inscrit et qu'aucune référence à un recueil sur support papier n'est indiquée), le jugement peut ne pas avoir été publié ailleurs. Utiliser la banque de données Quickcite, qui donne une liste de toutes les sources disponibles du jugement, pour confirmer qu'il n'a pas été publié ailleurs.
- **Westlaw** : La date comprise dans le code de désignation WESTLAW doit être mise entre crochets. Le code de désignation WESTLAW se situe au coin gauche supérieur de l'écran. Si le seul code de désignation reconnu est celui fourni par Westlaw (soit «WL»), le jugement n'est pas publié.

3.11.2.2.1 Lawnet

Exemple					
Intitulé,	code de désignation de la banque de données fourni par le service	date	(indication géographique et/ou cour),	référence précise	(service électronique)
Beryl Claire Clarke and Others c. Silkair (Singpore) Pte. Ltd.	Suit Nos. 1746, 1748-1752 of 1999,	24 octobre 2001,	(Sing. H.C.),	au para. 10	(Lawnet).

3.11.2.3 Services électroniques ne fournissant que le numéro de greffe de la décision

Exemples		
Référence traditionnelle pour les jugements non publiés sur support papier	(service électronique)	<adresse universelle> (si possible).
Caisse populaire de Trois-Pistoles c. April (31 janvier 2002), Kamouraska 250-22-001090-013 (C.Q. civ.)	(Azimut).	
R. v. Logan (15 décembre 1995), Port Hardy 9317 (B.C. Prov. Ct.),	en ligne : Electronic Frontier Canada	<http://www.efc.ca/pages/legal.html#court>.

- Fournir la référence de la décision comme si celle-ci n'était pas publiée. Voir la section 3.2.12.

4

DOCUMENTS GOUVERNEMENTAUX

4.1   CANADA

4.1.1   Débats législatifs

Exemples						
Indication géographique,	législature,	*titre*,	numéro	(date)	référence précise	(orateur).
		Débats de la Chambre des communes,	115	(15 juin 2000)	à la p. 8113	(Reed Elley).
Québec,	Assemblée nationale,	*Journal des débats*,	6	(24 mai 2001)	à la p. 12	(M. Marsan).
Nouvelle-Écosse,	House of Assembly,	*Debates and Proceedings*,	n° 85-29	(18 avril 1985)	à la p. 1343.	

• Pour les législatures provinciales, indiquer la province, à moins qu'elle ne fasse partie du titre du recueil des débats. L'information géographique n'est pas indiquée lorsqu'on renvoie aux débats de la Chambre des communes ou du Sénat.

- Indiquer le nom de la législature, à moins qu'il ne fasse partie du titre du recueil des débats.
- Indiquer le titre du recueil des débats en italique.
- Si le recueil est divisé en volume et/ou en numéro, l'indiquer après le titre précédé d'une virgule.
- Indiquer la date complète des débats entre parenthèses suivie d'une référence précise.
- Indiquer l'orateur entre parenthèses à la fin de la référence.

4.1.1.1 Procès-verbaux

Exemple					
Indication géographique,	législature,	*titre du recueil,*	numéro de la législature,	numéro du volume,	(date).
Québec,	Assemblée nationale,	*Procès-verbaux,*	35ᵉ lég.,	nᵒ 5	(5 décembre 1994).

- Pour les législatures provinciales, indiquer la province, à moins qu'elle ne fasse partie du titre du recueil des débats.
- Indiquer le nom de l'Assemblée législative, à moins qu'elle ne fasse partie du titre du recueil.
- Indiquer en italique le titre du recueil.
- Indiquer le numéro de la législature.
- Si le recueil est divisé en volume et/ou numéro, l'indiquer après le titre du recueil précédé d'une virgule.

4.1.2 Documents parlementaires et non parlementaires

Ces documents comprennent des rapports et des études rédigés par des comités, des commissions, des ministres et des auteurs particuliers pour des assemblées législatives ou divers organismes gouvernementaux.

Si le document se trouve dans une publication d'un organisme parlementaire, tel qu'un rapport de comité publié dans les journaux des débats, suivre les règles concernant les documents parlementaires, à la section 4.1.2.1.

Si le document n'est pas publié dans les journaux des débats ou s'il n'est pas publié par un organisme législatif, suivre les règles concernant les documents non parlementaires, à la section 4.1.2.2.

4.1.2.1 *Rapports parlementaires*

4.1.2.1.1 Débats

Exemple								
Indication géographique,	législature,	organisme,	«titre du rapport»	dans	*titre du recueil,*	volume, numéro	(date)	référence précise.
Québec,	Assemblée nationale,	Commission permanente de l'éducation,	«Étude détaillée du projet de loi n° 12 — Loi sur l'aide financière aux études»	dans	*Journal des débats de la Commission permanente de l'Éducation,*	vol. 37, n° 11	(1er juin 2001)	à la p. 1.

- Fournir l'indication géographique, s'il s'agit d'un rapport provincial.
- Suivre les règles concernant les débats législatifs, à la section 4.1.1, en y ajoutant les éléments suivants après le nom de l'assemblée législative : le nom de l'organisme dont émane le rapport ; le titre du rapport.
- Le titre du rapport se place entre guillemets.
- Fournir le numéro du rapport, s'il y en a un, après le titre du rapport, précédé d'une virgule.

4.1.2.1.2 *Sessional Papers*

Exemples								
Indication géographique,	législature,	«titre du rapport»	par	auteur	dans	*titre du recueil,*	numéro du *Sessional Paper*	(année)	référece précise.
Canada,	Parlement,	«Report of the Chief Inspector of Dominion Lands Agencies»	par	H.G. Cuttle	dans	*Sessional Papers,*	n° 25	(1920)	à la p. 3.
Ontario,	Assemblée législative,	«Report on Workmen's Compensation for Injuries»	par	James Mavor	dans	*Sessional Papers,*	n° 40	(1900)	à la p. 6.

- Inscrire l'indication géographique s'il s'agit d'un rapport provincial.

- Fournir le titre du rapport après la mention de l'assemblée législative.
- S'il y a un auteur, placer son nom après le titre du rapport.
- Si le rapport est numéroté, indiquer le numéro après le titre du recueil, précédé d'une virgule.

N.B. Depuis 1940, la plupart des juridictions ne publient plus de *Sessional Papers*.

4.1.2.2 *Rapports non parlementaires*

4.1.2.2.1 Modèle de base

Exemples						
Indication géographique,	organisme,	*titre,*	tome et/ou volume,	renseignements sur l'édition,	référence précise	(renseig-nements additionnels) (facultatif).
Québec,	Ministère de la Justice,	*Commentaires du ministre de la Justice : le Code civil du Québec,*	t. 2,	Québec, Publications du Québec, 1993	à la p. 5.	
	Conseil de la radiodiffusion et des télécom-munications canadiennes,	*Rapport annuel : 1978-79,*		Hull, Approvisionne-ments et Services Canada, 1979	à la p. 24.	
Québec,	Vérificateur général,	*Rapport à l'Assemblée nationale pour l'année 2000-2001,*	t. 1,	Québec, Publications du Québec, 2001	à la p. 169	(Vérificateur général : Guy Breton).

- Indiquer l'indication géographique, à moins qu'elle ne fasse partie du nom de l'organisme ou du titre du document.
- Indiquer l'organisme responsable à moins qu'il ne soit mentionné dans le titre.
- S'il y a un tome et/ou un volume, l'indiquer après le titre.
- Les renseignements sur l'édition sont donnés selon les règles concernant les monographies. Voir les sections 6.2.7-6.2.9.
- L'indication du nom du commissaire ou du président entre parenthèses à la fin de la référence est facultative.

4.1.2.2.2 Bulletins d'interprétation

Exemples					
Ministère,	Bulletin d'interprétation	numéro du bulletin,	«titre»	(date)	référence précise.
M.R.N.,	Bulletin d'interprétation	IT-459,	«Projet comportant un risque ou une affaire de caractère commercial»	(8 septembre 1980).	
M.R.N.,	Bulletin d'interprétation	IT-525R,	«Artistes de la scène»	(17 août 1995).	
M.R.N.,	Bulletin d'interprétation	IT-244R3,	«Dons de polices d'assurance-vie à des œuvres charitables»	(6 septembre 1991)	au n° 4.

- Si un bulletin a été révisé, le numéro de bulletin est suivi d'un «R». Le nombre de révisions est indiqué par le chiffre suivant le «R» (par ex. «R3»).
- Les bulletins d'interprétation étant divisés en paragraphes, renvoyer aux paragraphes.

4.1.2.2.3 Enquête parlementaire

Exemple				
Indication géographique,	Enquête parlementaire,	*titre,*	renseignements sur l'édition	référence précise.
Alberta,	Enquête parlementaire,	*Report on Comity and Parliamentary Practice in Municipal Bodies in Alberta,*	Edmonton, Queen's Printer, 1993	à la p. 2.

- Si le document est une enquête parlementaire, indiquer «Enquête parlementaire» avant le titre.

4.1.2.2.4   Rapport publié en plusieurs parties

4.1.2.2.4.1   Parties portant le même titre

Exemple				
Indication géographique,	*titre,*	livre ou cahier	renseignements sur l'édition	(président) (s'il y a lieu).
Canada,	*Rapport de la Commission royale d'enquête sur le bilinguisme et le biculturalisme,*	livres 1, 2	Ottawa, Imprimeur de la Reine, 1967	(Présidents : André Laurendeau et A. Davidson Dunton).

- Si les parties sont publiées séparément et portent le même titre, ajouter, après le titre, les éléments qui permettent de distinguer les différentes parties, tel le numéro de volume. Pour distinguer les parties du rapport, si un mot tel «livre» ou «cahier» paraît sur la page titre du document, l'utiliser plutôt que «vol.».

4.1.2.2.4.2   Parties portant des titres différents

Exemple		
Référence au livre 1	;	référence au livre 2.
Rapport de la Commission d'enquête sur la situation de la langue française et sur les droits linguistiques au Québec : la langue de travail, **livre 1,** Québec, Éditeur officiel, 1972 aux pp. 150, 300	;	*Rapport de la Commission d'enquête sur la situation de la langue française et sur les droits linguistiques au Québec : les droits linguistiques,* **livre 2,** Québec, Éditeur officiel, 1972 à la p. 38.

- Lorsqu'on renvoie à des parties distinctes portant des titres différents, on indique la référence complète pour chaque division, séparée d'un point-virgule. Indiquer le titre de la partie comme un sous-titre du document, c'est-à-dire précédé d'un deux-points.

4.1.2.2.5 Type de document

Exemple					
Organisme,	*titre*	(type de document)	auteur (s'il y a lieu),	renseignements sur l'édition	référence précise.
Commission de la santé et de la sécurité du travail,	*Planification des mesures d'urgence pour assurer la sécurité des travailleurs*	(Guide)		Québec, CSST, 1999	à la p. 53.

- Si le type de document (par ex. «Étude», «Document de travail») est indiqué sur la page titre, fournir ces renseignements entre parenthèses après le titre du document.

4.1.2.2.6 Auteur particulier

Exemple				
Organisme,	*titre*	par	auteur,	renseignements sur l'édition.
Ministère des Relations internationales,	*Des lois et des langues au Québec*	par	Marc Chevrier,	Québec, Ministère des Relations internationales, 1997.

- Si le document a été rédigé par un auteur particulier, indiquer son nom après le titre, précédé de «par».

4.1.3   Documents de conférences intergouvernementales

Exemples				
Conférence ou comité,	*titre,*	numéro du document,	lieu de la conférence,	date de tenue de la conférence.
Réunion fédérale-provinciale-territoriale des ministres responsables de la justice,	*Groupe de travail fédéral-provincial-territorial sur la provocation Rapport intérimaire,*	Doc. 830-600/020,	Montréal,	4-5 décembre, 1997.
Conférence fédérale-provinciale des Premiers ministres,	*Comte-rendu textuel de la Conférence fédérale-provinciale des Premiers ministres sur les questions constitutionnelles intéressant les autochtones,*	Doc. 800-18/004,	Ottawa,	8-9 mars 1984.

- Indiquer le nom complet de la conférence ou du comité, suivi du titre du document et le numéro du document.
- Indiquer le lieu et la date complète de la conférence.

4.2   ROYAUME-UNI

Indiquer que l'on renvoie à un document gouvernemental du Royaume-Uni en mettant «R.-U.» au début de la référence.

4.2.1 Débats

4.2.1.1 Avant 1803

Exemple						
R.-U.,	chambre,	*Parliamentary History of England,*	volume,	colonne	(date)	(orateur) (facultatif).
R.-U.,	H.C.,	*Parliamentary History of England,*	vol. 12,	col. 1327	(27 mai 1774).	

- Pour les débats qui datent d'avant 1803, renvoyer au recueil intitulé *Parliamentary History of England.*
- Après «R.-U.», indiquer la chambre. Abréger «*House of Commons*» par «H.C.» et «*House of Lords*» par «H.L.»
- L'orateur peut être indiqué entre parenthèses à la fin de la référence.

4.2.1.2 1803 et après

Exemples								
R.-U.,	chambre,	*titre,*	série,	volume,	colonne	référence précise	(date)	(orateur) (facultatif).
R.-U.,	H.L.,	*Parliamentary Debates,*	5ᵉ sér.,	vol. 442,	col. 3	à la col. 6	(3 mai 1983)	(Baroness Masham of Ilton).
R.U.,	S.P.,	*Official Report,*	session 1 (2000),	vol. 7, nᵒ. 6,	col. 634		(22 juin 2000)	(Peter Peacock).
R.U.,	N.I.A.,	*Official Report,*				à la p. 500	(24 octobre 2000).	
R.U.,	N.A.W.,	*Official Record,*				à la p. 27	(19 juillet 2001).	

- L'orateur peut être indiqué entre parenthèses à la fin de la référence.

Après «R.-U.», indiquer la chambre en utilisant les abréviations suivantes :

House of Lords	H.L.
House of Commons	H.C.
Scottish Parliament	S.P.
Northern Ireland Assembly	N.I.A.
National Assembly for Wales	N.A.W.

4.2.2 Journaux

Exemples				
R.-U.,	*journal,*	volume	(date)	référence précise.
R.-U.,	*Journal of the House of Commons,*	vol. 234	(9 décembre 1977)	à la p. 95.
R.-U.,	*Journal of the House of Lords,*	vol. 22	(10 janvier 1995)	à la p. 89.

• Ne pas répéter le nom de la chambre puisqu'il est indiqué dans le titre du journal.

4.2.3 Documents parlementaires

Exemples										
R.-U.,	chambre,	«titre»,	numéro sessionel ou *command number*	dans *Sessional Papers,*	vol.	(année)	1re page	référence précise	(président) (s'il y a lieu).
R.-U.,	H.C.,	«Report of the Committee on the Law Relating to Rights of Light»,	Cmnd 473	dans *Sessional Papers,*	vol. 17	(1957-58)	955		(Président : Sir C.E. Harman).
R.-U.,	H.C.,	«Monopolies and Mergers Commission Report on the Supply in the U.K. of the Services of Administering Performing Rights and Film Synchronisation Rights»,	Cm 3147	dans *Sessional Papers*		(1995-96)	1.		

- Indiquer le titre tel qu'il apparaît à la page titre du rapport.
- Indiquer le numéro sessionnel ou le numéro du *Command Paper* après le titre.
- Le nom du président peut être inscrit entre parenthèses à la fin de la référence.
- Renvoyer aux *Sessional Papers* de la *House of Commons*, à moins que le document n'apparaisse que dans les *Sessional Papers* de la *House of Lords*.
- L'abréviation du «*Command*» est essentielle à l'identification du document. Noter que l'abréviation appropriée apparaît à la première page de chaque *Command Paper* :

1833-1869	1re série (1-4222)	c.
1870-1899	2e série (1-9550)	C.
1900-1918	3e série (1-9239)	Cd
1919-1956	4e série (1-9889)	Cmd
1957-1986	5e série (1-9927)	Cmnd
1986 à aujourd'hui	6e série (1-)	Cm

- Indiquer la première page du document après la date.
- Pour les références précises, on renvoie à la pagination interne du document.
- Le nom du président du comité entre parenthèses à la fin de la référence est facultatif.

4.2.4 Documents non parlementaires

Exemples					
R.-U.,	organisme,	*titre,*	(type de document) (s'il y a lieu)	auteur (s'il y a lieu),	renseignements sur l'édition.
R.-U.,	Royal Commission on Criminal Procedure,	*Police Interrogation : The Psychological Approach,*			Londres, Her Majesty's Stationery Office, 1980.
R.-U.,	Royal Commission on the Press,	*Studies on the Press*	(Working Paper No. 3)	par Oliver Boyd-Barret, Colin Seymour-Ure et Jeremy Turnstall,	Londres, Her Majesty's Stationery Office, 1978.

- Suivre les règles concernant les documents non parlementaires canadiens, à la section 4.1.2.2.

4.3 ÉTATS-UNIS

Indiquer que l'on renvoie à un document gouvernemental des États-Unis en mettant «É.-U.» au début de le référence.

4.3.1 Débats

Exemples							
É.-U.,	*Cong. Rec.,*	édition,	tome,	partie,	référence précise	(date)	(orateur) (facultatif).
É.-U.,	*Cong. Rec.,*		t. 125,	15,	à la p. 18691	(1979).	
É.-U.,	*Cong. Rec.,*	daily ed.,	t. 143,	69,	à la p. H3176	(22 May 1977)	(Rep. Portman).

- Faire référence au *Congressional Record* pour les débats du congrès qui ont eu lieu après 1873.

- Pour savoir comment renvoyer aux débats plus anciens du Congrès, consulter *The Bluebook : A Uniform System of Citation*, 17ᵉ éd., Cambridge, Mass., Harvard Law Review Association, 2000.

4.3.2 Sessions des comités

4.3.2.1 Fédéral

Exemples					
É.-U.,	*titre,*	numéro du Congrès,	Renseignements sur l'édition	référence précise	(orateur) (facultatif).
É.-U.,	*Federal Property Campaign Fundraising Reform Act of 2000 : Hearing on H.R. 4845 Before the House Committee of the Judiciary,*	106ᵉ Cong.,	2000	à la p. 2-3.	
É.-U.,	*Assisted Suicide : Legal, Medical, Ethical and Social Issues : Hearing Before the Subcommittee on Health and Environment of the House Committee on Commerce,*	105ᵉ Cong.,	Washington, D.C., United States Government Printing Office, 1997	à la p. 2	(Dr C. Everett Koop).

- Toujours indiquer l'année de publication. Fournir plus de renseignements sur l'édition si possible.

4—Documents Gouvernementaux

4.3.2.2 État

Exemple							
É.-U.,	*titre,*	numéro du corps législatif (ou l'année),	numéro ou désignation de la session législative,	État	(renseignements sur l'édition)	référence précise	(orateur) (facultatif).
É.-U.,	*Rico Litigation : Hearing on S. 1197 Before the Senate Comm. on Commerce and Econ. Dev.,*	41ᵉ légis.,	1ʳᵉ sess. rég. 5	Ariz.	(1993)		(affirmé par Barry Wong, analyste politique).

- Voir la liste concernant les États à l'annexe B.
- Toujours indiquer l'année de publication. Fournir plus de renseignements sur l'édition si possible.

4.3.3 Rapports et documents

4.3.3.1 Fédéral

4.3.3.1.1 Documents et rapports numérotés

Exemple					
É.-U.,	organisme,	*titre*	(numéro),	renseignements sur l'édition	référence précise.
É.-U.,	Commission on Protecting and Reducing Government Secrecy,	*Secrecy: Report of the Commission on Protecting and Reducing Government Secrecy : Pursuant to Public Law 236, 103rd Congress*	(S. Doc. n° 105-2)	Washington, D.C., United States Government Printing Office, 1997	à la p. 3.

- Toujours indiquer l'année de publication. Fournir plus de renseignements sur l'édition si possible.
- Utiliser les abréviations suivantes pour le numéro :

Documents	Rapports
H.R. Doc. N°.	H.R. Rep. N°.
H.R. Misc. Doc. N°.	H.R. Conf. Rep. N°.
S. Doc. N°.	S. Rep. N°.
S. Exec. Doc. N°.	

4.3.3.1.2 Documents non numérotés et *Committee Prints*

Exemples					
É.-U.,	organisme,	titre,	Committee Print (si pertinent),	renseignements sur l'édition	référence précise.
É.-U.,	Staff of House Committee on Vetrans' Affairs, 105th Cong.,	Persian Gulf Illnesses: An Overview,	Committee Print,	1998	à la p. 15.
É.-U.,	National Commission on Children,	Beyond Rhetoric: A New American Agenda for Children and Families,		Washington, D.C., The Commission, 1991	à la p. 41.

- Indiquer le numéro du congrès avec l'organisme, si pertinent.
- Toujours indiquer l'année de publication. Fournir plus de renseignements sur l'édition si possible.

4.3.3.2 État

Exemples						
	É.-U.,	organisme,	*titre*	(numéro) (s'il y a lieu),	Renseignements sur l'édition	référence précise.
Documents et rapports numérotés	É.-U.,	California Energy Commission	*Existing Renewable Resources Account, vol. 1*	(500-01-014V1),	2001.	
Documents et rapports non numérotés	É.-U.,	Washington State Transport Commission,	*Washington's Transportation Plan 2003-2022,*		Washington State Department of Transportation, 2002.	

- Fournir le numéro du document, s'il y lieu.
- Toujours indiquer l'année de publication. Fournir plus de renseignements sur l'édition si possible.

4.4   FRANCE

Indiquer que l'on renvoie à un document gouvernemental de la France en mettant «France» au début de la référence.

4.4.1 Débats

4.4.1.1 De 1787 à 1860

Exemple						
France,	*Archives parlementaires,*	série,	tome,	date,	référence précise,	(orateur) (facultatif).
France,	*Archives parlementaires,*	1re série,	t. 83,	5 janvier 1794,	s. 3.	

- Abréger «Archives parlementaires : recueil complet des débats législatifs et politiques des chambres françaises» par «Archives parlementaires».

- Indiquer la série après le titre. La première série couvre les années 1787-1799, alors que la deuxième série couvre les années 1800-1860.
- Les références précises se font aux «sections» et non pas aux «articles».
- Le nom de l'orateur peut être ajouté entre parenthèses à la fin de la référence.

4.4.1.2 De 1871 à aujourd'hui

Exemples							
France,	journal,	chambre,	Débats parlementaires,	division,	numéro et date,	référence précise,	(orateur) (facultatif).
France,	*J.O.*,	Assemblée nationale,	Débats parlementaires,	Compte rendu intégral,	1re séance du 23 janvier 2001,	à la p. 635	(Gilbert Maurel).
France,	*J.O.*,	Sénat,	Débats parlementaires,	Compte rendu intégral,	séance du 3 avril 2001.		

- À partir de 1871, les débats parlementaires sont publiés dans le *Journal officiel de la République française*, abrégé «*J.O.*».
- Indiquer la chambre, suivie de «Débats parlementaires». Pour les périodes suivantes :
  - 1871-1880 : omettre la chambre et «Débats parlementaires».
  - 1943-1945, 1945-1946, 1947-1958 : indiquer seulement «Débats de [Chambre]».

Les chambres se nomment différemment selon les époques :

1881-1940	Chambre des députés		1880-1940	Sénat
1943-1945	Assemblée consultative provisoire		1946-1958	Conseil de la République
1945-1946	Assemblée constituante		1958 à aujourd'hui	Sénat
1947-1958	Assemblée de l'Union française			
1958 à aujourd'hui	Assemblée nationale			

- La division ne doit être indiquée qu'à partir de 1980 pour l'Assemblée nationale et à partir de 1983 pour le Sénat. Dans le cas de l'Assemblée nationale, les débats parlementaires se scindent en deux, soit «Compte rendu intégral» et en «Questions écrites remises à la Présidence de l'Assemblée nationale et réponses des ministres». Il existe également deux divisions pour le Sénat, soit «Compte rendu intégral» et «Questions remises à la Présidence du Sénat et réponses des ministres aux questions écrites».
- Terminer par le numéro (s'il y a lieu) et la date de la séance, puis par la référence précise à la page.
- Le nom de l'orateur peut être ajouté, entre parenthèses, à la fin de la référence.

4.4.2 Anciens journaux officiels

Exemple				
France,	*titre*,	année ou date de publication,	tome ou volume,	référence précise.
France,	*Journal officiel de l'Empire français*,	1868,	t. 1,	à la p. 14.

- Les débats parlementaires, les documents parlementaires et les documents non parlementaires précédant l'année 1871 sont généralement publiés à l'intérieur d'anciennes versions du *Journal officiel de la République française*.

1787-1810	*Gazette nationale* ou *Moniteur universel*
1811-1848	*Moniteur universel*
1848-1852	*Moniteur universel, Journal officiel de la République*
1852-1870	*Journal officiel de l'Empire français*

- Le mode de référence peut varier selon l'organisation du journal. Généralement, la référence devrait au moins inclure le titre du journal, l'année de référence ou la date de publication, le tome ou le volume (s'il y a lieu), de même que le numéro de la page.

4.4.3 Documents parlementaires

4.4.3.1 Travaux et réunions parlementaires

Exemples						
France,	chambre,	organisme,	«titre des travaux»,	Compte rendu ou *Bulletin*	(date)	(président) (facultatif).
France,	Assemblée nationale,	Délégation aux droits des femmes,	«Auditions sur le suivi de l'application des lois relatives à l'IVG et à la contraception»,	Compte rendu n° 4	(6 novembre 2001)	(présidente : Martine Lignières-Cassou).
France,	Sénat,	Commission des affaires culturelles,	«Auditions de M. Jack Lang, ministre de l'éducation nationale»,	*Bulletin* du 11 juin 2001	(13 juin 2001)	(président : Adrien Gouteyron).

- Indiquer le titre des travaux, puis le numéro du compte rendu ou du bulletin correspondant. Les «Comptes rendus» sont utilisés pour les travaux de l'Assemblée nationale, alors que les «Bulletins» sont utilisés pour les travaux du Sénat. Contrairement au terme «Compte rendu», le terme «Bulletin» doit être mis en italique.
- Terminer par la date, le président des travaux (facultatif), puis la référence précise à la page.

4—Documents Gouvernementaux

4.4.3.2 Rapports d'information

Exemple							
France,	chambre,	organisme,	*titre du rapport,*	par auteur(s),	numéro du rapport	(date)	référence précise.
France,	Sénat,	Commission des affaires étrangères,	*La réforme de la coopération à l'épreuve des réalités : un premier bilan 1998-2001,*	par Guy Penne, André Dulait et Paulette Brisepierre,	Rapport n° 46	(30 octobre 2001)	à la p. 7.

4.4.4   Documents non parlementaires

Exemples						
France,	organisme,	*titre,*	numéro, tome ou volume,	Renseigne-ments sur l'édition	référence précise	(renseigne-ments additionnels) (facultatif).
France,		*Commission d'enquête sur la sécurité du transport maritime des produits dangereux ou polluants,*	Rapport n° 2535, t. 1,			(5 juillet 2000 ; président : Daniel Paul).
France,	Conseil économique et social,	*La conjoncture économique et sociale à la fin de l'an 2000 : embellie et dangers,*		Avis et rapports du Conseil économique et social, *J.O.*, n° 2000-17	à la p. II-4	(20 décembre 2000 ; rapport présenté par Dominique Taddei).
France,	Ministère de la justice,	*Bulletin officiel,*	n° 82		à la p. 3	(du 1ᵉʳ avril au 30 juin 2001).

- La référence aux documents non parlementaires de France suit le même modèle de référence que celui qui prévaut pour les documents non parlementaires canadiens, à la section 4.1.2.2.

4.5 AUSTRALIE

Indiquer que l'on renvoie à un document gouvernemental de l'Australie en mettant «Austl.» au début de la référence.

4.5.1 Débats

Exemples						
Austl.,	indication géographique,	chambre,	*Parliamentary Debates*	(date)	référence précise	(orateur) (facultatif).
Austl.,	Commonwealth	House of Represen-tatives,	*Parliamentary Debates*	(17 septembre 2001)	à la p. 30739	(M. Howard, Premier Ministre).
Austl.,	Victoria,	Legislative Assembly,	*Parliamentary Debates*	(23 octobre 1968)	à la p. 1197.	

- Après «Austl.», inscrire l'indication géographique. Voir annexe C pour plus de détails.
- Utiliser *«Parliamentary Debates»* en tant que recueil.
- Le nom et le titre de l'orateur peuvent être indiqués entre parenthèses à la fin de la référence.

4.5.2 Rapports parlementaires

Exemple					
Austl.,	indication géographique,	*titre,*	numéro	(année)	référence précise.
Austl.,	Commonwealth,	*Department of Foreign Affairs Annual Report 1975,*	Parl. Paper n° 142	(1976)	à la p. 5.

- «Parl. Paper n°» précède le numéro.

4—Documents Gouvernementaux

4.5.3   Rapports non parlementaires

Exemples								
Austl.,	indication géograph- ique,	organisme,	*titre*	(type de docu- ment)	auteur(s) (s'il y a lieu),	Renseigne- ments sur l'édition	référence précise	(renseigne- ments supplément- aires).
Austl.,	Common- wealth,	Royal Commiss- ion into Aboriginal Deaths in Custody,	*Report of the Inquiry into the Death of Stanley John Gollan*		par Commiss- ioner Elliott Johnston, Q.C.,	Canberra : Australian Government Publishing Service, 1990	à la p. 31.	
Austl.,	Common- wealth,	Law Reform Commiss- ion,	*Annual Report 1998*	(Report n° 49),		Canberra : Australian Government Publishing Service, 1988.		

- Suivre les règles des rapports non parlementaires canadiens, à la section 4.1.2.2.

4.5.4   Documents des ministères

Exemple						
Auteur,	indication géographique,	*titre*,	service du document,	numéro	(date)	référence précise.
Paul Keating,	Commonwealth (Austl.),	*Opening of the Global Cultural Diversity Conference*,	Ministerial Document Service,	n° 172/94 -95	(27 avril 1995)	à la p. 5977.

- Si des renseignements supplémentaires sont nécessaires pour identifier précisément l'indication géographique, fournir l'indication géographique suivie de «Austl.» entre parenthèses et avant la virgule précédant le titre.

4.6   NOUVELLE-ZÉLANDE

Indiquer que l'on renvoie à un document gouvernemental de la Nouvelle-Zélande en mettant «N.-Z.» au début de la référence.

4.6.1   Débats

Exemple					
N.-Z.,	*Hansard,*	étape : sujet	(numéro de la question)	date	(orateur) (facultatif).
N.-Z.,	*Hansard,*	Questions To Ministers: Biosecurity Risk-Motor Vehicle and Equipment Imports	(n° 3)	1ᵉʳ mars 2000	(Ian Ewen-Street).

- Hansard fournit le type d'étape qui sera l'une des étapes suivantes : Questions to Ministers, Debate-General, Report of [ ] Committee ou Miscellaneous.
- Le sujet est le titre du débat, par ex. *Labour, Associate Minister-Accountability.*
- Le numéro de la question peut être indiqué, entre parenthèses, après «étape : sujet».
- Le nom de l'orateur peut être indiqué entre parenthèses à la fin de la référence.

4.6.2   Documents parlementaires

Exemples					
N.-Z.,	«titre»,	date,	session	(président)	préfixe et numéro (facultatif).
N.-Z.,	«Report of the Government Administration Committee, Inquiry into New Zealand's Adoption Laws»,	août 2001,	46ᵉ parle-ment	(Dianne Yates, présidente).	
N.-Z.,	«Report of the Game Bird Habitat Trust Board for the year ended 31 August 1999»,	février 2000,			C.22.

- Le nom du président peut être indiqué entre parenthèses après la session.
- La lettre qui précède le numéro (le préfixe) indique le sujet sur lequel porte le rapport.

4—Documents Gouvernementaux

Préfixe
A. Affaires politiques et étrangères
B. Finance et revenu
C. Environnement
D. Énergie et travaux
E. Bien-être et justice
F. Communications
G. Général
H. Commissions, «Royal Commissions»

4.7   SINGAPOUR

Indiquer que l'on renvoie à un document gouvernemental de Singapour en mettant «Sing.» au début de la référence.

4.7.1   Débats parlementaires

Exemple						
Sing.,	*Débats parlementaires,*	vol.,	colonne	référence précise	(date)	(nom de l'orateur) (facultatif).
Sing.,	*Débats parlementaires,*	v. 73,	col. 2436	à la col. 2437	(15 octobre 2001)	(Professeur S. Jayakumar).

4.8   SITES INTERNET

Exemple			
Référence complète,	en ligne :	nom du site	<adresse universelle>.
É.-U., Commission on Security and Cooperation in Europe, *Presidential Elections and Independence Referendums in the Baltic States, the Soviet Union and Successor States*, Washington (D.C.), The Commission, 1992 à la p. 53,	en ligne :	Commission on Security and Cooperation in Europe	<http://www.csce.gov/ reports.cfm>.

- Fournir la référence traditionnelle, suivie d'une virgule, de «en ligne :», du nom du site Internet et de l'adresse universelle (URL).
- Renvoyer à l'adresse universelle du document à moins que cette adresse ne soit propre à une session Internet, auquel cas renvoyer à la page d'accueil.
- Toutes les sources Internet ne sont pas fiables ; il faut donc porter une attention particulière lorsqu'on renvoie à de telles sources.
- Plusieurs textes en ligne disparaissent après un certain temps. Renvoyer à une source en ligne si cette source fournit des documents archivés remontant à quelques années.
- Inclure un numéro de paragraphe comme référence précise si possible. Si la pagination d'une source imprimée est reproduite dans une source électronique, renvoyer à la pagination utilisée par la source imprimée.

4—Documents Gouvernementaux

5

DOCUMENTATION INTERNATIONALE

5.1 TRAITÉS ET DOCUMENTS INTERNATIONAUX

5.1.1 Traités et autres accords internationaux

Exemples					
Titre,	parties (s'il y a lieu),	date de signature,	recueil de traités,	référence parallèle	(autre information) (facultatif).
Traité sur l'extradition,	Espagne et El Salvador,	10 mars 1997,	2010 R.T.N.U. 139.		
Convention de sauvegarde des droits de l'homme et des libertés fondamentales,		4 novembre 1950,	213 R.T.N.U. 221,	S.T.E. 5	[*Convention européenne des droits de l'homme*].

Pacte international relatif aux droits civils et politiques,		19 décembre 1966,	999 R.T.N.U. 171, art. 9-14,	R.T. Can. 1976 n° 47	(entrée en vigueur : 23 mars 1976, accession du Canada 19 mai 1976).
Accord de libre-échange nord-américain entre le gouvernement du Canada, le gouvernement des États-Unis et le gouvernement du Mexique,		17 décembre 1992,	R.T. Can. 1994 n° 2,	32 I.L.M. 289	(entrée en vigueur : 1er janvier 1994) [*ALÉNA*].
Accord général sur les tarifs douaniers et le commerce,		30 octobre 1947,	58 R.T.N.U. 187,	R.T. Can. 1947 n° 27	(entrée en vigueur : 1er janvier 1948) [*GATT de 1947*].

- Indiquer le titre complet du traité. Lorsque le nom des signataires est intégré dans le titre, abréger le nom afin de refléter l'usage (par ex. «Royaume-Uni» et non «Royaume-Uni de Grande-Bretagne et d'Irlande du Nord»). Le nom des parties ne devrait pas être abrégé (par ex. «R.-U.»).
- Si le nom des parties à un traité bilatéral ne fait pas partie du titre, le nom des parties devrait suivre le titre, entre virgules. Le nom des parties à un traité multilatéral peut être inclus comme information supplémentaire à la fin de la référence.
- Après le titre du traité, fournir la date précise de signature ou de présentation pour signature.
- Renvoyer aux recueils de traités selon l'ordre de préférence suivant : (1) *Recueil de traités des Nations Unies* (R.T.N.U.) ou *Recueil de traités de la Société des Nations* (R.T.S.N.) ; (2) Recueils de traités officiels des États pertinents (par ex. *Recueil des traités du Canada* (R.T. Can.), *United Kingdom Treaty Series* (U.K.T.S.)) ; (3) Autres recueils de sources internationaux (par ex. *International Legal Materials* (I.L.M.)).
- Des informations supplémentaires peuvent être fournies à la fin de la référence. Par exemple, on peut mentionner le nom des parties au traité, la date d'entrée en vigueur, le nombre de ratifications ou le statut de certains États.

Voici une liste des recueils de traités et leurs abréviations :

Air and Aviation Treaties of the World	A.A.T.W.
Australian Treaty Series	A.T.S.
Canada Treaty Series	Can. T.S.
Consolidated Treaty Series	Cons. T.S.
Documents juridiques internationaux	D.J.I.
European Treaty Series	Eur. T.S.
International Legal Materials	I.L.M.
Journal Officiel	J.O.
League of Nations Treaty Series	L.N.T.S.
Organization of American States Treaty Series	O.A.S.T.S.
Recueil des traités du Canada	R.T. Can.
Recueil des traités et accords de la France	R.T.A.F.
Recueil des traités des Nations Unies	R.T.N.U.
Recueil des traités de la Société des Nations	R.T.S.N.
Recueil général des traités de la France	Rec. G.T.F.
Recueil des traités d'alliance, de paix, de trêve, de neutralité, de commerce, de limites, d'échange, et plusieurs autres actes à la connaissance des relations étrangères des puissances et États de l'Europe	Rec. T.A.
Série des traités et conventions européennes	S.T.E.
United States Statutes at Large	U.S. Stat.
Treaties and other International Agreements of the United States of America 1776-1949	T.I. Agree (anciennement U.S.B.S.)
United States Treaties and Other International Acts Series	T.I.A.S.
British and Foreign State Papers	U.K.F.S.
United Kingdom Treaty Series	U.K.T.S.
United Nations Treaty Series	U.N.T.S.
United States Treaties and Other International Agreements	U.S.T.

5.1.2 Documents des Nations Unies

Le document auquel on renvoie ne contiendra pas toujours tous les éléments inclus dans les exemples ci-dessous. Il faut donc adapter les références en fournissant l'information nécessaire à l'identification du document.

Abréger les mots souvent utilisés dans les documents des Nations Unies de la façon suivante :

Décision	déc.
Document	doc.
Documents officiel	doc. off.
Extraordinaire	extra.
Miméographié	miméo.
Numéro	n$^\circ$
Pléniaire	plén.
Recommandation	rec.
Régulier	rég.
Résolution	rés.
Session	sess.
Spécial	spéc.
Supplément	supp.
Urgence	urg.

5.1.2.1 Charte des Nations Unies

Une référence complète n'est pas nécessaire pour la *Charte des Nations Unies*. On peut, néanmoins, renvoyer à la *Charte* de la façon suivante : *Charte des Nations Unies*, 26 juin 1945, R.T. Can. 1945 n$^\circ$7.

5.1.2.2 Documents officiels

Les documents officiels publiés par les organes des Nations Unies se divisent en trois parties, soit les séances, les suppléments et les annexes. Renvoyer aux documents officiels en inscrivant «Doc. off.» avant l'acronyme de l'organe qui en est responsable. Les abréviations officielles des principaux organes des Nations Unies sont :

Assemblée générale	AG
Conférence des Nations Unies sur le commerce et le développement	CNUCED

Conseil économique et social	CES
Conseil de sécurité	CS
Conseil de tutelle	CT
Conseil du commerce et du développement	CCED
Première commission, Deuxième commission, etc.	C.1, C.2, etc.

Fournir le nom complet des organes de l'ONU qui n'ont pas d'acronyme officiel.

5.1.2.2.1 Séances

Exemples					
Doc. off. et organe responsable,	numéro de sess. ou nombre d'années écoulées depuis la création de l'organe ou année civile,	numéro de séance,	numéro de doc. l'ONU et (numéro de vente) (s'il y a lieu)	(année du document)	référence précise ou a [provisoire].
Doc. off. CCED CNUCED,	23e sess.,	565e séance,	Doc. NU TD/B/SR.565	(1981).	
Doc. off. CS NU,	53e année,	3849e séance,	Doc. NU S/PV.3849	(1998)	[provisoire].
Doc. off. CES NU,	1984,	23e séance plén.,	Doc. NU E/1984/SR.23.		

- Au début de la référence, indiquer «Doc. off.» pour «documents officiels», suivi de l'abréviation de l'organe des Nations Unies et de la mention «NU», sauf si celle-ci fait partie de l'acronyme de l'organe.
- Après le nom de l'organe ou la mention «NU», indiquer le numéro de la session. Si le numéro de session n'est pas disponible, indiquer le nombre d'années écoulées depuis la création de l'organe. Si ni l'un ni l'autre n'est disponible, indiquer l'année civile.
- Indiquer le numéro de séance après le numéro de session ou l'année.
- Indiquer le numéro de document après le numéro de séance. Si un document a plusieurs numéros, il faut tous les indiquer, les séparant par une virgule. Le numéro de vente peut être inséré en l'indiquant entre parenthèses à la suite du numéro du document.
- Indiquer l'année civile du document entre parenthèses après le numéro du document, à moins qu'elle n'ait déjà été mentionnée précédemment dans la référence.

- Si le numéro de document est suivi d'une référence précise, insérer une virgule entre le numéro de document et la référence précise.
- Indiquer qu'un document est provisoire en indiquant «[provisoire]» à la fin de la référence.

5.1.2.2.2   Suppléments

Les résolutions, les décisions et les rapports paraissent dans les suppléments aux documents officiels.

Exemples									
	Auteur (s'il y a lieu),	*titre,*	Rés. ou Déc. et organe et n°,	doc. off.,	session ou année de l'organe ou année civile,	numéro de supp.,	numéro du document de l'ONU	(année civile) (s'il y a lieu)	1ʳᵉ page et référence précise
Résolutions		*Déclaration universelle des droits de l'Homme,*	Rés. AG 217(III),	Doc. Off. AG NU,	3ᵉ sess.,	supp. n° 13,	Doc. NU A/810	(1948)	71.
Décisions		*Protection of the heritage of indigenous people,*	Déc. CES 1998/277,	Doc. Off. CES NU,	1998,	supp. n° 1,	Doc. NU E/1998/ 98,		113.
Rapports		*Rapport du Secrétaire général Boutros-Ghali sur les travaux de l'Organisa-tion,*		Doc. off. AG NU,	46ᵉ sess.,	supp. n° 1,	Doc. NU A/46/1	(1991).	
	Commi-ssion on Crime prevent-ion and Criminal Justice,	*Report on the Ninth Session,*		Doc. Off. CES NU,	2000,	supp. n° 10,	Doc. NU E/2000/ 30.		

- Au début de la référence, indiquer le titre en italique. Pour les rapports, indiquer l'auteur s'il y a lieu.

- Dans le cas d'une décision ou d'une résolution, indiquer le numéro de décision ou de résolution après le titre.
- À la suite du numéro de décision ou de résolution, renvoyer aux documents officiels (par ex. «Doc. off. AG NU»).
- Indiquer le numéro de session ou le nombre d'années écoulées depuis la création de l'organe si le numéro de session n'est pas disponible. Si ni l'un ni l'autre n'est disponible, indiquer l'année civile.
- Un renvoi au numéro de supplément et au numéro de document doit suivre le numéro de session.
- Si l'année civile n'a pas été précédemment indiquée, l'inscrire entre parenthèses après le numéro de document.
- Placer ensuite le numéro de la première page du document et la référence précise, s'il y a lieu. Si rien n'est indiqué entre le numéro de document et le numéro de page, placer une virgule après le numéro de document, afin d'éviter toute confusion.

5.1.2.2.3   Annexes

Exemples						
Titre,	doc. off. et organe responsable	session ou année de l'organe ou année civile,	annexe, point numéro,	numéro de document de l'ONU	(année civile) (s'il y a lieu)	1re page et/ou référence précise.
Protectionism and structural adjustment,	Doc. off. CNUCED CCED,	32e sess.,	Annexe, point 6,	Doc. NU TD/B/1081	(1986)	23.
URSS : Projet de résolution,	Doc. off. CES NU,	3e année, 7e sess.,	Annexe, point 7,	Doc. NU E/884/Rev1	(1948)	29 au para. 3.

- À la suite du titre, renvoyer aux documents officiels de l'organe responsable.
- Indiquer le numéro de session ou l'année de l'organe (depuis sa création) si le numéro n'est pas disponible. Si ni l'un ni l'autre n'est disponible, indiquer l'année civile.
- Indiquer l'annexe et le point d'ordre du jour, suivis du numéro du document.
- Si l'année civile n'a pas été précédemment indiquée, l'inscrire après le numéro de document.
- Placer ensuite le numéro de la première page du document ou une référence précise. Si rien n'est indiqué entre le numéro de document et le numéro de page, placer une virgule après le numéro de document.

5.1.2.3 *Documents miméographiés*

Exemple
CES NU, Commission des droits de l'Homme, *République-Unie de Tanzanie : Projet de résolution révisé*, 24e sess., Doc. NU E/CN.4/L.991/Rev.1 (1968) [Miméo., limité].

- Si le document n'est disponible que sous forme miméographique, suivre les règles concernant les suppléments à la section 5.1.2.2.2. Abréger «miméographie» par «miméo.» entre crochets à la fin de la référence. S'il y a lieu, indiquer «limité», «restreint» ou «provisoire».

5.1.2.4 *Périodiques*

Exemple
«Emplois rémunérés dans les activités non agricoles» (1989) 63:9 Bulletin mensuel de statistiques 12 (NU, Département des affaires économiques et sociales internationales).

- Indiquer l'auteur si possible. Suivre les règles des références aux périodiques énoncées à la section 6.1. Si le titre n'indique pas que le périodique est publié par les Nations Unies, ajouter «NU» et l'organe responsable de la publication entre parenthèses à la fin de la référence.

5.1.2.5 *Annuaires*

Exemple
«Report of the Commission to the General Assembly on the work of its thirty-ninth Session» (Doc. NU A/42/10) dans *Yearbook of the International Law Commission 1987*, vol. 2, partie 2, New York, NU, 1989 à la p. 50 (Doc. NUA/CN.4/SER.A/1987/Add.1).

- Renvoyer aux articles d'annuaires des Nations Unies selon les règles énoncées pour les ouvrages collectifs à la section 6.3. Si possible, inclure le numéro de document. Omettre le nom de l'auteur et celui du directeur si ces informations ne sont pas disponibles.

5.1.2.6   Publications de vente

Exemple
NU, *Recommandations sur le transport des produits dangereux*, 9ᵉ éd., New York, NU, 1995 à la p. 118.

- Renvoyer aux éditions destinées à la vente selon les règles concernant les monographies à la section 6.2.

5.1.3 Communautés européennes

Les règlements, les directives, les décisions, les débats et les autres documents sont publiés dans le *Journal officiel des Communautés européennes*. Le *Journal officiel* est publié chaque jour de travail dans les onze langues officielles de l'Union Européenne. Il comprend deux séries (la série L pour la législation et la série C pour l'information et les annonces) ainsi qu'un supplément (la série S pour les offres publiques).

5.1.3.1 Règlements, directives et décisions

La législation des Communautés européennes comprend des instruments nommés règlements, directives et décisions qui sont publiés dans le *Journal officiel des Communautés européennes : Législation* (J.O. L.).

Exemples					
	CE,	*titre,*	[année du journal]	journal officiel et numéro de vol./1ʳᵉ page	référence précise.
Règlements	CE,	*Règlement 1148/99 de la Commission du 31 mai 1999, portant ouverture de ventes par adjudications simples à l'exportation d'alcools d'origine vinique,*	[1999]	J.O. L. 137/31	à la p. 39.
Directives	CE,	*Directive 99/59 du Conseil, du 17 juin 1999, modifiant la directive 77/388/CEE en ce qui concerne le régime de taxe sur la valeur ajoutée applicable aux services de télécommunications,*	[1999]	J.O. L. 162/63.	
Décisions	CE,	*Décision 98/85 de la Commission, du 16 janvier 1998, relative à certaines mesures de protection à l'égard des oiseaux vivants originaires de Hong Kong ou de la République populaire de Chine,*	[1998]	J.O. L. 15/45	à la p. 46.

- Indiquer «CE» suivi du titre descriptif de l'instrument complet en italique. Le numéro de l'instrument est inclus dans le titre. Les numéros de directives et de décisions sont composés des deux derniers chiffres de l'année et d'un numéro séquentiel (par ex. «98/85»). Les numéros de règlements sont composés, à l'inverse, d'un numéro séquentiel suivi des deux derniers chiffres de l'année (par ex. «1149/99»).
- Renvoyer au *Journal officiel des Communautés européennes : Législation* (J.O. L.) en séparant le numéro de volume et la première page de l'instrument par une barre oblique.

5.1.3.2 Débats du Parlement européen

Exemple				
CE,	*titre ou date de la séance,*	[année]	journal officiel et numéro de vol./1re page	référence précise.
CE,	*Niveaux maximaux admissibles de radioactivité,*	[1987]	J.O. D. 2-356/1	à la p. 6.

- Indiquer «CE» suivi du titre du document ou de la date de la séance du Parlement européen.
- Indiquer ensuite l'année du Journal officiel entre crochets. Renvoyer au *Journal officiel des Communautés européennes : Débats du Parlement européen* (J.O. D.) en séparant le numéro de volume et la première page du texte par une barre oblique. Noter que les numéros de volume ont deux composantes (par ex. 2-356). Une barre oblique sépare le numéro de volume de la première page (par ex. «2-356/1»).

5.1.3.3 Autres documents

Exemples	
Communications et Informations	CE, *Taux d'intérêt appliqué par la Banque centrale européenne à ses opérations de prise en pension : 300% au 1er janvier 1999 — Taux de change de l'euro 4 janvier 1999,* [1999] J.O. C. 2/1.
Publications générales	CE, Commission, *Les droits du citoyen européen,* Luxembourg, CE, 1990.
Périodiques	CE, *Commerce extérieur : statistiques mensuelles* (1994) n° 1 à la p. 16.

- Indiquer «CE» pour désigner les Communautés européennes comme étant l'organe responsable. Fournir des précisions sur l'auteur s'il y a lieu.
- Renvoyer au *Journal officiel des Communautés européennes : Communications et Informations* (J.O.C.) de la même manière que l'on renvoie aux autres sections du *Journal officiel.*
- Suivre les règles applicables établies au chapitre 6 pour renvoyer aux publications générales.
- Dans le cas des périodiques, mettre le titre en italique suivi de l'année et du numéro du périodique.

5.1.4 Conseil de l'Europe

Les documents émanant du Conseil de l'Europe sont publiés dans les publications officielles suivantes :

Bulletin d'information sur les activités juridiques	Bull. inf.
Comptes-rendus des débats	Débats
Documents de séance	Documents
Ordres du jour et procès-verbaux	Ordres
Textes adoptés par l'Assemblée	Textes adoptés

Exemples							
	Conseil de l'Europe,	organe,	information sur la session,	*titre* (s'il y a lieu),	publication officielle	(année)	référence précise.
Débats	Conseil de l'Europe,	A.P.,	2001 sess. ordinaire (1re partie),		Débats, vol. 1	(2001)	à la p. 67.
Textes adoptés	Conseil de l'Europe,	A.C.,	21e sess., partie 3,		Textes adoptés, Rec. 585	(1970)	à la 1.
Ordres du jour et procès-verbaux	Conseil de l'Europe,	A.C.,	21e sess., partie 2,		Ordres, 10e séance	(1969)	à la p.20.
Documents de séance	Conseil de l'Europe,	A.P.,	38e sess.,	*Déclaration écrite n° 150 sur la protection du site archéologique de Pompei,*	Documents, vol. 7, Doc. 5700	(1987)	à la p. 1.
Séries	Conseil de l'Europe,	Comité des Ministres,		*Recommandation R(82)1,*	(1980) 12 Bull. Inf. 58.		

• Indiquer «Conseil de l'Europe», suivi de l'organe responsable. Abréger «Assemblée parlementaire» par «A.P.» et «Assemblée consultative» par «A.C.».

- Fournir des renseignements sur la session, suivi du titre du document, s'il y a lieu.
- Renvoyer à la publication officielle.
- Indiquer entre parenthèses l'année de publication après la référence à la publication officielle.
- Noter que les références aux périodiques (par ex. Bull. Inf.) doivent se faire selon les règles de référence aux périodiques énoncées à la section 6.1.

5.1.5 Organisation des États américains

Exemples						
OÉA,	Organe,	numéro de session (s'il y a lieu),	*titre,*	numéro de document	(année)	référence précise.
OÉA,	Assemblée générale,	2ᵉ sess.,	*Draft Standards Regarding the Formulation of Reservations to Multilateral Treaties,*	Doc. off. OEA/Ser. P/AG/Doc .202	(1972).	
OÉA,	Commission Interaméricaine des Droits de l'Homme,		*Draft of the Inter-American Declaration on the Rights of Indigenous Peoples,*	Doc. off. OEA/Ser. L/V/II.90/ Doc.14, rev. 1	(1995)	à la p. 1.

- Indiquer «OÉA» suivi du nom complet de l'organe. L'Organisation des États américains et ses organes sont les auteurs de tous les documents de l'OÉA.
- S'il y a lieu, indiquer le numéro de session ou le numéro de séance après avoir indiqué l'organe responsable du document.
- Fournir le titre officiel du document.
- Placer la mention «Doc. off.» (Document officiel) devant le numéro du document commençant par «OEA». Le numéro du document débute avec les trois lettres «OEA» (Organización de los Estados Americanos) et non pas «OÉA» ou «OAS».
- Indiquer l'année de publication du document entre parenthèses à la fin de la référence. L'année peut être suivie d'une référence précise, s'il y a lieu.

5—Documentation Internationale

5.1.6   L'Organisation mondiale du commerce et l'Accord général sur les tarifs douaniers et le commerce (GATT)

Exemples						
	OMC ou GATT,	titre,	numéro de Déc., Rec. ou Doc.,	numéro de sess.	I.B.D.D.	service électronique (s'il y a lieu).
Décisions et recommandations		Accession of Guatemala,	GATT P.C. Déc. L/6824,	47ᵉ sess.,	supp. n° 38 I.B.D.D. (1991) 16.	
		Liberté de contrat en matière d'assurance,	GATT P.C. Rec. du 27 mai 1959,	15ᵉ sess.,	supp. n° 8 I.B.D.D. (1960) 26.	
Rapports	GATT,	Report of the Panel adopted by the Committee on Anti-Dumping Practices on 30 October 1995,	GATT Doc. ADP/137,		supp. n° 42 I.B.D.D. (1995) 17.	
	OMC,	Rapport du groupe de travail sur l'accession de la Bulgarie,	OMC Doc. WT/ACC/BGR/5 (1996),			en ligne : OMC <http://docs online.wto. org>.
Réunions	OMC, Conseil général,	Compte rendu de la réunion (tenue le 22 novembre 2000),	OMC Doc. WT/GC/M/60,			en ligne : OMC <http://docs online.wto. org>.

- Les décisions et les recommandations n'ont pas d'auteur. Le GATT et l'OMC, ainsi que les organes plus précis, doivent être indiqués comme étant les organes responsables des rapports du GATT et de l'OMC, à moins que cela ne soit indiqué dans le titre du rapport.

- Indiquer le numéro de décision ou de recommandation. S'il n'y a pas de numéro, indiquer la date complète de la décision ou de la recommandation. Indiquer «P.C.» pour désigner «Parties contractantes», «Déc.» pour désigner «Décision» et «Rec.» pour désigner «Recommandation».
- Si possible, renvoyer aux *Instruments de base et documents divers* (I.B.D.D.) du GATT. Indiquer l'année entre parenthèses et la première page du document.
- Si un rapport est publié indépendamment, sans numéro de document, suivre les règles énoncées à la section 6.2, par ex. GATT, *Les marchés internationaux de la viande : 1990/91*, Genève, GATT, 1991.

5.1.7   Organisation de coopération et de développement économique

Exemples						
	OCDE, organe (s'il y a lieu),	*titre,*	titre de la série,	numéro du document de travail,	numéro du document,	(renseignements sur l'édition).
Série	OCDE,	*Japon (n° 34),*	Examens en matière de coopération pour le développement,			Paris, ODCE, 1999.
Documents de travail	OCDE, Département économique,	*Pour une croissance écologiquement durable en Australie,*		Document de travail n° 309,	n° de doc. ECO/WKP (2001)35	(2001).
Périodiques	OCDE,	*Données OCDE sur l'environnement : Compendium 1995*				(1995).

- Indiquer «OCDE» et tout organe particulier, suivi du titre en italique.
- Si le document fait partie d'une série, fournir le titre de la série.
- Si le document est un document de travail, fournir le numéro du document de travail et le numéro du document. Noter que le numéro débute avec «OCDE» en français et en anglais.
- Par la suite, indiquer les renseignements sur l'édition entre parenthèses. Pour les périodiques, indiquer la date la plus précise possible.

5.2   JURISPRUDENCE

Voir les annexes E et G pour une liste des abréviations des organisations internationales et de leurs recueils.

5.2.1   Cour permanente de justice internationale (1922-1940)

Renvoyer aux lois et aux règles de la C.P.J.I. par titre, numéro du recueil et le nom de l'édition, suivis de la première page ou du numéro de document. Par exemple, *Revised Rules of the Court* (1926), C.P.J.I. 33 (sér. D) n° 1.

5.2.1.1   Jugements, ordonnances et avis consultatifs

Exemples						
	Intitulé (*nom des parties*)	(année),	type de décision,	recueil	numéro de la décision	référence précise.
Jugements	*Affaire des zones franches de la Haute-Savoie et du pays de Gex* (*France c. Suisse*)	(1932),		C.P.J.I. (sér. A/B)	n° 46	à la p. 167.
Avis consultatifs	*Trafic ferroviaire entre la Lituanie et la Pologne*	(1931),	Avis consulta-tif,	C.P.J.I. (sér. A/B)	n° 41	à la p. 3.
Ordonnances	*Chemin de fer Panevezys-Saldutiskis* (*Estonie c. Lituanie*),		Ordon-nance du 30 juin 1938,	C.P.J.I. (sér. A/B)	n° 75	à la p. 8.

- Fournir l'intitulé et le nom des parties entre parenthèses. Dans le cas des avis consultatifs, le nom des parties n'est pas indiqué puisqu'ils répondent à une demande d'une organisation internationale et ne règlent pas directement des différends inter-étatiques.
- Dans le cas des jugements et des avis consultatifs, indiquer l'année de la décision entre parenthèses après l'intitulé.
- Préciser s'il s'agit d'une ordonnance ou d'un avis consultatif. Fournir la date complète lorsqu'il s'agit d'une ordonnance.
- Renvoyer à une série de la C.P.J.I. et indiquer le numéro de la décision. Les jugements de la C.P.J.I. sont publiés dans *Série A : Recueil des arrêts* (C.P.J.I. (Sér. A)) et dans *Série A/B : Arrêts, ordonnances et avis consultatifs* (C.P.J.I. (Sér. A/B)). Les

ordonnances et les avis consultatifs sont publiés dans *Série A/B : Arrêts, ordonnances et avis consultatifs* (C.P.J.I. (Sér. A/B)) et dans *Série A/B : Arrêts, ordonnances et avis consultatifs* (C.P.J.I. (Sér. A/B)).

5.2.1.2 Plaidoiries, exposés oraux et autres documents

Exemples						
Intitulé (*nom des parties*),	«titre du document précis»	(date du document),	recueil	numéro de décision,	1re page	référence précise.
Affaire franco-hellénique des phares (*France c. Grèce*),	«Exposé oral de M. le professeur Basdevant»	(5 février 1934),	C.P.J.I. (sér. C)	n° 74,	222	à la p.227.
Affaire Pajzs, Csáky, Esterházy (*Hongrie c. Yougoslavie*),	«Requête introductive d'instance»	(1er décembre 1935),	C.P.J.I. (sér. C)	n° 79,	10	à la p.12.

- Fournir l'intitulé et, entre parenthèses, le nom des parties.
- Indiquer le titre officiel du document précis après l'intitulé de la cause, suivi de la date complète.
- Renvoyer à la série C.P.J.I. et indiquer le numéro de la décision. Les plaidoiries, les exposés oraux et les autres documents paraissent dans *Série C : Plaidoiries, exposés oraux et documents* (P.C.I.J. (Sér. C)).
- Insérer une virgule entre le numéro de la décision et le numéro de la première page.

5.2.2 Cour internationale de Justice (1945-présent)

Renvoyer aux lois et aux règles de la C.I.J. par titre, numéro de recueil et le nom de l'édition, suivis de la première page ou du numéro de document. Par exemple, *Travel and Subsistence Regulations of the International Court of Justice*, [1947] C.I.J. Acts & Doc. 94.

Les jugements, les ordonnances et les avis consultatifs ainsi que les plaidoiries et autres documents de la Cour internationale de Justice sont publiés dans le recueil officiel de la cour : *Recueil des arrêts, avis consultatifs et ordonnances* (C.I.J. Rec.) et dans *Mémoires, plaidoiries et documents* (C.I.J. Mémoires). La C.I.J. est également connue sous le nom de «Cour Mondiale».

5.2.2.1 *Jugements, ordonnances et avis consultatifs*

Exemples						
	Intitulé (*nom des parties*),	type de décision,	[année du recueil]	recueil	1re page	référence précise.
Jugements	*Affaire relative au Timor oriental* (*Portugal c. Australie*),		[1995]	C.I.J. rec.	90	à la p. 103.
Ordonnances	*Compétence en matière de pêcheries* (*Espagne c. Canada*),	Ordonnance du 8 mai 1996,	[1996]	C.I.J. rec.	58.	
Avis consutatifs	*Licéité de l'utilisation des armes nucléaires par un État dans un conflit armé*,	Avis consultatif,	[1996]	C.I.J. rec.	226	à la p. 230.

- Indiquer l'intitulé officiel ainsi que le nom des parties entre parenthèses. Bien que le C.I.J. Rec. sépare parfois le nom des parties par une barre oblique (par ex. *El Salvador/Honduras*), remplacer la barre oblique par un «c.» (par ex. *Portugal c. Australie*). Le nom des parties n'est pas indiqué dans le cas des avis consultatifs.
- Après l'intitulé, préciser s'il s'agit d'une ordonnance ou d'un avis consultatif. Fournir la date complète lorsqu'il s'agit d'une ordonnance.
- Renvoyer au recueil de la C.I.J. et indiquer la première page de la décision. Les jugements, les ordonnances et les avis consultatifs de la Cour internationale de Justice sont publiés dans le recueil officiel de la cour : *Recueil des arrêts, avis consultatifs et ordonnances* (C.I.J. Rec.).
- Renvoyer au site Internet de la C.I.J. selon les règles de la référence en ligne pour tout jugement, opinion et ordre de la C.I.J. qui n'est pas encore publié sur support papier.

5.2.2.2 Mémoires, plaidoiries et documents

Exemples						
Intitulé officiel (*nom des parties*),	«titre du document précis»	(date du document),	[année du recueil]	recueil et numéro de volume	1re page	référence précise.
Affaire du droit de passage sur le territoire indien (*Portugal c. Inde*),	«Plaidoirie de Shri M.C. Setalvad»	(23 septembre 1957),	[1960]	C.I.J. Mémoires (vol. 4)	14	à la p. 23.
Compétence en matière de pêcheries (*Espagne c. Canada*),	«Requête introductive d'instance par l'Espagne»	(28 mars 1995),		C.I.J. Mémoires	3.	

- Indiquer l'intitulé officiel ainsi que le nom des parties entre parenthèses.
- Fournir le titre officiel du document après l'intitulé, puis indiquer la date précise du document entre parenthèses.
- Renvoyer à la «C.I.J. Mémoires» et à la première page du document. La C.I.J. publie les mémoires et autres documents dans *Mémoires, plaidoiries et documents* (C.I.J. Mémoires). S'il y a un numéro de volume, l'inclure avant l'indication de la première page en chiffres arabes et entre parenthèses (par ex. «C.I.J. Mémoires (vol. 4)»).
- Noter qu'après 1981, les mémoires ne donnent aucune indication quant à la date de publication du recueil. Les volumes sont identifiés à partir du titre de la décision à laquelle le document se rapporte. Les mémoires sont disponibles sur le site de la C.I.J. : <http://www.icj-cij.org>.

5.2.3   Cour de Justice des Communautés européennes et Tribunal de première instance

Exemples								
	Intitulé,	numéro de décision,	[année du recueil]	recueil	1re page	référence précise,	référence parallèle.
C.J.E.	*Commission c. Luxembourg,*	C-26/99,	[1999]	E.C.R.	I-8987	à la p. I-8995.	
C.J. (1re inst.)	*Kesko c. Commission,*	T-22/97,	[1999]	E.C.R.	II-3775	à la p. II-3822.	

- Indiquer l'intitulé en utilisant la forme abrégée du nom des institutions (par ex. «Conseil» plutôt que «Conseil des Communautés européennes»).
- Indiquer le numéro de la décision. Un «C-» indique les décisions de la Cour de Justice des Communautés européennes (C.J.E.) et un «T-» indique celles du Tribunal de première instance (C.J. (1^{re}inst.)).
- Renvoyer au «Rec. C.E.» et indiquer la première page de la décision. Les décisions de la C.J.E. et les décisions de la C.J. (1re inst.) sont reproduites dans la publication officielle de la Cour, le *Recueil de la jurisprudence de la Cour et du Tribunal de première instance* couramment appelé *Recueil de la Cour européenne* (Rec. C.E.).
- Les numéros de page sont précédés par «I-» s'il s'agit de la C.J.E. et par «II-» s'il s'agit du Tribunal de première instance.
- Si possible, inclure une référence parallèle aux *Common Market Law Reports* (C.M.L.R.) ou au *Common Market Reporter* (C.M.R.).

5.2.4 Cour européenne des Droits de l'Homme et Commission européenne des Droits de l'Homme

Exemples					
Intitulé	(année du jugement),	numéro de vol.	recueil	1re page et référence précise,	référence parallèle.
Kurt c. Turquie	(1998),	74	Cour Eur. D.H. (Sér. A)	1152,	27 E.H.R.R. 373.
Larkos c. Chypre	(1999),	I	Cour Eur. D.H. (Sér. A)	557,	30 E.H.R.R. 597.
Spencer c. Royaume-Uni	(1998),	92A	Comm. Eur. D.H.D.R.	56,	41 Y.B. Eur. Conv. H.R. 72.

- Indiquer l'intitulé, suivi de l'année de la décision entre parenthèses.
- Indiquer le numéro de volume du recueil avant le nom du recueil, suivi du nom du recueil et de la première page de la décision. Renvoyer aux publications officielles de la Cour et de la Commission : *Cour européenne des Droits de l'Homme, Série A : Arrêts et décisions* (Cour Eur. D.H. (Sér. A)) ; *Recueil de décisions de la Commission européenne des Droits de l'Homme* (Comm. Eur. D.H. Rec. (de 1960 à 1974)) ; *Décisions et rapports de la Commission européenne des Droits de l'Homme* (Comm. Eur. D.H. D.R. (de 1975 à 1999)).
- Si possible, fournir une référence parallèle soit à l'*Annuaire de la Convention européenne des Droits de l'Homme* (Ann. Conv. Eur. D.H.), soit aux *European Human Rights Reports* (E.H.R.R.).

5.2.5   Cour Interaméricaine des Droits de l'Homme

5.2.5.1   Jugements et avis consultatifs

Exemples							
	Intitulé (*nom de l'État impliqué*)	(année de la décision),	type de décision et numéro,	recueil	numéro de décision,	référence précise,	référence parallèle.
Jugements	*Affaire Neira Alegría (Pérou)*	(1996),		Inter-Am. Ct. H.R. (Sér. C)	n° 29,	au para. 55,	*Annual Report of the Inter-American Court of Human Rights: 1996,* OEA/Ser.L/V/I II.19/doc.4 (1997) 179.
Avis consultatifs	*Reports of the Inter-American Commission on Human Rights (Art. 51 of the American Convention on Human Rights) (Chili)*	(1997),	Avis consult-atif OC-15/97,	Inter-Am. Ct. H.R. (Sér. A)	n° 15,	au para. 53,	*Annual Report of the Inter-American Commission on Human Rights : 1997,* OEA/Ser.L/V/I II.39/doc.5 (1998) 307.

- Inscrire l'intitulé suivi de l'année de la décision entre parenthèses. Si la cause implique un État individuel, indiquer le nom de celui-ci entre parenthèses avant l'année de la décision.
- Indiquer si la décision est un avis consultatif et fournir le numéro de la décision.
- Indiquer le recueil et le numéro de la décision. La Cour Interaméricaine des Droits de l'Homme publie ces décisions dans *Inter-American Court of Human Rights Series C : Decisions and Judgments* et ces avis consultatifs dans *Inter-American Court of Human Rights Series A : Judgments and Opinions.*
- Fournir une référence parallèle au rapport annuel de la Cour, aux *International Legal Materials* (I.L.M.) ou au *Inter-American Yearbook on Human Rights*, si possible.

5.2.5.2 Mémoires, plaidoiries et documents

Exemple					
Intitulé (nom de l'État impliqué),	type de décision et numéro,	«titre du document»	(date du document),	recueil et (série)	1ʳᵉ page et référence précise.
Proposed Amendments to the Naturalization Provisions of the Constitution of Costa Rica,	Avis consultatif OC-4/84,	«Verbatim Record of Public Hearing»	(7 Septembre 1983),	Inter-Am. Ct. H.R. (Sér. B)	203.

- Inscrire l'intitulé. Si la cause implique un État individuel, indiquer le nom de celui-ci entre parenthèses.
- Indiquer si la décision est un avis consultatif et fournir le numéro de la décision.
- Inclure le titre entre guillemets et la date du document entre parenthèses.
- Indiquer le recueil et la première page de la décision. La Cour Interaméricaine des Droits de l'Homme publie les mémoires, les plaidoiries et les documents dans *Inter-American Court of Human Rights Series B : Pleadings, Oral Arguments and Documents.*

5.2.6 Commission Interaméricaine des Droits de l'Homme

Exemple						
Intitulé	(année du jugement),	Inter-Am. Comm. H.R.	numéro de la décision,	référence précise,	rapport annuel,	numéro du document.
Sánchez c. Mexico	(1992),	Inter-Am. Comm. H.R.	No.27/92,		Annual Report of the Inter-American Commission on Human Rights : 1992-93,	OEA/Ser.L/ V/II.83/doc. 14 104.

- Inscrire l'intitulé suivi de l'année de la décision entre parenthèses.
- Inscrire «Inter-Am. Comm. H.R.» suivi du numéro de la décision.
- Les décisions de la Commission Interaméricaine des Droits de l'Homme sont publiées dans ses rapports annuels. Renvoyer au recueil annuel de la Commission et indiquer son numéro de document. Le numéro de document des publications de l'Organisation

des États américains débute toujours avec «OEA» et non pas «OÉA», quelle que soit la langue du document.

5.2.7   Tribunal pénal international pour l'ex-Yougoslavie

Exemple				
Intitulé	(année du jugement),	numéro de l'affaire	(tribunal),	référence parallèle.
Procureur c. Delalic	(2001),	Affaire n° IT-96-21-A	(Tribunal Pénal International pour l'ex-Yougoslavie, Chambre d'appel),	en ligne : Nations Unies <http://www.un.org/icty/jugements-f.htm>.

- Indiquer l'intitulé, suivi de l'année de la décision, du numéro de l'affaire et du nom du tribunal international. Des références à l'Internet peuvent être fournies en se conformant aux règles de la section 3.11.

5.2.8   Tribunal pénal international pour le Rwanda

Exemple				
Intitulé	(année du jugement),	numéro de l'affaire	(tribunal),	référence parallèle.
Procureur c. Ruggiu	(2000),	Affaire n° ICTR-97-32-I	(Tribunal pénal international pour le Rwanda, Chambre de 1re instance I),	en ligne : Nations Unies <http://www.ictr.org/>.

- Indiquer l'intitulé, suivi de l'année de la décision, du numéro de l'affaire et du nom du tribunal international. Des références à l'Internet peuvent être fournies en se conformant aux règles de la section 3.11.

5.2.9 Groupes spéciaux du GATT 1947

Intitulé (plainte(s))	(année du document),	numéro de doc. GATT,	vol. I.B.D.D. et (année)	1re page et référence précise,	référence parallèle.
République de Corée — Restrictions à l'importation de la viande de bœuf (*Plainte de la Nouvelle-Zélande*)	(1989),	GATT Doc. L/6505,	Supp. n° 36 I.B.D.D. (1990)	234,	en ligne : OMC <http://www.wto.org/french/tratop_f/dispu_f/gt47ds_f.htm>.
États-Unis — Droits compensateurs sur la viande de porc fraîche, réfrigérée et congelée en provenance du Canada (*Plainte du Canada*)	(1991),	GATT Doc. DS7/R,	Supp. n° 38 I.B.D.D. (1990-91)	30,	en ligne : OMC <http://www.wto.org/french/tratop_f/dispu_f/gt47ds_f.htm>.

- Fournir l'intitulé suivi du nom de l'État (ou des États) ayant déposé la plainte entre parenthèses.
- Indiquer la date de la décision entre parenthèses suivie d'une virgule et du numéro de document GATT.
- Renvoyer aux I.B.D.D. (*Instruments de base et documents divers*) du GATT en indiquant le numéro de volume suivi de «I.B.D.D.», de l'année entre parenthèses et de la première page du document.
- S'il y a lieu, renvoyer à la page et au paragraphe précis immédiatement après la référence au document.
- Une référence électronique peut être fournie en suivant les règles énoncées à la section 3.11.

5.2.10 Rapports de Groupes spéciaux et de l'Organe d'appel de l'OMC

Exemples						
	Intitulé (plainte(s))	(année de la décision),	numéro du document OMC	référence précise	(type de rapport),	référence parallèle.
Groupe spécial	*États-Unis – Articles 301 à 310 de la Loi de 1974 sur le commerce extérieur (Plainte des communautés européennes)*	(1999),	OMC Doc. WT/ DS152/R	au n° 3.1	(Rapport du Groupe spécial),	en ligne : OMC \<http://www. wto.org/ french/docs_f/ docs_f.htm\>.
Organe d'appel	*Inde — Protection conférée par un brevet pour les produits pharmaceutiques et les produits chimiques pour l'agriculture (Plaintes des États-Unis)*	(1997),	OMC Doc. WT/ DS50/ AB/R		(Rapport de l'Organe d'appel),	en ligne : OMC \<http://www. wto.org/ french/docs_f/ docs_f.htm\>.

- Fournir l'intitulé du rapport suivi du nom de l'auteur (ou des auteurs) de la plainte. Si les plaintes sont étudiées dans un seul rapport, indiquer le nom de tous les États ayant déposé une plainte après l'intitulé du rapport. Si par contre plusieurs États ont déposé des plaintes qui sont traitées séparément, indiquer le nom de l'État visé par le rapport. S'il y a plus de trois États, indiquer le nom d'un État suivi de «*et al.*».
- Après avoir indiqué l'année du rapport, fournir le numéro du document. Un rapport peut avoir plusieurs numéros de document (par ex. «WT/DS 8, 10, 11/AB/R»). Les lettres «AB» sont l'abréviation d'*Appellate Body*. Si un rapport est destiné à un État particulier parmi plusieurs ayant déposé une plainte, l'abréviation du nom de cet État apparaît dans le numéro de document (par ex. «OMC doc. WT/DS27/R/USA»).

- À la suite du numéro du document, indiquer entre parenthèses s'il s'agit d'un rapport d'un Groupe spécial ou d'un Organe d'appel.
- Une référence électronique peut être fournie en suivant les règles énoncées à la section 3.11.

5.2.11 Rapports de Groupes spéciaux de l'Accord de libre-échange canado-américain

Exemples						
	Intitulé	(année de la décision),	numéro du document,	recueil	(groupe spécial),	référence parallèle.
Publiés	*Re Framboises rouges du Canada*	(1990),	USA-89-1904-01,	3 T.C.T. 8175	(Groupe spéc. c. 19),	en ligne : Secrétariat de l'ALÉNA <http://www.nafta-sec-alena.org/french/index.htm>.
Non publiés	*Re Porc frais, frigorifié et congélé du Canada*	(1991),	ECC-91-1904-01 USA		(Comité con. extr.),	en ligne : Secrétariat de l'ALÉNA <http://www.nafta-sec-alena.org/french/index.htm>.

- À la suite de l'intitulé, indiquer l'année et le numéro du document. Renvoyer à un recueil si possible.
- Abréger les divers groupes spéciaux de la façon suivante : «Groupe spéc. c. 18» (Groupe spécial créé en vertu du chapitre 18), «Groupe spéc. c. 19» (Groupe spécial créé en vertu du chapitre 19) et «Comité con. extr.» (Comité pour contestation extraordinaire).
- Une référence électronique peut être fournie en suivant les règles énoncées à la section 3.11.

5.2.12 Rapports de Groupes spéciaux de l'Accord de libre-échange nord-américain

Exemples					
	Intitulé (*nom des parties*)	(année de la décision),	numéro du document	(groupe spécial),	référence parallèle.
Révision des décisions définitives d'organismes canadiens	*Re Ficelle synthétique pour ramasseuse-presse avec une résistance à la tension de 200LB ou moins, originaire ou exportée des États-Unis d'Amérique (États-Unis c. Canada)*	(1995),	CDA-94-1904-02	(Groupe spéc. c. 19),	en ligne : Secrétariat de l'ALÉNA <http://www.nafta-sec-alena.org/ french/index.htm>.
Révision des décisions définitives de l'organisme mexicain	*Re Polystyrène et cristale impacte en provenance des États-Unis d'Amérique (États-Unis c. Mexique)*	(1995),	MEX-94-1904-03	(Groupe spéc. c. 19),	en ligne : Secrétariat de l'ALÉNA <http://www.nafta-sec-alena.org/ french/index.htm>.
Révision des mesures canadiennes	*Re Tarifs douaniers appliqués par le Canada sur certains produits agricoles en provenance des États-Unis d'Amérique (États-Unis c. Canada)*	(1996),	CDA-95-2008-01	(Groupe arb. c. 20),	en ligne : Secrétariat de l'ALÉNA <http://www.nafta-sec-alena.org/ french/index.htm>.

- Après l'intitulé, indiquer le nom des parties entre parenthèses.
- Fournir l'année de la décision entre parenthèses. Inclure le numéro du document et renvoyer à un recueil si possible.
- Fournir des renseignements sur le chapitre dans lequel la plainte a été soumise. Indiquer «Groupe spéc. c. 19» pour désigner «Group spécial binational Chapitre 19 » et «Groupe Arb. c. 20» pour désigner le «Groupe arbitral créé en vertu du chapitre 20».
- Une référence électronique peut être fournie en suivant les règles énoncées à la section 3.11.

5.2.13 Décisions d'arbitrage international

Exemples					
	Intitulé ou numéro de la cause	(année de la décision),	recueil et référence précise	(cadre),	(arbitres) (facultatif).
Nom des parties divulgué	*Southern Pacific Properties c. Egypt*	(1992),	32 I.L.M. 933 à la p. 1008,	(International Center for Settlement of Investment Disputes),	(Arbitres : Dr Eduardo Jiménez de Aréchaga, Mohamed Amin El Mahdi, Robert F. Pietrowski Jr).
Parties anonymes	Déc. n° 6248	(1990),	19 Y.B. Comm. Arb. 124 à la p. 129	(International Chamber of Commerce).	

- Fournir l'intitulé avec le nom des parties, si disponible. Lorsque les parties sont anonymes, indiquer le numéro de la décision.
- Indiquer l'année de la décision entre parenthèses, suivie de la référence au recueil.
- Si possible, indiquer l'organisme qui a fourni le cadre ou le mécanisme d'arbitrage à la fin de la référence.
- Le nom des arbitres peut être indiqué entre parenthèses à la fin de la référence.

5.2.14 Décisions de droit international rendues devant des cours nationales

Exemples			
Intitulé,	recueil du pays d'origine,	recueil international	(pays et juridiction).
Re Noble et Wolf,	[1949] 4 D.L.R. 375,	[1948] Ann. Dig. I.L.C. 302	(Can., C.A. Ont.)
Lindon c. La Commonwealth de L'Australie (n° 2)	(1996), 136 A.L.R. 251,	118 I.L.R. 338	(Austl., H.C.).
Institute of Chartered Accountants in England and Wales c. Commissioners of Customs and Excise,	[1999] 2 All E.R. 449,	[1999] 2 C.M.L.R. 1333	(R.-U., C. des L.).

- Lorsqu'une décision de portée internationale est rendue par une cour nationale, fournir une référence à un recueil du pays d'origine. Étant donné la nature de la décision, il est toutefois nécessaire d'indiquer une référence à un recueil international tel que le *Annual Digest and Reports of Public International Law Cases* (Ann. Dig. I.L.C.), le *International Law Reports* (I.L.R.), les *Common Market Law Reports* (C.M.L.R.) ou le *Common Market Reporter* (C.M.R.).
- Indiquer le pays où la décision a été prise et préciser la cour qui a pris la décision.

5.3   SITES INTERNET

Exemple			
Référence traditionnelle,	en ligne :	nom du site	<adresse universelle>.
U.S., Commission on Security and Cooperation in Europe, *Presidential Elections and Independence Referendums in the Baltic States, the Soviet Union and Successor States*, Washington (D.C.), The Commission, 1992 à la p. 53,	en ligne :	Commission on Security and Cooperation in Europe	<http://www.csce.gov/ reports.cfm>.

- Fournir la référence traditionnelle, suivie d'une virgule, de «en ligne :», du nom du site Internet et de l'adresse universelle (URL).

- Renvoyer à l'adresse universelle du document à moins que cette adresse ne soit propre à une session Internet, auquel cas renvoyer à la page d'accueil.
- Toutes les sources Internet ne sont pas fiables, il faut donc porter une attention particulière lorsqu'on renvoie à de telles sources.
- Plusieurs textes en ligne disparaissent après un certain temps. Renvoyer à une source en ligne si cette source fournit des documents archivés remontant à quelques années.
- Inclure un numéro de paragraphe comme référence précise si possible. Si la pagination d'une source imprimée est reproduite dans une source électronique, renvoyer à la pagination utilisée par la source imprimée.

6

DOCTRINE ET AUTRES DOCUMENTS

6.1 PÉRIODIQUES

6.1.1 Modèle de base

Exemple							
Auteur,	«titre de l'article»	(année)	volume	Abréviation du périodique	première page	référence précise.	(service électronique) (s'il y a lieu).
Marie-Claude Prémont,	«La fiscalité locale au Québec : de la cohabitation au refuge fiscal»	(2001)	46	R.D. McGill	713	¶ 4	(QL).

6.1.2 Auteur

6.1.2.1 Un seul auteur

Exemple
Adrian Popovici, «La poule et l'homme : sur l'article 976 C.c.Q.» (1997) 99 R. du N. 214.

- Indiquer le nom de l'auteur tel que présenté. Indiquer tous les noms et les initiales utilisés. Ne pas mettre d'espace entre deux initiales. Ne pas inscrire un nom lorsque des initiales sont utilisées et ne pas inscrire d'initiales lorsqu'un nom est utilisé. Si, dans l'article, le nom de l'auteur est précédé d'un titre honorifique tel que «l'honorable», «Rabbin», «Professeur» ou «Lord», l'inclure dans la référence. Ne pas indiquer les diplômes ou toute autre référence.

6.1.2.2 Coauteurs

Exemple
Pascal Bascaron, Alexis Demirdjian et Ryhan Mansour, «La déclaration universelle des droits de l'homme : la torture et l'article 5 — 50 ans d'espoir» (1999) 6 R.E.J. 253.

- Ne pas indiquer plus de trois auteurs.
- Séparer le nom des deux derniers auteurs par «et».
- S'il y a plus de trois auteurs, indiquer le nom du premier auteur suivi de «*et al.*».

6.1.3 Titre de l'article

Exemple
Ghislain Otis, **«Les sources des droits ancestraux des peuples autochtones»** (1999) 40 C. de D. 591.

- Indiquer le titre de l'article entre guillemets.
- Ne pas mettre de virgule après le titre.
- Séparer un titre d'un sous-titre à l'aide d'un deux-points.
- Suivre les règles de mise en majuscules de la langue dans laquelle le titre est écrit.
- Pour plus de détails concernant les titres, voir la section 6.2.3 ci-dessous.

6.1.4   Année de publication

Exemples	
Le périodique est organisé par numéro de volumes	Michel Poirier, «La convention d'emphytéose peut-elle être à titre gratuit?» **(1998)** R. du B. 401.
Le périodique est organisé par année de publication	Frédéric Pollaud-Dulian, «À propos de la sécurité juridique» **[2001]** R.T.D. civ. 487.

- Si le périodique est divisé en volumes numérotés, indiquer la date de publication entre parenthèses.
- Si le périodique n'est pas divisé en volumes numérotés, indiquer l'année (telle qu'elle paraît sur la reliure) entre crochets.

6.1.5   Volume

Exemples	
Pagination consécutive	Cardine Simard, «La responsabilité civile pour la faute de la sage-femme : des projets pilotes à la législation» (2001) **32** R.D.U.S. 59.
Pagination non consécutive	Damian Powell, «Coke in Context : Early Modern Legal Observation and Sir Edward Coke's *Reports*» (2000) **21:3** J. Legal Hist. 33.

- Indiquer le numéro de volume entre l'année de publication et l'abréviation du titre du périodique.
- Lorsque la pagination des numéros d'un volume n'est pas consécutive (c'est-à-dire que chaque numéro commence à la page 1), indiquer le volume, suivi d'un deux-points et du numéro dans lequel se trouve l'article.

6.1.6   Titre du périodique

Exemples
Will Kymlicka, «Federalism and Secession : At Home and Abroad» (2000) 13 Can. J. L. & Jur. 207.
André Cellard et Gérald Pelletier, «Le Code criminel canadien, 1892-1927: étude des acteurs sociaux » (1998) 79 **Canadian Historical Review** 261.

- Abréger le titre du périodique selon la liste des abréviations à l'annexe H. Écrire le titre complet du périodique si aucune abréviation n'existe dans ce *Manuel* ou dans un autre manuel d'abréviation juridique.
- Ne pas mettre l'abréviation ou le titre en italique.

6.1.6.1 France

Exemple		
Auteur,	«titre»	renseignements sur l'édition.
Jean-Christophe Galloux,	«La loi du 6 mars 1998 relative à la sécurité et à la promotion d'activités sportives»	J.C.P. 1998.I.1085.

- Indiquer le nom et le titre des articles publiés dans les recueils généraux de France de la manière énoncée aux sections 6.1.2-6.1.3.
- Indiquer le recueil tel qu'indiqué aux sections 3.5.4-3.5.9.

Abréger les recueils de la manière suivante :

Actualité juridique de droit administratif	A.J.D.A.
Bulletin de la Cour de cassation, section civile	Bull. civ.
Gazette du Palais	Gaz. Pal.
Recueil des décisions du Conseil d'État ou *Recueil Lebon*	Rec.
Recueil Dalloz et *Recueil Dalloz et Sirey* (1945 – présent)	D.
Semaine Juridique (1937 – présent)	J.C.P.

6.1.7 Première page de l'article

Exemple
Marie-Josée Bernardi, «La diversité génétique humaine : éléments de politique canadienne» (2001) 35 R.J.T. **327**.

- Indiquer la première page de l'article après le titre de la revue.

6.1.7.1 Articles publiés en parties

Exemples	
Publication dans différents volumes	R.A. Macdonald, «Enforcing Rights in Corporeal Moveables : Revendication and Its Surrogates» (1986) 31 R.D. McGill 573 **et** (1986) 32 R.D. McGill 1.
Publication dans différentes parties d'un même volume	Roderick A. Macdonald, «L'image du Code civil et l'imagination du notaire» (1995) 74 R. du B. can. **97 et 330**.

- Si des parties de l'article ont été publiées dans plusieurs volumes, indiquer l'auteur et le titre, puis la référence complète pour chaque partie, les références étant séparées par «et».
- Si des parties de l'article ont été publiées dans un même volume, indiquer les premières pages de chaque partie, séparées par «et».

6.1.8 Référence précise

Exemple
Nicholas Kasirer, «Agapè et le devoir juridique de secours : qui est mon prochain?» [2001] R.I.D.C. 575 **à la p. 579**.

- Indiquer la référence précise à la fin de la référence.
- Indiquer la page ou le paragraphe. Lorsque les paragraphes sont numérotés, y renvoyer à l'aide de «au n°», «au para» ou ¶. Pour renvoyer à une page, utiliser «à la p.» et pour renvoyer à plusieurs pages, utiliser «aux pp.»
- Les pages et les paragraphes consécutifs sont séparés par un trait d'union, en conservant au moins les deux derniers chiffres (par ex. «32-35», et non «32-5»).
- Utiliser une virgule pour séparer les numéros non consécutifs (par ex. «aux pp. 21, 48»).
- Pour indiquer une partie générale inscrire «et s.» (abréviation de «et suivantes») immédiatement après le numéro. Il est toutefois préférable de renvoyer aux pages ou aux paragraphes précis.
- Lorsqu'on renvoie à une note, indiquer le numéro de la page où se trouve la note ainsi que le numéro de la note (par ex. «à la p. 99, n. 140»). Lorsqu'on renvoie à plusieurs notes, indiquer le numéro de la page où se trouvent les notes ainsi que les numéros des notes (par ex. «à la p. 142, nn. 73-75»). Si toutefois le numéro de la page n'est pas disponible parce qu'il s'agit d'un article en ligne, renvoyer au numéro de la note (par ex. n. 140).
- Utiliser des chiffres arabes pour renvoyer aux pages, aux paragraphes ou autres quel que soit le format des chiffres dans le texte (par ex. 5-6, v-vi).

6.2   MONOGRAPHIES

6.2.1 Modèle de base

Exemples									
Auteur,	*titre,*	édition,	autres éléments	lieu d'édition,	maison d'édition,	année d'édition	référence précise	(service électronique) (si utilisé).
Jean-Louis Baudouin et Pierre-Gabriel Jobin,	*Les obligations,*	5ᵉ éd.,		Cowansville (Qc),	Yvon Blais,	1998	au n° 52.	
J. Anthony VanDuzer,	*The Law of Partnerships and Corporations,*			Toronto,	Irwin Law,	1997,	c. 2 (B) (3)	(QL).

- D'autres éléments peuvent être indiqués, si nécessaire, selon les règles ci-dessous. Leur ordre de présentation est le suivant : nom du directeur d'un ouvrage collectif ; nom du traducteur ; numéro du volume ; titre du volume ; titre d'une collection et le numéro du volume dans cette collection (si nécessaire) ; feuilles mobiles.

6.2.2 Auteur

6.2.2.1 Un seul auteur

Exemples
Sylvio Normand, *Introduction au droit des biens*, Montréal, Wilson & Lafleur, 2000.
Jean-Pierre Baud, *L'affaire de la main volée : une histoire juridique du corps*, Paris, Seuil, 1993 à la p. 4.
Lucie Laflamme, *Le partage consécutif à l'indivision*, Montréal, Wilson & Lafleur, 1999.
Lord Denning, *What Next in the Law*, Londres, Butterworths, 1982.

- Indiquer le nom de l'auteur tel qu'il paraît sur la page couverture. Inclure tous les noms et initiales utilisés. Ne pas mettre d'espace entre deux initiales. Ne pas inscrire un nom lorsque des initiales sont utilisées et ne pas inclure d'intiales lorsqu'un nom est utilisé. Si le nom de l'auteur sur la page couverture est précédé d'un titre honorifique tel que «l'honorable», «Rabbin», «Professeur» ou «Lord», l'inclure dans la référence. Ne pas indiquer les diplômes ou autre références.

6.2.2.2 Coauteurs

Exemples
Jacques Bourdon, Jean-Marie Pontier et Jean-Claude Ricci, *Droit des collectivités territoriales*, Paris, Presses Universitaires de France, 1987.
Albert Chavanne et Jean-Jacques Burst, *Droit de la propriété industrielle*, 5ᵉ éd., Paris, Dalloz, 1998.

- Ne pas indiquer plus de trois auteurs.
- Séparer le nom des deux derniers auteurs par un «et».
- S'il y a plus de trois auteurs, indiquer le nom du premier auteur, suivi de «*et al.*».
- Mettre une virgule après «*et al.*».
- Pour les autres types de collaborations (par ex. «avec»), suivre la formule utilisée à la page titre.

6.2.2.3 Directeur d'un ouvrage collectif

Exemple
Denis Ferland et Benoît Emery, dir., *Précis de procédure civile du Québec*, 3ᵉ éd., Cowansville (Qc), Yvon Blais, 1997.

- Indiquer le nom du directeur avant le titre de l'ouvrage collectif, suivi de «dir.» entre virgules.
- Ne pas indiquer plus de trois directeurs. S'il y en a plus, indiquer le nom du premier, suivi de «*et al.*».
- L'abréviation «dir.», pour «directeur», vaut autant pour le singulier que pour le pluriel.
- Pour les auteurs des articles composant l'ouvrage, voir la section 6.3.

6.2.2.4 *Directeur ou correcteur de l'ouvrage d'un autre*

6.2.2.4.1   Le nom de l'auteur original fait partie du titre

Exemple				
Directeur,	dir.,	*titre,*	édition,	renseignements sur l'édition.
M. Dupin,	dir.,	*Oeuvres de Pothier*	2ᵉ éd.,	Paris, Pichon-Béchet, 1835.

- Si le nom de l'auteur fait partie du titre, renvoyer au directeur, suivi de «dir.» entre virgules.

6.2.2.4.2   Le nom de l'auteur original ne fait pas partie du titre

Exemple				
Auteur,	*titre,*	édition par	directeur,	renseignements sur l'édition.
Aubry et Rau,	*Droit civil français,*	8ᵉ éd. par	André Ponsard et Ibrahim Fadlallah,	Paris, Librairies techniques, 1989.

- Si le nom de l'auteur ne fait pas partie du titre, le nom du directeur se met après la mention de l'édition, introduit par «par».
- S'il y a plusieurs éditions, indiquer le numéro (par ex. «8ᵉ éd. par»).
- Indiquer l'information complète en ce qui concerne l'auteur et l'éditeur. Inscrire leur nom tel qu'utilisé par la maison d'édition.

6.2.2.5 *Traducteur*

N.B. Les textes en langues étrangères qui pourraient être méconnus des lecteurs devraient être traduits. Le texte original peut être inclus en note de bas de page.

6.2.2.5.1   Traduction professionnelle

Exemple				
Auteur,	*titre,*	trad. par	traducteur,	renseignements sur l'édition.
Jürgen Habermas,	*Droit et démocracie : entre faits et normes,*	trad. par	Rainer Rochlitz et Christian Bouchindhomme,	Paris, Gallimard, 1997.

- Si l'on utilise une version traduite par un professionnel, indiquer le nom du traducteur avant les renseignements sur l'édition, introduit par «trad. par».
- S'il est nécessaire de modifier la traduction, introduire la modification par «[modifiée par l'auteur]» après les renseignements sur l'édition.

6.2.2.5.2   Traduction faite par l'auteur du texte dans lequel on renvoie à l'ouvrage

Exemple
Comme le dit Kronby : «la cour fut convaincue par la preuve de l'épouse» [**notre traduction**][28].

- Il n'est pas nécessaire de traduire un passage tiré d'une source rédigée dans une autre langue que le français.
- Si, dans un texte, un ouvrage est traduit afin de le citer, l'indiquer par l'ajout de «[notre traduction]» ou «[traduction par l'auteur]» à la fin de la citation, après les guillemets et avant l'appel de note.

6.2.3 Titre

Exemples
B. Lefebvre, *La bonne foi dans la formation du contrat*, Montréal, Yvon Blais, 1998.
A.H. Oosterhoff et E.E. Gillese, *Text, Commentary and Cases on Trusts*, 5ᵉ éd., Toronto, Carswell, 1998.
Frédéric Garron, *La caducité du contrat : étude de droit privé*, Aix-en-Provence, Presses universitaires d'Aix-Marseille, 2000.

- Indiquer le titre principal en entier, en italique. Suivre l'orthographe et la ponctuation du titre publié en respectant les directives suivantes :
  - le sous-titre peut être indiqué, précédé d'un deux-points ;
  - mettre une virgule avant les dates comprise à la fin du titre ;
  - ne pas utiliser d'abréviations à moins qu'elles ne soient utilisées dans le titre publié.
- Respecter les règles de majuscules de la langue dans laquelle le titre est écrit.
- Si le titre de l'ouvrage est dans une langue autre que le français, l'anglais ou une langue familière au lecteur, il faut :
  - inscrire le titre original suivi d'une traduction en français. La traduction ne doit pas être mise en italique, mais entre crochets, sans ponctuation entre le titre original et la traduction. Si le titre originale n'est pas en caractères romains (s'il est chinois ou hébreux par exemple), le transcrire en écriture romaine.

- traduire le titre en français et le mettre en italique suivi de, par ex. «(en allemand)», afin d'indiquer la langue original du texte. Il n'y a pas de ponctuation entre la traduction du titre et les parenthèses.

6.2.3.1 *Procédures d'une conférence ou d'un symposium publiées*

Exemple
Marie-France Bich, «Petits éléments pour une réflexion polémique sur la solidarité en droit du travail » dans *Droits de la personne : solidarité et bonne foi. Actes des Journées strasbourgeoises de l'Institut canadien d'études juridiques supérieures 2000 tenues du 2 au 8 juillet 2000 à Strasbourg*, Cowansville (Qc), Yvon Blais, 2000.

- Toute information concernant la conférence ou le symposium devrait être traitée comme faisant partie du titre. Mettre cette information en italique après une virgule.

6.2.4 Numéro de volume

6.2.4.1 *Livres en français*

Exemples					
Auteur	*titre,*	tome et/ou volume,	édition	directeur (s'il y a lieu)	renseignements sur l'édition.
Jean Carbonnier,	*Droit civil: les obligations,*	t. 4,	22ᵉ éd.		Paris, Presses Universitaires de France, 2000.
Henri Mazeaud *et al.,*	*Leçons de droit civil,*	t. 3, vol. 1,	7ᵉ éd.	Yves Picod, dir.,	Paris, Montchrestien, 1999.

- Les ouvrages français peuvent être divisés en tomes, qui peuvent également être subdivisés en volumes.
- Utiliser «t.» pour abréger «tome» et «vol.» pour abréger «volume».
- Indiquer les numéros de tomes et de volumes en chiffres arabes.
- Les indications du tome et du volume suivent le titre et sont placées entre virgules.

6.2.4.2 Livres en anglais

6.2.4.2.1   Volumes publiés en livres distincts

Exemple				
Auteur,	*titre*,	volume,	renseignements sur l'édition	référence précise.
Anne F. Bayefsky,	*Canada's Constitution Act 1982 & Amendments : A Documentary History*,	vol. 2,	Toronto, McGraw-Hill, 1989	à la p. 669.

- Indiquer le numéro du volume avant les renseignements sur l'édition.
- Indiquer le numéro de volume en chiffres arabes.
- Insérer une virgule entre le titre et le numéro de volume.

6.2.4.2.2   Volumes publiés dans un seul livre

Exemple						
Auteur,	*titre*,	directeur, (s'il y a lieu),	traduction (s'il y a lieu),	renseignements sur l'édition	volume	référence précise
Karl Marx,	*Capital : A Critical Analysis of Capitalist Production*,	Friedrich Engels, dir.,	trad. par Samuel Moore et Edward Aveling,	Londres, Swan Sonnenschein, 1908,	vol. 1	à la p. 15.

- Lorsque le livre est publié en plusieurs volumes, indiquer le numéro du volume après les renseignements sur l'édition ; séparer par une virgule.
- Le numéro de volume est en chiffres arabes.

6.2.5   Édition

Exemple
Germain Brière, *Le nouveau droit des successions*, **2e éd.**, Montréal, Wilson & Lafleur, 1997.
Maurice Tancelin, *Des obligations : contrat et responsabilité*, **éd. rév.**, Montréal, Wilson & Lafleur, 1986.

- Indiquer le numéro de l'édition (par ex. «2e éd.») après le titre.

- Abréger «édition» par «éd.».
- Lorsque l'ouvrage a été révisé mais qu'aucun numéro d'édition n'est précisé, indiquer «éd. rév.» après le titre.

6.2.6   Livres présentés en feuilles mobiles

Exemple			
Auteur,	*titre,*	feuilles mobiles,	renseignements sur l'édition
Georges Audet *et al.,*	*Le congédiement en droit québécois en matière de contrat individuel de travail,*	feuilles mobiles,	Cowansville (Qc), Yvon Blais, 1991.

- Renvoyer aux livres présentés en feuilles mobiles de la même manière que celle adoptée pour les livres reliés en respectant les directives suivantes :
  - après le titre, indiquer que le livre est présenté en feuilles mobiles ;
  - utiliser la date d'édition qui paraît sur la page où sont indiquées les informations sur les droits d'auteur même si cette date diffère de la date qui se trouve ailleurs dans le livre ;
  - si possible, renvoyer à un numéro de paragraphe plutôt qu'à un numéro de page.

6.2.7   Lieu d'édition

Exemples
J.-L. Aubert, *La responsabilité civile des notaires*, 3ᵉ éd., **Paris**, Defrénois, 1998.
Andrée Lajoie, *Pouvoir disciplinaire et tests de dépistage de drogues en milieu de travail*, **Cowansville (Qc)**, Yvon Blais, 1995.

- Indiquer le lieu d'édition tel qu'il figure au recto ou au verso de la page titre. Utiliser la version française du nom de la ville si elle existe (par ex. écrire Londres et non *London*).
- S'il y a plus d'un lieu d'édition, ne mentionner que le premier.
- Si aucun lieu d'édition n'est fourni, utiliser «A.l.» pour désigner «aucun lieu».
- Si des renseignements supplémentaires sont requis pour identifier le lieu d'édition (par ex. la province, l'État ou le pays), les abréger entre parenthèses après le lieu d'édition.

6.2.8 Maison d'édition

Exemples	
	Pierre-Claude Lafond, *Précis du droit des biens*, Montréal, **Thémis**, 1999.
NON	Pierre-Claude Lafond, *Précis du droit des biens*, Montréal, **Les Éditions Thémis inc.**, 1999.
MAIS	Mireille D. Castelli et Dominique Goubau, *Précis de droit de la famille*, Sainte-Foy (Qc), **Presses de l'Université Laval**, 2000.

- Indiquer le nom de la maison d'édition tel qu'il figure à la page titre.
- Le nom de la maison d'édition ne doit pas être abrégé (par ex. on écrit «Presses de l'Université Laval» et non pas «P.U.L.»).
- Omettre l'article défini (le, la, les, l', *the*) même s'il est le premier mot faisant partie du nom.
- Omettre les expressions indiquant le statut corporatif.
- Omettre «Éditions», à moins que ce ne soit une partie inséparable du nom (par ex. «Éditions de l'Homme»). Suivre cette règle pour les autres langues (par ex. Verlag).
- Omettre également *«Publishing»* ou *«Publishers»* des noms d'éditeurs anglais.
- Indiquer «Presses» en français et *«Press»* en anglais.
- Fournir le lieu d'édition et le nom de chaque co-éditeur séparés d'un deux-points et suivis de l'année.
- Si un éditeur travaille pour une organisation, l'indiquer à l'aide de «pour».
- Si aucune maison d'édition n'est indiquée, utiliser «a.m.e.» signifiant «aucune maison d'édition».

6.2.9 Année d'édition

Exemple
Jean Pineau et Danielle Burman, *Théorie des obligations*, 2e éd., Montréal, Thémis, 1988.

- Indiquer l'année de l'édition actuelle, et non celle de la première édition. De façon générale, utiliser la date la plus récente de l'édition, à moins que l'année de publication ne soit indiquée de façon explicite.
- Ne pas indiquer l'année d'impression.
- Si aucune année n'est indiquée, utiliser «a.d.» signifiant «aucune date». Si l'année est connue ou peut être inférée mais n'est pas indiquée dans le livre, la mettre entre parenthèses suivie d'un point d'interrogation si nécessaire.

6.2.10 Référence précise

Exemples

Pierre-André Côté, *Interprétation des lois*, 3ᵉ éd., Montréal, Thémis, 1999 **à la p. 307**.

Jean-Louis Baudouin, *La responsabilité civile délictuelle*, 4ᵉ éd., Cowansville (Qc), Yvon Blais, 1994 **aux pp. 102-08, 121-25**.

Ronald Joseph Delisle et Don Stuart, *Learning Canadian Criminal Procedure*, 5ᵉ éd., Scarborough, Carswell, 1998, **c. 2 à la p. 377 et s.**

Francis Delpérée, *Le droit constitutionnel de la Belgique*, Belgique, Bruxelles, Bruylant, 2000 au nᵒ 257.

Isabelle Schulte-Tenckhoff, *La question des peuples autochtones*, Bruxelles, Bruylant, 1997 **à la p. 56, n. 61**.

- Indiquer la référence précise à la fin de la référence.
- Indiquer la page ou le paragraphe. Lorsque les paragraphes sont numérotés, y renvoyer à l'aide de «au nᵒ», «au para» ou ¶. Pour renvoyer à une page, utiliser «à la p.» et pour renvoyer à plusieurs pages, utiliser «aux pp.»
- Les pages et les paragraphes consécutifs sont séparés par un trait d'union, en conservant au moins les deux derniers chiffres (par ex. «32-35», et non «32-5»).
- Utiliser une virgule pour séparer les numéros non consécutifs (par ex. «aux pp. 21, 48»).
- Pour indiquer une partie générale indiquer «et s.» (abréviation de «et suivantes») immédiatement après le numéro. Il est toutefois préférable de renvoyer aux pages ou aux paragraphes précis.
- Abréger «chapitre» et «chapitres» par «c.».
- Lorsqu'on renvoie à une note, indiquer le numéro de la page où se trouve la note ainsi que le numéro de la note (par ex. «à la p. 99, n. 140»). Lorsqu'on renvoie à plusieurs notes, indiquer le numéro de la page où se trouvent les notes ainsi que les numéros des notes : (par ex. «à la p. 142, nn. 73-75»). Si toutefois le numéro de la page n'est pas disponible parce qu'il s'agit d'un article en ligne, renvoyer au numéro de la note (par ex. n. 140).
- Utiliser des chiffres arabes pour renvoyer aux pages, aux paragraphes ou autres quel que soit le format des chiffres dans le texte (par ex. 5-6, v-vi).

6.3   ARTICLES PUBLIÉS DANS DES OUVRAGES COLLECTIFS

Exemples

Auteur de l'article,	«titre de l'article»	dans	directeur (s'il y a lieu),	dir.,	*titre de l'ouvrage,*	Renseignements sur l'édition,	1re page de l'article	référence précise (s'il y a lieu).
Madeleine Cantin Cumyn,	«Le Code civil et la gestion des biens d'autrui»	dans	Jean-Louis Baudouin et Patrice Deslauriers,	dir.,	*La responsabilité civile des courtiers en valeurs mobilières et des gestionnaires de fortune : aspects nouveaux,*	Montréal, Yvon Blais, 1999,	121	à la p. 128.
Daniel Jutras,	«Le code et le ministre, essai sur les commentaires»	dans			*Mélanges offerts à Paul-André Crépeau,*	Cowansville (Qc), Yvon Blais, 1997,	451	à la p. 453.
Jocelyn Maclure,	«Introduction»	dans	Jocelyn Maclure et Alain-G. Gagnon,	dir.,	*Passages : l'identité, diversité et citoyenneté au Québec,*	Montréal, Québec Amérique 2001.		

- Indiquer le nom de l'auteur et le titre de l'article suivis de la référence à l'ouvrage collectif.
- Indiquer le nom du directeur, suivi de la mention «dir.» entre virgules. Omettre l'identité du directeur si celle-ci n'est pas fournie.
- Indiquer le titre de l'ouvrage collectif en italique suivi des renseignements sur l'édition.
- Indiquer ensuite la première page de l'article et la référence précise s'il y a lieu.
- Suivre les règles sur les articles qui font partie d'ouvrages collectifs, en utilisant comme titre d'article soit «Avant-propos», «Préface», «Introduction» ou «Conclusion», selon le cas.

6.4   DICTIONNAIRES

Exemples			
Titre,	édition ou année,	*s.v.*	«mot cherché».
Le nouveau petit Robert,	1990,	*s.v.*	«amphigourique».
Black's Law Dictionary,	6e éd.,	*s.v.*	«promissory estoppel».

- Indiquer le titre du dictionnaire en italique.
- Indiquer l'édition ou l'année.
- Abréger «*sub verbo*» par «*s.v.*», mot latin signifiant «au mot».

6.4.1   Dictionnaires spécialisés

Exemples						
Directeur ou auteur	dir. (s'il y a lieu)	*titre,*	édition (s'il y a lieu),	renseignements sur l'édition,	*s.v.*	«mot cherché».
Gérard Cornu,	dir.,	*Vocabulaire juridique,*	7e éd.,	Paris, Presses Universitaires de France, 1998,	*s.v.*	«minorité».
Agathe Van Lang,		*Dictionnaire de droit administratif,*		Paris, Dalloz, 1999.		

- Renvoyer au dictionnaire de la même manière que celle adoptée pour une monographie. Voir la section 6.2.
- Abréger «*sub verbo*» par «*s.v.*», mot latin signifiant «au mot».

6.5 ENCYCLOPÉDIES

6.5.1 France

6.5.1.1 Modèle de base

Exemples					
Titre du répertoire,	édition (s'il y a lieu),	identification de la rubrique,	par	auteur de la rubrique,	référence précise.
Juris-classeur civil,		art. 1354, fasc. A,	par	Roger Perrot.	
Encyclopédie juridique Dalloz : répertoire de droit commercial,	2ᵉ éd.,	«Ventes commerciales»,	par	Luc Bihl,	au n° 256.

- Si possible, renvoyer au *Juris-classeur civil*.
- Indiquer l'encyclopédie et le titre du répertoire au long en italique.
- Lorsque plus d'une édition a été publiée, indiquer le numéro de l'édition.
- Lorsqu'une même rubrique est publiée dans plus d'un répertoire du *Juris-classeur*, ne pas fournir de référence parallèle.
- Le titre abrégé est en italique.

Les abréviations des principaux répertoires sont :

Encyclopédie juridique Dalloz : Répertoire de droit administratif	*Rép. admin.*
Encyclopédie juridique Dalloz : Répertoire de droit civil	*Rép. civ.*
Encyclopédie juridique Dalloz : Répertoire de droit commercial	*Rép. com.*
Juris-classeur administratif	*J.-cl. admin.*
Juris-classeur civil	*J.-cl. Civ.*
Juris-classeur civil annexe	*J.-cl. civ. annexe*
Juris-classeur commercial	*J.-cl. Com.*
Juris-classeur commercial : Banque et crédit	*J.-cl. com. Banque et crédit*
Juris-classeur répertoire notarial	*J.-cl. rép. not.*
Juris-classeur responsabilité civile	*J.-cl. resp. civ.*

6.5.1.2 Rubriques

Exemples	
Classées par ordre alphabétique	*Encyclopédie juridique Dalloz : Répertoire de droit civil*, **«Personnalité (droits de la)»**, par D. Tallon au n° 153. *Juris-classeur civil annexes*, **«Associations»**, **fasc. 1-A**, par Robert Brichet.
Classées selon les articles d'un code	*Juris-classeur civil*, **app. art. 3, fasc. 4**, par Yves Luchaire. *Juris-classeur civil*, **art. 1315 à 1316,** par Daniel Veaux.
Classées selon un plan méthodique	*Juris-classeur commercial : Banque et crédit*, **vol. 2, fasc. 32**, par Jean Stoufflet.

- **Classées par ordre alphabétique** : indiquer les mots-clés qui identifient la rubrique entre guillemets. Ajouter «fasc.» et le numéro approprié après le nom de la rubrique, s'il y a lieu.
- **Classées par articles d'un code** : indiquer le numéro de l'article (ou des articles) sous lequel la rubrique est classée. Utiliser la même forme que celle du répertoire. Ajouter l'indication du fascicule après le numéro d'article s'il y a lieu.
- **Classées selon un plan méthodique** : indiquer le numéro du volume où se trouve la rubrique.
- Peu importe la méthode de classification des rubriques, indiquer le numéro du fascicule après celui du volume.
- Ne pas indiquer la date de révision du fascicule.

6.5.2 Common law

Exemples
Halsbury's Laws of England, 4ᵉ éd., vol. 34, Londres, Butterworths, 1980 à la p. 60, para. 71.
American Jurisprudence, 2ᵉ éd., vol. 17A, Rochester (N.Y.), Lawyer's Cooperative, 1991 au titre «Contracts», § 97.

- Suivre les règles pour les monographies à la section 6.2 sans indiquer le nom de l'auteur.
- Les références précises peuvent renvoyer à la page ou au numéro de paragraphe ou aux deux. L'abréviation de «paragraphe» est «para.». Utiliser le signe «§» pour les ouvrages américains.
- Si la partie a un titre, il peut également être indiqué.

6.6   RECENSIONS

Exemples						
Auteur,	«titre de la recension» (s'il y a lieu),	Recen-sion de	*titre de l'ouvrage recensé*	de	auteur de l'ouvrage recensé	renseignements sur l'édition.
Bjarne Melkevik,		Recen-sion de	*Démocratie et procéduralisa-tion du droit*	de	Philippe Coppens et Jacques Lenoblc	(2001) 42 C. de D. 337.
Yves-Marie Morissette,		Recen-sion de	*L'administrat-ion de la preuve*	de	Léo Ducharme	(2001) 46 R.D. McGill 1179.

- Si la recension porte un titre, l'indiquer après le nom de l'auteur.
- La mention «Recension de» précède le titre de l'ouvrage recensé.
- Après le titre de l'ouvrage recensé, le nom de son auteur est introduit par «de».
- Si le titre de la recension indique à la fois le titre de l'ouvrage recensé et son auteur, omettre ces informations du reste de la référence.

6.7   CHRONIQUES DE JURISPRUDENCE ET DE LÉGISLATION

Exemples						
	Auteur,	«titre» (s'il y a lieu),	type de chronique	de	*intitulé* ou nom de la loi ou du projet de loi	Renseigne-ments sur l'édition.
Commentaire d'arrêt	Léo Ducharme,	«La proclamation de l'existence en droit québécois de la règle de common law de l'engage-ment implicite de confident-ialité : *Lac d'amiante*, une décision judiciaire erronée»,	Chronique	de	*Lac d'amiante du Québec ltée c. 2858-0702 Québec inc.*	(2000) 79 R. du B. can. 435.
Chronique de législation	Jean-Pierre Colpron,	«Les nouvelles règles visant à réduire les pertes en capital»,	Chronique	de	l'art. 112 (3) de la *Loi de l'impôt sur le revenu*	(1996) 18 R.P.F.S. 177.

- Indiquer le titre du commentaire d'arrêt ou de la chronique de législation entre guillemets, s'il y en a un.
- Pour les commentaires d'arrêt, la mention «Commentaire de» précède l'intitulé de l'arrêt. Toutefois, si le titre indique le nom de l'arrêt, omettre «Commentaire de» et l'intitulé de l'arrêt du reste de la référence.
- Pour les chroniques de législation, la mention «Chronique de» précède le titre de la loi. Toutefois, si le titre indique le nom de la loi pertinente, omettre «Chronique de» et le titre de la loi du reste de la référence.

6.7.1 France

6.7.1.1 Notes

Exemple								
Auteur,	note sous	nom du tribunal,	date de la décision,	recueil.	année de publication.	titre abrégé ou numéro de la partie.	première page.
Danielle Corrignan-Carsin,	note sous	Cass. soc.,	10 mai 1999,	J.C.P.	1999.	II.	1425.

- Il y a un espace entre le recueil et l'année («Sem.Jur. 1991.»). Il n'y a toutefois pas d'espace entre l'année, le titre de la section et la première page («1991.Jur.21731.»).
- Après le nom de l'auteur et la mention «note sous», renvoyer à la décision et au recueil pertinents de la même manière que celle adoptée pour le référence à la jurisprudence française. Voir la section 3.5.

6.7.1.2 Chroniques publiées dans les recueils généraux

Exemples							
Auteur,	«titre»	recueil	année de publication.	titre abrégé ou numéro de la partie.	première page	référence précise.
Bertrand Mathieu et Michel Verpeaux,	Jurisprudence constitutionnelle»	J.C.P.	2000.	I.	2178	à la p. 2180.
Xavier Labbée,	«Esquisse d'une définition civiliste de l'espèce humaine»	D.	1999.	Chron.	437	à la p. 440.

- Il n'y a pas d'espace entre l'année de publication, la partie et la première page de la chronique (par ex. «D. 1972.Chron.137»).
- Indiquer l'information concernant les recueils français selon les règles de la section 3.5.4.

6.8 COMMENTAIRES, REMARQUES ET NOTES

Exemples			
Auteur (s'il y a lieu),	«titre» (s'il y a lieu),	genre du texte	renseignements sur l'édition.
Monroe Leigh,		Commentaire éditorial	(1996) 90 A.J.I.L. 235.
	«What We Talk About When We Talk About Persons : The Language of Legal Fiction »,	Note	(2001) 114 Harv. L. Rev. 1745.

- Inscrire le genre du texte (par ex. «Commentaire éditorial», «Note» ou «Remarque») avant les renseignements sur l'édition. Ne pas mettre entre guillemets les expressions telles que «Commentaire», «Remarque» ou «Note».

6.9 DOCUMENTS HISTORIQUES LÉGAUX

6.9.1 Droit romain

Collection	*Abréviation*	*Exemple*
Lois des douze tables	XII. Tab.	XII.Tab.8.2
Institutes de Gaius	G.	G. 3.220 (trad. Julien Reinach)
Code de Théodose	Cod. Th.	Cod. Th. 8.14.1
Institutes de Justinien	Inst.	Inst. 4.4 pr.
Digeste de Justinien	Dig.	Dig. 47.10.1 (Ulpian)
Codex de Justinien	Cod.	Cod. 6.42.16
Nouvelles	Nov.	Nov. 22.3

- Renvoyer à la division traditionnelle (généralement livre, titre, partie) et non au numéro de page de l'édition ou de la traduction. Il n'y a pas d'espace entre les numéros des différentes parties.
  - L'abréviation «pr.», précédée d'un espace, signifie «principium» ou «début» et renvoie au document non numéroté avant la première section d'un titre.
  - Pour le *Digeste* de Justinien, l'auteur du passage en question peut être indiqué entre parenthèses à la fin de la référence.

- Utiliser les chiffres arabes, suivis de points, pour indiquer les divisions quelle que soit l'utilisation de l'édition ou de la traduction.
- L'édition ou la traduction utilisée peu être indiquée entre parenthèses à la fin de la référence.

6.9.2   Droit canonique

Collection	Abréviation	Exemple
Decretum de Gratien	Decr. [facultatif]	1re partie : D.50 c.11 2e partie : C.30 q.4 c.5 2e partie, De poenitentia: De poen. D.1 c.75 3e partie : De cons. D.1 c.5
Décrétales de Grégoire IX (*Liber extra*)	X	X 5.38.12
Décrétales de Boniface VIII (*Liber sextus*)	VI	VI 5.2.16
Constitutions de Clément V (*Clementinae*)	Clem.	Clem. 3.7.2
Extravagantes de Jean XXII (*Extravagantes Johannis XXII*)	Extrav. Jo. XII	Extrav. Jo. XII 14.2
Extravagantes communes (*Extravagantes communes*)	Extrav. Com.	Extrav. Com. 3.2.9
Codex Iuris Canonici (1917)	1917 Code	1917 Code c.88, § 2
Codex Iuris Canonici (1983)	1983 Code	1983 Code c.221, § 1

- Renvoyer à la division traditionnelle et non au numéro de page de l'édition ou de la traduction utilisée.
- Utiliser les chiffres arabes pour indiquer les divisions quelle que soit l'utilisation de l'édition ou de la traduction.
- L'édition ou la traduction utilisée peut être indiquée entre parenthèses à la fin de la référence.

6.10 MANUSCRITS NON PUBLIÉS

6.10.1 Modèle de base

Exemple					
Auteur,	titre,	date	[non publié,	archivé	lieu].
J. Tremblay,	«Nouveaux développements en droit du travail»,	mai 1997	[non publié,	archivé	à la *Revue de droit de McGill*].

- Renvoyer au titre du manuscrit selon son genre. Pour les articles, placer le titre entre guillemets. Pour les monographies, inscrire le titre en italique.
- Faire suivre le titre du manuscrit de sa date de création.
- Indiquer que le manuscrit n'a pas été publié en mettant entre crochets «non publié» et «archivé», ainsi que l'endroit où le manuscrit se trouve.

6.10.2 Manuscrits à paraître

Exemple				
Auteur,	Titre,	renseignements sur l'édition	[à paraître en	date de publication prévue].
Eric Descheemaeker,	«Faut-il codifier le droit privé européen des contrats ?»	47 R.D. McGill	[à paraître en	2002].

- Renvoyer au titre du manuscrit selon son genre. Pour les articles, placer le titre entre guillemets. Pour les monographies, inscrire le titre en italique.
- Inscrire les renseignements sur l'édition selon le genre du manuscrit mais ne pas indiquer la date de publication.
- Indiquer que le manuscrit n'a pas encore été publié en ajoutant, entre crochets, «à paraître» et la date de publication prévue si disponible.

6.10.3 Thèses et dissertations

Exemple					
Auteur,	*titre,*	diplôme,	institution,	année	[non publié].
Louise Potvin,	*La personne et la protection de son image,*	thèse de doctorat en droit,	Université McGill,	1989	[non publiée].

- Après avoir indiqué l'auteur et le titre du document, inscrire le diplôme dans le cadre duquel il a été écrit. Y inclure la discipline étudiée (par ex. droit, science politique, économie), à moins qu'on puisse la déduire du diplôme ou du nom de l'institution.
- Après la mention de l'année de création du texte, inclure «non publié» entre crochets.
- Si le manuscrit a été publié, il faut alors renvoyer à la source publiée.
- Renvoyer aux thèses publiées sur support de microfiche tel que *University Microfilms International* de la même manière que celle adoptée pour les références aux thèses sur support papier.

6.11 ALLOCUTIONS ET TEXTES PRÉSENTÉS À DES CONFÉRENCES

Exemple					
Conférencier,	«titre» ou Allocution,	événement,	lieu ou institution,	date	renseignements sur l'édition ou [non publié].
Son excellence John Ralston Saul	Allocution d'ouverture,	Conférence d'ouverture de la conférence du Conseil international d'études canadiennes	Université d'Ottawa,	18 mai 2000	[non publiée]. Transcription disponible en ligne : La gouverneure générale du Canada <http://www.gg.ca/ speeches/ canadian studies_f.html>.

- Indiquer le titre de l'allocution, si possible ; si aucun titre n'est fourni, utiliser «Allocution».
- Inscrire l'événement dans le cadre duquel l'allocution a été prononcée.
- Indiquer le lieu ou l'institution où l'allocution a été faite.
- Inclure les renseignements sur l'édition.

- Pour les allocutions non publiées, inscrire «[non publiée]» à la fin de la référence.
- Pour les allocutions publiées dans une collection, respecter les mêmes règles de référence que celles qui prévalent pour les ouvrages collectifs. Voir la section 6.3.

6.12 REVUES

Exemples

Auteur (s'il y a lieu),	«titre de l'article»	titre de la revue	volume : numéro ou n°	(date)	1re page de l'article	référence précise	source électronique (s'il y a lieu).
Jacques Julliard,	«Requiem pour un "peuple interdit"»	Le Nouvel Observateur	n° 1740	(12 mars 1998)	47	à la p. 12.	
Julie Latour,	«Garde partagée, avis partagés»	Magazine National [de l'Association du Barreau canadien]		(mars 2001),			en ligne : <http://abc.cba.org/National/Cover2001_fr/MA01_fr.asp>.
Me Jean Lozeau et Me Paul Ryan,	«La faillite et la responsabilité fiscale des administrateurs et des tiers»	Le Monde Juridique	12 : 6		17	à la p. 19.	

- Indiquer le nom de l'auteur, s'il y a lieu, suivi du titre de l'article entre guillemets.
- Indiquer le nom de la revue en italique. Tout autre rensignement, tel que le lieu de publication, se place à la suite du titre, entre crochets.
- Indiquer le volume et/ou le numéro. Séparer ces informations par un deux-points.
- Indiquer la date complète entre parenthèses. Si la revue indique une période, n'indiquer que la première journée de cette période (par ex. pour un numéro couvrant du 22 au 28 novembre, n'indiquer que «22 novembre»).
- Indiquer la première page de l'article.
- Ne pas indiquer le numéro de la page de la source imprimée lorsqu'on renvoie à une source en ligne.
- Plusieurs textes disponibles en ligne disparaissent après un certain temps. Renvoyer aux sources en ligne seulement si la source fournit des documents archivés remontant à plusieurs années.

6.13 JOURNAUX, FILS DE PRESSE ET AUTRES SOURCES DE NOUVELLES

Exemples					
Auteur (s'il y a lieu),	«titre de l'article»	*journal [lieu d'édition]* (si nécessaire)	(date)	page	source électronique (s'il y a lieu).
Michel Venne,	«Pour un accès gratuit aux lois sur Internet»	*Le Devoir [de Montréal]*	(28 mai 1997)	A2.	
	«Un organisme d'aide juridique est menacé de fermeture par Québec»	*La Presse canadienne*	(8 août 2001)		(QL).
Sylvia Zappi,	«La Cour de cassation refuse de faire bénéficier les enfants isolés étrangers du droit des mineurs»	*Le Monde*	(11 novembre 2001),		en ligne : Le Monde.fr <http://www.lemonde.fr/recherche>.
	«Défaite des fabricants de tabac aux États-Unis»	*La Presse [de Montréal]*	(28 mai 1997)	B10.	

- Indiquer le nom de l'auteur, s'il y a lieu, suivi du titre de l'article entre guillemets.
- Indiquer le nom du journal, du fil de presse ou d'autres sources en italique. Tout autre renseignement, tel que le lieu de publication, se place à la suite du titre, entre crochets.
- Journaux:
  - L'indication de la page doit comprendre celle du cahier si les pages sont numérotées séparément dans chaque cahier (par ex. «B10»).
  - Pour les références précises, ne pas répéter le numéro de page si l'article ne paraît que sur une seule page.
- Fils de presse:
  - Remplacer le nom du journal (en italique) par le nom du fil de presse (également en italique).
  - Pour plus de renseignements sur la référence aux sources électroniques, voir la section 6.1.7.
- Autres sources:

- Plusieurs textes disponibles en ligne disparaissent après un certain temps. Renvoyer aux sources en ligne seulement si la source fournit des documents archivés remontant à plusieurs années.
- Ne pas inclure le numéro de la page de la source imprimée lorsqu'on fait référence à une source en ligne.
- Pour plus de renseignements sur la référence aux sources électroniques, voir la section 6.1.7.

6.13.1 Éditoriaux et lettres à la rédaction

Exemples				
Auteur,	type de document,	*journal*	(date)	page.
Jean Barrué,	Lettre à la rédaction,	*Le Monde diplomatique*	(avril 1997)	2.

- Indiquer «Lettre à la rédaction» après le nom de l'auteur de la lettre.
- Indiquer «Éditorial» après le titre d'un éditorial.
- Mettre en italique le nom du journal, de la revue ou de toute autre source. Placer à la suite du titre, entre crochets, tout autre renseignement tel que le lieu de publication (par ex. «La Presse [de Montréal]»).

6.14 COMMUNIQUÉS DE PRESSE

Exemples					
Organisme responsable,	genre du document	numéro (s'il y a lieu),	«titre» (facultatif)	(date)	source électronique (s'il y a lieu).
Organisation des Nations Unies,	Commu-niqué	CS/2284,	«Le conseil demande le retrait immédiat des troupes israéliennes des villes palestiniennes dont Ramallah et la coopération des parties avec l'Envoyé spécial de Washington»	(29 mars 2002),	en ligne : Recherche de communiqués de presse des Nations Unies <http://www.un.org/News/fr-press/>.
Cabinet du premier ministre du Québec	Commu-niqué		«Journée internationale des femmes : "Nouvelles réalités, solidarités nouvelles"»	(8 mars 2002),	en ligne : Site officiel du premier ministre du Québec <http://www.premier.gouv.qc.ca/premier/francais/communiques/index_communiques.html>.

- Indiquer le genre du document tel qu'énoncé sur le document (par ex. «Communiqué»).
- Indiquer le numéro du document immédiatement après le genre du document, s'il y a lieu.
- Si possible, fournir la date du document entre parenthèses à la fin de la référence.

6.15 LETTRES ET ENTREVUES

Exemples			
Lettre ou Entrevue	nom des personnes impliquées,	date	renseignements supplémentaires (archives, sources électroniques ou imprimées).
Lettre de	B. Diamond au Premier ministre R. Lévesque,	30 novembre 1982.	
Entrevue de	Edward Beauvais par Douglas Sanderson	(29 mai 1948)	sur *This Week*, CBC Radio, Toronto, CBC Radio Archives.
Lettre de	P.E. Moore, Acting Superintendent of Medical Services, Indian Affairs Branch, à Ellen L. Fairclough, Minister of Citizenship	[a.d. 1959?]	Hull, Affaires Indiennes et du Nord Canada (6-24-3, vol. 2).

- Inclure le nom des parties, suivi de la date à laquelle la lettre a été rédigée. Indiquer la date à laquelle la lettre a été rédigée. Si aucune date n'est fournie, inscrire «[a.d.]». Inscrire «[a.d.?]» pour indiquer une date probable.
- Identifier une lettre ou une entrevue en indiquant «Lettre de» ou «Entrevue de» suivi du nom des parties au début de la référence.
- Si le titre d'une personne impliquée n'est pas mentionné ou ne peut être inféré, fournir le plus de renseignements possible sur ce titre, précédé d'une virgule.
- Lorsque l'auteur est l'intervieweur, il n'est pas nécessaire d'identifier l'intervieweur.
- Lorsque l'auteur n'a pas personnellement fait l'entrevue, fournir le nom de l'intervieweur.
- Si la lettre ou l'entrevue est publiée, disponible en ligne ou archivée, inclure la référence.

6.16 DOCUMENTS ARCHIVÉS

Titre du document et autre information	Lieu des archives,	nom des archives,	(numéro de classification).
Lettres patentes du roi François 1er nommant Jacques Cartier capitaine général de l'expédition destinée au Canada (17 octobre 1540/Saint-Prix),	Ottawa,	Archives nationales du Canada	(MG 1-Série C11A).
Chief Andrew Paull à T.A. Crerar (22 juin 1944),	Ottawa,	Archives nationales du Canada	(RG 10, vol. 6826, file 496-3-2, pt. 1).

- Si un document se trouve dans des archives locales, fournir le plus de renseignements possible sur le document selon les règles de références (référence traditionnelle si possible), suivi de l'information des archives.

6.17 SOURCES ÉLECTRONIQUES

6.17.1 Services électroniques

Exemples	
Référence traditionnelle,	(service électronique et banque de données) (facultatif).
Denise Boulet, «Le traitement juridique du mineur suicidaire» (2002) 32 R.D.U.S. 317,	(QL).
Joseph Eliot Magnet, *Constitutional Law of Canada : Cases, Notes and Materials*, 8e éd., Kingston, Quicklaw, 2001	(QL).

- Fournir la référence complète, suivie du service électronique entre parenthèses.
- Si le document ne peut être facilement trouvé sur le service sans connaître la banque de données du service électronique, indiquer la banque de données dans laquelle le document a été trouvé (par ex. «(QL, MCGL)»).
- Si le nom de l'éditeur ne figure pas ou si le texte n'est publié que sur un serveur électronique, identifier le service en ligne comme l'éditeur (par ex. «Kingston : Quicklaw, 2001»).

- Cette forme de référence ne devrait être utilisée que pour les service électroniques qui exigent un abonnement ou pour les sites Internet qui ont une table des matières claire, des engins de recherche, des rédacteurs professionnels et une abréviation reconnue. Les renvois aux sites Internet gouvernementaux doivent inclure l'adresse Internet au complet.
- Inclure le numéro de paragraphe comme référence précise, si possible. Si la numérotation de la page d'une source sur support papier est reproduite sur le service électronique, renvoyer aux numéros de pages de la source sur support papier. Ne pas renvoyer à la référence précise des numéros de l'écran ou des pages du service électronique, car ces numéros sont propres au service électronique utilisé et la forme peut changer d'un format électronique à un autre (texte, html).
- Si possible, ne pas renvoyer à un service électronique auquel la majorité des lecteurs ne pourra accéder. Par exemple, ne pas renvoyer à Azimut lorsque l'auditoire ciblé n'est pas au Québec.

Voici une liste des abréviations des services électroniques :

Australian Legal Information Institute	AustLII
Azimut (produced by SOQUIJ)	Azimut
British and Irish Legal Information Institute	BILII
Butterworths Services	Butterworths
Institut canadien d'information juridique	IIJCan
*e*Carswell	eC
Jurifrance	JF
Lawnet	Lawnet
LexisNexis	Lexis
LexUM	LexUM
Quicklaw	QL
Westlaw	WL

6.17.2 Sites Internet

Exemples			
Référence traditionnelle,	en ligne :	Nom du site	\<adresse universelle\>.
Benoît Tabaka, «Internet et la diffusion des sondages électoraux : une réforme législative impossible?» (7 février 2002),	en ligne :	Juriscom.net	\<http://www.juriscom.net\>.
Jérôme Dupré, «Espionnage économique et droit : l'inutile création d'un bien informationnel» (été 2001),	en ligne :	Lex Electronica	\<http://www.lex-electronica.org/articles/v7-1/dupre.htm\>.

- Fournir la référence traditionnelle, suivie d'une virgule, de «en ligne :», du nom du site Internet et de l'adresse universelle (URL).
- Renvoyer à l'adresse universelle du document à moins que cette adresse ne soit propre à une session Internet, auquel cas renvoyer à la page d'accueil.
- Toutes les sources Internet ne sont pas fiables ; il faut donc porter une attention particulière lorsqu'on renvoie à de telles sources.
- Plusieurs textes en ligne disparaissent après un certain temps. Renvoyer à une source en ligne si cette source fournit des documents archivés remontant à quelques années.
- Inclure un numéro de paragraphe comme référence précise si possible. Si la numérotation de la page d'une source imprimée est reproduite dans une source électronique, renvoyer à la numérotation utilisée par la source imprimée.

6.17.3 CD-ROM et DVD

Exemples				
Référence traditionnelle,	CD-ROM ou DVD:	*Titre du disque si différent*	mise à jour (si nécessaire)	(renseignements sur l'édition).
P.W. Hogg et M.E. Turpel, «Implementing Aboriginal Self-Government : Constitutional and Jurisdictional Issues»,	CD-ROM :	*Pour sept générations: legs documentaire de la Commission royale sur les peuples autochtones,*		Ottawa, Libraxus, 1997.
B. Laghi, «Gay Seeks Rights-Code Protection» *The Globe and Mail* (4 novembre 1997) A4,	CD-ROM :	*The Globe and Mail on CD-ROM,*		Outremont, CEDROM-SNI, 1998.

- Fournir la référence traditionnelle du document auquel on renvoie.
- Mettre une virgule après la référence traditionnelle.
- Pour indiquer qu'un document est disponible sur disque, faire suivre la virgule de «CD-ROM :» ou «DVD :».
- Indiquer le titre du disque en italique, suivi d'une virgule.
- Fournir les renseignements sur l'édition du disque entre parenthèses en y incluant le lieu d'édition, l'éditeur et l'année d'édition.

INDEX

Index

APPENDICES/ANNEXES

APPENDICES ~ ANNEXES

A CANADA

This chart has been created to help illustrate the many different abbreviations in use for provinces and territories.

Jurisdiction	Statutes and Gazettes	Regulations	Courts and Journals	Neutral Citation	Law Reporters
Alberta	A.	Alta.	Alta.	AB	A. or Alta.
British Columbia	B.C.	B.C.	B.C.	BC	B.C.
Canada	C.	C.	C. or Can.	—	C. or Can.
Lower Canada	L.C.	L.C.	L.C.	—	L.C.
Manitoba	M.	Man.	Man.	MB	Man.
New Brunswick	N.B.	N.B.	N.B.	NB	N.B.
Newfoundland (Gazette: before 21 December 2001 / Regulations: before 13 December 2001 / before 6 December 2001 for most other purposes, including statutes)	N.	Nfld.	Nfld.	NF	Nfld.
Newfoundland & Labrador (Gazette: 21 December 2001 and after / Regulations: 13 December 2001 and after / 6 December 2001 and after for most other purposes, including statutes)	N.L.	N.L.	N.L. (if the name of the court or journal has changed)	NF (NL?)	Nfld.
Northwest Territories	N.W.T.	N.W.T.	N.W.T.	NWT	N.W.T.
Nova Scotia	N.S.	N.S.	N.S.	NS	N.S.
Nunavut	Nu.	Nu.	Nu.	NU	Nu.
Ontario	O.	O.	Ont.	ON	O.
Prince Edward Island	P.E.I.	P.E.I.	P.E.I.	PE	P.E.I.
Province of Canada	Prov. C.	Prov. C.	Prov. C.	—	—
Quebec	Q.	Q.	Q. (Journals), Qc. (Courts)	QC	Q.
Saskatchewan	S.	S.	Sask.	SK	Sask.
Upper Canada	U.C.	U.C.	U.C.	—	U.C.
Yukon	Y.	Y.	Y.	YK	Y.

Ce tableau a été créé pour faciliter la compréhension du système des abréviations utilisées dans les provinces et les territoires.

Lieu	Lois et Gazettes	Règlements	Cours et journaux	Référence neutre	Recueils de droit
Alberta	A.	Alta.	Alta.	AB	A. ou Alta.
Bas-Canada	B.-C.	B.-C.	B.-C.	—	B.-C.
Canada	C.	C.	C. ou Can.	—	C. ou Can.
Colombie-Britannique	B.C.	B.C.	B.C.	BC	B.C.
Haut-Canada	U.C.	U.C.	U.C.	—	U.C.
Île-du-Prince-Édouard	P.E.I.	P.E.I.	P.E.I.	PE	P.E.I.
Manitoba	M.	Man.	Man.	MB	Man.
Nouveau-Brunswick	N.-B.	N.-B.	N.-B.	NB	N.-B.
Nouvelle-Écosse	N.S.	N.S.	N.S.	NS	N.S.
Nunavut	Nu.	Nu.	Nu.	NU	Nu.
Ontario	O.	O. (refondus), Ont. (non refondus en français)	Ont.	ON	O.
Province du Canada	Prov. C.	Prov. C.	Prov. C.	—	—
Québec	Q.	Q.	Q. (Journaux), Qc (Cours)	QC	Q.
Saskatchewan	S.	S.	Sask.	SK	Sask.

Terre-Neuve (Gazette: avant le 21 décembre 2001 / Règlements: avant le 13 décembre 2001 / pour la plupart d'autres fins (ainsi que les lois): avant le 6 décembre 2001)	N.	Nfld.	Nfld.	NF	Nfld.
Terre-Neuve & Labrador (Gazette: le 21 décembre 2001 ou après / Règlements: le 13 décembre 2001 ou après / pour la plupart d'autres fins (ainsi que les lois) le 6 décembre 2001 ou après.	N.L.	N.L.	N.L. (si le nom du cour ou journal a changé)	NF (NL?)	Nfld.
Territoires du Nord-Ouest	T.N.-O.	T.N.-O.	T.N.-O.	NWT	N.W.T.
Yukon	Y.	Y.	Y.	YK	Y.

B UNITED STATES ~ ÉTATS-UNIS

Alabama	Ala.	Minnesota	Minn.
Alaska	Alaska	Mississippi	Miss.
Arizona	Ariz.	Missouri	Mo.
Arkansas	Ark.	Montana	Mont.
California	Cal.	Nebraska	Neb.
Californie	Cal.	Nevada	Nev.
Caroline du Nord	N.C.	New Hampshire	N.H.
Caroline du Sud	S.C.	New Jersey	N.J.
Colorado	Colo.	New Mexico	N. Mex.
Connecticut	Conn.	New York	N.Y.
Dakota du Nord	N. Dak.	North Carolina	N.C.
Dakota du Sud	S. Dak.	North Dakota	N. Dak.
Delaware	Del.	Nouveau Mexique	N. Mex.
District of Columbia	D.C.	Ohio	Ohio
District de Colombie	D.C.	Oklahoma	Okla.
États-Unis	É.-U.	Oregon	Or.
Florida	Fla.	Pennsylvania	Pa.
Floride	Fla.	Pennsylvanie	Pa.
Georgia	Ga.	Rhode Island	R.I.
Géorgie	Ga.	South Carolina	S.C.
Hawaii	Hawaii	South Dakota	S. Dak.
Idaho	Idaho	Tennessee	Tenn.
Illinois	Ill.	Texas	Tex.
Indiana	Ind.	United States	U.S.
Iowa	Iowa	Utah	Utah
Kansas	Kan.	Vermont	Vt.
Kentucky	Ky.	Virginia	Va.
Louisiana	La.	Virginie	Va.
Louisiane	La.	Virginie occidentale	W. Va.
Maine	Me.	Washington	Wash.
Maryland	Md.	West Virginia	W. Va.
Massachusetts	Mass.	Wisconsin	Wis.
Michigan	Mich.	Wyoming	Wyo.

C AUSTRALIA ~ L'AUSTRALIE

Jurisdiction *Indication géographique*	Legislation and Courts *Législation et cours*	Neutral citation *Référence neutre*
Australia	Austl.	
Commonwealth	Cth.	
Australian Capital Territory Territoire de la capitale australienne	A.C.T.	
New South Wales Nouvelle galles du sud	N.S.W.	NSW
Northern Territory Térritoire du nord	N.T.	NT
Queensland	Qld.	Q
South Australia Australie méridionale	S.A.	SA
Tasmania Tasmanie	Tas.	TAS
Victoria	Vic.	V
Western Australia Australie occidentale	W.A.	WA

D   OTHER JURISDICTIONS ~ AUTRES JURIDICTIONS

Afrique du sud	Afr. du sud
Écosse	Écosse
European Union	E.U.
France	France
Ireland	I.
Irelande du nord	I.N.
New Zealand	N.Z.
Northern Ireland	N.I.
Nouvelle-Zélande	N.-Z.
Royaume-Uni	R.-U.
Scotland	Scot.
Singapore / Singapour	Sing.
South Africa	S. Afr.
Union Européenne	U.E.
United Kingdom	U.K.

E INTERNATIONAL ORGANIZATIONS ~ ORGANISMES INTERNATIONAUX

Abbreviation Abréviation	Organization Organisme
A.C.	Assemblée consultative (Conseil de l'Europe)
A.P.	Assemblée parlementaire (Conseil de l'Europe)
AG	Assemblée générale (NU)
AIEA	Agence internationale de l'énergie atomique (NU)
APEC	Asia Pacific Economic Cooperation
Bur.	Bureau (NU)
C.1	Première Commission (NU)
C.2	Deuxième Commission (NU)
C.3	Troisième Commission (NU)
C.A.	Consultative Assembly (Council of Europe)
C.I.J.	Cour internationale de Justice
C.J. (1re inst.)	Tribunal de première instance (C.E.)
C.J.E.	Cour de Justice des Communautés européennes
C.P.J.I.	Cour permanente de justice internationale
CCED	Conseil du commerce et du dévoloppement (NU)
CDH	Commission des droits de l'homme (NU)
C.E.	Communautés européennes
CES	Conseil économique et social (NU)
CNUCED	Conférence des Nations Unies sur le commerce et le développement (NU)
CNUDCI	Commission des Nations Unies pour le droit commercial international
C.P.J.I.	Cour permanente de justice internationale
Comm. Eur. D.H.	Commission européenne des Droits de l'Homme
Comm. Interam. D.H.	Commission Interaméricaine des Droits de l'Homme
Conseil de l'Europe	Conseil de l'Europe
Council of Europe	Council of Europe
Cour Eur. D.H.	Cour européenne des Droits de l'Homme
Cour Interam. D.H.	Cour Interaméricaine des Droits de l'Homme
CS	Conseil de sécurité (NU)
CT	Conseil de tutelle (NU)
E.C.F.I.	European Court of First Instance
E.C.J.	Court of Justice of the European Communities
E.C.	European Communities

ESC	Economic and Social Council (UN)
E.U.	European Union
Eur. Comm. H.R.	European Commission of Human Rights
Eur. Ct. H.R.	European Court of Human Rights
FMI	Fonds monétaire international (NU)
GA	General Assembly (UN)
GATT	Accord général sur les tarifs douaniers et le commerce
	General Agreement on Tariffs and Trade
GC	General Committee (UN)
HCDH	Haut-Commissariat aux droits de l'homme (NU)
HCR	Haut-Commissariat des Nations Unies pour les réfugiés
HRC	Human Rights Committee (UN)
IAEA	International Atomic Energy Agency (UN)
ICJ	International Court of Justice
ICAO	International Civil Aviation Organization (NU)
ICTY	International Criminal Tribunal for the Former Yugoslavia (UN)
ICTR	International Criminal Tribunal for Rwanda (UN)
ILO	International Labor Organization (UN)
IMF	International Monetary Fund (UN)
Inter-Am. Comm. H.R.	Inter-American Commission on Human Rights
Inter-Am. Ct. H.R.	Inter-American Court of Human Rights
NATO	North Atlantic Treaty Organization
NU	Nations Unies
NUCED	Conférence des Nations Unies sur le commerce et le développement
OACI	Organisation de l'aviation civile internationale (NU)
O.A.S.	Organization of American States
O.É.A.	Organisation des États américains
OMC	Organisation mondiale du commerce
OTAN	Organisation du Traité de l'Atlantique Nord
OIT	Organisation internationale du Travail
P.A.	Parliamentary Assembly (Council of Europe)
P.C.I.J.	Permanent Court of International Justice
SC	Security Council
TC	Trusteeship Council
TDB	Trade and Development Board (UN)
TPIR	Tribunal pénal international pour le Rwanda (NU)

TPIY	Tribunal pénal international pour l'ex-Yougoslavie (NU)
U.E.	Union européenne
UN	Nations Unies
OHCHR	United Nations High Commissioner for Human Rights, Office of the (UN)
UNHCR	United Nations High Commissioner for Refugees
UNCITRAL	United Nations Commission on International Trade Law
UNCTAD	United Nations Conference on Trade and Development
WTO	World Trade Organization

F   COURTS AND TRIBUNALS ~ COURS ET TRIBUNAUX

Rules

This appendix contains a list of abbrevations of courts and tribunals, both current and historical. Place the jurisdictional abbreviation before or after the court abbreviation according to the rules below.

When to identify a court
- Identify a court unless it is obvious from the reporter (*e.g.* S.C.R.). See section 3.2.9.

When to identify the province, territory or state where a court is located
- Identify the jurisdiction unless it is obvious from the name of the court or the reporter (*e.g.* T.A.Q.).
- For English abbreviations, the abbreviation for the province, territory, or state normally precedes the abbreviation for the court (*e.g.* N.B.C.A., Ont. Gen. Div., Qc. Sup. Ct.).
- For French abbreviations, provide the abbreviation for the province after the abbreviation of the court for Ontario, New Brunswick and Quebec (*e.g.* Div. gén. Ont., C.A.N.-B., C.S. Qc.), otherwise follow the English rule.

When to identify the country in which a court is located
- Generally, courts located in a province, territory or state within a particular country are only identified using the abbreviation of that province, territory, or state.   For example, it would be incorrect to write "N.S.W.C.A. Austl." or "N.S.C.A. Can." The country may be indicated, however, if the province, territory or state is unfamiliar to the majority of readers and is not found in this *Guide*.
- Generally, federal, national, and unitary courts are identified by their country unless the country is obvious either from the reporter or from the abbreviation of the court itself. (The jurisdiction is obvious from the court's abbreviation when the name of the jurisdiction is contained in the abbreviation or when no other court shares the abbreviation.) Note:
    - When citing from the Citizenship Appeal Court of Canada, the Court Martial Appeal Court, or the Exchequer Court of Canada, include the abbreviation "Can." (*e.g.* Cit. A.C. Can.) For any other Canadian federal court, the jurisdiction is obvious and "Can." should not be included.
    - In most cases, the jurisdiction of French courts is obvious from the court abbreviation and the abbreviation "Fr." should not be included.
    - For Singapore, include the abbreviation "Sing." unless the citation is from the *Singapore Law Reports*.
- The country abbreviation normally follows the court abbreviation (*e.g.* Dist. Ct. Sing., D.C.N.Z.), but there are exceptions, especially if the name of the jurisdiction is part of the name of the court (*e.g.* N.Z.C.A.).

When to leave a space between abbreviations
- There should be no space between any abbreviations of courts consisting solely of upper case letters. Leave a space when an abbreviation consisting of upper case letters is placed next to an abbreviation consisting of both upper case and lower case letters (*e.g.* B.C.C.A., Ont. Div. Ct., N.S. Co. Ct., Alta. Q.B.).

Canadian federal and provincial administrative agencies and tribunals
- Include the abbreviation of the body or tribunal in parentheses at the end of the citation if it is not evident from the title of the cited reporter (if an abbreviation cannot be found, use the full name). Use the abbreviation as it is provided by the administrative body. These acronyms usually do not contain periods.   For further information, see section 3.2.12.

N.B. In English, the abbreviation for "Supreme Court" is "S.C.", and the abbreviation for Superior Court is "Sup. Ct." In French, these abbreviations are reversed. "Cour suprême" is abbreviated "C. supr." and "Cour supérieure" is abbreviated "C.S." Also, note that the American abbreviations are "Super. Ct." for "Superior Court" and "Sup. Ct." for a state Supreme Court.

Règles
Cet appendice comprend une liste des abréviations des cours et des tribunaux actuels ou historiques. Mettre l'abréviation des indications géographiques avant ou après l'abréviations des cours en respectant les règles ci-dessous.

Quand identifier une cour
- Identifier une cour à moins que le recueil n'indique l'information (par ex. R.C.S.). Voir section 3.2.9.

Quand identifier une province, un territoire ou un état où siège une cour
- Identifier la juridiction à moins que cette information soit inférée par le nom de la cour ou par le recueil (par ex. T.A.Q.).
- Pour abréviations en anglais, l'abréviation de la province, du territoire ou de l'état précède normalement l'abréviation de la cour (par ex. N.B.C.A., Ont. Gen. Div., Qc. Sup. Ct.).
- Pour les abréviations en français, fournir l'abréviation de la province après l'abréviation de la cour pour l'Ontario, le Nouveau-Brunswick et le Québec (par ex. Div. gén. Ont., C.A.N.-B., C.S. Qc), dans tous les autres cas respecter la règle d'abréviation en anglais.

Quand identifier le pays où siège la cour
- Généralement les cours qui siègent dans une province, un territoire ou un état dans un pays sont identifiées par l'abréviation de la province, du territoire ou de l'état. Par exemple, il serait faux d'écrire «N.S.W.C.A. Austl.» ou «N.S.C.A. Can.». Le pays

peut être indiqué si l'abréviation de la province, du territoire ou de l'état n'est pas connue des lecteurs ou n'est pas dans ce Manuel.

- Généralement, les cours fédérale, nationale et unitaire sont identifiées par le nom du pays à moins que celui-ci ne soit inféré par le recueil ou par l'abréviation de la cour. (Lorsque le nom de la juridiction est compris dans l'abréviation ou lorsqu'aucune autre cour ne partage l'abréviation, la juridiction peut être inférée). Noter :
  - Lorsqu'on renvoie à la Cour d'appel de citoyenneté, la Cour d'appel de la cour martiale du Canada, ou la Cour de l'Échiquier, il faut inclure l'abréviation «Can.» (par ex. C.A. cit.). Pour toute autre cour fédérale, l'indication géographique «Can.» est évidende et ne doit être incluse.
  - Dans la plupart des cas, la juridiction des cours en français est évidente et l'abréviation «Fr.» ne doit être incluses.
  - Pour Singapour, inclure l'abréviation «Sing.» à moins que la référence ne provienne des *Singapore Law Reports*.
- L'abréviation du pays suit l'abréviation de la cour (par ex. Dist. Ct. Sing., D.C.N.Z.), exception faite si le nom de la juridiction fait partie du nom de la cour (par ex. N.Z.C.A.).

Quand laisser un espace entre les abréviations
- Il n'y a pas d'espace entre les abréviations des cours quand l'abréviation est composée de lettres majuscules. Laisser un espace quand l'abréviation ne comprenant que des lettres majuscules est située après une abréviation qui contient des lettres majuscules et minuscules (par ex. B.C.C.A., Ont. Div. Ct., N.S. Co. Ct., Alta. Q.B.).

Organes et tribunaux administratifs provinciaux et fédéraux du Canada
- Indiquer l'abréviation de l'organe ou du tribunal administratif entre parenthèses à la fin de la référence, si on ne peut le déduire du titre du recueil (utiliser le nom si aucune abréviation n'est trouvée). Utiliser l'abréviation utilisée par l'organe administratif. Noter que ces acronymes sont composés de lettres simples identifiant chaque mot important du nom et ne prennent normalement pas de points. Voir la section 3.2.12.

N.B. En anglais, l'abréviation pour la «Supreme Court» est «S.C.» et les abréviations pour les cours supérieurs est «Sup. Ct.». En français, ces abréviations sont inversées, «Cour suprême» devient «C.S.» et «Cour supérieure» «C. sup.». De plus, noter que les abréviations américaines sont «Super. Ct.» pour «Superior Court» et «Sup. Ct.» pour la Cour suprême des états.

Court or Tribunal / Cour ou tribunal	Abbreviation / Abréviation
Admiralty Court	Adm. Ct.
Board of Tax Appeals (U.S. / É.-U.)	B.T.A.
Chancery Court	Ch.
Circuit Court	Cir. Ct.
Circuit Court of Appeals (state, U.S. / état, É.-U.)	Cir. Ct. App.
Circuit Court of Appeals (federal, U.S. / fédérale, É.-U.)	Cir.

Citizenship Appeal Court (Can.)	Cit. App. Ct.
Citizenship Appeals Court (U.S. / É.-U.)	Cit. A.C.
Common Pleas	C.P.
Coroners Court	Cor. Ct.
Conseil constitutionnel (France)	Cons. const.
Conseil d'État (France)	Cons. d'État
Constitutional Court of South Africa	S. Afr. Const. Ct.
County Court	Co. Ct.
County Court Judges' Criminal Court	Co. Ct. J. Crim. Ct.
Cour canadienne de l'impôt	C.C.I.
Cour d'appel	C.A.
Cour d'appel de citoyenneté	C.A. cit.
Cour de cassation : Assemblée plénière (France)	Cass. Ass. plén.
Cour de cassation : Chambre commerciale (France)	Cass. com.
Cour de cassation : Chambre criminelle (France)	Cass. crim.
Cour de cassation : Chambre des requêtes (France)	Cass. req.
Cour de cassation : Chambre mixte (France)	Cass. Ch. mixte
Cour de cassation : Chambre sociale (France)	Cass. soc.
Cour de cassation : Chambres réunies (France)	Cass. Ch. réun.
Cour de cassation : Première chambre civile (France)	Cass. civ. 1^e
Cour de cassation : Deuxième chambre civile (France)	Cass. civ. 2^e
Cour de cassation : Troisième chambre civile (France)	Cass. civ. 3^e
Cour de comté	C.c.
Cour des juges de la Cour de comté siégeant au criminel	C. j. C.c. crim.
Cour de district	C. dist.
Cour de l'Échiquier	C. de l'É.
Cour de l'Ontario, division générale	Div. gén. Ont.
Cour de magistrat	C. mag.
Cour de révision	C. rév.
Cour des divorces et des causes matrimoniales	C. div. & causes mat.
Cour des jeunes déliquants	C. jeun. dél.
Cour des petites créances	C. pet. cré.
Cour des Sessions de la paix	C.S.P.
Cour des successions	C. succ.
Cour divisionnaire	C. div.
Cour du Banc de la Reine	B.R.
Cour du Banc de la Reine, Division de la famille	B.R. (div. fam.)
Cour du Banc de la Reine, Division de première instance	B.R. (1re inst.)

Cour du Banc du Roi	B.R.
Cour du bien-être social	C.b.e.s.
Cour du recorder	C. rec.
Cour du Québec	C.Q.
Cour du Québec, Chambre de la jeunesse	C.Q. jeun.
Cour du Québec, Chambre de l'expropriation	C.Q. exp.
Cour du Québec, Chambre civile	C.Q. civ.
Cour du Québec, Chambre civile, petites créances	C.Q. civ. pet. cré.
Cour du Québec, Chambre criminelle et pénale	C.Q. crim. & pén.
Cour fédérale d'appel	C.F.A.
Cour fédérale, première instance	C.F. (1re inst.)
Cour municipale	C.M.
Cour provinciale	C.P.
Cour provinciale, Division civile	C.P. Div. civ.
Cour provinciale, Division criminelle	C.P. Div. crim.
Cour provinciale, Division de la famille	C.P. Div. fam.
Cour supérieure	C.S.
Cour supérieure, Chambre civile	C.S. civ.
Cour supérieure, Chambre criminelle	C.S. crim.
Cour supérieure, Division des petites créances	C.S. pét. cré.
Cour supérieure, Chambre de la famille	C.S. fam.
Cour supérieure, Chambre de la jeunesse	C.S. jeun.
Cour supérieure, Chambre du divorce	C.S. div.
Cour supérieure, Chambre de la faillite et de l'insolvabilité	C.S. fail. & ins.
Cour suprême, Division de la famille	C. supr. fam.
Cour suprême, Division d'appel	C. supr. A.
Cour suprême, Division de la Banc de la Reine	C. supr. B.R.
Cour suprême du Canada	C.S.C.
Court Martial Appeal Court	Ct. Martial App. Ct.
Cour d'appel de la cour martiale	C.A.C.M.
Court of Appeal	C.A.
Court of Appeal in Equity	C.A. Eq.
Court of Criminal Appeals	Ct. Crim. App.
Court of Divorce	Ct. Div.
Court of Divorce and Matrimonial Causes	Ct. Div. & Mat. Causes
Court of General Sessions of the Peace	Ct. G.S.P.
Court of Justice, General Division	Ct. J. (Gen. Div.)
Court of Justice, General Division, Small Claims Court	Ct. J. (Gen. Div. Sm. Cl.

	Ct.)
Court of Justice, General Division, Family Court	Ct. J. (Gen. Div. Fam. Ct.)
Court of Justice, Provincial Division	Ct. J. (Prov. Div.)
Court of Justice, Provincial Division, Youth Court	Ct. J. (Prov. Div. Youth Ct.)
Court of Justice (Scotland / Écosse)	Ct. Just.
Court of King's Bench	K.B.
Court of Quebec	C.Q.
Court of Quebec, Civil Division	C.Q. (Civ. Div.)
Court of Quebec, Civil Division, Small Claims	C.Q. (Civ. Div. Sm. Cl.)
Court of Quebec, Criminal & Penal Division	C.Q. (Crim & Pen. Div.)
Court of Quebec, Expropriation Division	C.Q. (Exp. Div.)
Court of Quebec, Youth Division	C.Q. (Youth Div.)
Court of Queen's Bench	Q.B.
Court of Queen's Bench, Family Division	Q.B. (Fam. Div.)
Court of Queen's Bench, Trial Division	Q.B. (T.D.)
Court of Review	Ct. Rev.
Court of Sessions (Scotland / Écosse)	Ct. Sess.
Court of Sessions of the Peace	Ct. Sess. P.
Distict Court (U.S Federal / É.U. fédéral)	D.
District Court (U.S. states / états des É.-U.)	Dist. Ct.
District Court Judges' Criminal Court	Dist. Ct. J. Crim. Ct.
District Court of New Zealand	D.C.N.Z.
Division Court	Div'n. Ct.
Divisional Court	Div. Ct.
Division provinciale	Div. prov.
Divorce and Matrimonial Causes Court	Div. & Mat. Causes Ct.
Environment Court	Env. Ct.
Exchequer Court	Ex. Ct.
Family Court of New Zealand	Fam. Ct. N.Z.
Family & Children's Court	Fam. & Child. Ct.
Family Court	Fam. Ct.
Federal Court, Appeal Division	F.C.A.
Federal Court, Trial Division	F.C.T.D.
Federal Court of Australia	F.C.A.
General Division	Gen. Div.
Haute Cour de justice	H.C.J.
High Court of Admiralty	H.C. Adm.

High Court of Australia	H.C.A.
High Court of Justice	H.C.J.
High Court: Chancery Division (U.K. / R.-U.)	Ch.D.
High Court: Family Division (U.K. / R.-U.)	Fam.D.
High Court: Queen's Bench Division (U.K./ R.-U.)	Q.B.D.
House of Lords (England / Angleterre)	H.L. (Eng.)
House of Lords (Scotland / Écosse)	H.L. (Scot.)
Judicial Committee of the Privy Council (Commonwealth)	P.C.
Justice de Paix (before 1958 / avant 1958) (France)	J.P.
Justice of the Peace Court	Just. P. Ct.
Juvenile Court	Juv. Ct.
Juvenile Delinquents' Court	Juv. Del. Ct.
Juvenile and Family Court	Juv. & Fam. Ct.
Labour Court	Lab. Ct.
Labour Court of South Africa	S. Afr. Labour Ct.
Labour Court of Appeal of South Africa	S. Afr. Labour C.A.
Maori Land Court / *Te Kooti Whenua Maori*	Maori Land Ct.
Maori Appellate Court	Maori A.C.
Master's Chambers	M.C.
Magistrates' Court	Mag. Ct.
Magistrates' Court of New Zealand	Mag. Ct. N.Z.
Municipal Court	Mun. Ct.
New Zealand Court of Appeal	N.Z.C.A.
New Zealand High Court	N.Z.H.C.
New Zealand Employment Court	N.Z. Empl. Ct.
New Zealand Youth Court	N.Z.Y.C.
Ontario Court, General Division	Ont. Ct. Gen. Div.
Privy Council	P.C.
Probate Court	Prob. Ct.
Provincial Court, Civil Division	Prov. Ct. (Civ. Div.)
Provincial Court, Civil Division, Small Claims Court	Prov. Ct. (Civ. Div. Sm. Cl. Ct.)
Provincial Court, Criminal Division	Prov. Ct. (Crim. Div.)
Provincial Court, Family Court	Prov. Ct. (Fam. Ct.)
Provincial Court, Family Division	Prov. Ct. (Fam. Div.)
Provincial Court, Juvenile Division	Prov. Ct. (Juv. Div.)
Provincial Court, Small Claims Division	Prov. Ct. (Sm. Cl. Div.)
Provincial Court, Youth Court	Prov. Ct. (Youth Ct.)

Provincial Court, Youth Division	Prov. Ct. (Youth Div.)
Provincial Division	Prov. Div.
Provincial Judges' Court, Criminal Division	Prov. J. Ct. Crim. Div.
Provincial Judges' Court, Family Division	Prov. J. Ct. Fam. Div.
Provincial Offences Court	Prov. Off. Ct.
Registrar of Trade Marks	Reg. T.M.
Recorder's Court	Rec. Ct.
Social Welfare Court	S.W. Ct.
Small Claims Court	Sm. Cl. Ct.
Small Debts Court	Sm. Debts Ct.
Stipendiary Magistrates' Court	Stip. Mag. Ct.
Superior Court (Canada)	Sup. Ct.
Superior Court, Bankruptcy and Insolvency Division	Sup. Ct. (Bank. & Ins. Div.)
Superior Court, Civil Division	Sup. Ct. (Civ. Div.)
Superior Court, Criminal Division	Sup. Ct. (Crim. Div.)
Superior Court, Divorce Division	Sup. Ct. (D. Div.)
Superior Court, Family Division	Sup. Ct. (Fam. Div.)
Superior Court, Small Claims Division	Sup. Ct. (Sm. Cl. Div.)
Superior Court, Youth Division	Sup. Ct. (Youth Div.)
Superior Court (U.S. / É.-U.)	Super. Ct.
Supreme Court (State, U.S. / état, É.-U.)	Sup. Ct.
Supreme Court of Canada	S.C.C.
Supreme Court, Appellate Division (Can. provincial / Can. Provinciale)	S.C. (A.D.)
Supreme Court, Appellate Division (state, U.S. / état, É.-U.)	Sup. Ct. App. Div.
Supreme Court, Chancery Division	S.C. (Ch. D.)
Supreme Court, Estates Division	S.C. (Est. Div.)
Supreme Court, Family Division	S.C. (Fam. Div.)
Supreme Court, King's Bench Division	S.C. (K.B. Div.)
Supreme Court Master	S.C. (Mast.)
Supreme Court, Queen's Bench Division	S.C. (Q.B. Div.)
Supreme Court Registrar	S.C. (Reg.)
Supreme Court Taxing Officer	S.C. (Tax.)
Supreme Court, Trial Division	S.C. (T.D.)
Supreme Court of the United States	U.S.S.C.
Surrogate Court	Surr. Ct.

Appendices/Annexes

Tax Court of Canada	T.C.C.
Territorial Court	Terr. Ct.
Territorial Court, Youth Court	Terr. Ct. Youth Ct.
Tribunal administratif (France)	Trib. admin.
Tribunal civil (before 1958 / avant 1958) (France)	Trib. civ.
Tribunal commercial (France)	Trib. com.
Tribunal correctionnel (France)	Trib. corr.
Tribunal d'instance (1958-present / 1958-présent) (France)	Trib. inst.
Tribunal de grande instance (France)	Trib. gr. inst.
Tribunal de première instance (avant 1958) (France)	Trib. civ.
Unified Family Court	Unif. Fam. Ct.
Youth Court	Youth Ct.
Waitangi Tribunal / *Te Rōpū Whakamana i te Tiriti o Waitangi*	Waitangi Trib.

G PRINTED CASELAW REPORTERS ~ RECUEILS DE JURISPRUDENCE IMPRIMES

Canadian Official Reporters ~ Recueils officiels canadiens

Always cite to these reporters first. Official reporters are published by the Queen's Printer. Whenever there is a discrepancy between two different versions of the same case, the version in the following reporters will be given precedence.

Toujours renvoyer aux recueils officiels d'abord. Les recueils officiels sont publiés par l'Imprimeur de la Reine. En cas de différence entre un recueil officiel et un autre recueil, la version du recueil officiel a préséance.

C.F.	Recueils des arrêts de la Cour fédérale du Canada (1971-présent)
Ex. C.R.	Canada Law Reports: Exchequer Court of Canada (1923-1970)
	Reports of the Exchequer Court of Canada (1875-1922)
F.C.	Federal Court Reports (1971-present)
R.C. de l'É.	Recueils des arrêts de la Cour de l'Échiquier (1875-1922)
	Rapports judiciaires du Canada : cour de l'Échiquier (1923-1970)
R.C.S.	Recueils des arrêts de la Cour suprême du Canada (1877-1922)
	Rapports judiciaires du Canada : cour suprême (1923-1969)
	Recueils des arrêts de la Cour suprême du Canada (1970-présent)
S.C.R.	Canada Supreme Court Reports (1970-present)
	Canada Law Reports: Supreme Court of Canada (1923-1969)
	Canada Supreme Court Reports (1876-1922)

Canadian Semi-Official Reporters ~ Recueils semi-officiels canadiens

The following reporters are published under the auspices of the local Law Society. Always cite to these reporters before any other, except the S.C.R., F.C., or Ex. C.R.

On renvoie toujours à ces recueils en premier lieu, mais après les recueils officiels. Les recueils suivants sont publiés sous l'égide du barreau de la province ou du territoire en question.

A.R.	Alberta Reports (1976-present / 1976-présent)
Alta. L.R.	Alberta Law Reports (only / seulement 1908-1932)
B.C.R.	British Columbia Reports (1867-1947)

B.R.	Recueils de jurisprudence du Québec : Cour du Banc de la Reine/du Roi (1942-1969)
	Rapports judiciaires officiels de Québec : Cour du Banc de la Reine/du Roi (1892-1941)
C.A.	Recueils de jurisprudence du Québec : Cour d'appel (1970-1985)
C.B.E.S.	Recueils de jurisprudence du Québec : Cour du bien-être social (1975-1985)
C.P.	Recueils de jurisprudence du Québec : Cour provinciale (1975-1985)
C.S.	Recueils de jurisprudence du Québec: Cour supérieure (1967-1985)
	Rapports judiciaires officiels de Québec : Cour supérieure (1892-1966)
C.S.P.	Recueils de jurisprudence du Québec : Cour des Sessions de la paix (1975-1985)
Man. R.	Manitoba Reports (1883-1961)
N.B.R.	New Brunswick Reports (2d) (only since 1969 / seulement depuis 1969)
N.S.R.	Nova Scotia Reports (2d) (1969-present/1969-présent)
	Nova Scotia Reports (1965-1969)
	N.B.: Not official from 1834-1929 / non- officielle de 1834 à 1929.
N.W.T.R.	Northwest Territories Reports (1983-1998)
Nfld. & P.E.I.R.	Newfoundland & Prince Edward Island Reports (1971-present/1971-présent)
O.L.R.	Ontario Law Reports (1900-1931)
O.R.	Ontario Reports (2d) (1973-present/1973-présent)
	Ontario Reports (1931-1973)
	N.B.: Not official from 1882-1900 / non-officielle de 1882 à 1900.
O.W.N.	Ontario Weekly Notes (1909-1962)
R.J.Q.	Recueils de jurisprudence du Québec (1975-present/1975-présent)
Sask. L.R.	Saskatchewan Law Reports (1907-1931)
T.J.	Recueils de jurisprudence du Québec: Tribunal de la jeunesse (1975-1985)
Terr. L.R.	Territories Law Reports (1885-1907)
Y.R.	Yukon Reports (1986-1989)

Abbreviations ~ Abréviations

- For a more detailed list of Law Reports, consult M.M. Prince, *Bieber's Dictionary of Legal Abbreviations*, 5th ed. (Buffalo, N.Y.: William S. Hein, 2001).
- If an English reporter is reprinted in whole or in part in the *English Reports*, the applicable volume(s) are indicated.
- For the most part, selected reporters with recent jurisprudence have been included from all countries represented in this *Guide*, while selected reporters with both historical and recent jurisprudence have been included for Canada and the U.K.

- French *Cahiers de droit* and yearbooks containing both doctrine and jurisprudence may be found in section Appendix H.
- Because reporters may cover a large time period during which many names have existed for a jurisdiction, the jurisdiction listed in the jurisdiction column is always the most recent name for the jurisdiction covered by the reporter.
- This list only contains printed reporters. Decisions of many courts and administrative bodies are now available online. Follow the rules in Chapter 3 when citing decisions obtained online.

- Pour une liste plus détaillée des *Law Reports*, consulter M.M. Prince, *Bieber's Dictionary of Legal Abbreviations*, 5ᵉ ed., Buffalo (N.Y.), William S. Hein, 2001.
- Si un recueil anglais est reproduit entièrement ou en partie dans les *English Reports*, le(s) volume(s) approprié(s) est indiqué.
- La plupart des recueils qui comprennet la jurisprudence récente est disponible dans ce Manuel. Les recueils qui contiennent de la jurisprudence plus anienne ou historique ont été inclus pour le Canada et le Royaume-Uni.
- Pour les *Cahiers de droit* et les annuaires français qui comprennent dc la doctrine et de la jurisprudence, voir L'annexe H.
- Puisque les recueils peuvent couvrir une longue période pendant laquelle des noms différents désignaient la juridiction, la liste des juridictions énumérées ci-dessous représente le nom le plus récent de la juridiction.
- Seuls les recueils imprimés sont inclus dans cette liste. Les décisions de plusieurs cours et organes administratifs sont maintenant diponibles en ligne. Respectes les règles du 3ᵉ chapitre pour les références aux décisions accédées en ligne.

Abbreviation Abréviation	Title of Reporter Titre du recueil	Jurisdiction Indication géographique	Dates
A.	Atlantic Reporter	U.S. / É.-U.	1855-1938
A.2d.	Atlantic Reporter, Second Series	U.S. / É.-U.	1938-
A. & N.	Alcock and Napier's Reports	I.	1831-1833
A. Crim. R.	Australian Criminal Reports	Austl.	1980-
A. imm. app.	Affaires d'immigration en appel	Can.	1967-1970
A. imm. app (n.s.)	Affaires d'immigration en appel (nouvelle série)	Can.	1969-1977
A. Int'l. L.C.	American International Law Cases	U.S. / É.-U.	1793-
A.N.W.T.Y.T.R.	Alberta, Northwest Territories & Yukon Tax Reporter	Can.	1973-
A.A.L.R.	Australian Argus Law Reports	Austl.	1960-1973
A.A.R.	Administrative Appeals Reports	Austl.	1984-
A.A.S.	Arbitrate – Santé et services sociaux	Can. (QC)	1983-
A.B.C.	Australian Bankruptcy Cases	Austl.	1928-1964
A.B.D.	Canada, Public Service Commission, Appeals and Investigation Branch, Appeal Board Decisions	Can.	1979 1999

A.C.	Law Reports, Appeal Cases	U.K. / R.-U.	1890-
A.C.A.	Australian Corporate Affairs Reporter	Austl.	1971-1982
A.C.L.C.	Australian Company Law Cases	Austl.	1971-
A.C.L.P.	Australian Company Law and Practice	Austl.	1981-1991
A.C.L.R.	Australian Company Law Reports	Austl.	1974-1989
A.C.L.R.	Australian Construction Law Reporter	Austl.	1982-1997
A.C.S.R.	Australian Corporations and Securities Reports	Austl.	1989-
A.C.T.R.	Australian Capital Territory Reports	Austl. (A.C.T.)	1973-
A.C.W.S.	All Canada Weekly Summaries	Can.	1970-1979
A.C.W.S. (2d)	All Canada Weekly Summaries (Second Series)	Can.	1980-1986
A.C.W.S. (3d)	All Canada Weekly Summaries (Third Series)	Can.	1986-
A.D.	South African Law Reports, Appellate Division	S. Afr. du sud	1910-1946
A.D.I.L.	Annual Digest and Reports of Public International Law Cases	Int'l	1919-1942
A.D.R.	Australian De Facto Relationships Law	Austl.	1985-
A.E.B.R.	Australian Business & Assets Planning Reporter	Austl.	1986-
A.E.B.C.N.	Australian Business & Estate Planning Case Notes	Austl.	1979-1981
A.E.U.B.	Alberta Energy and Utilities Board Decisions	Can (AB)	1995-
A.F.T.R.	Australian Federal Tax Reporter	Austl.	1969-
A.I.L.R.	Australian Indigenous Law Reporter	Austl.	1996-
A.I.N.	Australian Industrial and Intellectual Property Cases	Austl.	1982-
A.J.D.A.	Actualité juridique, droit administratif	France	1955-
A.J.D.I.	Actualité juridique, droit immobilier	France	1997-
A.J.D.Q.	Annuaire de jurisprudence et de doctrine du Québec	Can. (QC)	1997?-
A.J.P.I.	Actualité juridique, propriété immobilière	France	1955-1997
A.L.D.	Administrative Law Decisions	Austl.	1976-
A.L.J.R.	Australian Law Journal Reports	Austl.	1958-
A.L.L.R.	Australian Labour Law Reporter	Austl.	1977-
A.L.M.D.	Australian Legal Monthly Digest	Austl.	1967-
A.L.R.	Administrative Law Reports in the British Journal of Administrative Law	U.K. / R.-U.	1954-1957
A.L.R.	American Law Reports	U.S. / É.-U.	1919-1948
A.L.R.	Argus Law Reports	Austl.	1895-1959
A.L.R.	Australian Law Reports	Austl.	1973-

A.L.R.2d	American Law Reports (Second Series)	U.S. / É.-U.	1948-1965
A.L.R.3d	American Law Reports (Third Series)	U.S. / É.-U.	1965-1980
A.L.R.4th	American Law Reports (Fourth Series)	U.S. / É.-U.	1980-1991
A.L.R.5th	American Law Reports (Fifth Series)	U.S. / É.-U.	1992-
A.M.C.	American Maritime Cases	U.S. / É.-U.	1923-
A.P.R.	Atlantic Provinces Reports	Can.	1975-
A.R.	Alberta Reports	Can. (AB)	1976-
A.S.L.C.	Australian Securities Law Cases	Austl.	1971-
A.S.C. Sum.	Alberta Securities Commission Summaries	Can. (AB)	1975-
A.T.B.	Canada Air Transport Board Decisions	Can.	1944-1967
A.T.C.	Australian Tax Cases	Austl.	1969-
A.W.L.D.	Alberta Weekly Law Digest	Can. (AB)	1982-
Act.	Acton's Prize Cases (E.R. vol. 12)	U.K. / R.-U.	1809-1811
Ad. & El.	Adolphus & Ellis's Reports (E.R. vols. 110-113)	U.K. / R.-U.	1834-1842
Adam.	Adam's Justiciary Cases	Scot.	1893-1916
Add.	Addams's Reports (E.R. vol. 162)	U.K. / R.-U.	1822-1826
Admin. L.R.	Administrative Law Reports	Can.	1983-1991
Admin. L.R. (2d)	Administrative Law Reports (Second Series)	Can.	1992-1998
Admin. L.R. (3d)	Administrative Law Reports (Third Series)	Can.	1998-
Afr. L.R. (Comm.)	African Law Reports: Commercial	Afr.	1964-1980
Afr. L.R. (Mal.)	African Law Reports: Malawi Series	E. Afr. de l'est	1923-1972
Afr. L.R. (S.L.)	African Law Reports: Sierra Leone Series	W. Afr. de l'ouest	1920-1936 1957-1960 1964-1966 1972-1973
Al.	Aleyn's Select Cases (E.R. vol. 82)	U.K. / R.-U.	1646-1649
Ala.	Alabama Reports	U.S. / É.-U.	1840-1946
Ala. (N.S.)	Alabama Reports (New Series)	U.S. / É.-U.	1846-1975
Alaska Fed.	Alaska Federal Reports	U.E. / É.-U.	1869-1937
Alaska R.	Alaska Reports	U.S. / É.-U.	1884-1958
All E.R.	All England Reports	U.K. / R.-U.	1936-
All E.R. (Comm.)	All England Law Reports (Commercial Cases)	U.K. / R.-U.	1999-
All E.R. (E.C.)	All England Law Reports (European Cases)	U.K. / R.-U.	1995-
All E.R. Rep.	All England Reports Reprints	U.K. / R.-U.	1558-1935

All E.R. Rep. Ext.	All England Reprints Extension Volumes	U.K. / R.-U.	1895-1935
Alta. B.A.A.	Alberta Board of Arbitration, Arbitrations under the Alberta Labour Act	Can. (AB)	1980-
Alta. B.A.A.A.	Alberta Board of Adjudication, Adjudications and Arbitrations under the Public Service Employee Relations Act	Can. (AB)	1980-1986
Alta. B.I.R.	Alberta Board of Industrial Relations Decisions	Can. (AB)	1961-1982
Alta. E.R.C.B.	Alberta Energy Resources Conservation Board (Decisions and Reports) (formerly Alberta Oil and Gas Conservation Board)	Can. (AB)	1971-
Alta. H.R.C.R.	Alberta Human Rights Commission, Reports of Boards of Inquiry	Can. (AB)	1972-1982
Alta. L.R.	Alberta Law Reports	Can. (AB)	1908-1933
Alta. L.R. (2d)	Alberta Law Reports (Second Series)	Can. (AB)	1976-1992
Alta. L.R. (3d)	Alberta Law Reports (Third Series)	Can. (AB)	1992-
Alta. L.R.B.D.	Alberta Labour Relations Board Decisions	Can. (AB)	1982-1986
Alta. L.R.B.R.	Alberta Labour Relations Board Reports	Can. (AB)	1986-
Alta. O.G.C.B.	Alberta Oil and Gas Conservation Board Decisions (formerly Petroleum and Natural Gas Conservation Board of Alberta)	Can. (AB)	1957-1971
Alta. P.S.E.R.B.	Alberta Public Service Employee Relations Board Decisions	Can. (AB)	1981-1986
Alta. P.S.G.A.B.	Alberta Public Services Grievance Appeal Board Adjudications and Arbitrations	Can. (AB)	1980-1985
Alta. P.U.B.	Alberta Public Utilities Board Decisions	Can. (AB)	1976-
Amb.	Ambler's Reports, Chancery (E.R. vol. 27)	U.K. / R.-U.	1716-1783
And.	Anderson's Common Law Conveyancing and Equity (E.R. vol. 123)	U.K. / R.-U.	1534-1605
Andr.	Andrews' Reports (E.R. vol. 95)	U.K. / R.-U.	1738-1739
Ann. Conv. Eur. D.H.	Annuaire de la Convention européenne des droits de l'Homme	E.U. / U.E.	1958-
Anst.	Anstruther's Reports (E.R. vol. 145)	U.K. / R.-U.	1792-1797
App. Cas.	Appeal Cases	U.K. / R.-U.	1875-1890
App. Div.	New York Appellate Division Reports	U.S. / É.-U.	1896-1956

App. Div. 2d.	New York Appellate Division Reports (Second Series)	U.S. / É.-U.	1956-
Arb. Serv. Rep.	Arbitration Services Reporter	Can.	1977-
Ariz.	Arizona Reports	U.S. / É.-U.	1866-
Ark.	Arkansas Reports	U.S. / É.-U.	1837-
Ark. App.	Arkansas Appellate Reports	U.S. / É.-U.	1981-
Arn.	Arnold's Reports	U.K. / R.-U.	1838-1839
Arn. & H.	Arnold and Hodges's Reports	U.K. / R.-U.	1840-1841
Asp. M.L.C.	Aspinall's Maritime Law Cases	U.K. / R.-U.	1870-1940
Atk.	Atkyns's Reports, Chancery (E.R. vol. 26)	U.K. / R.-U.	1736-1755
Av. Cas.	Aviation Cases	U.S. / É.-U.	1822-
B. & Ad.	Barnewall & Adolphus's Reports, King's Bench (E.R. vols. 109-110)	U.K. / R.-U.	1830-1834
B. & Ald.	Barnewall & Alderson's Reports, King's Bench (E.R. vol. 106)	U.K. / R.-U.	1817-1822
B. & C.R.	Reports of Bankruptcy and Companies Winding-Up Cases	U.K. / R.-U.	1918-1941
B. & Cress.	Barnewall & Cresswell's Reports, King's Bench (E.R. vols. 107-109)	U.K. / R.-U.	1822-1830
B. & S.	Best & Smith's Reports (E.R. vols. 121-122)	U.K. / R.-U.	1861-1865
B. Const. L.R.	Butterworths Constitutional Law Reports	S. Afr. du sud	1994-
B.A.	Book of Awards (Arbtration Court, Court of Appeal)	N.Z. / N.-Z.	1894-1991
B.C. Empl. Standards Bd. Dec.	British Columbia Employment Standards Board Decisions	Can. (BC)	1981-1983
B.C. En. Comm'n Dec.	British Columbia Energy Commission Decisions	Can. (BC)	1977-1980
B.C.H.R.C. Dec.	British Columbia Human Rights Commission Decisions	Can. (BC)	1975-1982
B.C.S.C.W. Summ.	British Columbia Securities Commission Weekly Summary	Can. (BC)	1987-
B.C. Util. Comm'n.	British Columbia Utilities Commission Decisions	Can. (BC)	1980-
B.C.A.C.	British Columbia Appeal Cases	Can. (BC)	1991-
B.C.A.V.C.	British Columbia, Director of Trade Practices, Assurances of voluntary compliance pursuant to section 15 of the Trade Practices Act (Decisions)	Can. (BC)	1974-1978
B.C.D.	Bulletin des contributions directes, de la taxe sur la valeur ajoutée et des impôts indirects	France	1961-1974
B.C.L.R.	British Columbia Law Reports	Can. (BC)	1977-1986

B.C.L.R. (2d)	British Columbia Law Reports (Second Series)	Can. (BC)	1986-1995
B.C.L.R. (3d)	British Columbia Law Reports (Third Series)	Can. (BC)	1995-
B.C.L.R.B. Dec.	British Columbia Labour Relations Board Decisions	Can. (BC)	1979-
B.C.R.	British Columbia Reports	Can. (BC)	1867-1947
B.C.W.C.R.	British Columbia Workers' Compensation Reporter	Can. (BC)	1973-
B.D.M.	Bulletin de droit municipal	Can. (QC)	1994-
B.I.L.C.	British International Law Cases	U.K. / R.-U.	1964-
B.I.S.D.	Basic Instruments and Selected Documents	GATT	1952-
B.L.E.	Bulletin du libre-échange	Can.	1990-1996
B.L.R.	Business Law Reports	Can.	1977-1990
B.L.R. (2d)	Business Law Reports (Second Series)	Can.	1991-1999
B.L.R. (3d)	Business Law Reports (Third Series)	Can.	2000-
B.R.	Recueils de jurisprudence du Québec: Cour du Banc de la Reine / du Roi	Can. (QC)	1892-1941
B.R.	Rapports judiciaires officiels de Québec : Cour du Banc de la Reine / du Roi	Can. (QC)	1942-1969
B.R.E.F.	Décisions du Bureau de révision de l'évaluation foncière	Can. (QC)	1980-1998
Ball. & B.	Ball and Beatty's Reports	I.	1807-1814
Barn. C.	Barnardiston's Chancery Reports (E.R. vol. 27)	U.K. / R.-U.	1740-1741
Barn. K.B.	Barnardiston's King's Bench Reports (E.R. vol. 94)	U.K. / R.-U.	1726-1734
Barnes	Barnes's Notes (E.R. vol. 94)	U.K. / R.-U.	1732-1756
Batt.	Batty's Reports	I.	1825-1826
Bd. Rwy. Comm'rs Can.	Board of Railway Commissioners for Canada – Judgments, Orders, Regulations and Rulings	Can.	1911-1938
Bd. Trans. Comm'rs Can.	Board of Transport Commissioners for Canada – Judgments, Orders, Regulations, and Rulings (formerly Board of Railway Commissioners for Canada)	Can.	1938-1967
Beat.	Beatty's Reports	I.	1813-1830
Beaubien	Beaubien	Can. (QC)	1905-1906
Beav.	Beavan's Reports (E.R. vols. 48-55)	U.K. / R.-U.	1838-1866
Bel.	Bellewe's Reports (E.R. vol. 72)	U.K. / R.-U.	1378-1400
Bell	Bell's Reports (E.R. vol. 169)	U.K. / R.-U.	1858-1860
Ben. & D.	Benloe & Dalison's Reports (E.R. vol.	U.K. / R.-U.	1486-1580

	123)		
Benl.	Benloe's Reports (E.R. vol. 73)	U.K. / R.-U.	1531-1628
Bing.	Bingham's Reports (E.R. vols. 130-131)	U.K. / R.-U.	1822-1834
Bing. N.C.	Bingham's New Cases (E.R. vols. 131-133)	U.K. / R.-U.	1834-1840
Bla. H.	H. Blackstone Reports	U.K. / R.-U.	1788-1796
Bla. W.	W. Blackstone Reports	U.K. / R.-U.	1746-1779
Bli.	Bligh's Reports, House of Lords (E.R. vol. 4)	U.K. / R.-U.	1819-1821
Bli. N.S.	Bligh's Repors (New Series) (E.R. vols. 4-6)	U.K. / R.-U.	1826-1837
Bos. & Pul.	Bosanquet & Puller's Reports (E.R. vols. 126-127)	U.K. / R.-U.	1796-1804
Bos. & Pul. N.R.	Bosanquet & Puller's New Reports (E.R. vol. 127)	U.K. / R.-U.	1804-1807
Bridg.	Sir John Bridgman's Reports	U.K. / R.-U.	1613-1621
Bridg. Conv.	Sir Orlando Bridgman's Conveyances	U.K. / R.-U.	1600-1667
Bridg. J.	Sir J. Bridgman's Reports (E.R. vol. 123)	U.K. / R.-U.	1613-1621
Bridg. O.	Sir O. Bridgman's Reports (E.R. vol. 124)	U.K. / R.-U.	1660-1667
Bro. C.C.	Brown's Chancery Cases (by Belt) (E.R. vols. 28-29)	U.K. / R.-U.	1778-1794
Bro. P.C.	Brown's Parliamentary Cases (E.R. vols. 1-3)	U.K. / R.-U.	1702-1800
Brod. & Bing.	Broderip & Bingham's Reports (E.R. vol. 129)	U.K. / R.-U.	1819-1822
Brooke N.C.	Brooke's New Cases (E.R. vol. 73)	U.K. / R.-U.	1515-1558
Brown. & Lush.	Browning & Lushington's Admiralty Reports (E.R. vol. 167)	U.K. / R.-U.	1863-1865
Brownl.	Brownlow & Goldesborough's Reports (E.R. vol. 123)	U.K. / R.-U.	1569-1624
Bull. C.V.M.Q.	Bulletin – Commission des valeurs mobilières du Québec	Can. (QC)	1970?-
Bull. civ.	Bulletin des arrêts de la cour de cassation, Chambres civiles	France	1798-
Bull. Concl. fisc.	Bulletin des conclusions fiscales	France	1992-
Bull. Crim.	Bulletin des arrêts de la cour de cassation, Chambre criminelle	France	1798-
Bull. O.S.C.	Bulletin of the Ontario Securities Commission	Can. (ON)	1981-
Bulst.	Bulstrode's Reports, King's Bench (E.R. vols. 80-81)	U.K. / R.-U.	1609-1626

Bunb.	Bunbury's Reports, Exchequer (E.R. vol. 145)	U.K. / R.-U.	1713-1741
Burr.	Burrow's Reports (E.R. vols. 97-98)	U.K. / R.-U.	1756-1772
Burrell	Burrell Reports (E.R. vol. 167)	U.K. / R.-U.	1584-1839
C. & J.	Crompton & Jervis's Reports (E.R. vols. 148-149)	U.K. / R.-U.	1830-1832
C. & M.	Crompton & Meeson's Reports (E.R. vol. 149)	U.K. / R.-U.	1832-1834
C. & S.	Clarke and Scully's Drainage Cases	Can. (ON)	1898-1903
C.A.	Recueils de jurisprudence du Québec : Cour d'appel	Can. (QC)	1970-1985
C.A.C.	Canada Citizenship Appeal Court, Reasons for Judgment	Can.	1975-1977
C.A.C.M.	Recueil des arrêts de la Cour d'appel des cours martiales du Canada	Can.	1957-
C.A.E.C.	Commission d'appel des enregistrements commerciaux, Sommaires des décisions	Can. (ON)	1971-?
C.A.I.	Décisions de la Commission d'accès à l'information	Can. (QC)	1984-
C.A.L.P.	Décisions de la Commission d'appel en matière de lésions professionnelles	Can. (QC)	1986-
C.A.L.R.	Criminal Appeals Law Reporter	Can.	1993-
C.A.Q.	Causes en appel au Québec	Can. (QC)	1986-1995
C.A.R.	Commonwealth Arbitration Reports	Austl.	1905-
C.A.S.	Décisions de la Commission des affaires sociales	Can. (QC)	1975-1997
C.B.	Common Bench Reports (E.R. vols. 135-139)	U.K. / R.-U.	1845-1856
C.B. (N.S.)	Common Bench Reports (New Series) (E.R. vols. 140-144)	U.K. / R.-U.	1856-1866
C.B.E.S.	Recueils de jurisprudence du Québec : Cour du bien-être social	Can. (QC)	1975-1985
C.B.R.	Copyright Board Reports	Can.	1990-1994
C.B.R.	Canadian Bankruptcy Reports	Can.	1920-1960
C.B.R. (N.S.)	Canadian Bankruptcy Reports (New Series)	Can.	1960-1990
C.B.R. (3rd)	Canadian Bankruptcy Reports (Third Series)	Can.	1991-1998
C.B.R. (4th)	Canadian Bankruptcy Reports (Fourth Series)	Can.	1998-
C.C.C.	Cahiers du Conseil constitutionnel	France	1996-
C.C.C.	Canadian Criminal Cases	Can.	1898-1962
C.C.C. (N.S.)	Canadian Criminal Cases (New Series)	Can.	1963-1970
C.C.C. (2d)	Canadian Criminal Cases (Second	Can.	1971-1983

	Series)		
C.C.C. (3d)	Canadian Criminal Cases (Third Series)	Can.	1983-
C.C.E.L.	Canadian Cases on Employment Law	Can.	1983-1994
C.C.E.L. (2d)	Canadian Cases on Employment Law (Second Series)	Can.	1994-2000
C.C.E.L. (3d)	Canadian Cases on Employment Law (Third Series)	Can.	2000-
C.C.L.	Canadian Current Law	Can.	1948-1990
C.C.L.	Canadian Current Law: Jurisprudence / sommaires de la jurisprudence	Can.	1991
C.C.L.	Canadian Current Law: Case Law Digests / sommaires de la jurisprudence	Can.	1992-1996
C.C.L.	Canadian Current Law: Case Digests / sommaires de la jurisprudence	Can.	1996-
C.C.L. Législation	Canadian Current Law: Annuaire de la législation	Can.	1989-
C.C.L. Legislation	Canadian Current Law: Legislation Annual	Can.	1989-
C.C.L.I.	Canadian Cases on the Law of Insurance	Can.	1983-1991
C.C.L.I. (2d)	Canadian Cases on the Law of Insurance (Second Series)	Can.	1991-1998
C.C.L.I. (3d)	Canadian Cases on the Law of Insurance (Third Series)	Can.	1998-
C.C.L.R.	Canadian Computer Law Reporter	Can.	1983-1992
C.C.L.S.	Canadian Cases on the Law of Securities	Can.	1993-1998
C.C.L.T.	Canadian Cases on the Law of Torts	Can.	1976-1990
C.C.L.T. (2d)	Canadian Cases on the Law of Torts (Second Series)	Can.	1990-2000
C.C.L.T. (3d)	Canadian Cases on the Law of Torts (Third Series)	Can.	2000-
C.C.P.B.	Canadian Cases on Pensions and Benefits	Can.	1994-
C.C.R.I.	Conseil canadien des relations industrielles, motifs de décision	Can.	1999-
C.C.R.T.D.	Conseil canadien des relations du travail, décisions	Can.	1949-1974
C.C.R.T.D.I.	Conseil canadien des relations du travail, décisions et informations	Can.	1974-1998
C.C.T.C.T.D.	Commission canadienne des transports, comité des télécommunications – décisions	Can.	1973-1976
C.C.T.C.T.E.P.	Commission canadienne des transports, comité des transports par eau – permis	Can.	1976

C.C.T.C.T.O.	Commission canadienne des transports, comité des télécommunications – ordonnances	Can.	1975-1976
C.C.T.O.	Commission canadienne des transports – ordonnances	Can.	1972-1987
C.D.B.-C.	Collection de décisions du Bas-Canada	Can. (QC)	1847-1891
C.E.B.	Canadian Employment Benefits and Pension Guide Reports	Can.	1995-
C.E.G.S.B.	Crown Employees Grievance Settlement Board Decisions	Can. (ON)	1876-1997
C.E.L.R.	Canadian Environmental Law Reports	Can.	1978-1985
C.E.L.R. (N.S.)	Canadian Environmental Law Reports	Can.	1986-
C.E.R.	Canadian Customs and Excise Reports	Can.	1980-1989
C.F.	Recueils des arrêts de la Cour fédérale du Canada	Can.	1971-
C.F.L.C.	Canadian Family Law Cases	Can.	1959-1977
C.F.P.	Recueil des décisions des comités d'appel de la fonction publique	Can. (QC)	1980-1989
C.H.R.R.	Canadian Human Rights Reporter	Can.	1980-
C.I.C.B.	Criminal Injuries Compensation Board Decisions	Can. (ON)	1971-1989
C.I.J. Mémoires	Cour internationale de justice : Mémoires, plaidoiries et documents	Int'l	1946-
C.I.J. Rec.	Cour internationale de justice : Recueil des arrêts, avis consultatifs et ordonnances	Int'l	1946-
C.I.P.O.O. (M)	Commissaire à l'information et à la protection de la vie privée, Ontario, Orders, M Series	Can. (ON)	1988-1998
C.I.P.O.O. (P)	Commissaire à l'information et à la protection de la vie privée, Ontario, Orders, P Series	Can. (ON)	1992-1998
C.I.P.O.S.	Commissaire à l'information et à la protection de la vie privée, Ontario, Sommaires	Can. (ON)	1990-1992
C.I.P.R.	Canadian Intellectual Property Reports	Can.	1984-1990
C.I.R.B.	Canada Industrial Relations Board, Reasons for Decision	Can.	1999-
C.J.C.E.	Recueil de la jurisprudence de la cour et du tribunal de première instance, Cour de justice des communautés européennes	E.U. / U.E.	1954-
C.L.A.S.	Canadian Labour Arbitration Summaries	Can.	1986-
C.L.A.S.N.	Criminal Law Aid Scheme News	Sing.	
C.L.D.	Commercial Law Digest	Can.	1987-1990

C.L.L.	Canadian Current Law: Canadian Legal Literature	Can.	1991-
C.L.L.C.	Canadian Labour Law Cases	Can.	1944-
C.L.L.R.	Canadian Labour Law Reporter	Can.	1982-
C.L.P.	Décisions de la Commission des lésions professionnelles	Can. (QC)	1998
C.L.R.	Commonwealth Law Reports	Austl.	1903-
C.L.R.	Construction Law Reports	Can.	1983-1992
C.L.R. (2d)	Construction Law Reports (Second Series)	Can.	1992-2000
C.L.R. (3d)	Construction Law Reports (Third Series)	Can.	2000-
C.L.R.B.D.	Canada Labour Relations Board Decisions	Can.	1949-1974
C.L.R.B.R.	Canadian Labour Relations Board Reports	Can.	1974-1982
C.L.R.B.R. (N.S.)	Canadian Labour Relations Board Reports (New Series)	Can.	1983-1989
C.L.R.B.R. (2d)	Canadian Labour Relations Board Reports (Second Series)	Can.	1989-
C.M. & R.	Crompton, Meeson & Roscoe's Reports (E.R. vols. 149-150)	U.K. / R.-U.	1834-1835
C.M.A.R.	Canada Court Martial Appeal Reports	Can.	1957-
C.M.R.	Common Market Law Reports	E.U. / U.E.	1962-1988
C.M.R.	Common Market Reporter	E.U. / U.E.	1988-1997
C.N.L.C.	Canadian Native Law Cases	Can.	1763-1978
C.N.L.R.	Canadian Native Law Reporter	Can.	1979-
C.O.H.S.C.	Canadian Occupational Health and Safety Cases	Can.	1989-1993
C.P.	Recueils de jurisprudence du Québec : Cour provinciale	Can. (QC)	1975-1985
C.P.C.	Carswell's Practice Cases	Can.	1976-1985
C.P.C. (2d)	Carswell's Practice Cases (Second Series)	Can.	1985-1992
C.P.C. (3rd)	Carswell's Practice Cases (Third Series)	Can.	1992-1997
C.P.C. (4th)	Carswell's Practice Cases (Fourth Series)	Can.	1997-2001
C.P.C. (5th)	Carswell's Practice Cases (Fifth Series)	Can.	2001-
C.P.C. (Olmstead)	Canadian Constitutional Decisions of the Judicial Committee of the Privy Council (Olmstead)	Can.	1873-1954

C.P.C. (Plaxton)	Canadian Constitutional Decisions of the Judicial Committee of the Privy Council (Plaxton)	Can.	1930-1939
C.P.D.	Law Reports, Common Pleas Division	U.K. / R.-U.	1875-1880
C.P.D.R.	Cape Provincial Division Reports	S. Afr. du sud	1910-1946
C.P.J.I. (Sér. A.)	Publications de la Cour permanente de justice internationale: Série A: Recueil des arrêts	Int'l	1922-1930
C.P.J.I. (Sér. B.)	Publications de la Cour permamente de justice internationale : Série B : Recueil des avis consultatifs	Int'l	1922-1930
C.P.J.I. (Sér. A/B.)	Publications de la Cour permamente de justice internationale : Série A/B : Arrêts, ordonnances et avis consultatifs	Int'l	1931-1940
C.P.J.I. (Sér. C.)	Publications de la Cour permanente de justice internationale : Série C : Plaidoiries, exposés oraux et documents	Int'l	1922-1940
C.P.R.	Canadian Patent Reporter	Can.	1941-1971
C.P.R. (2d)	Canadian Patent Reporter (Second Series)	Can.	1971-1984
C.P.R. (3d)	Canadian Patent Reporter (Third Series)	Can.	1985-1999
C.P.R. (4th)	Canadian Patent Reporter (Fourth Series)	Can.	1999-
C.P.R.B.	Procurement Review Board of Canada, decisions	Can.	1990-?
C.P.T.A.	Décisions de la Commission de protection du territoire agricole	Can. (QC)	1984-1987
C.R.	Criminal Reports	Can.	1946-1967
C.R. (3rd)	Criminal Reports (Third Series)	Can.	1978-1991
C.R. (4th)	Criminal Reports (Fourth Series)	Can.	1991-1996
C.R. (5th)	Criminal Reports (Fifth Series)	Can.	1997-
C.R. (N.S.)	Criminal Reports (New Series)	Can.	1967-1978
C.R.A.C.	Canadian Reports: Appeal Cases: appeals allowed or refused by the Judicial Committee of the Privy Council	Can.	1828-1913
C.R.A.T.	Commercial Registration Appeal Tribunal – Summaries of Decisions	Can. (ON)	1971-1979
C.R.C.	Canadian Railway Cases	Can.	1902-1939
C.R.D.	Charter of Rights Decisions	Can.	1982-
C.R.M.P.C.	Commission de révision des marchés publics du Canada, décisions	Can.	1990-?
C.R.N.Z.	Criminal Reports of New Zealand	N.Z. / N.-Z.	1983-
C.R.R.	Canadian Rights Reporter	Can.	1982-1991
C.R.R. (2d)	Canadian Rights Reporter	Can.	1991-
C.R.R.B.D.I.	Canada Labour Relations Board	Can.	1974-1998

	Decisions and Information		
C.R.T.	Canadian Radio-Television and Telecommunications decisions and policy statements	Can.	1975-1985
C.R.T.C.	Canadian Railway and Transport Cases	Can.	1940-1966
C.R.N.Z.	Criminal Reports of New Zealand	N.Z. / N.-Z.	1993-
C.S.	Recueils de jurisprudence du Québec : Cour supérieure	Can. (QC)	1967-1985
C.S.	Rapports judiciaires officiels de Québec : Cour supérieure	Can. (QC)	1892-1966
C.S.D.	Canadian Sentencing Digest	Can.	1980-1994
C.S.P.	Recueils de jurisprudence du Québec : Cour des Sessions de la paix	Can. (QC)	1975-1985
C.T.	Jurisprudence en droit du travail : Décisions des commissaires du travail	Can. (QC)	1969-1981
C.T. Cases	Canadian Transport Cases	Can.	1966-1977
C.T.A.B.	Canada Tax Appeal Board Cases	Can.	1949-1966
C.T.A.B. (N.S.)	Canada Tax Appeal Board Cases (New Series)	Can.	1967-1971
C.T.B.R.	Canada Tarrif Board Reports	Can.	1937-1988
C.T.C.	Canada Tax Cases Annotated	Can.	1917-1971
C.T.C. (N.S.)	Canada Tax Cases (New Series)	Can.	1972-
C.T.C.	Canadian Transport Cases	Can.	1966-1977
C.T.C.A.T.C.	Canadian Transport Commission, Air Transport Committee Decisions	Can.	1967-1987
C.T.C.D.O.	Canadian Transport Commission, Decisions and Orders Summary	Can.	1970-1976
C.T.C.M.V.T.C.D.	Canadian Transport Commission, Motor Vehicle Transport Committee Decisions	Can.	1973-1987
C.T.C.M.V.T.C.O.	Canadian Transport Commission, Motor Vehicle Transport Committee Orders	Can.	1972-1987
C.T.C.O.Λ.	Canadian Transport Commission, Orders (Air)	Can.	1967-1987
C.T.C.R.	Canadian Transport Commission Reports	Can.	1978-1986
C.T.C.R.C.D.	Canadian Transport Commission, Review Committee Decisions	Can.	1971-1987
C.T.C.R.T.C.	Canadian Transport Commission. Railway Transport Committee – Judgments, Orders, Regulations, and Rulings (formerly Board of Transport Commissioners for Canada)	Can.	1967-1987

C.T.C.T.C.D.	Canadian Transport Commission, Telecommunication Committee Decisions	Can.	1973-1976
C.T.C.T.C.O.	Canadian Transport Commission, Telecommunication Committee Orders	Can.	1975-1976
C.T.C.W.T.C.D.	Canadian Transport Commission, Water Transport Committee, Decisions	Can.	1972-1987
C.T.C.W.T.C.L.	Canadian Transport Commission, Water Transport Committee, Licences	Can.	1976
C.T.C.W.T.C.O.	Canadian Transport Commission, Water Transport Committee, Orders	Can.	1979-1987
C.T.R.	Canadian Tax Reporter	Can.	1972-
C.T.R.	Cape Times Reports	S. Afr. du sud	1891-1910
C.T.R.	Commission du tarif registre	Can.	1981-1988
C.T.R.	De Boo Commodity Tax Reports	Can.	1987-1989
C.T.S.T.	Canada Trade and Sales Tax Cases	Can.	1989-1991
C.T.T.T.	Décisions du Commissaire du travail et du Tribunal du travail	Can. (QC)	1982-1993
C.T.T.T.C.R.A.A.	Décisions du Commissaire du travail, du Tribunal du travail et de la Commission de reconnaissance des associations d'artistes	Can. (QC)	1994-1997
Cal.	California Reports	U.S. / É.-U.	1850-1934
Cal.2d	California Reports (Second Series)	U.S. / É.-U.	1934-1969
Cal.3d	California Reports (Third Series)	U.S. / É.-U.	1969-1991
Cal.4th	California Reports (Fourth Series)	U.S. / É.-U.	1991-
Calth.	Calthrop's Reports (E.R. vol. 80)	U.K. / R.-U.	1609-1618
Cameron P.C.	Cameron's Constitutional Decisions of the Privy Council	Can.	1867-1915
Cameron S.C.	Cameron's Supreme Court Cases	Can.	1880-1900
Camp.	Campbell's Reports (E.R. vols. 170-171)	U.K. / R.-U.	1807-1816
Cape S.C.R.	Supreme Court Reports (Cape)	S. Afr. du sud	1880-1910
Car. & K.	Carrington & Kirwan Reports (E.R. vols. 174-175)	U.K. / R.-U.	1843-1853
Car. & M.	Carrington & Marshman Reports (E.R. vol. 174)	U.K. / R.-U.	1840-1842
Car. & P.	Carrington & Payne (E.R. vols. 171-173)	U.K. / R.-U.	1823-1841
Carey	Carey's Manitoba Reports	Can. (MB)	1875
Cart. B.N.A.	Cartwright's Cases on the British North America Act, 1867	Can.	1882-1897
Carter	Carter's Reports, Common Pleas (E.R. vol. 124)	U.K. / R.-U.	1664-1676
Carth.	Carthew's Reports, King's Bench (E.R.	U.K. / R.-U.	1686-1701

vol. 90)

Cary	Cary's Chancery Reports (E.R. vol. 21)	U.K. / R.-U.	1557-1604
Cas. t. Hard.	Cases temp. Hardwicke (E.R. vol. 95)	U.K. / R.-U.	1733-1738
Cas. t. Talb.	Cases temp. Talbot (E.R. vol. 25)	U.K. / R.-U.	1733-1738
Ch.	Law Reports, Chancery	U.K. / R.-U.	1891-
Ch. C.R.	Chancery Chambers Reports	Can. (ON)	1857-1872
Ch. Ca.	Cases in Chancery (E.R. vol. 22)	U.K. / R.-U.	1660-1698
Ch. R.	Chancery Reports (E.R. vol. 21)	U.K. / R.-U.	1625-1710
Ch. App.	Law Reports, Chancery Division	U.K. / R.-U.	1865-1874
Ch. D.	Law Reports, Chancery Division	U.K. / R.-U.	1875-1890
Chan. Cas.	Chancery Cases (E.R. vol. 22)	U.K. / R.-U.	1615-1710
Chit.	Chitty's Practice Reports, King's Bench	U.K. / R.-U.	1770-1822
Choyce. Ca.	Choyce Cases in Chancery (E.R. vol. 21)	U.K. / R.-U.	1557-1606
Cl. & F.	Clark & Finnelly's Reports, House of Lords (E.R. vols. 6-8)	U.K. / R.-U.	1831-1846
Co. Rep.	Coke's Reports, King's Bench (E.R. vols. 76-77)	U.K. / R.-U.	1572-1616
Coll.	Collyer's Reports (E.R. vol. 63)	U.K. / R.-U.	1844-1846
Colles	Colles's Reports, House of Lords (E.R. vol. 1)	U.K. / R.-U.	1697-1713
Com.	Comyns's Reports (E.R. vol. 92)	U.K. / R.-U.	1695-1740
Comb.	Comberbach's Reports (E.R. vol. 90)	U.K. / R.-U.	1685-1699
Comm. Eur. D.H.D.R.	Décisions et rapports de la Commission européenne des Droits de l'Homme	E.U. / U.E.	1975-1999
Comm. L.R.	Commercial Law Reports	Can.	1903-1905
Comp. Trib. dec.	Competition Tribunal, decisions	Can.	1986-?
Trib. conc. dec.	Tribunal de concurrence, décisions	Can.	1986-?
Conc. Bd. Rpts.	Conciliation Board Reports	Can.	1966-1974
Conc. Comm'r. Rpts.	Conciliation Commissioner Reports	Can.	1975
Cons. sup. N.-F.	Inventaire des jugements et déliberations du Conseil supérieur de la Nouvelle-France	Can. / U.S.	1717-1760
Cook Adm.	Cook's Vice-Admiralty Reports	Can. (QC)	1873-1874
Cooke C.P.	Cooke's Reports (Common Pleas) (E.R. vol. 125)	U.K. / R.-U.	1706-1747
Coop. Ch. Ch.	Cooper's Chancery Chamber's Reports	Can. (ON)	1866?
Coop. Pr. Ca.	Cooper's Practice Cases, Chancery (E.R. vol. 47)	U.K. / R.-U.	1822-1838
Coop. t. Br.	Cooper, temp. Brougham's Reports, Chancery (E.R. vol. 47)	U.K. / R.-U.	1833-1834
Coop. t. Cott.	Cooper, temp. Cottenham's Reports, Chancery (E.R. vol. 47)	U.K. / R.-U.	1846-1848

Coop., G.	Cooper's Cases in Chancery (E.R. vol. 35)	U.K. / R.-U.	1792-1815
Cour Eur. D.H. (Sér. A.)	Publications de la Cour européenne des Droits de l'Homme : Série A : Arrêts et décisions (autre titre / other title: Recueil des arrêt et décisions de la cour européenne des droits de l'homme).	E.U. / U.E.	1960-
Cour Eur. D.H. (Sér. B.)	Publications de la Cour européenne des Droits de l'Homme : Série B : Mémoires, plaidoiries et documents	E.U. / U.E.	1961-
Cowp.	Cowper's Reports (E.R. vol. 98)	U.K. / R.-U.	1774-1778
Cox.	Cox's Equity Reports (E.R. vols. 29-30)	U.K. / R.-U.	1783-1796
Cr. & Ph.	Craig and Phillips's Reports (E.R. vol. 41)	U.K. / R.-U.	1840-1841
Cro. Car.	Croke's Reports (Charles I) (E.R. vol. 79)	U.K. / R.-U.	1625-1641
Cro. Eliz.	Croke's Reports (Elizabeth I) (E.R. vol. 78)	U.K. / R.-U.	1582-1603
Cro. Jac.	Croke's Reports (James I) (E.R. vol. 79)	U.K. / R.-U.	1603-1625
Cun.	Cunningham's Reports (E.R. vol. 94)	U.K. / R.-U.	1734-1736
Curt.	Curteis's Reports (E.R. vol. 163)	U.K. / R.-U.	1834-1844
D.	Recueil Dalloz	France	1945-1965
D.A.	Recueil analytique de jurisprudence et de législation (Dalloz)	France	1941-1944
D.C.	Recueil critique Dalloz	France	1941-1945
D.C.A.	Canada, Commission de la fonction publique du Canada, décisions du comité d'appel	Can.	1979-1999
D.C.A.	Décisions de la cour d'appel / Queen's Bench Reports (Dorion)	Can. (QC)	1880-1886
D.C.D.R.T.	Décisions sur des conflits de droit dans les relations du travail	Can. (QC)	1964-1970
D.C.L.	Décisions de la Commission des loyers	Can. (QC)	1975-1981
D.C.R.	New Zealand District Court Reports	N.Z. / N.-Z.	1980-
D.C.R.M.	Commission de révision des marchés publics du Canada, décisions	Can.	1990-?
D.D.C.P.	Décisions disciplinaires concernant les corporations professionnels	Can. (QC)	1974-
D.D.O.P.	Décisions disciplinaires concernant les ordres professionnels	Can. (QC)	1995-
D.E.L.D.	Dismissal and Employment Law Digest	Can.	1986-
D.E.L.E.A.	Digest of Environmental Law and Environmental Assessment	Can.	1992-
D.F.Q.E.	Droit fiscal québécois express	Can. (QC)	1977-
D.H.	Recueil hebdomadaire Dalloz	France	1924-1940

D.J.C.	Canadian Current Law : Documentation juridique au Canada	Can.	1991-
D.J.G.	Dalloz jurisprudence général	France	1845-1923
D.L.Q.	Droits et libertés au Québec	Can. (QC)	1986-1987
D.L.R.	Dominion Law Reports	Can.	1912-1955
D.L.R. (2d)	Dominion Law Reports (Second Series)	Can.	1956-1968
D.L.R. (3d)	Dominion Law Reports (Third Series)	Can.	1969-1984
D.L.R. (4th)	Dominion Law Reports (Fourth Series)	Can.	1984-
D.O.A.L.	Décisions des orateurs, assemblé législative	Can. (NB)	1923-1982
D.P.	Recueil périodique et critique de jurisprudence (Dalloz)	France	1924-1940
D.R.L.	Décisions de la Régie du logement	Can. (QC)	1982-1993
D.S. / D.	Recueil Dalloz et Sirey	France	1965-
D.T.C.	Dominion Tax Cases	Can.	1920-
D.T.E.	Droit du travail Express	Can. (QC)	1982-
Dan.	Daniell's Reports (E.R. vol. 159)	U.K. / R.-U.	1817-1820
Davis	Davis's Reports (Ireland) (E.R. vol. 80)	I.	1604-1612
De G. & J.	De Gex & Jones's Reports (E.R. vols. 44-45)	U.K. / R.-U.	1857-1859
De G. & Sm.	De Gex & Smale's Reports (E.R. vols. 63-64)	U.K. / R.-U.	1846-1849
De G. F. & J.	De Gex, Fisher & Jones's Reports (E.R. vol. 45)	U.K. / R.-U.	1859-1862
De G. J. & S.	De Gex, Jones & Smith's Reports (E.R. vol. 46)	U.K. / R.-U.	1863-1865
De G. M. & G.	De Gex, Macnaghten & Gordon's Reports (E.R. vols. 42-44)	U.K. / R.-U.	1851-1857
Dea. & Sw.	Deane & Swabey's Reports (E.R. vol. 164).	U.K. / R.-U.	1855-1857
Dears.	Dearsly's Crown Cases (E.R. vol. 169)	U.K. / R.-U.	1852-1856
Dears. & B.	Dearsly and Bell's Crown Cases (E.R. vol. 169)	U.K. / R.-U.	1856-1858
Déc. B.-C.	Décisions des Tribunaux du Bas-Canada	Can. (QC)	1851-1867
Déc. trib. Mont.	Précis des décisions des tribunaux du district de Montréal	Can. (QC)	1853-1854
Den.	Denison's Crown Cases (E.R. vols. 1-2)	U.K. / R.-U.	1844-1852
Des. O.A.L.	Décisions des orateurs de l'Assemblée législative de la province de Québec (Desjardins)	Can. (QC)	1867-1901
Dick.	Dickens's Reports (E.R. vol. 21)	U.K. / R.-U.	1559-1798
Dods.	Dodson's Reports (E.R. vol. 165)	U.K. / R.-U.	1811-1822
Donn.	Donnelly's Reports (E.R. vol. 47)	U.K. / R.-U.	1836-1837

Doug.	Douglas's Reports (E.R. vol. 99)	U.K. / R.-U.	1778-1785
Dow	Dow's Reports (E.R. vol. 3)	U.K. / R.-U.	1812-1818
Dow & Cl.	Dow & Clark's Reports (E.R. vol. 6)	U.K. / R.-U.	1827-1832
Dowl. & Ry.	Dowling & Ryland's Reports (E.R. vol. 171)	U.K. / R.-U.	1821-1827
Drap.	Draper's King's Bench Reports	Can. (ON)	1829-1831
Drew.	Drewry's Reports (E.R. vols. 61-62)	U.K. / R.-U.	1851-1859
Drew. & Sm.	Drewry & Smale's Reports (E.R. vol. 62)	U.K. / R.-U.	1860-1865
Dy.	Dyer's Reports, King's Bench (E.R. vol. 73)	U.K. / R.-U.	1513-1582
E. & A.	Grant's Upper Canada Error and Appeals Reports	Can. (ON)	1846-1866
E. Afr. C.A.R.	Eastern Africa Court of Appeals Reports	Afr.	1934-1956
E. Afr. L.R.	Eastern Africa Law Reports	Afr.	1957-1967
E.C.H.R.	European Court of Human Rights	E.U. / U.E..	1960-
E.C.H.R. (Ser. A.)	Publications of the European Court of Human Rights : Series A : Judgments and Decisions	E.U. / U.E..	1960-
E.C.H.R. (Ser. B.)	Publications of the European Court of Human Rights: Series B. Pleadings, Oral Arguments and Documents	E.U. / U.E..	1961-
E.C.R.	European Court Reports : Reports of Cases before the Court	E.U. / U.E..	1954-
E. Distr. L.D.R.	Eastern Districts' Local Division Reports	S. Afr. du sud	1911-1946
E. Distr. R.	Eastern Districts' Reports	S. Afr. du sud	1880-1910
E.H.R.R.	European Human Rights Reports	E.U. / U.E..	1979-
E.L.L.R.	Employment and Labour Law Reporter	Can.	1991-
E.L.R.	Eastern Law Reporter	Can.	1906-1915
E.L.R.	Environmental Law Reporter of New South Wales	Austl.	1981-
E.M.L.R.	Entertainment and Media Law Reports	U.K. / R.-U.	1993-
E.R.	English Reports	U.K. / R.-U.	1210-1865
E.R.N.Z.	Employment Reports of New Zealand	N.Z. / N.-Z.	1991-
E.T.R.	Estates and Trusts Reports	Can.	1977-1994
E.T.R. (2d)	Estates and Trusts Reports (Second Series)	Can.	1994-
E.U.L.R.	European Union Law Reporter	E.U. / U.E.	1997-
East	East's Reports (E.R. vols. 102-104)	U.K. / R.-U.	1800-1812
Eden.	Eden's Reports, Chancery (E.R. vol. 28)	U.K. / R.-U.	1757-1766
Edw.	Edwards's Admiralty Reports (E.R. vol. 165)	U.K. / R.-U.	1808-1812

El. & Bl.	Ellis & Blackburn's Reports (E.R. vols. 118-120)	U.K. / R.-U.	1852-1858
El. & El.	Ellis & Ellis's Reports, King's Bench (E.R. vols. 120-121)	U.K. / R.-U.	1858-1861
El. Bl. & El.	Ellis, Blackburn & Ellis's Reports (E.R. vol. 120)	U.K. / R.-U.	1858
Eq. Ca. Abr.	Equity Cases Abridged, Chancery (E.R. vols. 21-22)	U.K. / R.-U.	1667-1744
Esp.	Espinasse's Reports	U.K. / R.-U.	1793-1807
Eur. Comm'n. H.R.C.D.	Collection of Decisions of the European Commission of Human Rights	E.U. / U.E.	1960-1974
Eur. Comm'n. H.R.D.R.	European Commission of Human Rights: Decisions and Reports	E.U. / U.E.	1975-1999
Ex. C.R.	Exchequer Court of Canada Reports	Can.	1875-1922
Ex. C.R.	Canada Law Reports : Exchequer Court	Can.	1923-1970
Ex. D.	Law Reports, Exchequer Division	U.K. / R.-U.	1875-1890
Exch. Rep.	Exchequer Reports	U.K. / R.-U.	1847-1856
F.	Federal Reporter	U.S. / É.-U.	1880-1924
F.2d.	Federal Reporter (Second Series)	U.S. / É.-U.	1925-1993
F.3d	Federal Reporter (Third Series)	U.S. / É.-U.	1993-
F.	Session Cases (Fifth Series) (Fraser)	Scot. / Écosse	1898-1906
F. & F.	Foster and Finalson's Reports (E.R. vol. 168)	U.K. / R.-U.	1856-1867
F. Cas.	Federal Cases	U.S. / É.-U.	1789-1880
F. Supp.	Federal Supplement	U.S. / É.-U.	1933-1998
F. Supp.2d	Federal Supplement (Second Series)	U.S. / É.-U.	1998-
F.C.	Canada Federal Court Reports	Can.	1971-
F.C.A.D.	Federal Court of Appeal Decisions	Can.	1981-1999?
F.L.D.	Family Law Digest	Can.	1968-1982
F.C.R.	Federal Court Reports	Austl.	1984-
F.L.R.	Federal Law Reports	Austl.	1956-
F.L.R.A.C.	Family Law Reform Act Cases	Can. (ON)	1978-1985
F.L.R.R.	Family Law Reform Reporter	Can.	1978-1987
F.P.R.	Fisheries Pollution Reports	Can.	1980?
F.T.L.R.	Financial Times Law Reports	U.K. / R.-U.	1981-
F.T.L.R.	Free Trade Law Reports	Can.	1989-1991
F.T.R.	Federal Trial Reports	Can.	1986-
F.T.U.	Free Trade Update	Can.	1990-1996
Fam.	Law Reports, Family Division	U.K. / R.-U.	1972-
Fam. L.R.	Family Law Reports	Austl.	1975-
Farm Products App. Trib. Dec.	Farm Products Appeal Tribunal Decisions	Can. (ON)	1990-1996?
Fitz-G.	Fitz-Gibbons' Reports (E.R. vol. 94)	U.K. / R.-U.	1727-1732

Foord	Foord's Reports	S. Afr	1880
Forrest	Forrest's Reports (E.R. vol. 145)	U.K. / R.-U.	1800-1801
Fort.	Fortescue's Reports (E.R. vol. 92)	U.K. / R.-U.	1695-1738
Fost.	Foster's Reports (E.R. vol. 168)	U.K. / R.-U.	1743-1761
Fox Pat. C.	Fox's Patent, Trade mark, Design and Copyright Cases	Can.	1940-1971
Freem. Ch.	Freeman's Reports, Chancery (E.R. vol. 22)	U.K. / R.-U.	1660-1706
Freem. K.B.	Freeman's Reports, King's Bench (E.R. vol. 89)	U.K. / R.-U.	1670-1704
G.L.R.	Gazette Law Reports	N.Z. / N.-Z.	1898-1953
G.S.T.R.	Canadian Goods and Services Tax Reporter / Reports / Monitor	Can.	1989-
G.T.C.	Canadian GST & Commodity Tax Cases	Can.	1993-
Gaz. L.R.	Gazette Law Reports	N.Z. / N.-Z.	1898-1952
Gaz. Pal.	Gazette du Palais	France	1886-
Ghana L.R.	Ghana Law Reports (West Africa)	W. Afr.	1959-1966 1971-1978
Giff.	Giffard's Reports (E.R. vols. 65-66)	U.K. / R.-U.	1858-1865
Gilb. Cas.	Gilbert's Cases in Law & Equity (E.R. vol. 93)	U.K. / R.-U.	1713-1715
Gilb. Rep.	Gilbert's Reports, Chancery (E.R. vol. 25)	U.K. / R.-U.	1705-1727
Godbolt	Godbolt's Reports (E.R. vol. 78)	U.K. / R.-U.	1575-1638
Gould.	Gouldsborough's Reports (E.R. vol. 75)	U.K. / R.-U.	1586-1602
Gow	Gow's Reports (E.R. vol. 171)	U.K. / R.-U.	1818-1820
Gr. / U.C. Ch.	Grant's Upper Canada Chancery Reports	Can. (ON)	1849-1882
Greg. R.	Gregorowski's Reports (Orange Free State)	S. Afr. du sud	1883-1887
Griq. W.R.	Griqualand West Reports (Cape of Good Hope)	S. Afr. du sud	1882-1910
H. & C.	Hurlstone & Coltman's Reports (E.R. vols. 158-159)	U.K. / R.-U.	1862-1866
H. & M.	Hemming & Miller's Reports (E.R. vol. 71)	U.K. / R.-U.	1862-1865
H. & N.	Hurlstone & Norman's Reports (E.R. vols. 156-158)	U.K. / R.-U.	1856-1862
H. & Tw.	Hall & Twells' Reports (E.R. vol. 47)	U.K. / R.-U.	1849-1850
H. & W.	Haszard & Warburton's Reports	Can. (PEI)	1850-1882
H.L. Cas.	Clark's House of Lords Cases (E.R. vols. 9-11)	U.K. / R.-U.	1847-1866
H.L. Cas.	House of Lords Cases	U.K. / R.-U.	1847-1866
Hag. Adm.	Haggard's Admiralty Reports (E.R. vol.	U.K. / R.-U.	1822-1838

	166)		
Hag. Con.	Haggard's Consistory Reports (E.R. vol. 161)	U.K. / R.-U.	1752-1821
Hag. Ecc.	Haggard's Ecclesiastical Reports (E.R. vol. 162)	U.K. / R.-U.	1827-1833
Hague Ct. Rep.	Hague Court Reports (1916)	Int'l	1899-1915
Hague Ct. Rep. (2d)	Hague Court Reports (Second Series) (1932)	Int'l	1916-1925
Hardr.	Hardres' Reports (E.R. vol. 145)	U.K. / R.-U.	1655-1669
Hare.	Hare's Reports (E.R. vols. 66-68)	U.K. / R.-U.	1841-1853
Harr. & Hodg.	Harrison and Hodgins Municipal Report	Can. (ON)	1845-1851
Hay & M.	Hay & Marriott's Reports (E.R. vol. 165)	U.K. / R.-U.	1776-1779
Her. Tr. Nor.	Heresy Trials in the Diocese of Norwich	U.K. / R.-U.	1428-1431
Het.	Hetley's Reports (E.R. vol. 124)	U.K. / R.-U.	1627-1632
Hob.	Hobart's Reports (E.R. vol. 80)	U.K. / R.-U.	1603-1625
Hodg.	Hodgins Election Cases	Can. (ON)	1871-1878
Hodges	Hodges' Reports	U.K. / R.-U.	1835-1837
Holt	Holt's Reports (E.R. vol. 171)	U.K. / R.U.	1815-1817
Holt, Eq.	Holt's Equity Reports (E.R. vol. 71)	U.K. / R.-U.	1845
Holt, K.B.	Holt's King's Bench Cases (E.R. vol. 90)	U.K. / R.-U.	1688-1711
Hut.	Hutton's Reports (E.R. vol. 123)	U.K. / R.-U.	1612-1639
I. Ch. R.	Irish Chancery Reports	I.	1852-1867
I.A.A.	Industrial Arbitration Awards	N.Z. / N.-Z.	1901-
I.A.R.	Industrial Arbitration Reports	Austl. (NSW)	1902-
I.B.D.D.	Instruments de base et documents divers	GATT	1952-
I.C.C.	Indian Claims Commission Decisions	U.S. / É.-U.	1948-1978
I.C.J. Pleadings	International Court of Justice: Pleadings, Oral Arguments, Documents	Int'l	1946-
I.C.J. Rep.	International Court of Justice: Reports of Judgments, Advisory Opinions and Orders	Int'l	1946-
I.C.L.R.	Irish Common Law Reports	I.	1852-1867
I.C.R.	Industrial Cases Reports	U.K. / R.-U.	1972-
I.C.R.	Industrial Court Reports	U.K. / R.-U.	1972-1974
I.C.S.I.D.	International Centre for Settlement of Investment Disputes (World Bank)	Int'l	1966-
I.L.R.	Canadian Insurance Law Reporter	Can.	1951-
I.L.R.	Insurance Law Reporter	Can.	1934-1950
I.L.R.	International Law Reports	Int'l	1950-

I.L.R.	Irish Law Reports	I.	1838-1850
I.L.R.M.	Irish Law Reports Monthly	I.	1981-
I.L.T.R.	Irish Law Times Reports	I.	1867-
I.M.A.	Institute of Municipal Assessors of Ontario, Court Decisions	Can. (ON)	1974-1986
I.R.	Irish Law Reports	I.	1892-
I.R. Eq.	Irish Reports, Equity Series	I.	1867-1878
I.R.C.L.	Irish Reports, Common Law Series	I.	1867-1878
Imm. A.B.D.	Immigration Appeal Board Decisions	Can.	1977-1988
Imm. A.C.	Immigration Appeal Cases	Can.	1968-1970
Imm. A.C (2d)	Immigration Appeal Cases (Second Series)	Can.	1969-1977
Imm. L.R.	Immigration Law Reporter	Can.	1985-1987
Imm. L.R. (2d)	Immigration Law Reporter (Second Series)	Can.	1987-1999
Imm. L.R. (3d)	Immigration Law Reporter (Third Series)	Can.	1999-
InfoCRTC	Broadcasting decisions, public notices and policy statements / Décisions, avis publics et énoncés de politique sur la radiodiffusion (CD-ROM) (also available on Internet / aussi disponible sur Internet)	Can.	1995-1998
Inter-Am. Ct. H.R. (Ser. A.)	Series A. Judgments and Opinions	Int'l	1982-
Inter-Am. Ct. H.R. (Ser. B.)	Series B: Pleadings, Oral Arguments and Documents	Int'l	1983-
Inter-Am. Ct. H.R. (Ser. C.)	Series C: Decisions and Judgments	Int'l	1987-
J. & H.	Johnson & Hemming's Reports (E.R. vol. 70)	U.K. / R.-U.	1860-1862
J.C.A.	Judgments Under the Competition Act	Can.	1984-
J.C.A.P.	Judgments Under the Competition Act and its Predecessors	Can.	1904-
J.C.P.	Semaine Juridique	France	1937-
J.-cl. Admin.	Juris-classeur Administratif	France	
J.-cl. B.C.	Juris-classeur Banque et Crédit	France	
J.-cl. Brev.	Juris-classeur Brevets d'Invention	France	
J.-cl. C.-C.	Juris-classeur Concurrence-Consommation	France	
J.-cl. C.-D.	Juris-classeur Contrats-Distribution	France	
J.-cl. Civ.	Juris-classeur Civil	France	Publication
J.-cl. Civ. Annexe	Juris-classeur Civil Annexe	France	créée en
J.-cl. Coll. terr.	Juris-classeur Collectivités territoriales	France	1907.
J.-cl. Com. gén.	Juris-classeur Commercial général	France	Mises à

J.-cl. Constr.	Juris-classeur Construction	France	jour
J.-cl. Coprop.	Juris-classeur Copropriété	France	trimestrielles
			.
J.-cl. Div.	Juris-classeur Divorce	France	
J.-cl. Dr. comp.	Juris-classeur Droit comparé	France	
J.-cl. Dr. de l'enfant	Juris-classeur Droit de l'enfant	France	
J.-cl. Dr. Intl.	Juris-classeur Droit International	France	
J.-cl. Env.	Juris-classeur Environnement	France	
J.-cl. Eur.	Juris-classeur Europe	France	
J.-cl. F. com.	Juris-classeur Fonds de commerce	France	
J.-cl. Fisc.	Juris-classeur Fiscal	France	
J.-cl. Fisc. imm.	Juris-classeur Fiscalité immobilière	France	
J.-cl. Fisc. intl.	Juris-classeur Fiscal international	France	
J.-cl. Foncier	Juris-classeur Foncier	France	
J.-cl. Impôt	Juris-classeur Impôt sur la Fortune	France	
J.-cl. M.D.M.	Juris-classeur Marques, Dessins et Modèles	France	
J.-cl. Not. Form.	Juris-classeur Notarial Formulaire	France	
J.-cl. Pén.	Juris-classeur Pénal	France	
J.-cl. Proc.	Juris-classeur Procédure	France	Publication
J.-cl. Proc. coll.	Juris-classeur Procédures collectives	France	founded
J.-cl. Proc. fisc.	Juris-classeur Procédures fiscales	France	in 1907.
J.-cl. Proc. pén.	Juris-classeur Procédure pénale	France	Quarterly
J.-cl. Prop. litt. art.	Juris-classeur Propriété littéraire et artistique	France	updates.
J.-cl. Rép. prat. Dr. priv.	Juris-classeur Répertoire pratique de Droit privé	France	
J.-cl. Resp. civ Ass.	Juris-classeur Responsabilité civile et Assurances	France	
J.-cl. Séc. Soc.	Juris-classeur Sécurité Sociale	France	
J.-cl. Sociétés	Juris-classeur Sociétés	France	
J.-cl. Trav.	Juris-classeur Travail	France	
J.E.	Jurisprudence Express	Can. (QC)	1977-
J.L.	Jurisprudence logement : Recueil trimestriel de jurisprudence sur le bail d'habitation comprenant des de la Régie du logement et des tribunaux judiciaires en matière de logement	Can. (QC)	1993-
J.L.	Jurisprudence Logement	Can. (QC)	1982-
J.M.	Décisions du juge des mines du Québec	Can. (QC)	1967-1972
J.S.S.T.	Jurisprudence en santé et sécurité du travail	Can. (QC)	1983-1985

J.S.S.T.I.	Jurisprudence en santé et sécurité du travail, décisions en matière d'inspection	Can. (QC)	1981-1983
Jac.	Jacob's Reports (E.R. vol. 37)	U.K. / R.-U.	1821-1822
Jac. & W.	Jacob & Walker's Reports (E.R. vol. 37)	U.K. / R.-U.	1819-1821
Jenk.	Jenkins's Reports (E.R. vol. 145)	U.K. / R.-U.	1220-1623
Johns.	Johnson's Reports (E.R. vol. 70)	U.K. / R.-U.	1859
Jones, T.	Jones, T., Reports (E.R. vol. 84)	U.K. / R.-U.	1667-1685
Jones, W.	Jones W., Reports (E.R. vol. 82)	U.K. / R.-U.	1620-1641
K. & J.	Kay & Johnson's Reports (E.R. vols. 69-70)	U.K. / R.-U.	1854-1858
K.B.	Law Reports, King's Bench	U.K. / R.-U.	1901-1951
K.L.R.	Kenya Law Reports	Afr.	1897-1956
Kay.	Kay's Reports (E.R. vol. 69)	U.K. / R.-U.	1853-1854
Keble	Keble's Reports (E.R. vols. 83-84)	U.K. / R.-U.	1661-1679
Keen	Keen's Reports (E.R. vol. 48)	U.K. / R.-U.	1836-1838
Keilway	Keilway's Reports (E.R. vol. 72)	U.K. / R.-U.	1496-1531
Kel. J. / Kel.	Kelyng, Sir John.'s Reports (E.R. vol. 84)	U.K. / R.-U.	1662-1669
Kel. W.	Kelynge, William's Reports (E.R. vol. 25)	U.K. / R.-U.	1730-1732
Keny.	Kenyon's Reports (E.R. vol. 96)	U.K. / R.-U.	1753-1759
Kenya L.R.	Kenya Law Reports	Kenya	1897-1956
Kn.	Knapp's Appeal Cases (E.R. vol. 12)	U.K. / R.-U.	1829-1836
L. Ed.	United States Supreme Court, Lawyers' Edition	U.S. / E.-U.	1790-1955
L. Ed.2d	United States Supreme Court, Lawyers' Edition (Second Series)	U.S. / E.-U.	1956-1979
L.A.C.	Labour Arbitration Cases	Can. (ON)	1948-1972
L.A.C. (2d)	Labour Arbitration Cases (Second Series)	Can. (ON)	1973-1981
L.A.C. (3d)	Labour Arbitration Cases (Third Series)	Can. (ON)	1982-1989
L.A.C. (4th)	Labour Arbitration Cases (Fourth Series)	Can. (ON)	1989-
L.A.R.	Labor Arbitration Reports	U.S. / É.-U.	1946-
L.C. Jur.	Lower Canada Jurist	Can. (QC)	1847-1891
L.C.B.D.	Land Compensation Board Decisions	Can. (ON)	1971-1983
L.C.R.	Land Compensation Reports	Can.	1969-
L.C.R.	Lower Canada Reports	Can. (QC)	1851-1867
L.N.	Legal News	Can. (QC)	1878-1897?
L.R. A. & E.	Law Reports, Admiralty and Ecclesiastical Cases (E.R. vols. 1-4)	U.K. / R.-U.	1865-1875
L.R. A. & E.	Law Reports, Admiralty and	U.K. / R.-U.	1865-1875

	Ecclesiastical Cases		
L.R. C.C.R.	Law Reports, Crown Cases Reserved	U.K. / R.-U.	1865-1875
L.R. C.P.	Law Reports, Common Pleas	U.K. / R.-U.	1865-1875
L.R. Ch. App.	Law Reports, Chancery Appeals	U.K. / R.-U.	1865-1875
L.R. Eq.	Law Reports, Equity Cases	U.K. / R.-U.	1865-1875
L.R. Ex.	Law Reports, Exchequer	U.K. / R.-U.	1865-1875
L.R.H.L.	Law Reports, English and Irish Appeal Cases	I./ U.K. / R.-U.	1865-1875
L.R. Ir.	Law Reports, Ireland	I.	1878-1893
L.R. P. & D.	Law Reports, Probate and Divorce	U.K. / R.-U.	1865-1875
L.R .Q.B.	Law Reports, Queen's Bench	U.K. / R.-U.	1865-1875
L.R. R.P.	Law Reports, Restrictive Practices	U.K. / R.-U.	1957-1972
L.R. Sc. & Div.	Scotch and Divorce Appeal Cases	U.K. / R.-U.	1866-1875
L.R.P.C.	Law Reports, Privy Council	U.K. / R.-U.	1865-1875
Lane	Lane's Reports (E.R. vol. 145)	U.K. / R.-U.	1605-1611
Lap. Sp. Dec.	Laperrier's Speakers' Decisions	Can.	
Latch.	Latch's Reports, King's Bench (E.R. vol. 82)	U.K. / R.-U.	1625-1628
Le. & Ca.	Leigh & Cave's Reports (E.R. vol. 169)	U.K. / R.-U.	1861-1865
Leach.	Leach's Cases on Crown Law (E.R. vol. 168)	U.K. / R.-U.	1730-1815
Lee.	Lee's Ecclesiastical Reports (E.R. vol. 161)	U.K. / R.-U.	1752-1758
Leo.	Leonard's Reports (E.R. vol. 74)	U.K. / R.-U.	1540-1615
Lev.	Levinz's Reports (E.R. vol. 83)	U.K. / R.-U.	1660-1697
Lewin.	Lewin's Crown Cases on the Northern Circuit (E.R. vol. 168)	U.K. / R.-U.	1822-1838
Ley.	Ley's Reports (E.R. vol. 80)	U.K. / R.-U.	1608-1629
Lilly	Lilly's Assize Cases	U.K. / R.-U.	1688-1693
Lit.	Littleton's Reports (E.R. vol. 120)	U.K. / R.-U.	1626-1632
Ll. L.R.	Lloyd's List Law Reports	U.K. / R.-U.	1919-1950
Lloyd's L.R.	Lloyd's Law Reports	U.K. / R.-U.	1968-
Lloyd's Rep.	Lloyd's List Law Reports	U.K. / R.-U.	1951-1967
Lloyd's Rep. Med.	Lloyd's Law Reports (Medical)	U.K. / R.-U.	1998-
Loc. Ct. Gaz.	Local Courts and Municipal Gazette	Can. (ON)	1865-1872
Lofft.	Lofft's Reports (E.R. vol. 98)	U.K. / R.-U.	1772-1774
Lush.	Lushington's Reports (E.R. vol. 167)	U.K. / R.-U.	1859-1862
Lut.	Lutwyche's Reports (E.R. vol. 125)	U.K. / R.-U.	1682-1704
M. & M.	Moody & Malkin (E.R. vol. 173)	U.K. / R.-U.	1826-1830
M. & Rob.	Moody & Robinson (E.R. vol. 174)	U.K. / R.-U.	1831-1844
M. & S.	Maule & Selwyn's Reports (E.R. vol. 105)	U.K. / R.-U.	1813-1817

M. & W.	Meeson & Welsby's Reports (E.R. vols. 150-153)	U.K. / R.-U.	1836-1847
M.A.C.M.L.C.	Digest of the Selected Judgements of the Maori Appellate Court and Maori Land Court	N.Z. / N.-Z.	1858-1968
M.C.	Malayan Cases	Sing.	1939-?
M.C.C.	Mining Commissioner's Cases	Can. (ON)	1906-1979?
M.C.D.	Magistrates' Court Decisions	N.Z. /N.-Z.	1939-1979
M.C.R.	Montreal Condensed Reports	Can. (QC)	1853-1854
M.C.R.	Précis des décisions des tribunaux du district de Montréal	Can. (QC)	1853-1854
M.C.R.	Magistrates' Court Reports	N.Z. / N.-Z.	1939-1979
M.H.R.C. Dec.	Manitoba Human Rights Commission Decisions	Can. (MB)	1971-1982
M.L.J.	Malayan Law Journal	Sing.	1932-
M.L.R. (K.B.)	Montreal Law Reports, King's Bench	Can. (QC)	1885-1891
M.L.R. (Q.B.)	Montreal Law Reports, Queen's Bench	Can. (QC)	1885-1891
M.L.R. (S.C.)	Montreal Law Reports, Superior Court	Can. (QC)	1885-1891
M.P.L.R.	Municipal and Planning Law Reports	Can.	1976-1990
M.P.L.R. (2d)	Municipal and Planning Law Reports (Second Series)	Can.	1991-
M.P.R.	Maritime Provinces Reports	Can.	1929-1968
M.V.R.	Motor Vehicle Reports	Can.	1979-1988
M.V.R. (2d)	Motor Vehicle Reports (Second Series)	Can.	1988-1994
M.V.R. (3d)	Motor Vehicle Reports (Third Series)	Can.	1994-2000
M.V.R. (4th)	Motor Vehicle Reports (Fourth Series)	Can.	2000-
M'Cle.	M'Cleland's Reports (E.R. vol. 148)	U.K. / R.-U.	1824
M'Cle. & Yo.	M'Cleland & Younge's Reports (E.R. vol. 148)	U.K. / R.-U.	1824-1825
Mac. & G.	M'Naghten & Gordon's Reports (E.R. vols. 41-42)	U.K. / R.-U.	1849-1851
Macl. & R.	Maclean & Robinson's Reports (E.R. vol. 9)	U.K. / R.-U.	1839
Madd.	Maddock's Reports (E.R. vol. 56)	U.K. / R.-U.	1815-1822
Man. & G.	Manning & Granger's Reports (E.R. vols. 133-135)	U.K. / R.-U.	1840-1844
Man. L.R.	Manitoba Law Reports (Queen's Bench)	Can. (MB)	1884-1890
M.L.B. Dec.	Manitoba Labour Board Decisions	Can. (MB)	1985-
Man. M.T.B.D.	Manitoba Motor Transport Board Decisions	Can. (MB)	1985-
Man. R.	Manitoba Reports	Can. (MB)	1883-1961
Man. R. (2d)	Manitoba Reports (Second Series)	Can. (MB)	1979-
Man. R. temp. Wood	Manitoba Reports temp. Wood (ed. Armour)	Can. (MB)	1875-1883

Maori L. Rev.	Maori Law Review	N.Z. / N.-Z.	1993-
March, N.R.	March's New Cases (E.R. vol. 82)	U.K. / R.-U.	1639-1642
Mer.	Merivale's Reports (E.R. vols. 35-36)	U.K. / R.-U.	1815-1817
Mod.	Modern Reports (E.R. vols. 86-88)	U.K. / R.-U.	1669-1732
Mont. Cond. Rep.	Montreal Condensed Reports	Can. (QC)	1853-1854
Moo. Ind. App.	Moore's Reports, Indian Appeals, Privy Council (E.R. vols. 18-20)	U.K. / R.-U.	1836-1872
Moo. K.B.	Moore's Reports, King's Bench (E.R. vol. 72)	U.K. / R.-U.	1519-1621
Moo. P.C.	Moore's Reports, Privy Council (E.R. vols. 12-15)	U.K. / R.-U.	1836-1862
Moo. P.C.N.S.	Moore's Reports, Privy Council, (New Series) (E.R. vols. 15-17)	U.K. / R.-U.	1862-1873
Mood.	Moody's Reports (E.R. vols. 168-169)	U.K. / R.-U.	1824-1837
Mos.	Mosely's Reports (E.R. vol. 25)	U.K. / R.-U.	1726-1731
My. & Cr.	Mylne & Craig's Reports (E.R. vols. 40-41)	U.K. / R.-U.	1835-1840
My. & K.	Mylne & Keen's Reports (E.R. vols. 39-40)	U.K. / R.-U.	1832-1835
N.A.C.D.	Native Appeal Court Selected Decisions (Natal and Transvaal)	S. Afr. du sud	1930-1948
N.A.C.R.	Native Appeal Court Reports	S. Afr. du sud	1951-
N.B. Eq.	New Brunswick Equity Reports (Trueman)	Can. (NB)	1894-1911
N.B. Eq. Cas.	New Brunswick Equity Cases (Trueman)	Can.. (NB)	1876-1893
N.B.E.S.T.D.	New Brunswick Employment Standards Tribunal Decisions	Can. (NB)	1986-
N.B.H.R.C. Dec.	New Brunswick Human Rights Commission Decisions	Can. (NB)	1974-1982
N.B.L.L.C.	New Brunswick Labour Law Cases	Can. (NB)	1965-1979
N.B.P.P.A.B.D.	New Brunswick Provincial Planning Appeal Board Decisions	Can. (NB)	1973-1983
N.B.R.	New Brunswick Reports	Can. (NB)	1825-1928
N.B.R. (2d)	New Brunswick Reports (Second Series)	Can. (NB)	1969-
N.E.	Northeastern Reporter	U.S. / É.-U.	1885-1936
N.E.2d	Northeastern Reporter (Second Series)	U.S. / É.-U.	1936-
N.E.B.D.	National Energy Board – Reasons for Decision	Can.	1970-
N.H.R.C. Dec.	Newfoundland Human Rights Commission Decisions	Can. (NF)	1971-1977
N.I.	Northern Ireland Law Reports	N.I. / I.N.	1925-
N.L.R.	Nigeria Law Reports	Nigeria	1881-1955

N.L.R.	Nyasaland Law Reports (Malawi)	Malawi	1922-1952
N.L.R. (O.S.)	Natal Law Reports (Old Series)	S. Afr. du sud	1867-1872
N.L.R. (N.S.)	Natal Law Reports (New Series)	S. Afr. du sud	1879-1932
N.P.D.R.	Natal Provincial Division Reports	S. Afr. du sud	1933-1946
N.R.	National Reporter	Can.	1973-
N.S.H.R.C. Dec.	Nova Scotia Human Rights Commissions Decisions	Can. (NS)	1972-1980
N.S.B.C.P.U. Dec.	Nova Scotia Board of Commissioners of Public Utilities Decisions	Can. (NS)	1923-1973
N.S.C.G.A. Dec.	Nova Scotia Compendium of Grievance Arbitration Decisions	Can. (NS)	1978-
N.S.R.	Nova Scotia Reports	Can.	1834-1929 1965-1969
N.S.R. (2d)	Nova Scotia Reports (Second Series)	Can. (NS)	1969-
N.S.R.U.D.	Reported and Unreported Decisions	Can. (NS)	1979-1984
N.S.W.S.C.R.	New South Wales Supreme Court Reports	Austl. (NSW)	1862-1976
N.S.W. St. R.	New South Wales State Reports	Austl. (NSW)	1901-1970
N.S.W.L.R.	New South Wales Law Reports	Austl. (NSW)	1880-1900 1971-
N.S.W.R.	New South Wales Reports	Austl. (NSW)	1960-1970
N.S.W.W.N.	New South Wales Weekly Notes	Austl. (NSW)	1884-1970
N.T.A.D. (Air)	National Transportation Agency Decisions (Air)	Can.	1988-1992
N.T.A.D. (Rwy)	National Transportation Agency Decisions (Railway)	Can.	1988-1991
N.T.A.O. (Air)	National Transportation Agency Orders (Air)	Can.	1988-1992
N.T.A.R.	National Transportation Agency of Canada Reports	Can.	1988-1995
N.T.J.	Northern Territory Judgments	Austl. (N.T.)	1951-1976
N.T.L.R.	Northern Territory Law Reports	Austl. (N.T.)	1992-
N.T.R.	Northern Territory Reports	Austl. (N.T.)	1978-
N.W.	Northwestern Reporter	U.S. / É.-U.	1879-1942
N.W.2d	Northwestern Reporter (Second Series)	U.S. / É.-U.	1942-
N.W.T.R.	Northwest Territories Reports	Can. (NWT)	1983-1998
N.W.T.S.C.R.	Northwest Territories Supreme Court Reports	Can. (NWT)	1889-1900
N.Y.	New York Reports	U.S. / É.-U.	1885-1955
N.Y.2d	New York Reports (Second Series)	U.S. / É.-U.	1956-
N.Y.S.2d	New York Supplement (Second Series)	U.S. / É.-U.	1956-
N.Z.H.R.C. Dec.	New Zealand Human Rights Commission Decisions	N.Z. / N.-Z.	1979-?
N.Z.A.C.	Judgments of the Arbitration Court of	N.Z. /N.-Z.	1979-1986

	New Zealand		
N.Z.A.R.	New Zealand Administrative Reports	N.Z. / N.-Z.	1976-
N.Z.B.L.C.	New Zealand Business Law Cases	N.Z. / N.-Z.	1984-
N.Z.F.L.R.	New Zealand Family Law Reports	N.Z. / N.-Z.	1981-
N.Z.I.L.R.	New Zealand Industral Law Reports	N.Z. / N.-Z.	1987-1990
N.Z.I.P.R.	New Zealand Intellectual Property Reports	N.Z. / N.-Z.	1967-1987
N.Z.L.R.	New Zealand Law Reports	N.Z. / N.-Z.	1883-
N.Z.P.C.C.	New Zealand Privy Council Cases	N.Z. / N.-Z.	1840-1932
N.Z.T.C.	New Zealand Tax Cases	N.Z. / N.-Z.	1973-
Nels.	Nelson's Reports, Chancery (E.R. vol. 21)	U.K. / R.-U.	1625-1693
Nfld. & P.E.I.R.	Newfoundland and Prince Edward Island Reports	Can. (NF/PEI)	1971-
Nfld. L.R.	Newfoundland Law Reports	Can. (NF)	1817-1949
Noy.	Noy's Reports (E.R. vol. 74)	U.K. / R.-U.	1559-1649
O.A.C.	Ontario Appeal Cases	Can.	1984-
O.A.R.	Ontario Appeal Reports	Can. (ON)	1876-1900
O.E.L.D.	Ontario Environmental Law Digest	Can. (ON)	1996-
O.F.L.R.	Ontario Family Law Reporter	Can. (ON)	1987-
O.H.R.C.B.I.	Ontario Human Rights Commission – Board of Inquiry	Can. (ON)	1963-1996
O.H.R.C. Dec.	Ontario Human Rights Commission Decisions	Can. (ON)	1956-1995?
O.H.R.C. Transcr.	Ontario Human Rights Commission, Trancripts of Selected Hearings	Can. (ON)	1968-1973
O.I.C. Arb.	Ontario Insurance Commission – Arbitration Cases	Can. (ON)	1995-
O.L.R.	Ontario Law Reports	Can. (ON)	1900-1931
O.L.R.B. Rep.	Ontario Labour Relations Board Reports	Can. (ON)	1944-
O.M.B. Dec.	Ontario Municipal Board Decisions	Can. (ON)	1953-1994
O.M.B. Index	Ontario Municipal Board Index to Applications Disposed of	Can. (ON)	1969-1992
O.M.B.E.A.B.	Joint Board of the Ontario Municipal Board and the Environmental Assessment Board Decisions	Can. (ON)	1984-
O.M.B.R.	Ontario Municipal Board Reports	Can. (ON)	1973-
O.N.E.D.	Office national de l'énergie, décisions	Can.	1970-
O.N.T.D. (aérien)	Office national des transports du Canada décisions (transport aérien)	Can.	1988-1992
O.N.T.D. (chemin de fer)	Office national des transports du Canada décisions (Chemin de fer)	Can.	1988-1991

O.N.T.O. (aérien)	Office national des transports du Canada arrêtés (transport aérien)	Can.	1988-1992
O.P.R.	Ontario Practice Reports	Can. (ON)	1848-1901
O.R.	Ontario Reports	Can. (ON)	1882-1900 1931-1973
O.R. (2d)	Ontario Reports (Second Series)	Can. (ON)	1973-1990
O.R. (3d)	Ontario Reports (Third Series)	Can. (ON)	1991-
O.S.C. Bull.	Ontario Securities Commission Bulletin	Can. (ON)	1949-
O.S.C.W.S.	Ontario Securities Commission Weekly Summary	Can. (ON)	1967-1980
O.W.C.A.T. Dec.	Ontario Workers' Compensation Appeals Tribunal Decisions	Can. (ON)	1986-1989
O.W.N.	Ontario Weekly Notes	Can. (ON)	1909-1962
O.W.R.	Ontario Weekly Reporter	Can. (ON)	1902-1916
Olmsted P.C.	Olmsted's Privy Council Decisions	Can.	1867-1954
Ont. Building Code Comm'n Rulings	Ontario Building Code Commission Rulings	Can. (ON)	1980-?
Ont. C.I.P. O.M.	Commissaire à l'information et à la protection de la vie privée de l'Ontario, ordonnances, série M	Can. (ON)	1988-1998
Ont. C.I.P. O.P.	Commissaire à l'information et à la protection de la vie privée de l'Ontario, ordonnances, série P	Can. (ON)	1989-1998
Ont. C.I.P. somm. app.	Commissaire à l'information et à la protection de la vie privée de l'Ontario, sommaires des appels	Can. (ON)	1990-1992
Ont. D. Crim.	Ontario Decisions – Criminal	Can. (ON)	1997-1999
Ont. D. Crim. Conv.	Ontario Decisions – Criminal Convictions Cases	Can. (ON)	1980-1996
Ont. D. Crim. Sent.	Ontario Decisions – Criminal Sentence Cases	Can. (ON)	1984-1996
Ont. Educ. Rel. Comm'n Grievance Arb.	Ontario Education Relations Commission Grievance Arbitrations	Can. (ON)	1970-1985
Ont. Elec.	Ontario Election Cases	Can. (ON)	1884-1900
Ont. En. Bd. Dec.	Ontario Energy Board Decisions	Can. (ON)	1961-
Ont. Envtl. Assessment Bd. Dec.	Ontario Environmental Assessment Board Decisions	Can. (ON)	1980-
Ont. Health Disciplines Bd. Dec.	Ontario Health Disciplines Board Decisions	Can. (ON)	1980-
Ont. I.P.C. O.M.	Ontario Information and Privacy Commissioner, Orders, M Series	Can. (ON)	1988-1998
Ont. I.P.C. O.P.	Ontario Information and Privacy	Can. (ON)	1989-1998

	Commissioner, Orders, P Series		
Ont. I.P.C. Sum. App.	Ontario Information and Privacy Commissioner, Summaries of Appeals	Can. (ON)	1990-1992
Ont. Lab.-Mgmt Arb. Comm'n Bull.	Ontario Labour-Management Arbitration Commission Bulletin	Can. (ON)	1978-1986
Ont. Liquor Licence App. Trib. Dec.	Ontario Liquor Licence Appeal Tribunal, Summaries of Decisions	Can. (ON)	1977-1981
Ont. Min. Community & Soc. Serv. Rev. Bd. Dec.	Ontario Ministry of Community and Social Services Review Board Decisions	Can. (ON)	1974-1978
Ont. Pol. R.	Ontario Police Reports	Can. (ON)	1980-
Orange Free State Prov. Div. R.	Orange Free State Provincial Division Reports	S. Afr. du sud	1910-1946
Ow.	Owen's Reports (E.R. vol. 74)	U.K. / R.-U.	1556-1615
P.	Law Reports, Probate, Divorce, and Admiralty Division	U.K. / R.-U.	1891-1971
P.	Pacific Reporter	U.S. / É.-U.	1883-1931
P.2d	Pacific Reporter (Second Series)	U.S. / É.-U.	1931-2000
P.3d	Pacific Reporter (Third Series)	U.S. / É.-U.	2000-
P. Wms.	Peere Williams's Reports (E.R. vol. 24)	U.K. / R.-U.	1695-1735
P.C.I.J. (Ser. A)	Publications of the Permanent Court of International Justice: Series A, Collection of Judgments	E.U. / U.E..	1922-1930
P.C.I.J. (Ser. B.)	Publications of the Permanent Court of International Justice: Series B, Collection of Advisory Opinions	E.U. / U.E..	1922-1930
P.C.I.J. (Ser. A/B)	Publications of the Permanent Court of International Justice: Series A/B, Judgments, Orders and Advisory Opinions	E.U. / U.E..	1931-1940
P.C.I.J. (Ser. C.)	Publications of the Permanent Court of International Justice, Series C, Pleadings, Oral Statements and Documents	E.U. / U.E..	1922-1940
P.D.	Law Reports, Probate and Divorce	U.K. / R.-U.	1875-1890
P.E.I.	Prince Edward Island Supreme Court Reports	Can. (PEI)	1850-1882
P.E.R.	Pay Equity Reports	Can. (ON)	1990-
P.F.P.	Pandectes françaises périodiques	France	1791-1844
P.N.G.C.B. Alta.	Petroleum and Natural Gas Conservation Board of Alberta	Can. (AB)	1938-1957
P.P.R.	Planning and Property Reports	Can. (ON)	1960-1963

P.P.S.A.C.	Personal Property Security Act Cases	Can.	1977-1990
P.P.S.A.C. (2d)	Personal Property Security Act Cases (Second Series)	Can.	1991-2000
P.P.S.A.C. (3d)	Personal Property Security Act Cases (Third Series)	Can.	2001-
P.R.B.C.	Procurement Review Board of Canada Decisions	Can.	1990-?
P.R.B.R.	Pension Review Board Reports	Can.	1972-1986
Palm.	Palmer's Reports (E.R. vol. 81)	U.K. / R.-U.	1619-1629
Park.	Parker's Reports (E.R. vol. 145)	U.K. / R.-U.	1743-1767
Patr. Elec. Cas.	Patrick's Election Cases (Upper Canada / Canada West)	Can. (ON)	1824-1849
Peake	Peake's Reports (E.R. vol. 170)	U.K. / R.-U.	1790-1812
Peake Add. Cas.	Peake's Reports (Additional Cases) (E.R. vol. 170)	U.K. / R.-U.	1790-1912
Per. C.S.	Extraits ou précédents des arrêts tirés des registres du Conseil supérieur de Québec (Perrault)	Can. (QC)	1727-1759
Perr. P.	Extraits ou précédents des arrêts tirés des registres de la prévosté de Québec	Can. (QC)	1753-1854
Peters	Peters' Prince Edward Island Reports	Can. (PEI)	1850-1872
Ph.	Phillips' Reports (E.R. vol. 41)	U.K. / R.-U.	1841-1849
Phill. Ecc.	Phillimore's Reports (E.R. vol. 161)	U.K. / R.-U.	1809-1821
Pl. Com.	Plowden's Commentaries (E.R. vol. 75)	U.K. / R.-U.	1550-1580
Pollex.	Pollexfen's Reports (E.R. vol. 86)	U.K. / R.-U.	1669-1685
Pop.	Popham's Reports (E.R. vol. 79)	U.K. / R.-U.	1592-1627
Prec. Ch.	Precedents in Chancery (T. Finch) (E.R. vol. 24)	U.K. / R.-U.	1689-1722
Price.	Price's Reports (E.R. vols. 145-147)	U.K. / R.-U.	1814-1824
Pyke	Pyke's Reports	Can. (QC)	1809-1810
Q. St. R.	Queensland State Reports	Austl. (Qld.)	1902-1957
Q.A.C.	Québec Appeal Cases	Can. (QC)	1986-1995
Q.B.	Queen's Bench Reports (E.R. vols. 113-118)	U.K. / R.-U.	1841-1852
Q.B.D.	Law Reports, Queen's Bench Division	U.K. / R.-U.	1875-1890
Q.L.R.	Quebec Law Reports	Can. (QC)	1875-1891
Q.P.R.	Québec Practice Reports	Can. (QC)	1896-1944
Q.R.	Queensland Reports	Austl. (Qld.)	1958-
Qc Comm. d.p. déc.	Québec Commission des droits de la personne, décisions des tribunaux	Can. (QC)	1977-1981
Qld. Lawyer Reps	Queensland Lawyer Reports	Austl. (Qld.)	1973-
R.A.C.	Ramsay, Appeal Cases	Can. (QC)	1873-1886
R.C. de l'É.	Recueil des arrêts de la Cour de l'Échiquier	Can.	1875-1922

R.C. de l'É.	Rapports judiciaires du Canada : Cour de l'Échiquier	Can.	1823-1970
R.A.T.	Recueil d'arrêts sur les transports	Can.	1966-1977
R.C.C.T.	Recueil des décisions de la Commission canadienne des transports	Can.	1978-1986
R.C.D.A.	Recueil des décisions de la Commission du droit d'auteur	Can.	1990-1994
R.C.D.A.	Recueil de jurisprudence canadienne en droit des assurances	Can.	1983-1991
R.C.D.A. (2ᵉ)	Recueil de jurisprudence canadienne en droit des assurances (deuxième série)	Can.	1991-1998
R.C.D.A. (3ᵉ)	Recueil de jurisprudence canadienne en droit des assurances (troisième série)	Can.	1998-
R.C.D.E.	Recueil de jurisprudence canadienne en droit de l'environnement	Can.	1978-1985
R.C.D.E. (n.s.)	Recueil de jurisprudence canadienne en droit de l'environnement (nouvelle série)	Can.	1986-
R.C.D.F.	Recueil de jurisprudence canadienne en droit de la faillite		1920-1960
R.C.D.F. (2ᵉ)	Recueil de jurisprudence canadienne en droit de la faillite (deuxième série)	Can.	1960-1990
R.C.D.F. (3ᵉ)	Recueil de jurisprudence canadienne en droit de la faillite (troisième série)	Can.	1991-1998
R.C.D.F. (4ᵉ)	Recueil de jurisprudence canadienne en droit de la faillite (quatrième série)	Can.	1998-
R.C.D.S.S.T.	Recueil de jurisprudence canadienne en droit de la santé et de sécurité au travail	Can.	1989-1993
R.C.D.T.	Recueil de jurisprudence canadienne en droit du travail	Can.	1983-1994
R.C.D.T. (2ᵉ)	Recueil de jurisprudence canadienne en droit du travail (deuxième série)	Can.	1994-2000
R.C.D.T. (3ᵉ)	Recueil de jurisprudence canadienne en droit du travail (troisième série)	Can.	2000-
R.C.D.V.M.	Recueil de jurisprudence canadienne en droit des valeurs mobilières	Can.	1993-1998
R.C.E. / Rec. / Recueil Lebon	Recueil des arrêts du Conseil d'Etat statuant au contentieux et du Tribunal des conflits, des arrêts des cours administratives d'appel et des jugements des tribunaux administratifs (ceci est le nom le plus récent du recueil / this is the most recent name of the reporter)	France	1821-

R.C.R.A.S.	Recueil de jurisprudence canadienne en matière de retraite et d'avantages sociaux	Can.	1994-
R.C.R.C.	Recueil de jurisprudence canadienne en responsabilité civile	Can.	1976-1990
R.C.R.C. (2ᵉ)	Recueil de jurisprudence canadienne en responsabilité civile (deuxième série)	Can.	1990-2000
R.C.R.C. (3ᵉ)	Recueil de jurisprudence canadienne en responsabilité civile (troisième Série)	Can.	2000-
R.C.R.P.	Recueil des arrêts du Conseil de révision des pensions	Can.	1972-1986
R.C.S.	Rapports judiciaires du Canada : cour suprême	Can.	1923-1969
R.C.S.	Recueils des arrêts de la Cour suprême du Canada	Can.	1877-1922 1970-
R.C.T.C.	Rapports de la Commission de Tarif	Can.	1937-1988
R.D.C.C.	Recueil des décisions du Conseil constitutionnel	France	1959-
R.D.C.F.Q.	Recueil des décisions, Commission de la fonction publique et Comité d'appel de la fonction publique	Can. (QC)	1990-
R.D.F.	Recueil de droit de la famille	Can.	1986-
R.D.F.Q.	Recueil de droit fiscal québécois	Can. (QC)	1977-
R.D.I.	Recueil de droit immobilier	Can. (QC)	1986-
R.D.J.	Revue de droit judiciaire	Can. (QC)	1983-1996
R.D.J.C.	Recueil de droit judiciaire de Carswell	Can.	1976-1985
R.D.J.C. (2ᵉ)	Recueil de droit judiciaire de Carswell (deuxième série)	Can.	1985-1992
R.D.J.C. (3ᵉ)	Recueil de droit judiciaire de Carswell (troisième série)	Can.	1992-1997
R.D.J.C. (4ᵉ)	Recueil de droit judiciaire de Carswell (quatrième série)	Can.	1997-2001
R.D.J.C. (5ᵉ)	Recueil de droit judiciaire de Carswell (cinquième série)	Can.	2001-
R.D.P.	Revue de droit pénal	Can. (QC)	1978-1983
R.D.R.T.Q.	Recueil des décisions, Regie des télécommunication du Québec	Can. (QC)	1990-
R.D.T.	Revue de droit du travail	Can. (QC)	1963-1976
R.E.C.J.	Records of the Early Courts of Justice of Upper Canada	Can. (ON)	1789-1984
R.F.L.	Reports of Family Law	Can.	1971-1978
R.F.L. (2d)	Reports of Family Law (Second Series)	Can.	1978-1986
R.F.L. (3d)	Reports of Family Law (Third Series)	Can.	1986-1994
R.F.L. (4th)	Reports of Family Law (Fourth Series)	Can.	1994-2000
R.F.L. (5th)	Reports of Family Law (Fifth Series)	Can.	2000-

R.I.A.A.	Report of International Arbitral Award	Int'l	1948-
R.J. imm.	Recueil de jurisprudence en droit de l'immigration	Can.	1985-1987
R.J. imm. (2e)	Recueil de jurisprudence en droit de l'immigration (deuxième série)	Can.	1987-1999
R.J. imm. (2e)	Recueil de jurisprudence en droit de l'immigration (deuxième série)	Can.	1999-
R.J.C.	Revue de jurisprudence commerciale	France	1957-
R.J.C.	Recueil de jurisprudence en droit criminel	Can.	1946-1967
R.J.C. (n.s.)	Recueil de jurisprudence en droit criminel (nouvelle série)	Can.	1967-1978
R.J.C. (3e)	Recueil de jurisprudence en droit criminel (troisième série)	Can.	1978-1991
R.J.C. (4e)	Recueil de jurisprudence en droit criminel (quatrième série)	Can.	1991-1996
R.J.C. (5e)	Recueil de jurisprudence en droit criminel (cinquième série)	Can.	1997-
R.J.D.A.	Recueil de jurisprudence en droit des affaires	Can.	1977-1990
R.J.D.A. (2e)	Recueil de jurisprudence en droit des affaires (deuxième série)	Can.	1991-
R.J.D.A. (2e)	Recueil de jurisprudence en droit des affaires (deuxième série)	Can.	1991-1999
R.J.D.A. (3e)	Recueil de jurisprudence en droit des affaires (troisième série)	Can.	2000-
R.J.D.C.	Recueil de jurisprudence en droit de la construction	Can.	1983-1992
R.J.D.C. (2e)	Recueil de jurisprudence en droit de la construction (deuxième série)	Can.	1992-2000
R.J.D.C. (3e)	Recueil de jurisprudence en droit de la construction (troisième série)	Can.	2000-
R.J.D.I.	Recueil de jurisprudence en droit immobilier	Can.	1977-1989
R.J.D.I. (2e)	Recueil de jurisprudence en droit immobilier (deuxième série)	Can.	1989-1996
R.J.D.I. (3e)	Recueil de jurisprudence en droit immobilier (troisième série)	Can.	1996-
R.J.D.M.	Recueil de jurisprudence en droit municipal	Can.	1976-1990
R.J.D.M. (2e)	Recueil de jurisprudence en droit municipal (deuxième série)	Can.	1991-
R.J.D.T.	Recueil de jurisprudence en droit du travail	Can. (QC)	1998-

R.J.F.	Revue de jurisprudence fiscale (ancien titre / former title : Bulletin des contributions directes, de la taxe sur la valeur ajoutée et des impôts indirects)	France	1975-
R.J.F.	Recueil de jurisprudence en droit de la famille	Can.	1971-1978
R.J.F. (2ᵉ)	Recueil de jurisprudence en droit de la famille (deuxième série)	Can.	1978-1986
R.J.F. (3ᵉ)	Recueil de jurisprudence en droit de la famille (troisième série)	Can.	1986-1994
R.J.F. (4ᵉ)	Recueil de jurisprudence en droit de la famille (quatrième série)	Can.	1994-2000
R.J.F. (5ᵉ)	Recueil de jurisprudence en droit de la famille (cinquième série)	Can.	2000-
R.J.O. (3ᵉ)	Recueil de jurisprudence de l'Ontario. (troisième série) (1882-1991 : voir *Ontario Reports*)	Can. (ON)	1991-
R.J.Q.	Recueils de jurisprudence du Québec	Can. (QC)	1875-1891 1975-
R.J.S.	Revue de jurisprudence sociale	France	1989-
R.L.	Revue légale	Can. (QC)	1869-1892
R.L.	Revue légale	Can. (QC)	1943-
R.L. (n.s.)	Revue légale (nouvelle série)	Can. (QC)	1895-1943
R.N.B. (2d)	Recueil des arrêts du Nouveau Brunswick (deuxième série) (1825-1928 : voir *New Brunswick Reports*)	Can. (NB)	1969-
R.O.N.T.C.	Recueil des décisions de l'office national des transports du Canada	Can.	1988-
R.P.C.	Reports of Patent Cases	U.K. / R.-U.	1884-1955
R.P.C.	Reports of Patent, Design and Trademark Cases	U.K. / R.-U.	1957-
R.P.E.I.	Reports of cases determined in the Supreme Court, Court of Chancery and Court of Vice-Admiralty of Prince Edward Island	Can. (PEI)	1850-1872
R.P.Q.	Rapports de pratique de Québec	Can. (QC)	1897-1982
R.P.R.	Real Property Reports	Can.	1977-1989
R.P.R. (2d)	Real Property Reports (Second Series)	Can.	1989-1996
R.P.R. (3d)	Real Property Reports (Third Series)	Can.	1996-
R.P.T.A.	Recueil en matière de protection du territoire agricole	Can. (QC)	1990-
R.R.	Revised Reports	U.K. / R.-U.	1785-1865
R.R.A.	Recueil en responsabilité et assurance	Can. (QC)	1986-
R.S.	Recueil Sirey	France	1955?-1965
R.S.A.	Recueil de sentences arbitrales	Can. (QC)	1981-1983
R.S.E.	Recueil des sentences de l'éducation	Can. (QC)	1974-

R.S.F.	Recueil de jurisprudence en droit des successions et des fiducies	Can	1977-1994
R.S.F. (2e)	Recueil de jurisprudence en droit des successions et des fiducies (deuxième série)	Can.	1994-
R.S.P.	Recueil des ordonnances de la régie des services publics	Can. (QC)	1973-1978
R.T.C.	Décisions et énoncés de politique sur la radiodiffusion et les télécommunications canadiennes	Can.	1975-1985
Raym. Ld.	Raymond, Lord Reports (E.R. vols. 91-92)	U.K. / R.-U.	1694-1732
Raym. T.	Raymond, Sir T. Reports (E.R. vol. 83)	U.K. / R.-U.	1660-1684
Rép pén. & proc. pén.	Encyclopédie juridique Dalloz : Répertoire de droit pénal et de procédure pénale	France	1951-
Rép. admin.	Encyclopédie juridique Dalloz : Répertoire de contentieux administratif	France	1951-
Rep. Ch.	Reports in Chancery (E.R. vol. 21)	U.K. / R.-U.	1615-1710
Rép. civ.	Encyclopédie juridique Dalloz: Répertoire de droit civil	France	1951-
Rép. com.	Encyclopédie juridique Dalloz : Répertoire de droit commercial	France	1951-
Rép. commun.	Encyclopédie juridique Dalloz : Répertoire de droit communautaire	France	1957-
Rép. proc. civ.	Encyclopédie juridique Dalloz : Répertoire de procédure civile	France	1951-
Rép. soc.	Encyclopédie juridique Dalloz : Répertoire des sociétés	France	1951-
Rep. t. Finch	Reports, temp. Finch (Nelson's folio Reports) (E.R. vol. 23)	U.K. / R.-U.	1673-1681
Rép. tr.	Encyclopédie juridique Dalloz: Répertoire de droit du travail	France	1951-
Rev. serv. arb.	Revue des services d'arbitrage	Can.	1977-
Rhod. & N.L.R.	Rhodesia & Nyasaland Law Reports	E. Afr.	1956-1963
Rhod. L.R.	Rhodesian Law Reports	Zimb.	1964-1979
Ridg. t. Hard.	Ridgeway, temp. Hardwicke's Reports (E.R. vol. 27)	U.K. / R.-U.	1733-1745
Ritch. Eq. Rep.	Ritchie's Equity Reports	Can. (N.S.)	1873-1882
Rob. / Rob. Chr.	Robinson, C.'s Reports (E.R. vol. 165)	U.K. / R.-U.	1798-1808
Rob. Ecc.	Robertson's Ecclesiastical Reports (E.R. vol. 163)	U.K. / R.-U.	1844-1853
Rolle.	Rolle's Reports (E.R. vol. 81)	U.K. / R.-U.	1614-1625
Roscoe	Roscoe's Reports	S. Afr. du sud	1861-1878
Russ.	Russell's Reports (E.R. vol. 38)	U.K. / R.-U.	1823-1829

Russ. & M.	Russell & Mylne's Reports (E.R. vol. 39)	U.K. / R.-U.	1829-1831
Russ. & Ry.	Russell & Ryan's Crown Cases (E.R. vol. 168)	U.K. / R.-U.	1799-1823
Russ. E.R.	Russell's Election Reports	Can. (NS)	1874
S. Afr. L.R.	South African Law Reports	S. Afr. du sud	1947-
S. Ct.	Supreme Court Reporter	U.S. / É.-U.	1882-
S.A.F.P.	Sentences arbitrales de la fonction publique	Can. (QC)	1983-
S.A.G.	Sentences arbitrales de griefs	Can. (QC)	1970-1981
S.A.L.R.	South Australia Law Reports	Austl.	1865-
S.A.R.B. Dec.	Social Assistance Review Board Selected Decisions	Can. (ON)	1975-1986
S.A.R.B. Sum.	Social Assistance Review Board Summaries of Decisions	Can. (ON)	1988-1994
S.A.S.R.	South Australia State Reports	Austl. (S.A.)	1921-
S.C.C. Cam.	Canada Supreme Court Cases (Cameron) (Published / publié 1918)	Can.	1887-1890
S.C.C. Cam. (2d)	Canada Supreme Court Reports (Cameron) (Published / publié 1925)	Can.	1876-1922
S.C.C. Coutl.	Canada Supreme Court Cases (Coutlée)	Can.	1875-1907
S.C.C.B.	Supreme Court of Canada Bulletin of Proceedings	Can.	1970-
S.C.C.D.	Supreme Court of Canada Decisions	Can.	1978-
S.C.C.R.	Supreme Court of Canada Reports Service	Can.	1971-
S.C.R.	Canada Law Reports: Supreme Court of Canada	Can.	1923-1969
S.C.R.	Canada Supreme Court Reports	Can.	1877-1922 1970-
S.E.	South Eastern Reporter	U.S. / É.-U.	1887-1939
S.E.2d	South Eastern Reporter (Second Series)	U.S. / É.-U.	1939-1988
S.E.C. Dec.	Securities and Exchange Commission Decisions	U.S. / É.-U.	1934-
S.L.L.R.	Sierra Leone Law Reports	W. Afr.	1960-1963
S.L.T.	Scots Law Times	Scot. / Écosse	1893-
S.N.B. & B.	Sarawak, North Borneo and Brunei Supreme Court Reports	Malay.	1952-1963
S.O.L.R.	Sexual Offences Law Reporter	Can.	1994-
S.R.L.A.	Speakers' Rulings, Legislative Assembly	Can. (NB)	1923-1982
S.S.C.	Sarawak Supreme Court Reports	Malay.	1928-1953
S.S.L.R.	Straits Settlements Law Reports	Sing.	1893-1942
S.T.R.	Canadian Sales Tax Reporter	Can.	1968-1989
S.W.	South Western Reporter	U.S. / É.-U.	1979-

S.W. 2d.	South Western Reporter (Second Series)	U.S. / É.-U.	1928-
Salk.	Salkeld's Reports (E.R. vol. 91)	U.K. / R.-U.	1689-1712
Sarbah	Sarbah's Fanti Law Reports	Ghana	1845-1903
Sask. C. Comp. B.	Saskatchewan Crimes Compensation Board, Awards	Can. (SK)	1968-1992
Sask. Human Rights Comm'n Dec.	Saskatchewan Human Rights Commission Decisions	Can. (SK)	1973-1981
Sask. L.R.	Saskatchewan Law Reports	Can. (SK)	1907-1931
Sask. L.R.B.D.	Saskatchewan Labour Relations Board Decisions	Can. (SK)	1945-1977
Sask. L.R.B.D.C.	Saskatchewan Labour Relations Board, Decisions and Court Cases	Can. (SK)	1945-1964
Sask. L.R.B.R.	Saskatchewan Labour Relations Board, Report of Meetings	Can. (SK)	1967-1973
Sask. R.	Saskatchewan Reports	Can.	1980-
Sask. S.C. Bull.	Saskatchewan Securities Commission Monthly Bulletin	Can. (SK)	1984-
Sav.	Savile's Reports (E.R. vol. 123)	U.K. / R.-U.	1580-1594
Say.	Sayer's Reports (E.R. vol. 96)	U.K. / R.-U.	1751-1756
Scot. L.R.	Scottish Law Reporter	Scot. / Écosse	1865-1924
Searle	Searle's Reports	S. Afr. du sud	1850-1867
Sel. Ca. t. King.	Select Cases, temp. King (E.R. vol. 25)	U.K. / R.-U.	1724-1733
Sem. Jur	Semaine Juridique	France	1927-1936
Sess. Cas.	Session Cases	U.K. / R.-U.	1710-1748
Sess. Cas.	Session Cases	Scot. / Écosse	1906-
Sess. Cas. S.	Session Cases (Shaw & Balantine)	Scot. / Écosse	1821-1838
Sess. Cas. D.	Session Cases (Second Series) (Dunlop)	Scot. / Écosse	1838-1862
Sess. Cas. F.	Session Cases (Fifth Series) (Fraser)	Scot. / Écosse	1898-1906
Sess. Cas. M.	Session Cases (Third Series) (Macpherson)	Scot. / Écosse	1862-1873
Sess. Cas. R.	Session Cases (Fourth Series) (Rettie)	Scot. / Écosse	1873-1898
Show. K.B.	Shower's Reports, King's Bench (E.R. vol. 89)	U.K. / R.-U.	1678-1695
Show. P.C.	Shower's Reports, Privy Council (E.R. vol. 1)	U.K. / R.-U.	1694-1699
Sid.	Siderfin's Reports, King's Bench (E.R. vol. 82)	U.K. / R.-U.	1657-1670
Sim.	Simons's Reports (E.R. vols. 57-60)	U.K. / R.-U.	1826-1852
Sim. (N.S.)	Simons's New Reports (E.R. vol. 61)	U.K. / R.-U.	1850-1852
Sim. & St.	Simons & Stuart's Reports (E.R. vol. 57)	U.K. / R.-U.	1822-1826
Sing. L.R.	Singapore Law Reports	Sing.	1946-

Skin.	Skinner's Reports (E.R. vol. 90)	U.K. / R.-U.	1681-1698
Sm. & G.	Smale & Giffard's Reports (E.R. vol. 65)	U.K. / R.-U.	1852-1857
Sm. & S.	Smith and Sager's Drainage Cases	Can. (ON)	1901-1913
So.	Southern Reporter	U.S. / É.-U.	1887-1941
So.2d	Southern Reporter (Second Series)	U.S. / É.-U.	1941-
Sp. Ecc. & Ad.	Spinks's Ecclesiastical & Admiralty Reports (E.R. vol. 164)	U.K. / R.-U.	1853-1855
Sp. P.C.	Spinks' Prize Court Cases (E.R. vol. 164)	U.K. / R.-U.	1854-1856
St.-M.S.D.	Saint-Maurice's Speakers' Decisions	Can. (QC)	1868-1885
Stark.	Starkie's Reports (E.R. vol. 171)	U.K. / R.-U.	1814-1820
Str.	Strange's Reports (E.R. vol. 93)	U.K. / R.-U.	1716-1749
Stu. Adm.	Stuart's Vice-Admiralty Reports (Lower Canada)	Can. (QC)	1836-1874
Stu. K.B.	Stuart's Reports (Lower Canada)	Can. (QC)	1810-1835
Sty.	Style's Reports (E.R. vol. 82)	U.K. / R.-U.	1646-1655
Sudan. L.R.	Sudan Law Reports	Sudan	1956-1971
Sw. & Tr.	Swabey & Tristram's Reports (E.R. vol. 164)	U.K. / R.-U.	1858-1865
Swab.	Swabey's Reports (E.R. vol. 166)	U.K. / R.-U.	1855-1859
Swans.	Swanston's Reports (E.R. vol. 36)	U.K. / R.-U.	1818-1819
T.A.	Décisions du Tribunal d'arbitrage	Can. (QC)	1982-1997
T.A.A.T.	Tribunal d'appel des accidents du travail	Can. (ON)	1985-1997
T.A.Q.	Décisions du Tribunal administratif du Québec	Can. (QC)	1998-
T.B.R.	Tariff Board Reports	Can.	1937-1988
T.B.R.D.	Taxation Board of Review Decisions	Austl.	1939-1949
T.B.R.D. (N.S.)	Taxation Board Review Decisions (New Series)	Austl.	1950-1968
T.C.D.	Tribunal de la Concurrence, décisions	Can.	1986-
T.C.T.	Canadian Trade and Commodity Tax Cases	Can.	1989-1992
T.E.	Recueils de jurisprudence du tribunal de l'expropriation	Can. (QC)	1972-1986
T.J.	Recueils de jurisprudence du Québec : Tribunal de la jeunesse	Can. (QC)	1975-1985
T.L.L.R.	Tenant and Landlord Law Repors	Can. (ON)	1983-1988
T.L.R.	Times Law Reports	U.K. / R.-U.	1884-1952
T.M.R.	Trademark Reporter	U.S. / É.-U.	1911-
T.P.E.I.	Tucker's Select Cases of Prince Edward Island	Can. (PEI)	1817-1828
T.R.	Term Reports (E.R. vols. 99-101)	U.K. / R.-U.	1785-1800

T.S.P.A.A.T.	Tribunal d'appel de la sécurité professionnelle et de l'assurance contre les accidents du travail	Can. (ON)	1998-
T.T.C.	Hunter's Torrens Title Cases	Austl., Can., N.Z. N.-Z., U.K. R.-U	1865-1893
T.T.J.	Jurisprudence en droit du travail : Tribunal du travail	Can. (QC)	1970-1981
T.T.R.	Trade and Tariff Reports	Can.	1990-1996
T.T.R.	Trade and Tariff Reports	Can.	1990-1996
T.T.R. (2d)	Trade and Tarrif Reports (Second Series)	Can.	1996-
Talb.	Talbot's Cases temp. (E.R. vol. 25)	U.K. / R.-U.	1733-1738
Taml.	Tamlyn's Reports (E.R. vol. 48)	U.K. / R.-U.	1829-1830
Tas. L.R.	Tasmanian Law Reports	Austl. (Tas.)	1896-1940
Tas. R.	Tasmania Reports	Austl. (Tas.)	1979-
Tas. S.R.	Tasmania State Reports	Austl. (Tas.)	1941-1978
Taun.	Taunton's Reports (E.R. vols. 127-129)	U.K. / R.-U.	1807-1819
Tax A.B.C.	Tax Appeal Board Cases	Can.	1949-1966
Tax A.B.C. (N.S.)	Tax Appeal Board Cases (New Series)	Can.	1967-1972
Terr. L.R.	Territories Law Reports	Can. (NWT)	1885-1907
Toth.	Tothill's Reports (E.R. vol. 21)	U.K. / R.-U.	1559-1646
Turn. & R.	Turner & Russell's Reports, Chancery (E.R. vol. 37)	U.K. / R.-U.	1822-1824
U.C. Chamb. Rep.	Upper Canada Chambers Reports	Can. (ON)	1846-1852
U.C.C.P.	Upper Canada Common Pleas Reports	Can. (ON)	1850-1882
U.C.E. & A.	Upper Canada Error and Appeal Reports (Grant)	Can. (ON)	1846-1866
U.C.K.B.	Upper Canada King's Bench Report (Old Series)	Can. (ON)	1831-1844
U.C.Q.B.	Upper Canada Queen's Bench Reports (New Series)	Can. (ON)	1842-1882
U.C.Q.B. (O.S.)	Upper Canada Queen's Bench Reports (Old Series)	Can. (ON)	1831-1838
U.I.C. Dec. Ump.	Unemployment Insurance Commission – Decisions of the Umpire	Can.	1943-
U.I.C. Selec. Dec. Ump.	Unemployment Insurance Commission – Selected Decisions of the Umpire	Can.	1943-1949
U.S.	United States Reports	U.S. / É.-U.	1754-
U.S. App. D.C.	United States Court of Appeals Reports	U.S. / É.-U.	1941-
U.S.L.W.	United States Law Week	U.S. / É.-U.	1933-
Uganda L.R.	Uganda Law Reports	E. Afr.	1904-1973
V.L.R.	Victorian Law Reports	Austl. (Vic.)	1886-1956

V.R.	Victorian Reports	Austl. (Vic.)	1870-1872 1957-
Vaugh.	Vaughan's Reports (E.R. vol. 124)	U.K. / R.-U.	1665-1674
Vent.	Ventris's Reports (E.R. vol. 86)	U.K. / R.-U.	1666-1688
Vern.	Vernon's Reports (E.R. vol. 23)	U.K. / R.-U.	1680-1719
Ves. & Bea.	Vesey & Beames' Reports (E.R. vol. 35)	U.K. / R.-U.	1812-1814
Ves. Jr.	Vesey Junior's Reports (E.R. vols. 30-34)	U.K. / R.-U.	1789-1817
Ves. Sr.	Vesey Senior's Reports (E.R. vols. 27-28)	U.K. / R.-U.	1746-1755
W. Rob.	W. Robinson's Reports (E.R. vol. 166)	U.K. / R.-U.	1838-1850
W. W. & A'B.	Wyatt, Webb & A'Beckett's Reports (Supreme Court of Victoria)	Austl.	1866-1871
W.A.C.	Western Appeal Cases	Can.	1991-
W.A.L.R.	Western Australia Law Reports	Austl. (W.A.)	1899-1959
W.A.R.	Western Australia Reports	Austl. (W.A.)	1960-1990
W.A.R. (N.S.)	Western Australia Reports (New Series)	Austl. (W.A.)	1990-
W.C.A.T. Dec.	Workers' Compensation Appeal Tribunal Decisions	Can. (NF)	1987-
W.C.A.T.R.	Workers Compensation Appeals Tribunal Reporter	Can. (ON)	1986-1997
W.C.B.	Weekly Criminal Bulletin	Can.	1976-1986
W.C.B. (2d)	Weekly Criminal Bulletin (Second Series)	Can.	1986-
W.D.C.P.	Weekly Digest of Civil Procedure	Can.	1985-1989
W.D.C.P. (2d)	Weekly Digest of Civil Procedure (Second Series)	Can.	1990-1994
W.D.C.P. (3d)	Weekly Digest of Civil Procedure (Third Series)	Can.	1994-
W.D.F.L.	Weekly Digest of Family Law	Can.	1982-
W.L.A.C.	Western Labour Arbitration Cases	Can.	1966-1985
W.L.R.	Weekly Law Reports	U.K. / R.-U.	1953-
W.L.R.	Western Law Reporter	Can.	1905-1917
W.L.R.B.D.	Canadian Wartime Labour Relations Board Decisions	Can.	1944-1948
W.L.T.R.	Western Law Times and Reports	Can.	1890-1896
W.S.I.A.T.R	Workplace Safety and Insurance Appeals Tribunal Reporter	Can. (ON)	1998-
W.W.R.	Western Weekly Reports	Can.	1911-1950 1971-
W.W.R. (N.S.)	Western Weekly Reports (New Series)	Can.	1951-1970
Welsb. H. & G.	Welsby, Hurlstone & Gordon's Exchequer Reports (E.R. vols. 154-156)	U.K. / R.-U.	1847-1856
West, t. Hard.	West, temp. Hardwicke Reports (E.R.	U.K. / R.-U.	1736-1739

	vol. 25)		
West.	West's Reports (E.R. vol. 9)	U.K. / R.-U.	1839-1841
West's Alaska	West's Alaska Digest	Can (AB)	1987-
Wight.	Wightwick's Reports (E.R. vol. 145)	U.K. / R.-U.	1810-1811
Will. Woll. & H.	Willmore, Wollaston & Hodges's Reports	U.K. / R.-U.	1838-1839
Willes.	Willes's Reports (E.R. vol. 125)	U.K. / R.-U.	1737-1760
Wilm.	Wilmot's Reports (E.R. vol. 97)	U.K. / R.-U.	1757-1770
Wils. Ch.	Wilson's Reports, Chancery (E.R. vol. 37)	U.K. / R.-U.	1818-1819
Wils. Ex.	Wilson's Reports, Exchequer (E.R. vol. 159)	U.K. / R.-U.	1805-1817
Wils. K.B.	Wilson's Reports, King's Bench (E.R. vol. 95)	U.K. / R.-U.	1742-1774
Winch.	Winch's Reports (E.R. vol. 124)	U.K. / R.-U.	1621-1625
Wms. Saund.	Williams' & Saunders's Reports (E.R. vol. 85)	U.K. / R.-U.	1666-1673
Y. & C. Ex.	Younge & Collyer's Reports (E.R. vol. 160)	U.K. / R.-U.	1834-1842
Y. & C.C.C.	Younge & Collyer's Chancery Cases (E.R. vols. 62-63)	U.K. / R.-U.	1841-1843
Y. & J.	Younge & Jervis's Reports (E.R. vol. 148)	U.K. / R.-U.	1826-1830
Y.A.D. / Young Adm.	Young's Admiralty Decisions	Can. (NS)	1864-1880
Y.B. Eur. Conv. H.R.	Yearbook of the European Convention on Human Rights	E.U. / U.E.	1955-
Y.R.	Yukon Reports	Can.	1986-1989
Yel.	Yelverton's Reports (E.R. vol. 80)	U.K. / R.-U.	1603-1613
You.	Younge's Reports (E.R. vol. 159)	U.K. / R.-U.	1830-1832

H PERIODICALS AND YEARBOOKS / PÉRIODIQUES ET ANNUAIRES

Name of Periodical or Yearbook /Nom du périodique ou de l'annuaire	Abbreviation /Abréviations
Across Borders	Across Borders
Acta Criminologica	Acta Crim.
Actualités du droit	Actualités
Actualités juridiques, droit administratif	Actualités jur. dr. admin.
Actualités-Justice	Actualités-Justice
Actualité et droit international	Actualité & dr. int.
Actualités de la délégation pour l'Union Européen	Actualités dél. U.E..
Actualités d'Unidroit	Actualités d'Unidroit
Adelaide Law Review	Adel. L.R.
Adelphia Law Journal	Adelphia. L.J.
Administrative & Regulatory Law News	Admin. & Reg. L. News
Administrative Law Journal of the American University (formerly Administrative Law Journal)	Admin. L.J. Am. U.
Administrative Law Review	Admin. L. Rev.
Advocate (Idaho)	Advocate (Idaho)
Advocate (British Columbia)	Advocate (B.C.)
Advocates' Quarterly	Advocates' Q.
Advocates' Society Journal	Advocates' Soc. J.
African-American Law and Policy Report	Afr.-Am. L. & Pol'y Rep.
Air Force Law Review	A.F.L. Rev.
Air & Space Law	Air & Space L.
Air & Space Lawyer	Air & Space Law.
Akron Law Review	Akron L. Rev.
Akron Tax Journal	Akron Tax J.
Alabama Law Review	Ala. L. Rev.
Alaska Law Review	Alaska L. Rev.
Albany Law Environmental Outlook	Alb. L. Envtl. Outlook
Albany Law Journal of Science & Technology	Alb. L.J. Sci. & Tech.
Albany Law Review	Alb. L. Rev.
Alberta Law Quarterly	Alta. L. Q.
Alberta Law Review	Alta. L. Rev.
Alternatives Journal	Alt. J.
American Association of Law Libraries Spectrum	A.A.L.L. Spec.
American Bankruptcy Institute Journal	Am. Bankr. Inst. J.
American Bankruptcy Institute Law Review	Am. Bankr. Inst. L. Rev.
American Bankruptcy Law Journal	Am. Bank. L.J.
American Bar Association Antitrust Law Journal	A.B.A. Antitrust L.J.

American Bar Association Criminal Justice	A.B.A. Criminal J.
American Bar Association Entertainment & Sports Lawyer	A.B.A. Ent. & Sports Law.
American Bar Association Family Advocate	A.B.A. Fam. Advocate
American Bar Association Family Law Quarterly	A.B.A.Fam. L.Q.
American Bar Association Journal	A.B.A. J.
American Bar Association Law Practice Management	A.B.A.P.M.
American Bar Association Section of Intellectual Property Law	A.B.A.I.P.L.
American Bar Association Tort and Insurance Law Journal	A.B.A. Tort & Ins. L.J.
American Business Law Journal	Am. Bus. L.J.
American Criminal Law Review	Am. Crim. L. Rev.
American Indian Law Review	Am. Indian L. Rev.
American Intellectual Property Law Association Quarterly Journal	A.I.P.L.A.Q.J.
American Journal of Comparative Law	Am. J. Comp. L.
American Journal of Criminal Law	Am. J. Crim. L.
American Journal of International Arbitration	Am. J. Int'l Arb.
American Journal of International Law	A.J.I.L. / Am. J. Int'l L.
American Journal of Jurisprudence	Am. J. Juris.
American Journal of Law & Medicine	Am. J. L. & Med.
American Journal of Legal History	Am. J. Legal Hist.
American Journal of Tax Policy	Am. J. Tax Pol'y
American Journal of Trial Advocacy	Am. J. Trial Advoc.
American Law and Economics Review	Am. L. & Econ. Rev.
American Review of International Arbitration	Am. Rev. Int'l Arb.
American Society International Law Review	Am. Soc. Int'l L. Rev.
American University International Law Review *(formerly American University Journal of International Law & Policy)*	Am. U. Int'l L. Rev.
American University Journal of Gender, Social Policy & the Law *(formerly American University Journal of Gender & the Law)*	Am. U. J. Gender Soc. Pol'y & L.
American University Journal of International Law & Policy	Am. U. J. Int'l L. & Pol'y
American University Law Review	Am. U. L. Rev.
Analyse de politiques	Anal. de pol.
Anglo-American Law Review	Anglo-Am. L. Rev.
Animal Law	Animal L.
Annales de droit aérien et spacial	Ann. Air & Sp. L.
Annals of Air and Space Law	Ann. Air & Sp. L.
Annales de droit de Louvain	Ann. dr. Louv.
Annales de la propriété industrielle artistique et littéraire	Ann. pr. ind. art. & lit.
Annales de l'Université des sciences sociales de Toulouse	Ann. de l'U.s.s.T.
Annals of Health Law	Annals Health L
Annuaire canadien de droit international	A.C.D.I.

Annuaire canadien des droits de la personne	A.C.D.P.
Annuaire de la Convention européenne des droits de l'Homme	Ann. Conv. Eur. D.H. l'Homme
Annuaire de droit aérien et spatial	Ann. dr. aér. & spat.
Annuaire de droit maritime et aérien	Ann. dr. marit. & aér.
Annuaire de droit maritime et aéro-spatial	Ann. dr. marit. & aéro-spat.
Annuaire des collectivités locales	Ann. coll. loc.
Annuaire français de droit international	A.F.D.I.
Annuaire français des droits de l'Homme	Ann. fr. D.H.
Annuaire français du transport aérien	Ann. fr. transp. aér.
Annuaire de la Haye de droit international	Ann. Haye dr. int.
Annuaire de l'Institut de droit international	Ann. inst. dr. int.
Annuaire international de justice constitutionnelle	Ann. int. j. c.
Annuaire de la Société des Nations	Ann. S.N.
Annuaire de la Société française de droit aérien et spatial	Ann. S. fr. dr. aér. & spat.
Annuaire de législation étrangère	Ann. lég. étrang.
Annuaire de législation française	Ann. lég. fr.
Annuaire de philosophie de droit	Ann. phil. dr.
Annuaire des Nations Unies	Ann. N.U.
Annuaire suisse de droit international	Ann. suisse dr. int.
Annual Review of Banking Law	Ann. Rev. Banking L.
Annual Survey of American Law	Ann. Surv. Am. L.
Annual Survey of Australian Law	Ann. Surv. Austl. L.
Annual Survey of Commonwealth Law	Ann. Surv. Commonwealth L.
Annual Survey of English Law	Ann. Surv. Engl. L.
Annual Survey of International & Comparative Law	Ann. Surv. Int'l & Comp. L.
Annual Survey of South African Law	Ann. Surv. S. Afr. L.
Antitrust	Antitrust
Antitrust Law and Economics Review	Antitrust L. & Econ. Rev.
Antitrust Law Journal	Antitrust L.J.
Appeal: Review of Current Law and Law Reform	Appeal
Arab Law Quarterly	Arab L.Q.
Arbitration International	Arb. Int'l
Arizona Bar Journal	Ariz. Bar. J.
Arizona Journal of International & Comparative Law	Ariz. J. Int'l & Comp. L.
Arizona Law Review	Ariz. L. Rev.
Arizona State Law Journal	Ariz. St. L.J.
Arkansas Law Review	Ark. L. Rev.
Art, Antiquity, and the Law	Art. Ant. & L.
Artificial Intelligence and Law	A.I. & L.
Army Lawyer	Army Law.
Asian Law Journal	Asian L.J.

Asia Pacific Journal of Environmental Law	Asia Pac. J. Envtl L.
Asia-Pacific Journal of Human Rights and the Law	Asia Pac. J. H.R. & L.
Asia Pacific Journal of International Law	Asia Pac. J. Int'l L.
Asia Pacific Law Review	Asia Pac. L. Rev.
Asian-Pacific American Law Journal	Asian Pac. Am. L.J.
(formerly Asian American Pacific Islands Law Journal)	
Asian-Pacific Law & Policy Journal	Asian Pac. L. & Pol'y J.
Atomic Energy Law Journal	A.E.L.J.
Auckland University Law Review	Auckland U.L. Rev.
Australian & New Zealand Journal of Criminology	Austl. Crim. & N.Z.J.
Australian Bar Review	Austl. Bar Rev.
Australian Business Law Review	Austl. Bus. L. Rev.
Australian Competition and Consumer Law Journal	Austl. Comp. & Cons. L.J.
Austalian Insurance Law Journal	Austl. Ins. L.J.
Australian Journal of Contract Law	Austl. J. Contract L.
Australian Journal of Corporate Law	Austl. J. Corp. L.
Australian Journal of Family Law	Austl. J. Fam. L.
Australian Journal of Labour Law	Austl. J. Lab. L.
Australian Property Law Journal	Austl. Prop. L.J.
Australian Torts Law Journal	Aust. Torts L.J.
Austrian Journal of Public and International Law	Aus. J. Pub. & Int'l L.
Austrian Review of International and European Law	Aus. Rev. Int'l & Eur. L.
Baltimore Law Review	Baltimore L. Rev.
Banking and Finance Law Review	B.F.L.R.
Banking Law Journal	Banking L.J.
Banking Policy Report	Banking Pol'y Rep.
Bankruptcy Developments Journal	Bankr. Dev. J.
Banque et droit	B. & dr.
Bar & Bench News Digest	Bar & Bench N.D.
Baylor Law Review	Baylor L. Rev.
Barrister	Barrister
Behavioural Sciences and the Law	Behav. Sci. & L.
Berkeley Journal of Employment and Labour Law	Berkeley J. Emp. & Lab. L.
Berkeley Journal of Health Care Law	Berkeley J. Health Care L.
Berkeley Journal of International Law	Berkeley J. Int'l L.
Berkeley Technology Law Journal	Berkeley Tech. L.J.
Berkeley Women's Law Journal	Berkeley Women's L.J.
Biotechnology Law Report	Biotech. L. Rep.
Bureau of National Affairs Patent, Trademark and Copyright Journal	B.N.A. Patent, T.M. & Copyright J.
Boston Bar Journal	Boston Bar J.
Boston College Environmental Affairs Law Review	B.C. Envtl. Aff. L. Rev.

Boston College International & Comparative Law Review	B.C. Int'l. & Comp. L. Rev.
Boston College Law Review	B.C.L. Rev.
Boston College Third World Law Journal	B.C. Third World L.J.
Boston University International Law Journal	B.U. Int'l L.J.
Boston University Journal of Science & Technology Law	B.U.J. Sci. & Tech. L.
Boston University Journal of Tax Law	B.U.J. Tax L.
Boston University Law Review	B.U.L. Rev.
Boston University Public Interest Law Journal	B.U. Pub. Int. L.J.
Brandeis Law Journal	Brandeis L.J.
Briefly Speaking	Brief. Speaking
Brigham Young University Education & Law Journal	B.Y.U. Educ. & L.J.
Brigham Young University Law Review	B.Y.U.L. Rev.
British Columbia Law Notes	B.C.L.N.
British Institute of International and Comparative Law	Brit. Inst. Int'l & Comp. L.
British Journal of Criminology	Brit. J. Crim.
British Tax Review	Brit. Tax Rev.
British Yearbook of International Law	Brit. Y.B. Int'l L.
Brooklyn Journal of International Law	Brook. J. Int'l L.
Brooklyn Law Review	Brook. L. Rev.
Buffalo Criminal Law Review	Buff. Crim. L. Rev.
Buffalo Environmental Law Journal	Buff. Envtl. L.J.
Buffalo Human Rights Law Review	Buff. H.R.L. Rev.
Buffalo Law Review	Buff. L. Rev.
Buffalo Public Interest Law Journal	Buff. Pub. Int. L.J.
Buffalo Women's Law Journal	Buff. Women's L.J.
Bulletin canadien VIH-SIDA et droit	Bull can. VIH-SIDA & D.
Bulletin of Legal Developments	Bull.
Bulletin d'information sur les activités juridiques (Conseil de l'Europe)	Bull. info.
Business and the Law	Bus. & L.
Business Law Review	Bus. L. Rev.
Business Lawyer	Bus. Law.
Business Quarterly	Bus. Q.
BYU Journal of Public Law	B.Y.U.J. Pub. L.
Cahiers de droit	C. de D.
Cahiers de droit de l'entreprise	C. de D. entr.
Cahiers de Droit européen	C. de D. eur.
Cahiers du Conseil Constitutionnel	C. du Cons. Const.
Cahiers de l'Institut québécois d'administration judiciaire	C.I.Q.A.J.
Cahiers de propriété intellectuelle	C.P.I.
California Bankruptcy Journal	Cal. Bankr. J.
California Criminal Law Review	Cal. Crim. L. Rev.
California Law Review	Cal. L. Rev.

California Regulatory Law Reporter	Cal. Reg. L. Rep.
California State Bar Journal	Cal. St. B.J.
California Western International Law Journal	Cal. W. Int'l L.J.
California Western Law Review	Cal. W.L. Rev.
Cambridge Law Journal	Cambridge L.J.
Cambridge Yearbook of European Legal Studies	Cambridge Y.B. Eur. Legal Stud.
Campbell Law Review	Campbell L. Rev.
Canada Law Journal	Can. L.J.
Canada-United States Law Journal	Can.-U.S.L.J.
Canadian Bar Association Papers	C.B.A. Papers
Canadian Bar Association Year Book	C.B.A.Y.B.
Canadian Bar Journal	Can. Bar J.
Canadian Bar Review	Can. Bar Rev.
Canadian Bioethics Report	Can. Bioethics R.
Canadian Business Law Journal	Can. Bus. L.J.
Canadian Business Review	Can. Bus. Rev.
Canadian Communications Law Review	Can Comm. L. Rev.
Canadian Community Law Journal	Can. Community L.J.
Canadian Competition Policy Record	Can. Compet. Pol'y Rec.
Canadian Competition Record	Can. Comp. Rec.
Canadian Council on International Law: Proceedings	Can. Council Int'l L. Proc.
Canadian Criminal Law Review	Can. Crim. L. Rev.
Canadian Criminology Forum	Can. Crim. Forum
Canadian Current Tax	Can Curr. Tax
Canadian Environmental Law News	Can. Envtl. L.N.
Canadian Family Law Quarterly	Can. Fam. L.Q.
Canadian HIV/AIDS Policy & Law Review	Can. HIV/AIDS Pol'y & L. Rev.
Canadian Human Rights Advocate	Can H.R. Advoc.
Canadian Human Rights Yearbook	Can. Hum. Rts. Y.B.
Canadian Intellectual Property Review	C.I.P.R.
Canadian International Lawyer	Can. Int'l. Law.
Canadian Journal of Administrative Law & Practice	Can. J. Admin. L. & Prac.
Canadian Journal of Corrections	Can. J. Corr.
Canadian Journal of Criminology	Can. J. Crim.
Canadian Journal of Criminology and Corrections	Can. J. Crim. & Corr.
Canadian Journal of Family Law	Can. J. Fam. L.
Canadian Journal of Insurance Law	Can. J. Ins. L.
Canadian Journal of Law and Jurisprudence	Can. J.L. & Jur.
Canadian Journal of Law and Society	C.J.L.S.
Canadian Journal of Law and Technology	C.J.L.T.

Canadian Journal of Women and the Law	C.J.W.L.
Canadian Labour & Employment Law Journal	C.L.E.L.J.
Canadian Law Review	Can. L. Rev.
Canadian Law Times	Can. L.T.
Canadian Lawyer	Can. Law.
Canadian Legal Studies	Can. Legal Stud.
Canadian Municipal Journal	Can. Mun. J.
Canadian Native Law Bulletin	Can. N.L. Bull.
Canadian Public Policy	Can. Pub. Pol'y
Canadian Tax Foundation (Conference Report / Rapport de conférence)	Can. Tax Found.
Canadian Tax Highlights	Can. Tax. Highlights
Canadian Tax Journal	Can. Tax J.
Canadian Tax News	Can. Tax N.
Canadian Taxation: A Journal of Tax Policy	Can. Tax'n: J. Tax Pol'y
Canadian Yearbook of International Law	Can. Y.B. Int'l Law
Capital University Law Review	Capital U.L. Rev.
Cardozo Arts & Entertainment Law Journal	Cardozo Arts & Ent. L.J.
Cardozo Electronic Law Bulletin	Cardozo E.L. Bull.
Cardozo Journal of International & Comparative Law (*formerly New Europe Law Review*)	Cardozo J. Int'l. & Comp. L.
Cardozo Law Review	Cardozo L. Rev.
Cardozo Studies in Law and Literature	Cardozo Stud. L. & Lit.
Cardozo Women's Law Journal	Cardozo Women's L.J.
Carolina Law Journal	Car. L.J.
Case Western Reserve Journal of International Law	Case W. Res. J. Int'l L.
Case Western Reserve Law Review	Case W. Res. L. Rev.
Catholic Lawyer	Cath. Law.
Catholic University Law Review	Cath. U. L. Rev.
Chapman Law Review	Chapman L. Rev.
Chicago Journal of International Law	Chicago J. Int'l L.
Chicago-Kent Law Review	Chicagio-Kent L. Rev.
Chicano-Latino Law Review (*formerly Chicano Law Review*)	Chicano-Latino L. Rev.
Chicago Lawyer	Chicago Law.
Chicago Legal Forum	Chicago Legal F.
Children's Legal Rights Journal	Child. Legal Rts. J.
Chinese Yearbook of International Law and Affairs	Chinese Y.B. Int'l L. & Aff.
Chitty's Law Journal	Chitty's L.J.
Circles: Buffalo Women's Journal of Law & Social Policy	Circles
Civil Liberties Review	Civ. Lib. Rev.
Civil Justice Quarterly	C.J.Q.
Cleveland State Law Review	Clev. St. L. Rev.

Cleveland-Marshall Law Review   Clev.-Marshall L. Rev.
Clinical Law Review   Clinical L. Rev.
Codicillus   Codicillus
Colorado Journal of International Environmental Law & Policy   Colo. J. Int'l Envtl. L. & Pol'y

Colorado Lawyer   Colo. Law.
Columbia Business Law Review   Colum. Bus. L. Rev.
Columbia Human Rights Law Review   Colum. H.R.L. Rev.
Columbia Journal of Asian Law   Colum. J. Asian Law
(formerly Journal of Chinese Law)

Columbia Journal of East European Law   Colum. J. E. Eur. L.
Columbia Journal of Environmental Law   Colum. J. Envtl. L.
Columbia Journal of European Law   Colum. J. Eur. L.
Columbia Journal of Gender and Law   Colum. J. Gender & L.
Columbia Journal of Law and Social Problems   Colum. J.L. & Soc. Probs.
Columbia Journal of Transnational Law   Colum. J. Transnat'l L.
Columbia Law Review   Colum. L. Rev.
Columbia Science and Technology Law Review   Colum. Sci. & Tech. L. Rev.
Columbia-V.L.A. Journal of Law & the Arts   Colum.-V.L.A. J. L. & Arts
Commercial Law Journal   Com. L.J.
Commercial Leasing Law and Strategy   Com. Leasing L. & Strategy
Common Market Law Review   C.M.L. Rev.
Commonwealth Law Bulletin   Commonwealth L. Bull.
Commonwealth Legal Education   Commonwealth Legal Educ.
Communication Law & Policy   Comm. L. & Pol'y
Communications Lawyer   Comm. Law.
Communique – International Court of Justice   Communique I.C.J.
Comparative and International Law Journal of Southern Africa   Comp. & Int'l L.J.S. Afr.
Comparative Labor Law & Policy Journal   Comp. Lab. L. & Pol'y J.
(formerly Comparative Labor Law Journal)

Comparative Juridical Review   Comp. Jurid. Rev.
Comptes rendus sténographiques des débats (Conseil de l'Europe) Débats
Computer Law and Security Report   Computer L. & Sec. R.
Computer Law Review and Technology Journal   Computer L. Rev. & T. J.
Computer Lawyer   Computer Law.
Congressional Digest   Cong. Dig.
Connecticut Bar Journal   Conn. B.J.
Connecticut Insurance Law Journal   Conn. Ins. L.J.
Connecticut Journal of International Law   Conn. J. Int'l L.
Connecticut Law Review   Conn. L. Rev.
Connecticut Probate Law Journal   Conn. Prob. L.J.
Constitutional Commentary   Const. Commentary

Constitutional Forum Constitutionnel	Const. Forum Const.
Constitutional Review	Const. Rev.
Consumer Finance Law Quarterly Report	Cons. Fin. L.Q. Rep.
Construction Law Journal	Construction L.J.
Construction Lawyer	Construction Law.
Copyright Bulletin	Copyright Bull.
Cooley Law Review	Cooley L. Rev.
Cornell International Law Journal	Cornell Int'l L.J.
Cornell Journal of Law & Public Policy	Cornell J. L. & Pub. Pol'y
Cornell Law Review	Cornell L. Rev.
Cornell Law Journal	Cornell L.J.
Corporate Management Tax Conference	Corp. Mgmt. Tax Conf.
Corporate Taxation	Corp. Tax'n.
Corpus Juris Secundum	C.J.S.
Correspondances judiciaires	Corr. jud.
Counsellor : The New York Law School Journal	Counsellor
Cours de perfectionnement du notariat	C.P. du N.
Creighton Law Review	Creighton L. Rev.
Crime, Law and Social Change	Crime, L. & Soc. Change
Criminal Law Forum	Crim. L.F.
Criminal Law Quarterly	Crim. L.Q.
Criminal Law Review	Crim. L. Rev.
Criminologie	Criminol.
Criminology	Criminol.
Critical Criminology	Crit. Criminol.
Croation Arbitration Yearbook	Croation Arb. Y.B.
Croatian Critical Law Review	Croat. Crit. L. Rev.
Crown Counsel's Review	Crown Coun. Rev.
Cumberland Law Review	Cumb. L. Rev.
Current Law Yearbook	Curr. L.Y.B.
Current Legal Problems	Curr. Legal Probs.
Current Medicine for Attorneys	Current Med. for Att'ys
Currents: International Trade Law Journal	Currents
Cyberspace Law Journal	Cyberspace L.J.
Cyberspace Lawyer	Cyberspace Law.
Dalhousie Journal of Legal Studies	Dal. J. Leg. Stud.
Dalhousie Law Journal	Dal. L.J.
Defense Counsel Journal	Def. Couns. J.
Delaware Journal of Corporate Law	Del. J. Corp. L.
Delaware Law Review	Del. L. Rev.
Delaware Lawyer	Del. Law
Denver Journal of International Law & Policy	Denv. J. Int'l L. & Pol'y

Denver University Law Review   Denv. U.L. Rev.
(formerly Denver Law Journal)
Department of State Bulletin   Dep't St. Bull.
DePaul Business Law Journal   DePaul Bus. L.J.
DePaul International Law Journal   DePaul Int'l L.J.
DePaul Journal of Health Care Law   DePaul J. Health Care L.
DePaul Law Review   DePaul L. Rev.
DePaul-L.C.A. Journal of Art and Entertainment Law and Policy   DePaul-L.C.A. J. Art & Ent. L. & Pol'y

Deutsches und Europäisches Familienrecht   D.E.F.R.
Dickinson Journal of Environmental Law & Policy   Dick. J. Envtl. L. & Pol'y
Dickinson Journal of International Law   Dick. J. Int'l L.
Dickinson Law Review   Dick. L. Rev.
Digital Technology Law Journal   D.T.L.J.
Dispute Resolution Journal   Disp. Resol. J.
(formerly Arbitration Journal)
District of Columbia Law Review   D.C.L. Rev.
Documents juridiques internationaux   D.J.I.
Documents (Working Papers) (Council of Europe)   Documents
Documents de séance (Conseil de l'Europe)   Documents
Drake Journal of Agricultural Law   Drake J. Agric. L.
Drake Law Review   Drake L. Rev.
Droit et pratique du commerce international   D.P.C.I.
Droit des sociétés   Dr. soc.
Droit et patrimoine   Dr. et pat.
Droit et Société   Dr. et Soc.
Droit Maritime Français   Dr. Marit. Fr.
Droit polonais contemporain   Dr. polon. contemp.
Droit Social   Dr. social
Droit européen des transports   Dr. eur. transp.
Droits   Droits
Duke Environmental Law & Policy Forum   Duke Envtl L. & Pol'y F.
Duke Journal of Comparative & International Law   Duke J. Comp. & Int'l L.
Duke Journal of Gender Law & Policy   Duke J. Gender L. & Pol'y
Duke Law Journal   Duke L.J.
Duquesne Business Law Journal   Duq. Bus. L.J.
Duquesne Law Review   Duq. L. Rev.
East European Business Law   E. Eur. Bus. L.
East European Constitutional Review   E. Eur. Const. Rev.
East European Human Rights Review   E. Eur. H.R. Rev.
Ecology Law Quarterly   Ecology L. Q.
Edinburgh Law Review   Ed. L. Rev.

Education & Law Journal	Educ. & L.J.
Elder Law Journal	Elder L.J.
Electronic Journal of Comparative Law	E.J.C.L.
Emory International Law Review	Emory Int'l L. Rev.
(formerly Emory Journal of International Dispute Resolution)	
Emory Law Journal	Emory L.J.
Employee Rights & Employment Policy Journal	Employee Rts. & Employment Pol'y J.
Energy Law Journal	Energy L.J.
Entertainment & Sports Lawyer	Ent. & Sports Law.
Entertainment Law & Finance	Ent. L. & Fin.
Environmental Law	Envtl. L.
Environmental Law and Management	Envtl. L. & Mgmt
Environmental Law and Policy Journal	Envtl. L. & Pol'y J.
Environmental Law Journal	Envtl. L.J.
Environmental Lawyer	Envtl. Law.
Environmental Policy and Law	Envtl. Pol'y & L.
Environmentally Friendly: The Journal of the Pace Center for Environmental Legal Studies	Envtlly Friendly
Environs Environmental Law and Policy Journal	Environs Envtl. L. & Pol'y J.
Estates and Trusts Journal	E. & T.J.
Estates and Trusts Quarterly	E. & T.Q.
Estates Trusts & Pensions Journal	E.T.P.J.
Ethics	Ethics
Europarecht	EuR.
Europäische Zeitschrift für Privatrecht	E.Z.P.R.
European Business Law Review	Eur. Bus. L. Rev.
European Competition Law Review	Eur. Comp. L. Rev.
European Environmental Law Review	Eur. Envtl. L. Rev.
European Environment Yearbook	Eur. Env. Y.B.
European Human Rights Law Review	Eur. H.R.L. Rev.
European Intellectual Property Review	Eur. I.P. Rev.
European Journal of Health Law	Eur. J. Health L.
European Journal of Law & Economics	Eur. J. L. & Econ.
European Journal of Law Reform	Eur. J. L. Ref.
European Journal of International Law	E.J.I.L.
European Journal for Education Law and Policy	Eur. J. Educ. L. & Pol'y
European Journal of Migration and Law	Eur. J. Migr. & L.
European Journal of Social Security	Eur. J. Soc. Sec.
European Journal of Criminal Policy & Research	Eur. J. Crim. Pol'y & Research
European Journal of Crime, Criminal Law, and Criminal Justice	Eur. J. Crime, Crim. L. &

	Crim. J.
European Law Journal	Eur. L.J.
European Law Review	Eur. L. Rev.
European Review of Private Law	E.R.P.L.
European Transport Law	Eur. Transp. L.
Examiner	Examiner
F.A.A. Aviation News	F.A.A. Av. N.
Family Court Review	Fam. Ct. Rev.
(formerly Family & Conciliation Courts Review)	
Family Law Quarterly	Fam. L.Q.
Family Law Review	Fam. L. Rev.
Federal Bar News & Journal	Fed. B. News & J.
Federal Circuit Bar Journal	Fed. Circuit B.J.
Federal Communications Law Journal	Fed. Comm. L.J.
Federal Courts Law Review	Fed. Cts. L. Rev.
Federal Lawyer	Fed. Law.
Federal Litigator	Fed. Litigator
Federal Rules Decisions	F.R.D.
Feminist Legal Studies	Fem. Legal Stud.
Florida Bar Journal	Fla. B.J.
Florida Coastal Law Journal	Fla. Coastal L.J.
Florida International Law Journal	Fla. Int'l L.J.
Florida Journal of International Law	Fla. J. Int'l L.
Florida Law Review	Fla. L. Rev.
(formerly University of Florida Law Review)	
Florida State Journal of Transnational Law & Policy	Fla. St. J. Transnat'l L. & Pol'y
Florida State University Journal of Land Use & Environmental Law	Fla. St. U.J. Land Use & Envtl. L.
Florida State University Law Review	Fla. St. U.L. Rev.
Florida Tax Review	Fla. Tax Rev.
Food & Drug Law Journal	Food & Drug L.J.
Fordham Environmental Law Journal	Fordham Envtl. L.J.
Fordham Finance, Securities & Tax Law Forum	Fordham Fin. Sec. & Tax L.F.
Fordham Intellectual Property, Media & Entertainment Law Journal	Fordham I.P. Media & Ent. L.J.
Fordham International Law Journal	Fordham Int'l L.J.
Fordham Journal of Corporate and Finance Law	Fordham J. Corp. & Fin. L.
Fordham Law Review	Fordham L. Rev.
Fordham Urban Law Journal	Fordham Urb. L.J.
International Law FORUM du droit international	FORUM

George Mason Law Review	Geo. Mason L. Rev.
(formerly George Mason University Law Review and George Mason Independent Law Review)	
George Mason University Civil Rights Law Journal	Geo. Mason U. Civ. Rts. L.J.
George Washington International Law Review	Geo. Wash. Int'l L. Rev.
(formerly George Washington Journal of International Law and Economics)	
George Washington Law Review	Geo. Wash. L. Rev.
Georgetown Immigration Law Journal	Geo. Immig. L.J.
Georgetown International Environmental Law Review	Geo. Int'l Envtl. L. Rev.
Georgetown Journal of Gender and the Law	Geo. J. Gender & L.
Georgetown Journal of Legal Ethics	Geo. J. Legal Ethics
Georgetown Journal on Poverty Law & Policy	Geo. J. on Poverty L. &
(formerly Georgetown Journal on Fighting Poverty)	Pol'y
Georgetown Law Journal	Geo. L.J.
Georgetown Public Policy Review	Geo. Pub. Pol'y Rev.
Georgia Journal of International and Comparative Law	Ga. J. Int'l. & Comp. L.
Georgia Law Review	Ga. L. Rev.
Georgia State University Law Review	Ga. St. U. L. Rev.
Golden Gate University Law Review	Golden Gate U.L. Rev.
Gonzaga Law Review	Gonz. L. Rev.
Great Plains Natural Resources Journal	Great Plains Nat. Resources J.
Griffith Law Review	Griffith L.R.
Hague Yearbook of International Law	Hague Y.B. Int'l L.
Hamline Journal of Public Law and Policy	Hamline J. Pub. L. & Pol'y
Hamline Law Review	Hamline L. Rev.
Harvard BlackLetter Law Journal	Harv. BlackLetter L.J.
Harvard Civil Rights-Civil Liberties Law Review	Harv. C.R.-C.L.L. Rev.
Harvard Environmental Law Review	Harv. Envtl. L. Rev.
Harvard Human Rights Journal	Harv. Hum. Rts. J.
(formerly Harvard Human Rights Yearbook)	
Harvard International Law Journal	Harv. Int'l L.J.
Harvard Journal of Law and Public Policy	Harv. J.L. & Pub. Pol'y
Harvard Journal of Law & Technology	Harv. J.L. & Tech.
Harvard Journal on Legislation	Harv. J. on Legis.
Harvard Law Review	Harv. L. Rev.
Harvard Negotiation Law Review	Harv. Negot. L. Rev.
Harvard Women's Law Journal	Harv. Women's L.J.
Hastings Communications & Entertainment Law Journal	Hastings Comm. & Ent. L.J.
Hastings Constitutional Law Quarterly	Hastings Const. L.Q.
Hastings International and Comparative Law Review	Hastings Int'l & Comp. L. Rev.

Hastings Law Journal	Hastings L.J.
Hastings West-Northwest Journal of Environmental Law and Policy	Hastings W.-Nw. J. Envtl. L. & Pol'y
Hastings Women's Law Journal	Hastings Women's L.J.
Hawaii Bar Journal	Haw. B.J.
Hawaill Law Review	Haw. L. Rev.
Health and Human Rights	Health & Hum. Rts.
Health Law in Canada	Health L. Can.
Health Law Journal	Health L.J.
Health Lawyer	Health Law.
Health Matrix	Health Matrix
Heidelberg Journal of International Law	Heidelberg J. Int'l L.
High Technology Law Journal	High Tech. L.J.
Hitotsubashi Journal of Law and Politics	H.J.L.P.
Hofstra Law Review	Hofstra L. Rev.
Hofstra Labor & Employment Law Journal	Hofstra Lab. & Empl. L.J.
Hofstra Law Review	Hofstra L. Rev.
Hofstra Property Law Journal	Hofstra Prop. L.J.
Holdsworth Law Review	Hold. L.R.
Hong Kong Law Journal	Hong King L.J.
Houston Journal of International Law	Hous. J. Int'l L.
Houston Law Review	Hous. L. Rev.
Howard Journal of Criminal Justice	How. J. Crim. Justice
Howard Law Journal	How. L.J.
Howard Scroll: The Social Justice Law Review	How Scroll.
Human Rights Internet Reporter	H.R.I.R.
Human Rights Law Journal	H.R.L.J.
Human Rights Case Digest	Hum. Rts. Case Digest
Human Rights in Development	Hum. Rts. Dev.
Human Rights in Developing Countries	Hum. Rts. Dev. Countries
Human Rights Journal	Hum. Rts. J.
Human Rights Quarterly	Hum. Rts. Q.
Human Rights Tribune	Hum. Rts. Trib.
Humboldt Forum Recht	Humboldt F.R.
Idaho Law Review	Idaho L. Rev.
IDEA: The Journal of Law and Technology	IDEA
ILSA Journal of International & Comparative Law	ILSA J. Int'l & Comp. L.
Illinois Bar Journal	Ill. B.J.
Illinois Law Quarterly	Ill. L.Q.
Immigration and Nationality Law Review	Immig. & Nat'lity L. Rev.
Impact Labour Law & Management Practices	Impact
Indiana International and Comparative Law Review	Ind. Int'l & Comp. L. Rev.

Indiana Journal of Global Legal Studies	Ind. J. Global Legal Stud.
Indiana Law Journal	Ind. L.J.
Indiana Law Review	Ind. L. Rev.
Indigenous Law Journal	Indigenous L.J.
Industrial Law Journal	Indus. L.J.
Industrial Relations Law Journal	Indus. Rel. L.J.
Industrial & Labor Relations Review	Indus. & Lab. Rel. Rev.
Information Bulletin on Legal Affairs (Council of Europe)	Inf. Bull.
Information and Communications Technology Law	I. & Comm. T. L.
Insolvency Bulletin	Ins. Bull.
Intellectual and Comparative Law Quarterly	I.C.L.Q.
Intellectual Property Journal	I.P.J.
Intellectual Property Law Bulletin	I.P.L. Bull.
Intellectual Property Law Newsletter	I.P.L. Newsl.
Intellectual Property & Technlology Forum	I.P. & T. F.
Intellectual Property & Technology Law Review	I.P. & T. L. Rev.
International Arbitration Law Review	Int'l. Arb. L. Rev.
International Business Law Journal	I.B.L.J.
International Business Lawyer	Int'l Bus. Law.
International Commercial Litigation	Int'l Com. Lit.
International Commission of Jurists Review	Int'l Comm. Jur. Rev.
International Company and Commercial Law Review	Int'l Co. & Com. L. Rev.
International and Comparative Corporate Law Journal	Int'l & Comp. Corp. L.J.
International and Comparative Law Quarterly	I.C.L.Q.
International and Comparative Law Review	Int'l. & Comp. L. Rev.
International Criminal Law Review	Int'l. Crim. L. Rev.
International Financial Law Review	Int'l. Fin. L. Rev.
International Insights	Int'l Insights
International Insurance Law Review	Int'l Ins. L. Rev.
International Journal	Int'l J.
International Journal for the Semiotics of Law	Int'l J. Sem. L.
International Journal of Children's Rights	Int'l J. Child. Rts.
International Journal of Communications Law & Policy	Int'l J. Comm. L. & Pol'y.
International Journal of Comparative Labour Law and Industrial Relations	Int'l J. Comp. Lab. L. & Ind. Rel.
International Journal of Conflict Management	Int'l J. Confl. Mgmt
International Journal of Cultural Property	Int'l J. Cult. Prop.
International Journal of Franchising and Distribution Law	Int'l J. Franch. & Distrib. L.
International Journal of Human Rights	Int'l J.H.R.
International Journal of Offender Therapy and Comparative Criminology	Int'l J. Off. Ther. & Comp. Crim.
International Journal of Law Policy and the Family	Int'l J.L. Pol'y & Fam.
International Journal of Law and Information Technology	Int'l J.L. & I.T.

International Journal of Law and Psychiatry	Int'l J. L. & Psychiatry
International Journal of Legal Information	Int'l J. Legal Info.
International Journal of Marine and Coastal Law	Int'l J. Mar. & Coast. L.
International Journal of the Sociology of Law	Int'l J. Soc. L.
International Journal of Refugee Law	Int'l J. Refugee. L.
International Journal of the Sociology of Law	Int'l J. Soc. L.
International Lawyer	Int'l Law.
International Legal Materials	I.L.M.
International Legal Perspectives	Int'l Legal Persp.
International Legal Practitioner	Int'l Leg. Practitioner
International Legal Theory	Int'l L. Theory
International Review of Criminal Policy	Int'l Rev. Crim. Pol'y
International Review of Industrial Property and Copyright Law	Int'l Rev. Ind. Prop & C'right L.
International Review of Law Computers & Technology	Int'l Rev. L. Comp. & Tech.
International Review of Law & Economics	Int'l Rev. L. & Econ.
International Review of the Red Cross	Int'l Rev. Red Cross
International Tax and Business Lawyer	Int'l Tax & Bus. Law.
International Trade Law and Practice	Int'l Trade L. & Pract.
International Trade Law & Regulation	Int'l Trade L. Reg.
International Trade Law Quarterly	I.T.L.Q.
Iowa Law Review	Iowa L. Rev.
Irish Jurist	Ir. Jur.
Islamic Law & Society	Islamic L. & Soc.
Israel Law Review	Isr. L.R.
Issues in Law & Medicine	Issues L. & Med.
Jewish Law Report	Jewish L.R.
John Marshall Journal of Computer & Information Law	J. Marshall J. Computer & Info. L.
John Marshall Law Quarterly	J. Marshall L.Q.
John Marshall Law Review	J. Marshall L. Rev.
Journal des Tribunaux	J. Tribun
Journal des Tribunaux – Droit Européen	J. Tribun. Droit. Eur.
Journal des juges provinciaux	J.J. prov.
Journal du Barreau	J. Barreau
Journal du droit des jeunes	J. dr. jeunes
Journal du droit international	J.D.I.
Journal of Affordable Housing & Community Development Law	J. Aff. Housing & Community Dev. L.
Journal of African Law	J. Afr. L.
Journal of Agricultural Law	J. Agric. L.
Journal of Air Law	J. Air L.

Journal of Air Law and Commerce	J. Air L. & Com.
Journal of Appellate Practice & Process	J. App. Pr. & Pro.
Journal of Art & Entertainment Law	J. Art. & Ent. L.
Journal of BioLaw & Business	J. BioLaw & Bus.
Journal of Business Law	J. Bus. L.
Journal of Chinese Law	J. Chinese L.
Journal of College & University Law	J.C. & U.L.
Journal of Comparative Business and Capital Market Law	J. Comp. Bus. & Cap. Mkt. L.
Journal of Conflict and Security Law	J. Confl. & Sec. L.
Journal of Conflict Resolution	J. Confl. Resolution
Journal of Constitutional Law in Eastern and Central Europe	J. Const. L.E. & Cent. Eur.
Journal of Contemporary Health Law & Policy	J. Contemp. Health L. & Pol'y
Journal of Contemporary Law	J. Contemp. L.
Journal of Contemporary Legal Issues	J. Contemp. Legal Issues
Journal of Corporate Taxation	J. Corp. Tax'n
Journal of Corporation Law	J. Corp. L.
Journal of Criminal Justice Education	J. Crim. J. Educ.
Journal of Criminal Law & Criminology	J. Crim. L. & Criminology
Journal of Dispute Resolution	J. Disp. Resol.
Journal of Energy Law & Policy	J. Energy L. & Pol'y
Journal of Energy, Natural Resources & Environmental Law	J. Energy, Nat'l Res. & Envtl. L.
Journal of Environmental Law	J. Envtl. L.
Journal of Environmental Law & Practice	J. Envtl. L. & Prac.
Journal of Environmental Law & Litigation	J. Envtl. L. & Litig.
Journal of European Integration	J. Eur. Int.
Journal of Family Law	J. Fam. L.
Journal of Gender, Race & Justice	J. Gender Race & Just.
Journal of Health and Hospital Law	J. Health & Hosp. L.
Journal of Health Care Law & Policy	J. Health Care L. & Pol'y
Journal of Health Politics, Policy & Law	J. Health Pol.
Journal of the History of International Law	J. Hist. Int'l L.
Journal of the Indian Law Institute	J.I.L.I.
Journal of Informaion, Law and Technology	J. Info. L. & T.
Journal of the Institute for the Study of Legal Ethics	J.I.S.L.E.
Journal of Intellectual Property	J. Intell. Prop.
Journal of Intellectual Property Law	J. Intell. Prop. L.
Journal of International Arbitration	J. Int'l Arb.
Journal of International Banking Law	J.I.B.L.
Journal of International Economic Law	J. Int'l Econ. L.
Journal of International Financial Markets	J. Int'l. Fin. Markets

Journal of International Law & Business	J. Int'l L. & Bus.
Journal of International Legal Studies	J. Int'l Legal Stud.
Journal of International Taxation	J. Int'l Tax.
Journal of International Wildlife Law and Policy	J. Int'l Wildlife L. & Pol'y
Journal of Juvenile Law	J. Junvenile L.
Journal of Land Use & Environmental Law	J. Land Use & Envtl. L.
Journal of Land, Resources & Environmental Law *(formerly Journal of Energy, Natural Resources & Environmental Law)*	J. Land Resources & Envtl. L.
Journal of Law & Commerce	J.L. & Com.
Journal of Law & Economics	J.L. & Econ.
Journal of Law, Economics & Organization	J.L. Econ. & Org.
Journal of Law & Education	J.L. & Educ.
Journal of Law and Environment	J.L. & Env't
Journal of Law and Equality	J.L. & Equality
Journal of Law & Family Studies	J.L. & Fam. Stud.
Journal of Law & Health	J.L. & Health
Journal of Law & Policy	J.L. & Pol'y
Journal of Law & Politics	J.L. & Pol.
Journal of Law & Religion	J.L. & Religion
Journal of Law and Social Policy	J. L. & Soc. Pol'y
Journal of Law and Society	J.L. & Soc'y
Journal of Law in Society	J.L. in Soc'y
Journal of Law & Technology	J.L. & Tech.
Journal of Law, Medicine & Ethics	J.L. Med. & Ethics
Journal of Legal Advocacy & Practice	J. Legal Advoc. & Prac.
Journal of Legal Economics	J. Legal Econ.
Journal of Legal Education	J. Legal Educ.
Journal of Legal History	J. Legal Hist.
Journal of Legal Medicine	J. Legal Med.
Journal of Legal Pluralism	J. Legal Pluralism
Journal of Legal Studies	J. Legal Stud.
Journal of Legislation	J. Legis.
Journal of Legislation & Public Policy	J. Legis. & Pub. Pol'y
Journal of Maritime Law & Commerce	J. Mar. L. & Com.
Journal of Medicine and Law	J. Med. & L.
Journal of Mineral Law & Policy	J. Min. L. & Pol'y
Journal of Multistate Taxation	J. Multistate Tax'n
Journal of Natural Resources & Environmental Law *(formerly Journal of Mineral Law & Policy)*	J. Nat. Resources & Envtl. L.
Journal of Partnership Taxation	J. Partnership Tax'n
Journal of Personal Injury Litigation	J. Pers. Inj. Lit.

Journal of Pharmacy & Law	J. Pharmacy & L.
Journal of Planning & Environmental Law	J. Plan. & Envtl. L.
Journal of Products Liability	J. Prod. Liab.
Journal of Proprietary Rights	J. Proprietary Rts.
Journal of Small & Emerging Business Law	J. Small & Emerging Bus. L.
Journal of Science & Technology Law	J. Sci. & Tech. L.
Journal of Social Welfare Law	J. Soc. Welfare L.
Journal of Social Welfare and Family Law	J. Soc. Welfare & Fam. L.
Journal of South Pacific Law	J. S. Pac. L.
Journal of Southern Legal History	J.S. Legal Hist.
Journal of Space Law	J. Space L.
Journal of Taxation	J. Tax'n
Journal of Technology Law & Policy	J. Tech. L. & Pol'y
Journal of the Institute for the Study of Legal Ethics	J. Inst. for Study Legal Ethics
Journal of the Law Society of Scotland	J.L.S.S.
Journal of the Legal Profession	J. Legal Prof.
Journal of the Patent & Trademark Office Society	J. Pat. & Trademark Off. Soc'y
Journal of the Suffolk Academy of Law	J. Suffolk Academy L.
Journal of Transnational Law & Policy	J. Transnat'l L. & Pol'y
Journal of World Trade	J. World Trade.
Journal of World Trade Law, Economics and Policy	J. World Trade L. Econ. & Pol'y
Journal Officiel des Communautés européennes: Communications et Informations	J.O.C.
Journal Officiel des Communautés européennes: Débats du Parlement européen	J.O.D.
Journal Officiel des Communautés européennes: Législation	J.O.L.
Judicature	Judicature
Kansas Journal of Law & Public Policy	Kan. J.L. & Pub. Pol'y
Kansas Law Review	Kan. L. Rev.
Kentucky Children's Rights Journal	Ky. Children's Rts. J.
Kentucky Law Journal	Ky. L.J.
Korean Journal of Air and Space Law	Korean J. Air & Sp. L.
Korean Journal of International and Comparative Law	Korean J. Int'l & Comp. L.
Korean Journal of Comparative Law	Korean J. Comp. L.
La Raza Law Journal	La Raza L.J.
Labor Law Journal	Lab. L.J.
Labor Lawyer	Lab. Law.
Land and Water Law Review	Land & Water L. Rev.
Law & Contemporary Problems	Law & Contemp. Probs.

Law & Inequality	Law & Inequality
Law and History Review	L.H.R.
Law and Philosophy	Law & Phil.
Law and Philosophy: an International Journal for Jurisprudence and Legal Philosophy	Law & Phil. Int'l J.
Law & Policy	Law & Pol'y
Law & Policy in International Business	Law & Pol'y Int'l Bus.
Law and Politics Book Review	Law & Pol. Book Rev.
Law & Practice of International Courts & Tribunals	Law & Prac. Int'l Courts & Trib.
Law & Psychology Review	Law & Psychol. Rev.
Law & Sexuality: A Review of Lesbian & Gay Legal Issues	Law & Sexuality
Law & Social Inquiry	Law & Soc. Inquiry
Law & Society Review	Law & Soc'y Rev.
Law Department Management	Law Dep't Mgmt
Law Firm Partnership & Benefits Report	Law Firm Partnership & Ben. Rep.
Law Librarian	Law. Librn.
Law Library Journal	Law Libr. J.
Law Office Management & Administration Report	Law Off. Mgmt & Admin. Rep.
Law Office Technology Review	Law Off. Tech. Rev.
Law Practice Management *(formerly Legal Economics)*	Law Prac. Mgmt
Law Quarterly Review	Law Q. Rev.
Law Review of Michigan State University Detroit College of Law	Law Rev. Mich. St. U. Det. C.L.
Law Society Gazette (Law Society of Upper Canada)	L. Soc'y Gaz.
Law Society's Gazette and Guardian Gazette	L. Soc'y Gaz. & Guardian Gaz.
Law Technology and Insurance	Law Tech. & Ins.
Lawyers Journal *(formerly Pittsburgh Legal Journal)*	Pittsburgh Legal J.
Legal History Review	Legal Hist. Rev.
Legal Issues of Economic / European Integration	L.I.E.I.
Legal Medical Quarterly	L. Med. Q.
Legal Reference Services Quarterly	Legal Ref. Serv. Q.
Legal Studies	L.S.
Legal Theory	Legal Theory
Leiden Journal of International Law	Leiden J. Int'l L.
Lex Electronica: Revue du droit des technologies de l'information	Lex Electronica
Lloyd's Maritime and Commercial Law Quarterly	L.M.C.L.Q.
Local Courts' and Municipal Gazette (Toronto)	Local Ct. Gaz.

Los Angeles Lawyer	L.A. Law.
Louisiana Bar Journal	La. B.J.
Louisiana Law Review	La. L. Rev.
Lower Canada Jurist	L.C. Jurist
Lower Canada Law Journal	L.C.L.J.
Loyola Consumer Protection Journal	Loy. Con. Prot. J.
Loyola Law Review (New Orleans)	Loy. L. Rev.
Loyola of Los Angeles Entertainment Law Journal	Loy. L.A. Ent. L.R.
Loyola of Los Angeles International & Comparative Law Journal	Loy. L.A. Int'l & Comp. L.J.
Loyola of Los Angeles Law Review	Loy. L.A. L. Rev.
Loyola Poverty Law Journal	Loy. Poverty L.J.
Loyola University of Chicago Law Journal	Loy. U. Chicago L.J.
Maastricht Journal of European and Comparative Law	M.J.E.C.L.
Maine Law Review	Me. L. Rev.
Malaya Law Review	Mal. L. Rev.
Malayan Law Journal	M.L.J.
Manitoba Bar News	Man. Bar N.
Manitoba Law Journal	Man. L.J.
Maori Law Review	Maori L. Rev.
Marquette Intellectual Property Law Review	Marq. Intell. Prop. L. Rev.
Marquette Law Review	Marq. L. Rev.
Marquette Sports Law Review	Marq. Sports L.J.
Maryland Journal of Contemporary Legal Issues	Md. J. Contemp. Legal Issues
Maryland Journal of International Law and Trade	Md. J. Int'l L. & Trade
Maryland Law Review	Md. L. Rev.
Massachusetts Law Review	Mass. L. Rev.
McGeorge Law Review (*formerly Pacific Law Journal*)	McGeorge L. Rev.
McGill Law Journal	McGill L.J.
Media Law & Policy	Media L. & Pol'y
Medicine, Science and the Law	Med. Sci. Law.
Medical Law Review	Med. L. Rev.
Medicine & Law	Med. & L.
Melbourne University Law Review	Melbourne U.L. Rev.
Mercer Law Review	Mercer L. Rev.
Mexico Trade & Law Reporter	Mex. Trade & L. Rep.
Michigan Bar Journal	Mich. B.J.
Michigan Business Law Journal	Mich. Bus. L.J.
Michigan Journal of Gender & Law	Mich. J. Gender & L.
Michigan Journal of International Law	Mich. J. Int'l L.
Michigan Journal of Law Reform	Mich. J.L. Reform

Michigan Journal of Race & Law	Mich. J. Race & L.
Michigan Law & Policy Review	Mich. L. & Pol'y Rev.
Michigan Law Journal	Mich. L.J.
Michigan Law Review	Mich. L. Rev.
Michigan State University – D.C.L. Journal of International Law	MSU-DCL J. Int'l L.
Michigan Telecommunications & Technology Law Review	Mich. Telecomm. & Tech. L. Rev.
Military Law Review	Mil. L. Rev.
Minnesota Intellectual Property Review	Minn. Intell. Prop. Rev.
Minnesota Journal of Global Trade	Minn. J. Global Trade
Minnesota Law Review	Minn. L. Rev.
Mississippi College Law Review	Miss. C.L. Rev.
Mississippi Law Journal	Miss. L.J.
Mississippi Law Review	Miss. L. Rev.
Missouri Environmental Law & Policy Review	Mo. Envtl. L. & Pol'y Rev.
Missouri Law Review	Mo. L. Rev.
Modern Law Review	Mod. L. Rev.
Monash University Law Review	Monash U.L. Rev.
Monde Juridique	Monde Jur.
Money Laundering Law Report	Money Laundering L. Rep.
Montana Law Review	Mont. L. Rev.
Montana Lawyer	Mont. Law
Monthly Labor Review	Monthly Lab. Rev.
Murdoch University Electronic Journal of Law	Murdoch U.E.J.L.
NAFTA: Law & Business Review of the Americas	NAFTA L. & Bus. Rev. Am.
National Banking Law Review	Nat'l Banking L. Rev.
National Black Law Journal	Nat'l Black L.J.
National Insolvency Review	Nat'l Insolv. Rev.
National Institute of Justice Journal	Nat'l Inst. Just. J.
National Journal of Constitutional Law	N.J.C.L.
National Journal of Sexual Orientation Law	Nat'l J. Sexual Orientation. L.
National Law Journal	Nat'l L.J.
National Law Review	Nat'l L. Rev.
National Real Property Law Review	Nat'l Real P.L.R.
Natural Resources & Environment	Nat. Resources & Env't
Naval Law Review	Nav. L. Rev.
Nebraska Law Review	Neb. L. Rev.
Neptunus: Maritime and Oceanic Law Review	Neptunus
Netherlands International Law Review	Nethl. Int'l L. Rev.
Netherlands Quarterly of Human Rights	Nethl. Q.H.R.

New England International and Comparative Law Annual	New Eng. Int'l & Comp. L. Ann.
New England Journal of Medicine	New Eng. J. Med.
New England Journal on Criminal & Civil Confinement	New Eng. J. on Crim. & Civ. Confinement
New England Law Review	New Eng. L. Rev.
New Europe Law Review	New Eur. L. Rev.
New Jersey Lawyer	N.J. Law.
New Law Journal	New L.J.
New Mexico Law Review	N.M.L. Rev.
New York City Law Review	N.Y. City L. Rev.
New York International Law Review	N.Y. Int'l L. Rev.
New York Law Journal	N.Y.L.J.
New York Law Review	N.Y.L. Rev.
New York Law School Journal of Human Rights	N.Y.L. Sch. J. Hum. Rts.
New York Law School Journal of International & Comparative Law	N.Y.L. Sch. J. Int'l & Comp. L.
New York Law School Law Review	N.Y.L. Sch. L. Rev.
New York State Bar Journal	N.Y. St. B.J.
New York University Clinical Law Review	N.Y.U. Clin. L. Rev.
New York University East European Constitutional Review	E. Eur. Const. Rev.
New York University Environmental Law Journal	N.Y.U. Envtl. L.J.
New York University International Journal of Constitutional Law	N.Y.U. Int'l J. Cont. L.
New York University Journal of International Law & Politics	N.Y.U.J. Int'l L. & Pol.
New York University Journal of Legislation & Public Policy	N.Y.U.J. Legis. & Pub. Pol'y
New York University Law Review	N.Y.U.L. Rev.
New York University Review of Law & Social Change	N.Y.U. Rev. L. & Soc. Change
New Zealand Law Review	N.Z.L. Rev.
New Zealand Universities Law Review	N.Z.U.L. Rev.
NEXUS: A Journal of Opinion	NEXUS: J. Opinion
Non-State Actors and International Law	Non-State Act. & Int'l L.
Nordic Journal of International Law	Nordic J. Int'l L.
North Carolina Central Law Journal	N.C. Centr. L.J.
North Carolina Journal of International Law & Commercial Regulation	N.C.J. Int'l L. & Com. Reg.
North Carolina Law Review	N.C.L. Rev.
North Dakota Law Review	N.D.L. Rev.
Northern Illinois University Law Review	N. Ill. U.L. Rev.
Northern Ireland Legal Quarterly	N. Ir. Legal Q.
Northern Kentucky Law Review	N. Ky. L. Rev.
Northwestern Journal of International Law & Business	Nw. J. Int'l L. & Bus.

Northwestern University Law Review	Nw. U.L. Rev.
Notre Dame International Law Review	Notre Dame Int'l L. Rev.
Notre Dame Journal of Law Ethics & Public Policy	Notre Dame J.L. Ethics & Pub. Pol'y
Notre Dame Law Review	Notre Damc L. Rev.
Nova Law Review	Nova L. Rev.
Nuclear Law	Nuclear L.
Ocean & Coastal Law Journal *(formerly Territorial Sea Journal)*	Occan & Coastal L.J.
Ocean Development& International Law	Ocean Devel. & Int'l L.
OECD Journal of Competition Law and Policy	OECD J. Comp. L. & Pol'y
Official Journal of the European Communities: Debates of the European Parliament	O.J.D.
Official Journal of the European Communities: English Special Edition	O.J. Sp. Ed.
Official Journal of the European Communities: Information and Notices	O.J.I.
Official Journal of the European Communities: Legislation	O.J.L.
Official Report of Debates (Council of Europe)	Debates
Ohio Northern University Law Review	Ohio N.U.L. Rev.
Ohio State Journal on Dispute Resolution	Ohio St. J. Disp. Resol.
Ohio State Law Journal	Ohio St. L.J.
Oklahoma City University Law Review	Okla. City U.L. Rev.
Oklahoma Law Review	Okla. L. Rev.
Ombudsman Journal	Ombudsman J.
Ontario Family Law Bulletin	Ont. Fam. L. Bull.
Ontario Lawyers Gazette	Ont. Law. Gaz.
Ontario Securities Commission Bulletin	O.S.C. Bull.
Orders of the Day and Minutes of Proceedings (Council of Europe)	Orders
Ordres du jour et procès-verbaux (Conseil de l'Europe)	Ordres
Oregon Law Review	Or. L. Rev.
Osaka University Law Review	Osaka U.L. Rev.
Osgoode Hall Law Journal	Osgoode Hall L.J.
Osteuropa-Recht	Osteurop.-R.
Otago Law Review	Otago L. Rev.
Ottawa Law Review	Ottawa L. Rev.
Oxford Journal of Legal Studies	Oxford J. Legal Stud.
Pace Environmental Law Review	Pace Envtl. L. Rev.
Pace International Law Review *(formerly Pace Yearbook of InternationalLaw)*	Pace Int'l L. Rev.
Pace Law Review	Pace Y.B. Int'l L.
Pacific Law Journal	Pac. L.J.

Pacific Rim Law & Policy Journal	Pac. Rim L. & Pol'y J.
Patent Law Annual	Pat. L. Ann.
Pepperdine Law Review	Pepp. L. Rev.
Philippine Law Journal	Philippine L.J.
Pittsburgh Legal Journal	Pittsburgh Legal J.
Polish Contemporary Law	Polish Contemp. L.
Potomac Law Review	Potomac L. Rev.
Probate & Property	Prob. & Prop.
Probate Law Journal	Prob. L.J.
Procurement Lawyer	Procurement Law.
Products Liability Law Journal	Prod. Liab. L.J.
Provincial Judges Journal	Prov. Judges J.
Psychology, Public Policy & Law	Psychol. Pub. Pol'y & L.
Public Contract Law Journal	Pub. Cont. L.J.
Public Interest Law Review	Pub. Int. L. Rev.
Public Land Law Review	Pub. Land L. Rev.
Public Land & Resources Law Review	Pub. Land & Resources L. Rev.
Public Law	P.L.
QLR	QLR
(formerly Bridgeport Law Review)	
Queen's Law Journal	Queen's L.J.
Quinnipiac Health Law Journal	Quinnipiac Health L.J.
Quinnipiac Law Review	Quinnipac L. Rev.
Quinnipiac Probate Law Journal	Quinnipiac Prob. L. J.
(formerly Connecticut Probate Law Journal)	
Ratio Juris	Ratio Juris
Real Estate Law Journal	Real Est. L.J.
Real Estate Law Report	Real Est. L. Rep.
Real Property, Probate & Trust Journal	Real Prop. Prob. & Tr. J.
Recueil des Cours	Rec. des Cours
Reform	Reform
Regent University Law Review	Regent U.L. Rev.
Relations Industrielles	R.I.
Res Communes: Vermont's Journal of the Environment	Res Communes: Vermont's J. Env't
Responsabilité civile et assurances	Resp. civ. et assur.
Restitution Law Review	R.L.R.
Review of Central and East European Law	Rev. cent. & E. Eur. L.
Review of Constitutional Studies	Rev. Const. Stud.
Review of European Community and International Environmental Law	R.E.C.I.E.L.
Review of Litigation	Rev. Litig.

Revista Europea de Derecho de la Navegacion Maritima y Aeuronautica	R.E.D.N.M.A.
Revista Juridica de la Universidad Interamiricana de Puerto Rico	Rev. Jur. U.I.P.R.
Revista Juridica Universidad de Puerto Rico	Rev. Jur. U.P.R.
Revue administrative	Rev. admin.
Revue africaine de droit international et comparé	R.A.D.I.C.
Revue algérienne des sciences juridiques, économiques et politiques	Rev. A.S.J.E.P.
Revue belge de droit international	Rev. B.D.I.
Revue canadienne de criminologie	Rev. can. dr. crim.
Revue canadienne de droit communautaire	Rev. can. dr. commun.
Revue canadienne de droit de commerce	Rev. can. dr. comm.
Revue canadienne de Droit Familial	Rev. Can. D. Fam.
Revue canadienne de droit pénal	R.C.D.P.
Revue canadienne de droit international	R.C.D.I.
Revue canadienne droit et société	R.C.D.S.
Revue canadienne de propriété intellectuelle	R.C.P.I.
Revue canadienne du droit d'auteur	R.C.D.A.
Revue critique	Rev. crit.
Revue critique de droit international privé	Rev. crit. dr. int. privé
Revue critique de jurisprudence belge	R.C.J.B.
Revue critique de législation et de jurisprudence du Canada	R.C.L.J.
Revue de la common law en français	R.C.L.F.
Revue de droit de l'ULB	Rev. dr. ULB
Revue de droit d'Ottawa	R.D. Ottawa
Revue de droit de l'Université de Sherbrooke	R.D.U.S.
Revue de droit de l'Université du Nouveau-Brunswick	R.D. U.N.-B.
Revue de droit de McGill	R.D. McGill
Revue de droit des affaires internationales	R.D.A.I.
Revue de droit immobilier	R.D. imm.
Revue de droit international, de sciences diplomatiques et politiques	R.D.I.S.D.P.
Revue de droit international et dc droit comparé	Rev. D.I. & D.C.
Revue de droit social	R.D.S.
Revue de droit uniforme	Rev. D.U.
Revue de jurisprudence	R. de J.
Revue de l'arbitrage	Rev. arb.
Revue de législation et de jurisprudence	R. de L.
Revue de planification fiscale et successorale	R.P.F.S.
Revue du Barreau	R. du B.
Revue du Barreau canadien	R. du B. can.
Revue d'études constitutionnelles	R. études const.

Revue d'études juridiques	R.E.J.
Revue d'histoire du droit	Rev. hist. dr.
Revue d'histoire du droit international	Rev. hist. dr. int.
Revue d'intégration européenne	R.I.E.
Revue du droit	R. du D.
Revue du droit de l'union européenne	R.D.U.E.
Revue du droit public et de la science politique en France et à l'étranger	Rev. D.P. & S.P.
Revue du Notariat	R. du N.
Revue de la recherche juridique	R.R.J.
Revue de planification fiscale et successorale	R.P.F.S.
Revue des Juristes de l'Ontario	Rev. juristes de l'Ont.
Revue des sociétés	Rev. sociétés
Revue égyptienne de droit international	Rev. E.D.I.
Revue européenne de droit privé	R.E.D. privé
Revue européenne de droit public	R.E.D. public
Revue européenne de philosophie et droit	R.E.P.D.
Revue Femmes et Droit	R.F.D.
Revue française de droit administratif	Rev. fr. dr. admin.
Revue française de droit aérien et spatial	Rev. fr. dr. aérien
Revue française de droit constitutionnel	Rev. fr. dr. constl.
Revue générale de droit	R.G.D.
Revue générale de droit international public	R.G.D.I.P.
Revue générale du droit des assurances	R.G.D.A.
Revue hellénique de droit international	R.H.D.I.
Revue historique de droit français et étranger	Rev. hist. dr. fr. & étran.
Revue internationale de droit comparé	R.I.D.C.
Revue internationale de droit pénal	Rev. I.D.P.
Revue internationale de la Croix-Rouge	R.I.C.R.
Revue internationale de la propriété industrielle et artistique	R.I.P.I.A.
Revue internationale de politique criminelle	Rev. I.P.C.
Revue internationale du droit d'auteur	R.I.D.A.
Revue internationale de Sémiotique Juridique	R.I.S.J.
Revue juridique de l'environnement	R.J.E.
Revue juridique des étudiants et étudiantes de l'Université Laval	R.J.E.U.L.
Revue juridique La femme et le droit	Rev. jur. femme dr.
Revue juridique Thémis	R.J.T.
Revue nationale de droit constitutionnel	R.N.D.C.
Revue québécoise de droit international	R.Q.D.I.
Revue suisse de droit international et de droit européen	S.Z.I.E.R.
Revue suisse de jurisprudence	R.S.J.
Revue trimestrielle de droit civil	R.T.D. civ.
Revue trimestrielle de droit commercial et de droit économique	Rev. trim. dr. com.

Revue trimestrielle de droit européen	R.T.D. eur.
Revue nationale de droit constitutionnel	N.J.C.L.
Revue universelle des droits de l'homme	R.U.D.H.
Richmond Journal of Global Law & Business	Rich. J. Global L. & Bus.
Richmond Journal of Law & Technology	Rich. J.L. & Tech.
Richmond Journal of Law and the PUblic Interest	Rich. J.L. & Pub. Int.
Rivista di Dritto Internazionale	R.D.I.
Roger Williams University Law Review	Roger Williams U. L. Rev.
Rutgers Computer & Technology Law Journal	Rutgers Computer & Tech. L.J.
Rutgers-Camden Law Journal	Rutgers-Camden. L.J.
Rutgers Journal of Law and Religion	Rutgers J.L. & Religion
Rutgers Law Journal	Rutgers L.J.
Rutgers Law Review	Rutgers L. Rev.
Rutgers Race and the Law Review	Rutgers Race & L. Rev.
Saint John's Journal of Legal Commentary	St. John's J. Legal Comment.
Saint John's Law Review	St. John's L. Rev.
Saint Louis University Law Journal	Saint Louis U.L.J.
Saint Louis University Public Law Review	St. Louis U. Pub. L. Rev.
Saint Louis-Warsaw Transatlantic Law Journal	St. Louis-Warsaw Transatlantic L.J.
Saint Mary's Law Journal	St. Mary's L.J.
Saint Thomas Law Review	St. Homas L. Rev.
San Diego Law Review	San Diego L. Rev.
San Joaquin Agricultural Law Review	San Joaquin Agric. L. Rev.
Santa Clara Computer & High Technology Law Journal	Santa Clara Computer & High Tech. L.J.
Santa Clara Law Review	Santa Clara L. Rev.
Saskatchewan Bar Review	Sask. Bar Rev.
Saskatchewan Law Review	Sask. L. Rev.
Scandinavian Studies in Law	Scand. Stud. L.
Scottish Current Law Yearbook	Scot. Curr. L.Y.B.
Schweizerische Juristen-Zeitung	S.J.Z.
Schweizerische Zeitschrift für internationales und europäisches Recht	S.Y.I.E.R.
Seattle University Law Review (formerly University of Puget Sound Law Review)	Seattle U.L. Rev.
Securities Regulation Law Journal	Sec. Reg. L.J.
Seton Hall Constitutional Law Journal	Seton Hall Const. L.J.
Seton Hall Journal of Sport Law	Seton Hall J. Sport L.
Seton Hall Law Review	Seton Hall L. Rev.

Seton Hall Legislative Journal	Seton Hall Legis. J.
Sherbrooke Law Review	Sherbrooke. L. Rev.
Singapore Academy of Law Journal	Sing. Ac. L.J.
Singapore Journal of International & Comparative Law	S.J.I.C.L.
Singapore Journal of Legal Studies	S.J.L.S.
Singapore Law Review	Sing. L. Rev.
SMU Law Review	SMU L. Rev.
South African Journal on Human Rights	S.A.J.H.R.
South African Yearbook of International Law	S.A.Y.B. Int'l L.
South Carolina Environmental Law Journal	S.C. Envtl. L.J.
South Carolina Law Review	S.C.L. Rev.
South Dakota Law Review	S.D.L. Rev.
South Texas Law Review	S. Tex. L. Rev.
(formerly South Texas Law Journal)	
Southern California Interdisciplinary Law Journal	S. Cal. Interdisciplinary L.J.
Southern California Law Review	S. Cal. L. Rev.
Southern California Review of Law and Women's Studies	S. Cal. Rev. L. & Women's Stud.
Southern California Sports & Entertainment Law Journal	S. Cal. Sports & Ent. L.J.
Southern Illinois University Law Journal	S. Ill. U.L.J.
Southern University Law Review	S.U.L. Rev.
Southwestern Journal of Law & Trade in the Americas	Sw. J. Trade Am.
Southwestern University Law Review	Sw. U.L. Rev.
Space Policy	Space Pol'y
Special Lectures of the Law Society of Upper Canada	Spec. Lect. L.S.U.C.
Sports Lawyers Journal	Sports Law. J.
Stanford Environmental Law Journal	Stan. Envtl. L.J.
Stanford Journal of International Law	Stan. J. Int'l L.
Stanford Journal of Law, Business & Finance	Stan. J.L. Bus. & Fin.
Stanford Journal of Legal Studies	Stan. J. Legal Stud.
Stanford Law & Policy Review	Stan. L. & Pol'y Rev.
Stanford Law Review	Stan. L. Rev.
Stanford Technology Law Review	Stan. Tech. L. Rev.
Statute Law Review	Stat. L. Rev.
Stetson Law Review	Stetson L. Rev.
Studia Canonica	Stud. Canon.
Suffolk Journal of Trial & Appellate Advocacy	Suffolk J. Trial & Appellate Advoc.
Suffolk Transnational Law Review	Suffolk Transnat'l L. Rev.
(formerly Suffolk Transnational Law Journal)	
Suffolk University Law Review	Suffolk U.L. Rev.
Supreme Court Economic Review	Sup. Ct. Econ. Rev.
Supreme Court Review	Sup. Ct. Rev.

Supreme Court Economic Review	Sup. Ct. Econ. Rev.
Supreme Court Law Review	Sup. Ct. L. Rev.
Sydney Law Review	Sydney L. Rev.
Syracuse Journal of International Law & Commerce	Syracuse J. Int'l L. & Com.
Syracuse Law Review	Syracuse L. Rev.
Syracuse University Law and Technology Journal	Syracuse U.L. & T.J.
Tax Law Review	Tax L. Rev.
Telecommunications & Space Journal	Telecom. & Space J.
Temple Environmental Law & Technology Journal	Temp. Envtl. L. & Tech. J.
Temple International & Comparative Law Journal	Temp. Int'l & Comp. L.J.
Temple Law Review *(formerly Temple Law Quarterly)*	Temp. L. Rev.
Temple Political & Civil Rights Law Review	Temp. Pol. & Civ. Rts. L. Rev.
Tennessee Law Review	Tenn. L. Rev.
Texas Bar Journal	Tex. B.J.
Texas Forum on Civil Liberties & Civil Rights	Tex. F. on C.L. & C.R.
Texas Hispanic Journal of Law & Policy *(formerly Hispanic Law Journal)*	Tex. Hispanic J. L. & Pol'y
Texas Intellectual Property Law Journal	Tex. Intell. Prop. L.J.
Texas International Law Journal	Tex. Int'l L.J.
Texas Journal of Business Law	Tex. J. Bus. L.
Texas Journal of Women & the Law	Tex. J. Women & L.
Texas Law Review	Tex. L. Rev.
Texas Review of Law & Politics	Tex. Rev. L. & Pol.
Texas Wesleyan Law Review	Tex. Wesleyan L. Rev.
Texas Tech Law Review	Tex. Tech L. Rev.
Textes adoptés par l'Assemblée (Conseil de l'Europe)	Textes adoptés
Texts Adopted by the Assembly (Council of Europe)	Texts Adopted
Theoretical Inquiries in Law	Theor. Inq. L.
Third World Legal Studies	Third World Legal Stud.
Thomas Jefferson Law Review	Thomas Jefferson L. Rev.
Thomas M. Cooley Journal of Practical & Clinical Law	T.M. Cooley J. Prac. & Clinical L.
Thomas M. Cooley Law Review	T.M. Cooley L. Rev.
Thurgood Marshall Law Review	T. Marshall L. Rev.
Toledo Journal of Great Lakes' Law, Science & Policy	Tol. J. Great Lakes' L. Sci. & Pol'y
Tolley's Communications Law	Tolley's Comm. L.
Tort & Insurance Law Journal	Tort & Ins. L.J.
Touro Environmental Law Journal	Touro Envtl. L.J.
Touro International Law Review	Touro Int'l L. Rev.

Touro Law Review	Touro L. Rev.
Trade Law Topics	Trade L. Topics
Transnational Law & Contemporary Problems	Transnat'l L. & Contemp. Probs.
Transnational Lawyer	Transnat'l Law.
Transportation Law Journal	Transp. L.J.
Travaux de l'association Henri Capitant des amis de la culture juridique française	Travaux de l'assoc. Henri Capitant
Tribal Law Journal	Tribal L.J.
Tribune des droits humaine	Trib. dr. hum.
Trusts & Estates	Trusts & Est.
Tulane European & Civil Law Forum	Tul. Eur. & Civ. L.F.
Tulane Environmental Law Journal	Tul. Envtl. L.J.
Tulane Journal of International & Comparative Law	Tul. J. Int'l. & Comp. L.
Tulane Journal of Law and Sexuality	Tul. J.L. & Sexuality
Tulane Law Review	Tul. L. Rev.
Tulane Maritime Law Journal	Tul. Mar. L.J.
Tulsa Journal of Comparative & International Law	Tulsa J. Comp. & Int'l L.
Tulsa Law Journal	Tulsa L.J.
U.C. Davis Journal of International Law & Policy	U.C. Davis J. Int'l L. & Pol'y
U.C. Davis Law Review	U.C. Davis L. Rev.
UCLA Asian Pacific American Law Journal	UCLA Asian Pac. Am. L.J.
UCLA Bulletin of Law and Technology	UCLA Bull. L. & T.
UCLA Entertainment Law Review	UCLA Ent. L. Rev.
UCLA Journal of Environmental Law & Policy	UCLA J. Envtl. L. & Pol'y
UCLA Journal of International Law and Foreign Affairs	UCLA J. Int'l L. & Foreign Aff.
UCLA Law Review	UCLA L. Rev.
UCLA Pacific Basin Law Journal	UCLA Pac. Basin L.J.
UCLA Women's Law Journal	UCLA Women's L.J.
UMKC Law Review	UMKC L. Rev.
Uniform Law Conference of Canada: Proceedings	Unif. L. Conf. Proc.
Uniform Law Review	Unif. L. Rev.
United States-Mexico Law Journal	U.S.-Mex. L.J.
University of Arkansas at Little Rock Law Review	U. Ark. Little Rock L. Rev.
University of Baltimore Intellectual Property Law Journal	U. Balt. Intell. Prop. L.J.
University of Baltimore Journal of Environmental Law	U. Balt. J. Envtl. L.
University of Baltimore Law Forum	U. Balt. L.F.
University of Baltimore Law Review	U. Balt. L. Rev.
University of British Columbia Law Review	U.B.C. L. Rev.
University of California at Davis Law Review	U.C. Davis L. Rev.
University of Chicago Law Review	U. Chicago L. Rev.

University of Chicago Law School Roundtable — U. Chicago L. Sch. Roundtable

University of Chicago Legal Forum — U. Chicago Legal F

University of Cincinnati Law Review — U. Cin. L. Rev.

University of Colorado Law Review — U. Colo. L. Rev.

University of Dayton Law Review — U. Dayton L. Rev.

University of Detroit Mercy Law Review — U. Det. Mercy L. Rev.

University of Florida Journal of Law & Public Policy — U. Fla. J.L. & Pub. Pol'y

University of Ghana Law Journal — U.G.L.J.

University of Hawaii Law Review — U. Haw. L. Rev.

University of Illinois Law Review — U. Ill. L. Rev.

University of Kansas Law Review — U. Kan. L. Rev.

University of Malaya Law Review — U. Mal. L. Rev.

University of Memphis Law Review — U. Mem. L. Rev.

University of Miami Business Law Review — U. Miami Bus. L. Rev.

University of Miami Entertainment & Sports Law Review — U. Miami Ent. & Sports L. Rev.

University of Miami Inter-American Law Review — U. Miami Inter-Am. L. Rev.

University of Miami International & Comparative Law Review (formerly University of Miami Yearbook of International Law) — U. Miami Int'l & Comp. L. Rev.

University of Miami Law Review — U. Miami L. Rev.

University of Michigan Journal of Law Reform — U. Mich. J.L. Ref.

University of New Brunswick Law Journal — U.N.B.L.J.

University of New South Wales Law Journal — U.N.S.W.L.J.

University of Pennsylvania Journal of Constitutional Law — U. Pa. J. Const. L.

University of Pennsylvania Journal of International Economic Law — U. Pa. J. Int'l Econ. L.

University of Pennsylvania Journal of Labor and Employment Law — U. Pa. J. Lab. & Employment L.

University of Pennsylvania Law Review — U. Pa. L. Rev.

University of Pittsburgh Law Review — U. Pitt. L. Rev.

University of Queensland Law Jounal — U.Q.L.J.

University of Richmond Law Review — U. Rich. L. Rev.

University of San Francisco Law Review — U.S.F. L. Rev.

University of San Francisco Journal of Law and Social Challenges — U.S.F. J.L. & Soc. Challenges

University of San Francisco Maritime Law Journal — U.S.F. Mar. L.J.

University of Tasmania Law Review — U. Tasm. L. Rev.

University of the District of Columbia Law Review (formerly District of Columbia Law Review) — U.D.C. L. Rev.

University of Toledo Law Review — U. Tol. L. Rev.

University of Toronto Faculty of Law Review — U.T. Fac. L. Rev.

University of Toronto Law Journal — U.T.L.J.

University of Western Australia Law Review	U.W.A. L. Rev.
University of Western Ontario Law Review	U.W.O. L. Rev.
Upper Canada Law Journal	U.C.L.J.
Utah Bar Journal	Utah B.J.
Valparaiso University Law Review	Val. U. L. Rev
Vanderbilt Journal of Entertainment Law & Practice	Vand. J. Ent. L. & Prac.
Vanderbilt Journal of Transnational Law	Vand. J. Transnat'l L.
Vanderbilt Law Review	Vand. L. Rev.
Vermont Bar Journal	Vt. B.J.
Vermont Law Review	Vt. L. Rev.
Victoria University of Wellington Law Review	V.U.W.L.R.
Vietnam Law & Legal Forum	Vietnam L. & Legal Forum
Villanova Environmental Law Journal	Vill. Envtl. L.J.
Villanova Law Review	Vill. L. Rev.
Villanova Sports and Entertainment Law Journal	Vill. Sports & Ent. L.J.
Virginia Environmental Law Journal	Va. Envtl. L.J.
Virginia Journal of International Law	Va. J. Int'l L.
Virginia Journal of Law & Technology	Va. J.L. & Tech.
Virginia Journal of Social Policy & Law	Va. J. Soc. Pol'y & L.
Virginia Journal of Sports and the Law	Va. J. Sports & L.
Virginia Law Review	Va. L. Rev.
Virginia Tax Review	Va. Tax Rev.
Waikato Law Review: Taumauri	Waikato L. Rev.
Wake Forest Law Review	Wake Forest L. Rev.
Waseda Bulletin of Comparative Law	Waseda Bull. Comp. L.
Washburn Law Journal	Washburn L.J.
Washington & Lee Race & Ethnic Ancestry Law Journal *(formerly Race & Ethnic Ancestry Law Journal and Race & Ethnic Ancestry Law Digest)*	Wash. & Lee Race & Ethnic Ancestry L.J.
Washington & Lee Law Review	Wash. & Lee L. Rev.
Washington Law Review	Wash. L. Rev.
Washington University Journal of Law & Policy	Wash. U.J.L. & Pol'y
Washington University Journal of Urban and Contemporary Law	Wash. U.J. Urb. & Contemp. L.
Washington University Law Quarterly	Wash. U.L.Q.
Wayne Law Review	Wayne L. Rev.
Web Journal of Current Legal Issues	Web J.C.L.I.
West Virginia Journal of Law & Technology	W. Va. J. L. & T.
West Virginia Law Review	W. Va. L. Rev.
West Virginia Lawyer	W. Va. Law.
West's Education Law Reporter	Ed. Law Rep.
Western Law Review (San Francisco)	West. L. Rev.
Western Law Review (Canada)	West. L.R.

Western Ontario Law Review	West. Ont. L. Rev.
Western New England Law Review	W. New Eng. L. Rev.
Western State University Law Review	W. St. U. L. Rev.
Widener Journal of Public Law	Widener J. Pub. L
Widener Law Symposium Journal	Widener L. Symp. J.
Willamette Journal of International Law & Dispute Resolution	Willamette J. Int'l & Disp. Resol.
Willamette Law Review	Willamette L. Rev.
William & Mary Bill of Rights Journal	Wm. & Mary Bill Rts. J.
William & Mary Environmental Law & Policy Review	Wm. & Mary Envtl. L. & Pol'y Rev.
William & Mary Journal of Women and the Law	Wm. & Mary J. Women & L.
William & Mary Law Review	Wm. & Mary L. Rev.
William Mitchell Law Review	Wm. Mitchell L. Rev.
Windsor Review of Legal and Social Issues	Windsor Rev. Legal Soc. Issues
Windsor Yearbook of Access to Justice	Windsor Y.B. Access Just.
Wisconsin Environmental Law Journal	Wis. Envtl. L.J.
Wisconsin International Law Journal	Wis. Int'l L.J.
Wisconsin Law Review	Wis. L. Rev.
Wisconsin Women's Law Journal	Wis. Women's L.J.
World Arbitration and Mediation Report	World Arb. & Mediation Rep.
World Trade and Arbitration Materials	W.T.A.M.
Wyoming Law Review	Wyo. L. Rev.
(formerly Land & Water Law Review)	
Yale Human Rights & Development Law Journal	Yale Human Rts. & Dev. L.J.
Yale Journal of International Law	Yale J. Int'l L.
Yale Journal of Law & Feminism	Yale J.L. & Feminism
Yale Journal of Law & the Humanities	Yale J.L. & Human.
Yale Journal on Regulation	Yale J. on Reg.
Yale Law & Policy Review	Yale L. & Pol'y Rev.
Yale Law Journal	Yale L.J.
Yearbook : Commercial Arbitration	Y.B. Comm. Arb.
Yearbook of Air and Space Law	Y.B. Air & Sp. L.
Yearbook of Copyright and Media Law	Y.B. Copyright & Media L.
Yearbook of European Law	Y.B. Eur. L.
Yearbook of International Law	Y.B. Int'l L.
Yearbook of International Environmental Law	Y.B. Int'l Env. L.
Yearbook of International Humanitarian Law	Y.B. Int'l Human. L.
Yearbook of Maritime Law	Y.B. Marit. L.

Yearbook of the Canadian Bar Association	Y.B. C.B.A.
Yearbook of the European Convention on Human Rights	Y.B. Eur. Conv. H.R.
Yearbook of the Institute of International Law	Y.B. Inst. Int'l L.
Yearbook of the International Court of Justice	Y.B.I.C.J.
Yearbook of the United Nations	Y.B.U.N.
Yearbook on Human Rights	Y.B.H.R.
Zeitschrift für ausländisches öffentliches Recht und Völkerrecht	Z.a.ö.R.V.
Zeitschrift für das gesamte Familienrecht	Fam. R. Z
Zeitschrift für Europäisches Privatrecht	Z. Eu. P.
Zeitschrift für Luft- und Weltraumrecht	Z.L.W.
Zeitschrift für Rechtspolitik	Z.R.P.
Zeitschrift für Rechtsvergleichung	Z.R.V.
Zeitschrift für Unternehmens und Gesellschaftsrecht	Z.U.G.
Zeitschrift für Vergleichende Rechtswissenschaft	Z. Vgl. RWiss.
Zeitschrift für Wirtschaftsrecht	Z.W.